THE GARRETT ENIGMA
AND THE EARLY SUBMARINE PIONEERS

THE GARRETT ENIGMA
AND THE EARLY SUBMARINE PIONEERS

PAUL BOWERS

Resurgam

Airlife
England

Copyright © 1999 Paul Bowers

First published in the UK in 1999
by Airlife Publishing Ltd

British Library Cataloguing-in-Publication Data
A catalogue record for this book
is available from the British Library

ISBN 1 84037 066 1

Typeset by Servis Filmsetting Ltd, Manchester
Design by Design/Section, Frome
Printed and bound in Great Britain by Butler & Tanner Limited, Frome and London

Airlife Publishing Ltd
101 Longden Road, Shrewsbury, SY3 9EB, England
E-mail: airlife@airlifebooks.com
Website: www.airlifebooks.com

CONTENTS

ACKNOWLEDGEMENTS

Because I started my research into *Resurgam* over 20 years ago with no intention of committing my thoughts to paper, the list of all those who helped me is bound to be incomplete; for this I apologise.

My thanks must go to: Commander Richard Compton-Hall, MBE, RN (Retd) who, when he was Director of the Royal Navy Submarine Museum, gave me much support and help and in particular started me on my quest when he asked me to build a model of *Resurgam* for the museum; Major Kenneth Macksey, MC, RTR, (Retd) who persevered with his encouragement for me to write the book; my sons Jonathan and Richard who removed the excuses I had always managed to produce with their computer help and advice.

The librarians, archivists and staff of many firms and sources of reference who have shown much patience and have been so helpful. These include Vickers Shipbuilding and Engineering Ltd, Cochran Boilers Ltd, Messrs Plenty Ltd, the Royal Navy Submarine Museum, the Science Museum, Liverpool City and Merseyside County Museums, the Public Libraries and Information Services of the cities of Manchester, Liverpool, Portsmouth and Chichester; Clwyd County Council and Havant and Emsworth libraries; the British Library, Public Records Office, Companies Record Office; the libraries of the Ministry of Defence and Royal Naval College Greenwich; the library of Lambeth Palace and Diocese of Manchester; the Royal Institute of Naval Architects; the Universities of Oxford, Cambridge and Dublin and the Archaeological Diving Unit of the University of St Andrew; Manchester Grammar and Rossall Schools; and more recently the *Resurgam* and *Hunley* Web Sites.

Much help was received from overseas, contact being established through the Naval staff of the Embassies of the United States of America, Turkey and Denmark; in the United States of America the Department of the Navy, United States National Archives, United States Naval Historical Section and both the Smithsonian Institution and the Memorial Submarine Force Museums.

Many individuals have been most helpful. I would particularly like to thank: Captain P.B. Archer, RN (Retd), Commander H. Manners, RN (Retd), Adrian Lloyd, Alan Collins (Cochran Boilers Ltd), Ken Wellings (late of VSEL), the late Commander J. Maber, RN, and the late Gus Britton who was the archivist at the Royal Navy Submarine Museum.

I would also like to express my appreciation to my editor, Peter Coles.

Finally my sincere thanks to my wife for her support and tolerance.

PROLOGUE

On 22 September 1914 three lone British Cressy Class cruisers, H.M.S. *Aboukir,* H.M.S. *Hogue* and H.M.S. *Cressy*, were patrolling the south-eastern part of the North Sea off the Dutch coast, in an area known as the Broad Fourteens. The two destroyer flotillas, which had been accompanying the cruisers, had been forced, by a gale, to find shelter while the cruisers continued the patrol alone.

The German submarine *U9*, under the command of *Kapitanleutnant* Otto Weddingen, had been despatched on 20 September to patrol the Flanders Bight to prevent the British from landing troops on the Belgian coast. During the voyage there were navigation problems because the gyro compass was faulty and, on the evening of 21 September, the boat was off the Dutch coast some fifty miles from her patrol area when she too was forced to take shelter from the gale by submerging.

At dawn on the 22nd, by which time the weather had improved, *U9* surfaced to recharge her batteries. Visibility was good and the masts of the three cruisers were sighted. At this time *U9* was running on her Korting diesel engines which tended to produce a lot of smoke. To avoid advertising his presence and alerting the enemy, Weddingen submerged his submarine and used her electric motors. The cruisers, which were two miles (3.2 km) apart and travelling line abreast, maintained a steady and closing course at 10 knots (18.5 kph). At 6.20am, at a range of 500 yards (457 metres), Weddingen fired one bow torpedo, hitting H.M.S. *Aboukir* which immediately stopped. Her captain, under the impression that his ship had hit a mine, summoned the other cruisers to come to his assistance.

In the meantime *U9* submerged deeper and reloaded the empty torpedo tube. On returning to periscope depth Weddingen could see the *Aboukir* sinking with both the other cruisers in attendance and stationary. At 6.55am a second attack was launched and at a range of 300 yards (274 metres) the two bow tubes were fired at H.M.S. *Hogue*. *U9* had to withdraw by going astern and broke surface. Sighted, she was engaged by H.M.S. *Hogue* but managed to submerge and reload one of her forward tubes. H.M.S. *Hogue* sank ten minutes later.

Coming to periscope depth again Weddingen manoeuvred his boat to fire at H.M.S. *Cressy* with his stern tubes. As the submarine was about to fire, her periscope was sighted and the cruiser went full ahead, but one of the two torpedoes, which had been fired, hit her and stopped her dead in the water. Weddingen turned his boat and fired his last torpedo which hit and sank the cruiser.

U9 withdrew to the north and managed to evade the British destroyers, which, by then were on their way to rejoin the cruisers and had been ordered to cut her off. Weddingen returned safely to Germany and a hero's welcome.

In one hour the British had lost three, albeit old, armoured cruisers and 1459 officers and men. The incident clearly highlighted the effectiveness and potential of the submarine while emphasising the folly of earlier British policy which was against the introduction of submarines. Great Britain had absolute command of the seas with the most powerful surface fleet in the world but there were those who realised that even small nations armed with the submarine could pose a threat to her position. This threat was not taken all that seriously at the beginning of World War I, and consequently the three cruisers were taking no evasive action against the potential threat and paid the price.

Great Britain did have her own submarine fleet but this was largely deployed in a harbour and coast defensive role which was considered to be of subsidiary importance. Later in the war British submarines were used aggressively and very successfully.

It was not until the end of the nineteenth century that the submarine came of age and navies started to arm themselves with this new weapon. The French were certainly ahead of the field at this time because of Government interest and backing. The situation in Great Britain was completely different. There had been no official support or financial aid because, with the most powerful navy in the world, an additional submarine fleet was considered unnecessary. Indeed, when it was eventually realised that submarines were being introduced into other navies the British were forced to buy designs from abroad, as they were not in a position to build their own.

This was not because there had been a lack of inventiveness in the United Kingdom. There had been numerous submarines built over the years and perhaps the best known British inventor was George William Garrett who designed and built a steam-driven submarine in 1879 and later helped to build others which were exported. Garrett had many titles and has even been referred to as the 'Father of the British Submarine'. In fact, he never built a submarine for the Royal Navy, although it can be argued that at one time he, and therefore by association the United Kingdom, was well in advance of the rest of the world in submarine development. To understand the reasons why this technological lead was not exploited it is necessary to go back to Garrett's early days and even further back in time.

CHAPTER 1

BACKDROP

George William Littler Garrett was born in London on 4 July 1852 and died, nearly half a century later, on 26 February 1902 in New York. He was a Victorian, the son of a clergyman, who had been groomed to fit into the normal pattern of life expected of him.

Garrett is not famous; not many people have even heard of him, but he carved an important niche for himself in history by building his submarine the *Resurgam* (I shall rise again). Ironically, the thing that made *Resurgam* well known is not that she was a success but that she sank. Thus his place in history is largely emotive, although he should really be remembered for some of the more innovative inventions which can be attributed to him, but which he unfortunately failed to develop and market.

Resurgam was built in 1879 and was fitted with an ingenious steam-powered system to propel the boat both on the surface and under the water. She was lost off the North Wales coast early the following year. For various reasons there was some mystery about the loss of this boat. Indeed, Garrett himself may well have deliberately contributed to the confusion. Since then the story has been regularly resurrected and elaborated as rumours and false hopes that the boat had been located were circulated. Often, selective reporting, based on previously published articles, changed the story and added even more mystery. But there was much more to Garrett's life; later he was closely involved in designing, building, developing and testing other submarines; not only had he been made a deacon but was later granted a commission in the Turkish Navy, served as a soldier in the U.S. Army as well as being in the Revenue Service of that country. Several writers credited him with having invented the first real submarine, and having built the first practical sub-

marine. These are exaggerations, but the story of *Resurgam* was always an interesting gap filler when there was little news.

The submarine really came of age with the combination of three new inventions: the petrol engine for surface running, the electric motor to propel the submarine underwater, and the development of a suitable submarine-launched weapon system. The first submarines were accepted into Naval service at the beginning of the twentieth century, having been finally developed in the preceding twenty years by civilians, such as Garrett, who, unlike those in authority, had the foresight to see the potential of an underwater warship. During the last two decades of the nineteenth century there was much submarine building activity. Boats were being developed in different ways in Russia, France, Spain and the United States. Garrett was amongst the leaders, indeed he was ahead of the field when *Resurgam* was built. He achieved much but he has been lionised by journalists and writers for his designs were never generally adopted. It was others who built the first submarines to be generally accepted by the major navies of the world. The father of the British and United States Submarine Services was undoubtedly John P. Holland, an Irish-American, whose designs were accepted and used. Other countries would lay claim that their own inventors such as Drzewieki in Russia, Lake of the United States, Goubet, de Lome, Zede, and Laubeuf of France could qualify for that title as far as they were concerned.

Garrett was a remarkable man. He was an innovator, an engineer, a designer and submarine builder. But later in his life he became a jack-of-all-trades, as the following abridged *curriculum vitae* shows, but it also gives an indication of the breadth of his participation in life.

He was educated at Rossall School, in Lancashire, which he attended for one year before going on to Manchester Grammar School and thence to Trinity College, Dublin. He became headmaster of a school in Ireland, attended a course at the South Kensington Museum (in the Science and Art Department) and became an instructor at the Manchester Mechanics Institution. He spent a year travelling around the world during which time he familiarised himself with and taught navigation. He was made deacon to the curacy of Christchurch, Manchester which necessitated him obtaining a theological qualification. He was married and had a family. He designed, built and captained several submarines some of which were sold abroad where he was responsible for their re-assembly, fitting out, crew training and work-up.

So that he could train the Turkish submariners he was granted a commission in the Turkish navy and committed himself to help that country in time of war. He was one of the first true international commuters travelling between England, Greece and Turkey but he also had business interests in France and Russia, although he never visited that country. For some time he lived and worked in Sweden. He must have had some linguistic capability as he had to deal with local (submarine) builders and crews in Sweden, Greece and Turkey. As an engineer he was involved in the building of Milford Haven Docks in Wales. At the age of thirty-eight he emigrated to the United States but failed to settle down. He first purchased land in Florida where he became a farmer. Later he joined the U.S. Customs and Revenue Service, after which he spent some time in the United States Army and served in Puerto Rico. He was also a rigger and a fireman in New York, where he died six months before his fiftieth birthday.

This was the man who built *Resurgam*.

About twenty years ago I was invited to make a cut-away model of *Resurgam* by the Director of the Royal Navy Submarine Museum, Commander Richard Compton-Hall. Until then I had special-ised. All the models I had made for the Museum were of World War II submarines. I remember the conversation with the Director well because I agreed to make the model with only the vaguest idea of what *Resurgam* looked like or when she was built. I was starting off with a completely blank piece of paper, which is a challenging way to start a model.

My initial research concerned the vessel herself. For many months I searched and acquired information, much of it brought with it other facts about Garrett himself and his other submarines. The time to start work on the drawings, and then the model, comes when it is realised that as thorough a search as possible has been carried out and it is unlikely that anything else new or significant will surface. The model was made and delivered and the paperwork I had acquired filed away.

Resurgam was drawn to my attention again some months ago. But when I dug out the Garrett files it was only to realise that there was an enormous amount of information but that it was in an untidy mess. Under the impression that it would only take a couple of hours to sort out, work started. As the papers were ordered and assembled I became interested in Garrett's philosophy and the developments that took place as he was evolving the different boats. As the information was assembled more research was carried out. Then it seemed necessary to broaden the base to establish what developments had taken place before Garrett started his work; what happened after he withdrew; and how he and his work fitted into the scheme of things. My research concentrated on submarine development and largely ignored Garrett's private life. It only touches upon the finances involved and does not examine the backgrounds of, and tries to avoid comment on, the many interesting people with whom Garrett came into contact. This has been covered by others.

The more I delved the more I realised how complicated the subject was. Often there was considerable overlap in developments taking place; frequently there was a tantilising piece of information about an invention but nothing else. There was no steady progression.

I also felt guilty criticising the work of men who had the ability, determination and courage to build their dream and then, taking their lives in their own hands, testing it. I also found it hard to relegate years of work by some of the inventors to a few short paragraphs, dismissing their achievements in a few words, when their efforts merited more. The story cannot be related without some criticism and because of the large number of submarines designed and built it is necessary to gloss over the work of many men.

As the background and research is submarine-biased, it is felt that it would be appropriate to describe, in principle and in very simple terms, how a submarine works as this is germane to some of the arguments put forward later.

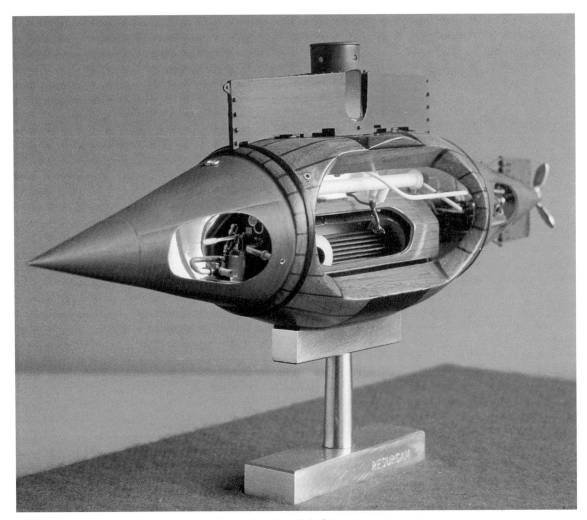

The author's model of *Resurgam*

CHAPTER 2

THE SUBMARINE

Purely for the record and to try and clarify the situation it is best to start with an authorised, precise meaning and the *Compact Oxford Dictionary* gives one definition of submarine as: 'operating or operated, constructed or laid, intended for use under water. A submarine (boat) is a boat designed that it can be submerged and propelled when under water.' A submersible, on the other hand, is defined: 'that can be submerged, covered with and plunged into or made to remain under water esp a submarine boat.' Although both 'submarine' and 'submersible' can be used to describe a 'submarine boat' the difference between the two terms would appear to be that submarine implies that it is under water permanently whereas submersible describes a temporary condition.

Submarines, using the everyday meaning of the word, are surface-dependent in that they have to surface periodically. There are a number of reasons for this (although the emphasis on each has altered as development has taken place). The stale air in the vessel has to be changed otherwise the crew would be asphyxiated. An internal combustion engine has to be run to recharge the batteries and this can only be used when fresh air can be drawn into the submarine. There has to be refuelling, revictualling and maintenance of equipment and machinery. In the past, it was necessary to at least break the surface with a periscope to see the enemy so that an attack could be carried out. Finally the crew, unlike that of Captain Nemo[1], would probably appreciate some shore leave. A true submarine would submerge after launching and continue to operate under water *ad infinitum*. This is not impossible although it may be impractical and costly.

The nuclear-powered submarines are the closest thing that man has to a true submarine as they can remain submerged for weeks on end, whilst travelling many thousands of miles. If necessary, an enemy can be engaged without the vessel surfacing or breaking the surface. They are no longer as surface-dependent as submarines used to be.

The difference between what we call a submarine and a submersible is dependent on how long the vessel can remain under water. This is a very grey area and it is not proposed to offer a definition now but to leave it to the judgement of the reader.

The definition of the semi-submersible presents less of a problem. This is a surface vessel which, by taking on ballast, is able to lower its freeboard thereby exposing a minimum amount of the vessel above water. The essence being that part of the vessel is always visible above the surface.

Traditionally submarines are always referred to as 'boats' irrespective of their size.

Hull and Fittings

The fundamental components of a submarine, which are shown in Figs 1 and 2, are:

1 The hull, which is water-tight and in which the crew work and live. This is now called the pressure hull.
2 Ballast tanks which can be filled with water and emptied to make the vessel submerge.
3 The means of propulsion.
4 A vertical rudder to steer the vessel in the horizontal plane and horizontal rudders to steer it in the vertical plane.
5 Navigation equipment.
6 Weapon system(s) which can be fired under water.
7 The means for the crew to acquire targets, observe and fire the weapon system(s) when the submarine is submerged.

1 *Twenty Thousand Leagues Under the Sea* by Jules Verne.

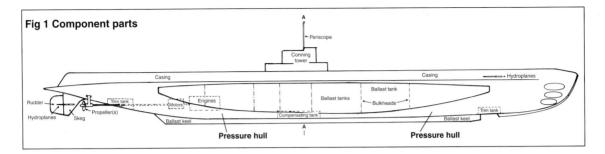

Fig 1 Component parts

Hull Design

The cross-section of the pressure hull of a modern submarine is circular and the longitudinal section is cigar shaped. Various structures are attached to the hull such as the conning tower, hatches, gun, ballast tanks, and keel; much of this will be covered by a streamlining structure particularly at the bow and stern which is open to the sea or free flooding.

There are three types of hull; this is governed by the position of the ballast tanks. These are illustrated in Fig 3. The 'Single Hull' encompasses the ballast tanks which are internal; in the 'Saddle Tank' hull the ballast tanks are strapped to the hull like a saddle; In the 'Double Hull' the tanks are outside the pressure hull but conform to the streamlining of the vessel and the pressure hull itself is in a form of cocoon.

Displacement

When the submarine is put in the water it should float on a level keel because it has been designed to do this although it may be necessary to make a few weight adjustments to make it balance perfectly in the water. The submarine floats because it is lighter than the weight of the total volume of the water it would displace if submerged (submerged displacement). This can be worked out mathematically by establishing the volume bounded by the external shape of the complete submarine (this excludes free flooding areas) in cubic feet; 35 cubic feet of sea water is equivalent to 1 ton. In surface trim the water displaced by the vessel equals the complete weight of the boat. This can be expressed either in cubic feet or tons. The positive buoyancy is the

Fig 2 Section AA

Submarine Section

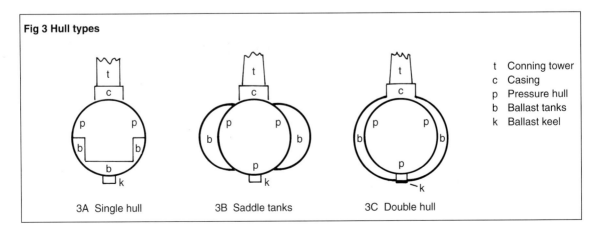

Fig 3 Hull types

t	Conning tower
c	Casing
p	Pressure hull
b	Ballast tanks
k	Ballast keel

3A Single hull   3B Saddle tanks   3C Double hull

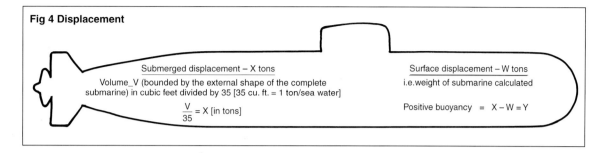

Fig 4 Displacement

Submerged displacement – X tons
Volume_V (bounded by the external shape of the complete
submarine) in cubic feet divided by 35 [35 cu. ft. = 1 ton/sea water]

$$\frac{V}{35} = X \text{ [in tons]}$$

Surface displacement – W tons
i.e. weight of submarine calculated

Positive buoyancy $= X - W = Y$

difference between the submerged displacement and surfaced displacement.

Buoyancy

Figs 4 and 5 illustrate displacement. It will be assumed that the weight of the example submarine is W and the positive buoyancy is Y. When she is put in the water she weighs W and she floats. If the ballast tanks inside the vessel are filled with Y amount of water the positive buoyancy is neutralised and the vessel will be exactly the same weight as the water she displaces and will float, but just below the surface. By adding more ballast the submarine will sink; conversely, if water is blown or pumped out the boat will rise. Theoretically the submarine can be made to float at different levels in the water by continually adjusting the amount of ballast in her tanks.

In most modern submarines the ballast tanks themselves are relatively simple. At the bottom is a free flood hole which is open to the sea and at the top of the tank is a valve. To submerge, the valve is opened, the air can escape and water enters through the free flood holes. Closing the valve effectively stops both the air escaping and the water entering the tank. To surface, high pressure compressed air is fed into the tanks forcing the water out through the free flood holes. Once the conning tower has been opened the tanks can be cleared with a low pressure blower taking air from the atmosphere. Although the final part of surfacing is slower, it conserves the limited bottled compressed air supply. In the very early submarines ballast tanks were cleared in a variety of ways including steam instead of compressed

air, hand and mechanically-driven pumps.

Another method of altering the buoyancy of a submarine is by having a 'variable displacement' hull (Fig 6). Several submarines have incorporated a variation of this system which can best be explained as having two cylinders which fit together telescopically with their outside ends sealed. Displacement can be changed by compressing or extending the cylinders. In doing this the submerged displacement of the tube can be altered without changing its weight.

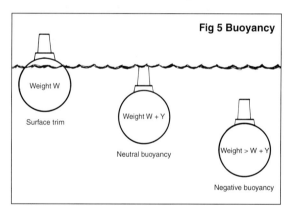

Fig 5 Buoyancy

Weight W
Surface trim

Weight W + Y
Neutral buoyancy

Weight > W + Y
Negative buoyancy

Longitudinal Stability/Compensation

One of the most difficult problems the early submarine designers had to overcome was the longitudinal stability of the submarine when it was submerged. Under water the submarine is practically weightless and when trimmed or on an even keel its centre of gravity is normally in the centre of the vessel. Any redistribution of weight or movement in the boat, for instance a crewman moving from one end of the submarine to the other, or the sudden loss of weight

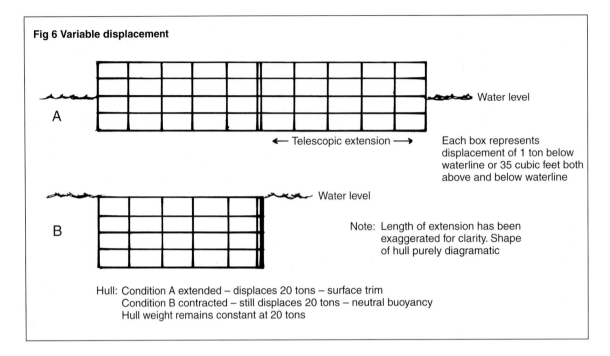

Fig 6 Variable displacement

A

Water level

← Telescopic extension →

Each box represents displacement of 1 ton below waterline or 35 cubic feet both above and below waterline

Water level

B

Note: Length of extension has been exaggerated for clarity. Shape of hull purely diagramatic

Hull: Condition A extended – displaces 20 tons – surface trim
Condition B contracted – still displaces 20 tons – neutral buoyancy
Hull weight remains constant at 20 tons

when a torpedo was discharged from the bow, would upset the equilibrium. The smaller the submarine, the smaller the weight which would adversely effect it. Compensation can be made in several ways: by using the hydroplanes; by readjusting the distribu-tion of water between the various ballast tanks; by having a moveable counter-weight which can be quickly and easily adjusted; or by taking on addi-tional ballast to compensate for fuel used or weapons fired.

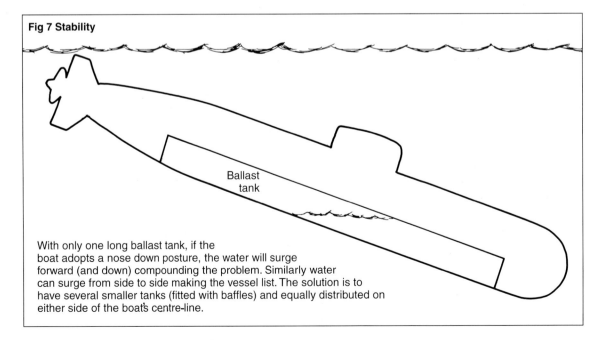

Fig 7 Stability

Ballast tank

With only one long ballast tank, if the boat adopts a nose down posture, the water will surge forward (and down) compounding the problem. Similarly water can surge from side to side making the vessel list. The solution is to have several smaller tanks (fitted with baffles) and equally distributed on either side of the boat's centre-line.

Trim

As submarines developed, more sophisticated methods of maintaining stability were introduced. In addition to the ballast tanks there are now trim tanks within the submarine; these work on an independent and separate system. Water is transferred between these tanks first to achieve and then to maintain the correct balance between weight distribution and buoyancy. Particularly in the smaller submarines trimming is a continuous and necessary process to compensate for movement within the submarine.

Stability

Imagine that there was just one long ballast tank in the submarine, as illustrated in Fig 7, which was partly filled with water. Should the submarine, for some reason, become even slightly bow heavy, the water in the tank would surge towards the bow making the bow even heavier and this could have disastrous results on the stability of the vessel which it could be very difficult to correct. Therefore a submarine normally has tanks along her length and on either side of the centre line. The tanks are separate or they are suitably divided to minimise water surge.

Steerage Way

The submarine is given forward momentum by turning the propeller. Only when she is moving will she have steerage way, that is the vessel can be turned to port and starboard using the rudder.

Hydroplanes

Similarly a boat can be steered in the vertical plane using the hydroplanes, which in British submarines, are fitted at the bow and at the stern (Figs 1 and 8). The hydroplanes have to exert less force if the submarine is in a state of negative buoyancy when she is diving, or positive buoyancy when rising. But if the boat is dived when she is in a state of positive buoyancy the planes would also have to counteract the strong upward pull as the boat tried to remain on the surface thus dissipating the forward thrust of the propeller. The converse applies to a surfacing boat with negative buoyancy.

Hydroplanes were often described as 'side rudders' by the early submarine engineers.

Air Supply

Within the closed hull there is only a limited quantity of air to sustain human life. The crew use the oxygen from the air and expel carbon dioxide; this used to govern how long a boat could remain submerged. Various methods to replace or clean the foul air have been introduced.

Motive Power

If the propelling and auxiliary machinery within the boat is to be driven mechanically, an adequate power plant, that can work when the submarine is submerged, is required. This should not be dependent on or contaminate the crew's available air supply.

Weapons

Before the end of the nineteenth century when the torpedo, as we know it, was invented, the term torpedo was used to describe an explosive mine or charge. This original definition of torpedo is used extensively where original documents are quoted.

The 'modern' self-propelled torpedo is fired from either a tube fitted within the pressure hull, which can be re-loaded, or from a single shot external tube. Torpedo tubes are normally fitted at the bow, but can also be fitted at the stern and midships. Some of the early submarines carried torpedoes in external brackets from which they could be launched.

Complications

In designing, building and operating submarines

Fig 8 Position of hydroplanes

		Stern hydroplanes		Forward hydroplanes
Diving	A	Stern held up		Bow forced down
	B	Stern forced down		Bow forced down
	C	Cruising at selected depth		
Surfacing	D	Stern held down		Bow forced up
	E	Stern forced up		Bow forced up

N.B. Hydroplanes are used in conjunction with ballast taken on and its distribution there are many more considerations such as the enormous static water pressure the hull is subjected to as it descends; salinity and temperature changes in the water; navigation; communications; etc. But these, as far as the Garrett story is concerned, are for a future age.

Submarine Development

To set Garrett's achievements and influence into the scheme of things it is important to put his work into context. To this end it is necessary to see what submarine development had taken place before he started his work; what was going on while he was developing submarines; and the path developments took after he had finished his work. Each of these phases could be the subject of vast tomes. Indeed vast tomes have been written about them but it is not the intention to repeat them here but purely to set the scene.

The development of the submarine was not clear cut. There was not a steady, progressive development as there was, for instance, for the aeroplane after the first powered flight. The success of the first powered flight was dependent on the necessary technology being in place. Before this, man had wanted to fly but did not have the wherewithal to build an aeroplane which worked and could be further developed. Similarly with the submarine, until the right components were available a really effective submarine could not be built. Man's optimistic endeavours to travel under water can be traced back at least 2,300 years. Between then and 1900 there had been many further attempts. Numerous problems had to be overcome before a true submarine could be constructed, and one of the most pressing was the development of a suitable motor or engine which could propel the vessel underwater without using up the crew's oxygen supply.

In the early development stages the pioneers often duplicated experiments, or seemed to be slow in the progress they were making. This can be attributed to the poor circulation of information because of the lack of good communications and also because some of the inventors were secretive or badly disciplined in the way in which they carried out and wrote up their various trials. Even so progress was made and this accelerated towards the end of the nineteenth century.

During the early development of the submarine there was a very close relationship between vessels that could be submerged and have no underwater mobility; those that could submerge and travel under water; and those which could reduce their freeboard and run awash on the surface. The lessons learned from the three modes contributed to the overall development and therefore the three types of vessel will be considered where appropriate. As the reader has already been warned, to further confuse the issue all three are often referred to by their inventors as submarine-boats, although such terms as a diving bell – submersibles – or semi-submersibles would be more appropriate.

Development was spasmodic, and we only have details of those vessels which were successful; those which failed publicly; those which were very well publicised; and those which were involved in a tragedy or were particularly bizarre. Many moderately successful submarines were probably built yet details about them were never published and consequently we may know nothing about them. The final group is that of the paper submarine; many treatises were written (although in many cases it is most fortunate that they were never built because the end results could have been fatal); but some good designs were never tested. The most successful inventors were those who had Government sponsorship or backing, but this was often difficult or more likely impossible to obtain. As development costs were prohibitively high, and because of a lack of Government interest, there was not an easy market for the speculator.

CHAPTER 3

EARLIEST DAYS TO THE SEVENTEENTH CENTURY

Aristotle (384–322BC) the Greek philosopher recorded that Alexander the Great used diving bells in the siege of Tyre in 332BC. Later, during the fourth century, Vegece, a Latin historian, described various diving suits, some of which were connected to the surface allowing the diver to breathe freely. Much later Bohaddin, a twelfth century Arab historian, recorded that divers using some sort of bellows attachment were able to enter a town which was under siege by the Crusaders. Man had started to harness an ability to go under water as an aid or weapon of war, although there were to be other attractions such as the recovery of treasure; harvesting both food and wealth from the sea and allowing him to build foundations under water for buildings and bridges.

Roger Bacon (1214–94), a Franciscan philosopher, alluded to: 'devices with which men could walk on the sea bed or under rivers without danger'.

Water obstacles have impeded armies and if the bridges have been destroyed commanders have had to find alternative methods of crossing. This is less of a problem if the crossing is unopposed. Robert Valturio in his *De Re Militari* in the fifteenth century produced two interesting drawings (Fig 9). The first shows what appear to be surface vessels fitted with hand-cranked paddle wheels but they were later credited with being a precursor of the submarine although the unshrouded paddle wheels, once submerged, would not be very effective. The second vessel appears to be a sealable container which would be useful for transporting equipment, particularly if it had to be kept dry, over or through a river. Again, the vessel is fitted with what appears to be a hand-cranked paddle wheel which would not have been a very effective motive power under water. These drawings were first produced in 1472 and are therefore not as clear as they could be. One thought that comes to mind is that if ropes had been previously laid across the obstacle, the paddle-like appendages could have been used as a form of winch, to drag the vessel to the other side.

Royalty was often interested in scientific progress and, in the sixteenth century, Charles V of Spain, together with 10,000 spectators, witnessed Greeks diving in the fast-flowing River Toja near

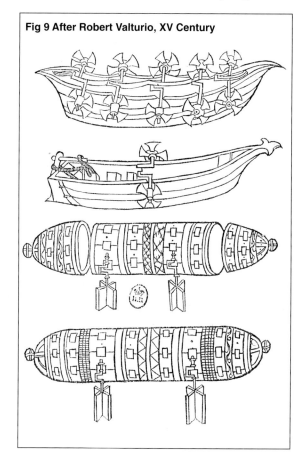

Fig 9 After Robert Valturio, XV Century

Toledo. They used a diving bell in the form of a reversed cauldron suspended by ropes and fitted with an interior platform. 'Not only did the divers not get wet but a candle they took with them was not extinguished.'

Francis Bacon (1561–1626), the English philosopher, wrote in *Novum Organum Scientiarum* (1620) that he had heard rumours that a machine had been invented, in the form of a small boat in which men could travel under water. Often there is some substance to a rumour of this sort and thus it could well have been the very first submarine or submersible. Regrettably there does not appear to be anything more substantial.

There are records of specific events. In 1552 there was a demonstration, attended by the Doge of Venice and other dignitaries of that city, by Adriatic fishermen using a bell, which measured 3 metres by 3 metres; one of the divers remained underwater for nearly two hours.

Nicolo Tartalea, a sixteenth century Italian mathematician, recorded an idea for a device consisting of a wooden structure with two platforms. Within the device was a winch connected to a heavy weight which was dropped in the water like an anchor; the device could then be winched down to any required depth. Fitted within the wooden structure was a glass bowl containing air; the aperture at the bottom permitted the diver to insert his head and breathe as and when required. Tartalea developed his idea and also proposed enclosing the diver completely in a glass sphere (presumably a larger version of his first device). Finally he considered that he could make his apparatus out of wood and fitted with glass ports so that the diver could see in all directions. It is not known if these 'machines' were ever built.

Unfortunately, up to the end of the sixteenth century, the few available records are very vague. There is no credible data showing if they were ever built and if so, how successful they had been. During the years which followed, many more developments took place and fortunately many of these have been well documented.

However, before proceeding with the evolution of the submarine, it is worth digressing to consider man's endeavour to work physically under water on the sea bed.

Diving Bells

The way men went about this can be grouped under three broad categories: the diving bell, which carried its own supply of air and was only connected to the surface with lifting tackle; the diving chamber, which was directly linked to the surface for its air supply; and the diving suit, which drew its air supply from a portable container, a diving bell, diving chamber or directly from the surface. All these had two limitations: firstly they were very restricted in how far they could move once in position, and secondly they were limited in the depth of water in which they could work.

To give just a little background on diving bells there is one that is worth mentioning not because it was particularly advanced, but it was designed by the famous astronomer Edmund Halley and the description is in his own words. It was whilst at Oxford reading mathematics that he became interested in astronomy and later, on the recommendation of King Charles II, he went to St Helena to catalogue the stars of the Southern hemisphere. On returning to Europe he settled for a time in Paris to pursue his scientific studies. Halley's popular fame is linked to his prediction, in 1682, that a comet, named after him, would return every seventy-six years. But his fame is much greater because of his work on trade winds, monsoons and terrestial magnetism. He is considered to be the father of modern geophysics.

Like so many great scientists, Halley's work was very wide ranging, and he made significant contributions in several disciplines. It was in 1690 that he developed a diving bell. This is how he described it:

> The Art of Living under Water: Or, a discourse concerning the Means of furnishing Air at the Bottom of the sea, in any ordinary depths. By Edm.

Halley, LL.D. Secretary to the Royal Society.

The Bell I made use of was of Wood, containing about 60 Cubick Foot in its concavity, and was of the form of a Truncate-Cone, whose Diameter at Top was three foot, and at Bottom five. This I coated with Lead so heavy that it would sink empty, and I distributed the weight so about its bottom, that it would go down in a perpendicular situation and no other. In the Top I fixed a strong but clear Glass, as a Window to let in the Light from above, and likewise a Cock to let out the hot Air that had been Breathed; and below, about a Yard under the Bell, I placed a Stage which hung by three Ropes, each of which was charged with about one Hundred Weight, to keep it steady. This Machine I suspended from the Mast of a Ship, by a Spritt which was sufficiently secured by Stays to the Mast-head, and was directed by Braces to carry it over board clear of the Ship side, and to bring it again within-board as occasion required.[1]

Fig 10 Edmund Halley's Bell, 1690

Halley himself experimented with the diving bell and remained submerged with several other passengers, on one occasion, for an hour. Improvements were considered, but it is not known if they were implemented. To replenish the air in the bell, Halley proposed using weighted barrels which would be lowered and connected to the interior of the bell by a pipe; a hole in the bottom of the barrel would allow the air to be replaced by water. As the bell was very heavy and not very manoeuvrable he considered using divers fitted with glass helmets and connected to the bell by a breathing tube.

There is something romantic about the diving bell: adventure, the search for treasure in the South Seas with the associated *Boy's Own* terrors of the deep in the form of a giant octopus, but it is not so easy to link them with a Hollywood musical in which, at the drop of a hat, the hero bursts into song. However, in March 1774, the King of Sweden, accompanied by Princess Sophie-Albertine, attended a demonstration of a diving bell in Lake Vattern. Jonas Dahlberg, the

Inspector of Diving, submerged with the designer of the bell and could be seen moving below the water by the royal party. The Inspector then 'sang a song of many couplets', which the king listened to using a tube connected to the bell, after which Dahlberg then serenaded the princess. The king and the princess then 'gave flattering praise to the talents of the inspector and the genius of the inventor.' Hollywood musicals will never be the same . . . they do depict real life after all.

The diving bell later developed into other forms of diving machine such as the bathysphere and its uses covered exploration, scientific studies as well as submarine rescue. Although of great interest, these static diving bells and chambers are only of peripheral relevance to submarine development.

1 *Philosophical Transactions of the Royal Society of London* Vol. 29, 1716.

Establishing the Principles

William Bourne was an English mathematician who wrote several books on science and philosophy at the end of the sixteenth century. In one of his early publications he outlined the theory that if a vessel floated and its displacement was reduced sufficiently, without altering its weight, it would sink. Conversely the vessel would float again if the submerged displacement was increased without altering its weight. In the previous chapter this was described as 'variable displacement'. In *Inventions or Devices*, published in London in 1578, (the book had the very modest subtitle: 'Very necessary for all Generals and Captains or Leaders of men as well by sea as by land'), he expanded his ideas showing how he could apply his theory in a ship.

The design was based on the hull of a then current sailing vessel. The practice of blistering designs or ideas onto existing hull forms was quite common, although such a hull would have been most unsatisfactory as a submarine. However, it would have been of a proven design, readily available should it be decided to build. But perhaps, most importantly, those to whom the project was presented (and who it was hoped would finance development), could easily relate to a shape which was so familiar.

Bourne's intention was to have large bellows, constructed from leather and controlled by screwed winches within the hull. First, the hull would be made watertight and an access hatch for the crew fitted on the deck. The bellows would be positioned on either side of the vessel and would draw water in through holes bored through the hull. Bourne particularly emphasised that the bellows and the joint with the hull would have to be completely watertight. The hull of the vessel would be ballasted with rocks and stones, to reduce the freeboard, so that by filling the bellows with water, thereby reducing the displacement, the vessel would submerge. By reversing the procedure and forcing the water from the bellows, the minimal freeboard would be re-established as the vessel surfaced.

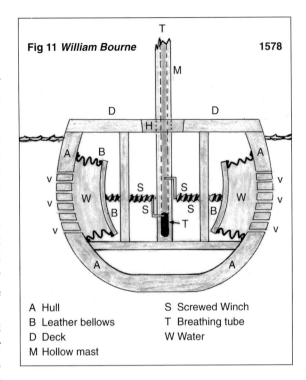

Fig 11 *William Bourne* 1578

A Hull	S Screwed Winch
B Leather bellows	T Breathing tube
D Deck	W Water
M Hollow mast	

Bourne also addressed the problem of air supply by having a hollow mast fitted so that the crew could breathe. Bearing in mind that this was purely a theoretical exercise, his submerging procedure would be as follows. Before anchoring, plumb the depth of the water to ensure that the top of the mast remained above water once the vessel was submerged and resting on the sea bed. Drop the anchor, seal the hatches and draw water into the bellows; the vessel would submerge. To surface, the water would be forced from the bellows.

This was one of the first written records of a serious study into submerging a vessel. No consideration appears to have been given, at this stage, to underwater navigation, Bourne having limited himself to considering how his theory of 'variable hull displacement' (not his words) could be put into practice. Had such a vessel been built there could have been problems with hull leakage: water seeping in through the bellows (which would have had to be quite large), and the associated joints with the hull. This would have become a greater problem as the vessel submerged and the water pressure increased. It would have been necessary to fit pumps to clear the bilges and to circulate the air which, with one narrow tube to the surface, would have been difficult. The important fact is that Bourne had identified the requirement and had produced a solution, which could later be adopted, adapted and refined by others.

Seventeenth Century

Cornelius van Drebel (sometimes spelled Drebbel), a Dutchman, built his first submarine in London around 1620 and some contemporary but contradictory comment on his vessel has been recorded. He was born in 1572 and in due course was apprenticed as an engraver. For him this lacked a challenge and he started to study philosophy in the disciplines which we would group as: science, mathematics and chemistry. He soon became an academic of some repute.

He travelled within Europe and in 1604 moved to England and the court of James I. In 1610, with the agreement of the king, van Drebel moved to Prague where he became the tutor to the children of the Emperor Ferdinand II. Two years later Ferdinand was deposed; van Drebel managed to escape and returned to England where he became the tutor to the son of James I.

Whilst in England van Drebel designed a perpetual motion machine; he is reputed to have invented the thermometer and introduced both the telescope and microscope to England. He made some form of machine which could produce rain, thunder and cold temperatures; he also built a magic lantern for projecting pictures.

A contemporary writer recorded how van Drebel's interest in submarine navigation came about. Apparently, whilst walking along the banks of the River Thames he saw some ships towing baskets filled with fish. He noted that the bows of these vessels were forced down into the water as they strained to pull the baskets, but periodically, as the rope tension slackened, the bows rose up. Van Drebel thought that using this principle he could design a boat which could be held under water using oars and rods.

James I was an intellectual and a rapport developed between the two men. James encouraged van Drebel in his research into underwater navigation. The outcome was that a submarine was designed and built. Motivated by his initial successful experiments van Drebel built a second, larger submarine. The vessel must have been of a reasonable size as there were twelve oarsmen, as well as 'other passengers'. One commentator recorded that 'the boat could only submerge to a depth of twelve – fifteen feet, for beyond this depth there was a danger that she would sink'. A contemporary sketch shows the vessel with the typical lines of a seventeenth century sailing vessel with a high prow and stern but no masts and rigging. The vessel appears to have a large internal ballast tank with associated pumps. However, another written description suggests that she was 'made of wood covered in oiled or greased leather and was egg-shaped'.

Van Drebel had devised a method of purifying the air on board using what he called 'the quintessence of air a few drops of which freshened the atmosphere in the vessel as though one had been transported to the most beautiful hill'. Aristotle's four fundamental elements of life were: Fire, Earth, Water and Air. There was also a fifth, magical and unknown element, on which all life depended and this was known as the 'quintessence of life'. Unfortunately van Drebel left no written records of his work and so his secret died with him. There were those who were sceptical about the 'quintessence'. They suggested that the boat was fitted with two tubes connected to the surface with pumps within the vessel to draw in fresh air and expel stale air. If this was the case it would have been an improvement or development of Bourne's hollow mast.

It is worth considering, at this stage, the problem of breathing in a confined space. In the early seventeenth century it was realised that there was some form of 'quintessence of life' and in a confined space this could be used up and therefore needed to be replaced. Air had not been defined and certainly its composition was not known because its component gases (oxygen and nitrogen) had not been isolated as such for gas had not been identified. Furthermore although it was recognised that air was depleted it was not understood what had occurred. Indeed it was not until after van Drebel's death that the study of air became a major subject for scientific research.

In an article published in 1997 in *History Today* (Volume 47, January 1997) Zbigniew Sydlo and Richard Brzezinski put forward some very interesting ideas on the subject which are directly related to alchemy. They suggest that the alchemist of the seventeenth century may have been well ahead of some of the scientists who are credited with major discoveries very much later concerning the identification and isolation of oxygen and gases generally.

Alchemy, medieval forerunner to chemistry, was primarily 'the pursuit of the transmutation of base metals into gold'. It was an academic discipline and there is a close affinity between alchemists and philosophers. Intelligent men were seeking answers to the riddles and mysteries of nature but they often foundered through lack of understanding or knowledge. Fundamental facts, which are taken for granted by small children at school today, had at this time not been discovered or identified.

Unlike the scientists who followed and published their findings so that others could benefit and further their work the alchemists were more secretive. Protecting their discoveries by recording their findings in picturesque language and mysterious ways which made it difficult if not impossible for the uninitiated to decipher. The popular concept that the prototype alchemist was a charlatan or trickster trying to turn base metal into gold was reinforced by numerous, well documented confidence tricks based on making gullible people wealthy. This all helped to give alchemy the aura of being a false art without firm foundations, but in fact it was a serious discipline. This was recognised by some of the greatest scientists who were fascinated by their work and tried to decipher their writings.

With the support of Rudolph II, Prague had become the alchemy centre of Europe where the greatest alchemists gathered. One of those working there during van Drebel's stay at the court was Michael Sendivogius. He had put forward the theory that the all important element in air which was fundamental to life was related to saltpetre. He had identified that air was made up of different components but science (and probably alchemy) had not advanced sufficiently to allow him to isolate and define them any further. It is suggested in the *History Today* article that oxygen may have been produced, by accident or design, from saltpetre and stored in a container. If either Sendivogius or van Drebel had achieved this and it had been used in the submersible it could account for the euphoric feeling of 'being transported to the most beautiful hill'.

It is reputed that James I accompanied van Drebel in a trip on or under the Thames. In the light of the encouragement given by the king and probable rapport between these two men this is quite possible. However, even with the king's support there appears to have been no further development of the submersible by either van Drebel or the Government. It is not known if this is because of the vessel's limitations, a lack of Government interest or a shortage of money.

One of the earliest patents taken out in England relating to submarine activities was taken out by Richard Norwood on 2 April 1632. He claimed to have found out 'a special means to dive into the sea or other deep waters, there to discover, and thence by an engine to raise or bring up such goods as are lost or cast away by shipwreck or otherwise.' His patent conferred on him sole use of his invention for fourteen years. He fails to explain, in the patent, how he intends to achieve his aim but it was probably some form of diving bell. Furthermore we do not know whether or not he made his fortune with his invention.

In 1640 in France, Jean Barie made a very similar request for a vague patent covering a machine to recover fish and wrecks from the sea bed. He did have some success salvaging part of a wreck off Dieppe.

The clergy, who were amongst the élite educated minority of the time, contributed significantly to the development of the submarine. In France, Father Mersenne, proposed that the hulls of submarines should be made of metal and should be fish-shaped. In 1644 this was fairly forward thinking although metal had been used for diving bells. He also considered arming the submarine with an upward firing cannon; the submarine went below its target, the muzzle was placed close to its hull, a watertight door opened, the gun fired and the recoil automatically closed the door. Little consideration seems to have been given to the ingress of water when the door was opened and the effects of fatally holing the enemy vessel which was immediately above the submarine. But it really is the thought that counts (however uncharitable), for although man had, from the earliest times, tried to use the cover of water to gain advantage in warfare, the thoughts of the Jesuit priests were perhaps the first seeds of an idea to use the mobility of the submarine truly aggressively.

A few years later there was more clerical input from Bishop Wilkins who wrote a philosophical treatise in which he considered submarine navigation with the advantages of privacy, security from pirates, and shelter from storms. Again this is a demonstration of the available knowledge. Anyone who has been taken to sea for a day in a submarine in rough conditions will know how uncomfortable it can be on the surface, particularly to those prone to seasickness, and what a blessing it is to submerge into the tranquility below the storm.

In 1653 another documented vessel was built at Rotterdam by de Son, a French engineer. His boat was driven by a paddle-wheel and was 72 feet (22 metres) long with a height of 12 feet (3.7 metres) and an 8 foot (2.4 metres) beam (Fig 12). The builder, who was supported by the State in his endeavours, made numerous claims:

'in one day to destroy one hundred ships, can go from Rotterdam to London and back again in one day, & in six weeks to goe to the East Indiens, and run as Swift as a bird can flye, no fire, no Storme, or Bullets, can hinder her, unless it please God. Although the Ships meane to be safe in their havens, it is in vaine, for shee shall come to them in any place, it is impossible for her to be taken, unlese by treacherie, and then can not bee governed by any but himselfe.'

With such a promise there is no wonder he was given Government backing. There was a central paddle-wheel which was to have some form of clockwork motor or spring to drive it, which was wound manually by the crew. The vessel was built of wood.

On 14 October 1653 thousands of people arrived to see the launch but the inventor claimed that the vessel would not be ready for a further eight to ten days. Eventually a new date for the ceremony was arranged; the vessel was to be launched into the River Meuse on 6 July 1654 and many invitations to witness the event were sent out. However, the launching was again put off by de Son who issued a statement to the effect that he had been unable to obtain a particular type of iron that was necessary for the completion of the boat.

Apparently a number of people had warned the Dutch that de Son 'was short of a few marbles' (*qu'il avait besoin de quelques grains d'ellebore*). But de Son was convinced that his submarine would work and although he had had no previous theoretical or practical experience he was able to convince the Dutch that his invention merited support. Had it ever been tested, it would probably

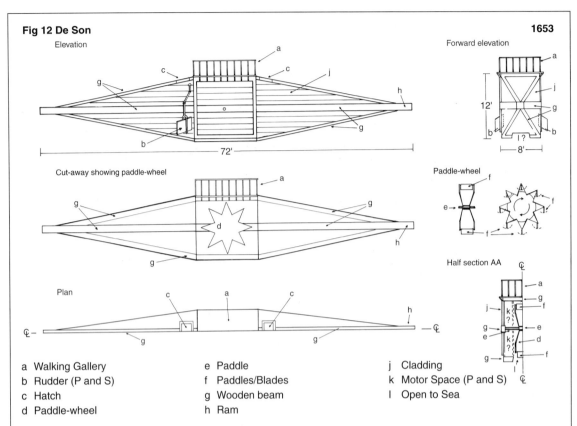

Fig 12 De Son   1653

Elevation

Forward elevation

Cut-away showing paddle-wheel

Paddle-wheel

Plan

Half section AA

a Walking Gallery
b Rudder (P and S)
c Hatch
d Paddle-wheel

e Paddle
f Paddles/Blades
g Wooden beam
h Ram

j Cladding
k Motor Space (P and S)
l Open to Sea

Three drawings of this vessel have been seen. One shows the vessel to be a catamaran with the paddle-wheel between the two hulls; another has paddle-wheels on either flank mounted in sponsons; but what appears to be the most authentic and accurate representation of the vessel has one paddle-wheel contained within the single hull. It is on this last description that the above drawings have been prepared and developed but unfortunately there are no details of the interior of the vessel or the projected power plant. De Son's very innovative concept was optimistically too ambitious. His idea of using a paddle-wheel, with paddles or blades that feathered and (presumably) locked in the driving position, driven by a motor rather than by manpower was well ahead of his time. The shape of the vessel was also quite revolutionary. As will be seen, for many years the inventors and builders of submersibles based their hull design on the then current surface vessels. De Son designed a vessel for a new environment.

only have been able to run awash and the paddle-wheel arrangement would not have been very efficient. His claims of speed and endurance could well have landed him in trouble had there been a 'Trades Description Act' in force. However, de Son did produce a hull shape which would be adapted by others.

Father Borelli was born near Naples in 1608. He studied mathematics at Pisa and later researched and published works on the laws of movement of animals. He retired to a monastery where he wrote

about astronomy and geometry. It was only after his death in 1680 that his paper describing his submarine was published. His idea for submerging a vessel was a practical refinement of Bourne's variable displacement concept.

Borelli's submarine was of wooden construction, completely enclosed and fitted with four oars on either side. The oars themselves were a complete innovation, designed to work permanently under water. The blades were hinged in such a manner that after the pulling stroke, which imparts movement to the vessel, the blades collapsed as they were

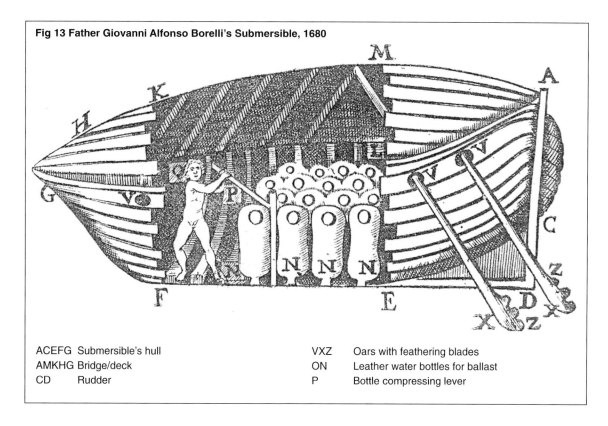

Fig 13 Father Giovanni Alfonso Borelli's Submersible, 1680

ACEFG	Submersible's hull	VXZ	Oars with feathering blades
AMKHG	Bridge/deck	ON	Leather water bottles for ballast
CD	Rudder	P	Bottle compressing lever

pushed back for the next stroke, making it stream-lined and able to pass through the water more easily. Borelli based his idea on the way the webbed feet of a goose or swan collapse as they are moved forward through the water.

Borelli changed the volume of his craft by having leather bottles connected directly to the sea through the bottom of the boat. The necks of these containers were permanently open and water ingress was controlled by levers which either allowed water to enter or forced it out. The levers would have been fitted with some form of locking arrangement so that they could maintain a selected level of water.

Without even building a submarine, Borelli had made a significant contribution to the development of the submarine. His folding oar was an innovation which would be adopted by others; and placing the numerous bottles low down in the hull was an improvement of Bourne's concept.

Many claims, some quite ambiguous, were made and submitted to monarchs and governments in the hope that the inventor would be given patronage and financial backing. It is recorded that an Italian Jesuit priest, Joseph M. Ciminus wrote to the King of France in November 1685: 'his invention provided the means for men and ships to rise and sink at will to the bottom of the sea, fully armed and with all the limbs free to stop, move, sit down, walk about and run for the space of seven hours or a whole day.' Three years later Royer Doligny also made a similar vague proposal to the king. His 'machine' was designed to go under water where work could be carried out without inconvenience. With his machine he could enter ports, go under ships, and move like a fish; sufficient food, for several days, could be carried and eaten under water, in his device. Those travelling in it could move about freely and hold conversations. There is no indication of how all this was to be achieved, but if the idea could

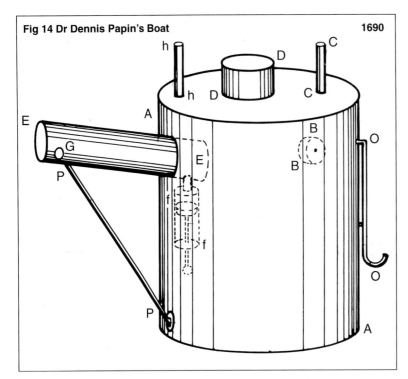

Fig 14 Dr Dennis Papin's Boat 1690

Eighteenth Century

Periodicals were not only sources of information for the general public but also an outlet to exchange views through their correspondence columns. Sometimes they could be misleading. In December 1747, *The Gentleman's Magazine* published a historical piece about a submersible built by Dr Dennis Papin, in about 1690.

Dr Papin was a Frenchman and a practising doctor, although his true interest was in the sciences, physics and mathematics. A Calvinist, he was persecuted for his religious beliefs, left France and moved to England. There he soon settled down and became associated with the prominent physicist and chemist Dr Boyle, both men sharing a common interest in research into respiration and air. Later he became a member of the Royal Society of which Boyle had been a founder

have been sold to a gullible senior-officer with ambition (had there been one), it would be an attractive proposition for furthering his career!

member. Dr Papin then moved to Marburg where Charles, Landgrave of Hesse, offered him the chair of mathematics and physics 'which he held brilliantly'.

The Landgrave had read about van Drebel's submarine and invited Dr Papin to build something similar. Two submarines were constructed.

The magazine article was limited to a description of the second vessel and in it there is no mention of Dr Papin the designer. The boat was made of wood and measured 6 feet (1.8 metres) high, 6 feet (1.8 metres) long and 3 feet (.9 metre) wide. The small craft was forced under the water using the two rowing oars which were fitted on the flanks; submerging was assisted by admitting a limited amount of water ballast. Immediately the rowers felt they could easily manage to force the vessel below the surface and hold her there the ballast water cock was closed; it would appear that this water went straight into the bilges. Theoretically the vessel always retained a small degree of positive buoyancy. (The ballasting arrangements are not at all clear in either the article or descriptions of the vessel elsewhere.) The oars were used to bring the vessel to the surface as water was pumped out. (No water pump is shown in the drawing (Fig 14) although it is mentioned in the text.) The spout (EE) was to allow a crewman to 'use his arm to ruin enemy ships' (again there is no indication how this was to be achieved except that it was possible to build up the air pressure within the tube to prevent water pouring in). There was an air pump (BB) which would circulate air through tubes (CC) and (HH). (The air pump, known as: 'the Hessian rotary sucker and forcer,' had been

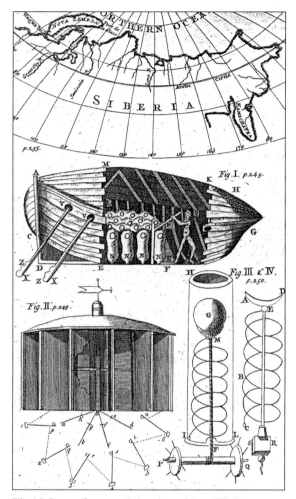

Fig 15 Copy of reversed drawing of Borelli's Boat

variable displacement had been achieved to submerge his vessel rather than water ballast. Mr Marriott having already got hold of the wrong end of the stick, went on to explain that one needed oars, the blades of which were like the foot of a goose but this was to move the vessel sideways. However, he did suggest that an oar with a flexible blade, mounted at the stern, would drive the vessel like a fish.

Mr Marriott's explanation, complete with a reversed copy of Borelli's drawing, was published in June 1749, possibly confusing some of the readers (Fig 15). However, it did do some good because it encouraged Samuel Ley to write a letter to the magazine in July 1749 in which he commented that he knew of a diving-ship far superior to the one illustrated in the magazine (Borelli's). He referred to the submarine built by Nathaniel Symons in 1729. Ley had not actually seen this vessel but he had met the builder who had told him about it twenty years previously.

Symons was a carpenter from Harbeston, near Totnes in Devonshire, and the submarine he built was in two parts which fitted together telescopically. The seal between the two halves was of leather and the vessel could be extended or contracted by screw winches within the boat. Entry into the vessel was through two watertight doors; Ley's actual description of how Symons entered the vessel is interesting: 'he made a false door in the side, which, when he was in, shut very tight; and tho' his going in admitted a small quantity of water, it was no inconvenience; after this outer door was shut, he opened the inner one to get into his boat.'

Mr Ley gave no indication how or even if the boat was to be propelled or steered, but it did carry lead to reduce its freeboard and make it more stable.

The craft was demonstrated on the River Dart. The vessel went out to the middle of the river where Symons, by himself, entered the boat, contracted the hulls and submerged. He remained below for 45 minutes and then he extended the

designed previously by Dr Papin, initially to feed air to a candle in an enclosed space and later to replenish the air in a diving bell.) The boat was fitted with a barometer (OO) to show the depth of the vessel. Although it is known that the vessel was tested there are no details about its performance.

In response to this brief article a certain Mr T.M. wrote to the magazine saying that he had failed to understand how the water was pumped out of the vessel, but that he had consulted a Mr Marriott who had clarified the situation. Unfortunately, Mr Marriott based his explanation on a drawing of Borelli's boat and explained how hulls and the boat surfaced. After this experiment he reported that the air 'began to be thick but it was still bearable'. Although there were hundreds of spectators including 'a great number of gentlemen of worth', who witnessed his demonstration, he received but a crown piece from them all.

Considering the problem now, the way Symons chose to alter the displacement of his boat was quite straightforward. But what he accomplished was quite remarkable; not only in the way he had been able to achieve variable displacement but that he was able to construct the vessel and make it work successfully. Ley actually described Symons as 'a common carpenter' but he must certainly have been very skilful and knowledgeable. Later he also built a diving bell but 'his cousin and some others, deprived him of both the honour and the profit'.

We must be grateful to *The Gentleman's Magazine* for drawing our attention to Symons' telescopic submarine but it is worth noting the confusion that these three articles caused, possibly because of problems in translation. One French historian was under the impression that M.T. (he reversed the initials at the bottom of T.M.'s letter to the magazine) was claiming to have designed Borelli's submarine. His suspicion was strengthened because Borelli's original drawing had been reversed when printed in the magazine but all the letters had been re-engraved so that they were the right way round. The Frenchman was particularly upset because he felt the 'pseudo-inventor' was retaining his anonymity because of his guilty conscience hiding behind initials and not offering his true identity. He did not realise that T.M. was purely submitting Marriott's explanation in which Borelli's drawing was used, to make a point.

But this was not the end of the confusion. Another French historian, writing in 1900, was befuddled by the articles. He attributed Borelli's boat to Simons (Symons) and went so far as to report that it was egg-shaped, powered by four pairs of oars, submerged by the method described by Borelli and implied that the vessel was seen in the Thames in 1774.

These incidents serve to show how easily a development, such as Symons', may never have been recorded for posterity. They also highlight, in the historical context, how an unintentional error can wrongly attribute work to someone else or misinterpret how equipment is designed to work, and how easily this can be perpetuated.

CHAPTER 4

BUSHNELL'S *TURTLE*

Some inventors and their inventions come to prominence all too briefly to disappear, even after glowing reports on their success, never to be heard of again. One such was a member of the Bordeaux Academy called Dionis who, in 1772, invented a submarine with eight oars. On 28 May, he is reputed to have sailed, with ten people on board, into the Bay of Biscay. There for four and a half hours the vessel was submerged and travelled five leagues (twenty kilometres). At the end of the submerged part of the voyage the passengers had had no breathing difficulties. This is attributed to the use of 'an artificial water' which was used to purify the air when it was no longer fit to breathe, the residue being expelled through a tube into the sea. This is rather reminiscent of the experiments carried out by van Drebel over one hundred years previously.

Others achieve prominence because they are very innovative, successful, or historically important. One, which falls into this category, was Bushnell's *Turtle* of 1773–1776. Her design was well thought out, she was (bearing in mind when she was built) successful, and historically she can be considered important.

Born in 1742 in Connecticut, Bushnell entered Yale in 1771 and on graduating in 1775 devoted his time to developing a submarine. His boat, the *Turtle*, was ready in 1776.

In 1787 Bushnell wrote to Thomas Jefferson, who later became the third President of the United States, giving a very full description of the general principles of how his submarine was designed and built. The letter was written eleven years after the *Turtle* was built, and may have included a few modifications based on experience, but it gives a very clear idea of how the boat was constructed and used. The letter is long and only a precis of the

more important parts is given below.

A set of drawings was prepared, nearly one hundred years after the boat was launched, by Lieutenant F.M.Barber, U.S. Navy, who needed them for a lecture (Fig 16). These appear to be the most accurate when compared to Bushnell's own description, and the precis below is directly related to this drawing. Other drawings exist but their provenance and accuracy is not known and they are shown, but purely for interest.

The hull was in the shape of two upper halves of a turtle shell joined together. The small conning tower was at the top (where the reptile's head would have emerged) and this had a water-tight lid to allow the crewman to enter the vessel and portholes so that he could see where he was going. There was lead ballast within and at the bottom of the compartment, but the main part of the lead ballast was fixed outside the hull and could be jettisoned from within should it be necessary to surface in an emergency. In the bottom of the compartment there were two ballast tanks and pumps so that they could be emptied.

The operator, who sat upright on a bench, had a cranked handle immediately to his front and another slightly higher. Both connected to Archimedes screws outside the hull, the former with a horizontal shaft and the latter with a vertical shaft. Behind him, and penetrating the rear hull, a cranked tiller connected to the rudder.

The armament of the submarine consisted of a large, wooden-encased explosive charge of 150 lb (68 kg) with a clockwork timing device that could be set for any duration under two hours. The canister was fixed to the back of the hull above the rudder and could be detached from within. On top of the vessel was an auger which could be screwed into the underparts of a ship and then released from the submarine. The auger was attached by rope to the charge and once they were both released the wooden canister, which was buoyant, would float up under the ship's hull where it would be detonated by the timer.

The procedure for submerging was very simple. The vessel would have had its internal ballast adjusted to cater for the weight of the operator. Once closed down the helmsman would allow water into the ballast tanks using a foot control which would open a sea cock. Fine adjustments could be made by pumping ballast out or allowing a little more in. It was also possible to use the vertical screw to make adjustments to the depth. To move forward or astern he could use the horizontal screw and the rudder for horizontal direction. It was also possible to use the rudder, which was in a flexible mounting, to propel the vessel forward or to adjust its horizontal orientation.

Bushnell's very full description of the *Turtle*
may have included modifications which would have been made after the vessel was first tested and used in 1776. But it shows quite clearly, how advanced Bushnell was in his thinking and development. Oars have been replaced with Archimedes screws; this was a quantum leap forward in thinking and application, for the propeller, as we know it, was not developed as such until about 1800. Probably not very efficient, Bushnell's screw had possibly proved to be passably satisfactory during the initial trials, although it produced insufficient thrust to counter a tideway. Although the 'propeller' is shown in the drawing as being hand operated Bushnell indicated, in his letter, that it could be adapted to be turned by the operator using his feet.

Unlike his predecessors, who had opted for variable displacement, Bushnell had fitted ballast tanks. With his foot valve to allow water in and

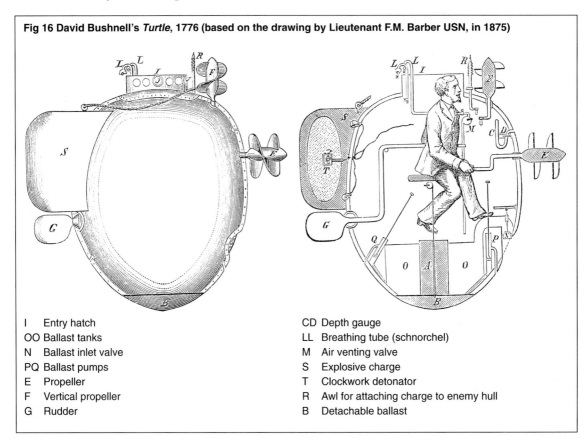

Fig 16 David Bushnell's *Turtle*, 1776 (based on the drawing by Lieutenant F.M. Barber USN, in 1875)

I	Entry hatch	CD	Depth gauge
OO	Ballast tanks	LL	Breathing tube (schnorchel)
N	Ballast inlet valve	M	Air venting valve
PQ	Ballast pumps	S	Explosive charge
E	Propeller	T	Clockwork detonator
F	Vertical propeller	R	Awl for attaching charge to enemy hull
G	Rudder	B	Detachable ballast

pumps to expel it he had control over his buoyancy but this was further refined using the vertical Archimedes screw which, he claimed, could adjust the depth keeping of the small vessel.

The hull of the submarine was designed to withstand the pressure of the sea but it was not an ideal shape for a boat. It must have been very difficult to maintain a steady course. The various hull penetrations were very carefully constructed. The pumps had double valves, and both air and water inlets were covered with perforated metal so that foreign bodies did not enter the system causing a blockage. In addition the water inlets also had screw down taps so they could be sealed in an emergency.

He had considered that it would be dark in the boat and had fitted luminous dials to the compass and the depth gauge. The controls had been laid out ergonomically, and Bushnell explained in his letter to Jefferson, exactly how the component parts of the vessel would be operated by the helmsman. Even so, in the dark, it would have been very hectic for the operator who would have been required to operate various pieces of equipment at the same time if he was to survive.

Bushnell considered that the air in the submarine would last for about half an hour before it needed to be 'freshened'. The vessel was fitted with two self-sealing ventilation pipes, which extended vertically just above the side of the conning tower and these could be used to ventilate the boat when it was awash.

Considering Bushnell's own description of the vessel, it would appear that Lieutenant Barber's drawing, accurately depicts what the small submarine looked like. Two other drawings are shown but these are considered to be less accurate (Figs 17 & 18). Immediately after completion in 1776 she was tested. This included diving the vessel at the end of a rope so that she could be

rescued should there be a problem.

The purpose of the submarine was to attack the British and surprise could be achieved by doing this submerged at night. He had devised an explosive device which could be detonated, by timer, under water. This had been tested and found satis-

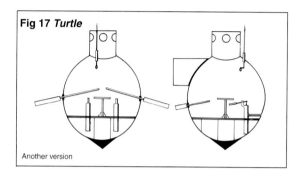

Fig 17 *Turtle*

Another version

Fig 17 The configuration of this simple drawing is similar to the previous plan but with a fundamental difference in the vessel's means of propulsion. Two possible explanations come to mind immediately. Firstly that a contemporary draughtsman or historian, who had not seen the vessel, was unable to come to terms with a description of Bushnell's revolutionary propulsion system and consequently drew something which he understood. A second possibility is that this was a very early drawing, by Bushnell himself, before he had fully developed his ideas. Like the next drawing it does not convey a true representation of the final version of the submersible as described by Bushnell.

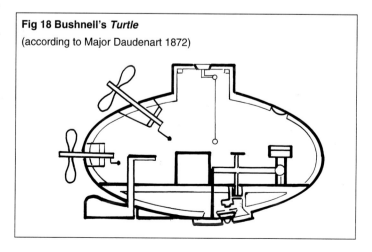

Fig 18 Bushnell's *Turtle*
(according to Major Daudenart 1872)

factory. The method of fixing the explosive charge to an enemy hull, using the detachable auger, is somewhat suspect. He may well have tested this and found that he could fix the screw into the hull of a wooden ship, but this is questionable. Would the submarine have provided a suitably firm base from which the auger could be forced into the wooden hull or, as pressure was applied, instead of the auger penetrating the hull would the small submarine, offering the least resistance, have been pushed away from its target?

It was decided that *Turtle* should be used in an attack against the British, but the operator, who had been involved in the trials and was by then very experienced and competent in the operation of the craft, became ill. It took Bushnell some time to find a suitable replacement and it was Sergeant Ezra Lee, a soldier, who was selected to carry out the first submarine attack.

To precis Bushnell's own report: 'The submarine was despatched from New York towards a fifty-gun ship (probably H.M.S. *Eagle*). Submerged, Lee tried to fix the auger in the wooden bottom of the ship but he came up against some iron near the keel. Had he moved a few inches I (Bushnell) am sure that he would have found some wood in which the auger could be set; even if the vessel had a copper bottom this could have been pierced easily. Because Lee was not adept at manoeuvring the small craft he moved away from the ship; after a futile search to find her again he surfaced, but as dawn was breaking he did not dare to make a further attempt. Withdrawing to New York, as Lee passed Governor's Island, he thought he had been seen and jettisoned the explosive charge which was slowing him down; an hour later this exploded. Afterwards Lee reported that he could have fixed the charge under the prow of the English ship as he approached; 150 lb (68 kg) of explosive so positioned would have sunk her.'

The submarine was used in two further attacks but these both failed. On the first occasion, as the submarine approached the enemy, the operator, again Ezra Lee, lost sight of his target and went well beyond her. During the second attack the boat was carried away by the tide while she was submerged below the enemy vessel trying to locate her keel.

After these abortive attempts Bushnell, who was in poor health, felt that he was not getting the necessary official backing and temporarily abandoned his project hoping that he could return to it later. He was convinced that he could have succeeded if the submarine operators were more skilful.

Historically the attacks carried out by the *Turtle* were significant. Although the submarine had been a failure, in that no British ship was sunk or damaged, this was the first occasion when a submarine attack was carried out. Within limitations the small vessel was manoeuvrable, she could submerge and gain surprise, and she had the means to sink the target. If Sergeant Ezra Lee had been able to make the auger penetrate the hull the first attack could have resulted in the sinking of an important British ship.

On her operational debut the submarine had not had a great impact and certainly did not influence the outcome of the war. One hundred years would pass before a successful attack would be carried out against a surface ship, and this too would happen in North America.

CHAPTER 5

THE DAY WAGER

One of the most bizarre events happened in 1773 when J. Day lost his life in an underwater accident in Plymouth harbour. This is slightly out of chronological order but this is intentional, for having just considered the advances that Bushnell had made, Day's contribution to submarine development was non-existent, although some lessons could be learned from his mistakes.

As far as Day was concerned his vessel had no functional purpose except to make money. Day's story started in Norfolk where he built a watertight compartment into a small boat. He sealed himself in the chamber and allowed the tide to submerge the vessel and he remained in the compartment for several hours. (One historian recorded that he remained under water for 24 hours at a depth of 30 feet [9 metres].) Having successfully survived, Day devised a way of making money from his stunt and the way in which he solved the problem was quite original.

He approached a potential sponsor, who was a gambler. Day's proposal was that he could build a large submersible in three months, and sink it, with himself on board, '100 yards (91 metres) deep in the sea, where he would remain for 24 hours and then return to the surface'. The concept was that the gambler, Mr Christopher Blake, would take bets on the success of Day's venture, and Day would be paid ten per cent of the winnings. Blake agreed, and bets were laid, but the wager was lost

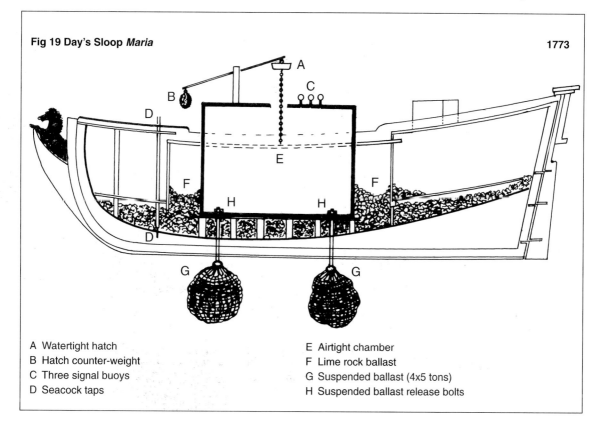

Fig 19 Day's Sloop _Maria_   1773

A Watertight hatch
B Hatch counter-weight
C Three signal buoys
D Seacock taps

E Airtight chamber
F Lime rock ballast
G Suspended ballast (4x5 tons)
H Suspended ballast release bolts

because the vessel was not ready in the stipulated three months. However, Blake agreed to underwrite the experiment which was in an advanced stage of development, but the depth would be limited to 20 fathoms (36.6 metres) for a submerged period of twelve hours.

Day had acquired a fifty-ton sloop. The mast and rigging were removed and the vessel made sound by Mr Sparks, a shipwright of Plymouth, where the event was to take place. A watertight chamber measuring about 12 feet (3.7 metres) long, 9 feet (2.7 metres) wide and 8 feet (2.4 metres) high was built into the hold of the vessel. It was heavily framed and covered with two layers of 2 inch (5 cm) thick planks running at right angles to each other. The planks in both layers were caulked. Access to the chamber was through a door in its top which when closed formed a watertight seal and was locked with chains from the inside.

Two sea cocks were fitted which could be controlled from the forecastle. Ten tons of lime rock were loaded as additional ballast into the hold. Four holes were drilled through the lower part of the hull and into the airtight chamber. Through these were fitted four ring bolts the shafts of which were secured inside the watertight container with bolts. Attached to each of the rings additional ballast, in the form of five tons of rock, was suspended. The concept was that the sea cocks would be opened, the hull flooded and the sloop would sink with Day in the airtight chamber. At the end of the experiment Day would unfasten the bolts holding the suspended twenty tons of ballast thereby restoring a level of positive buoyancy to the vessel, which would then rise.

On the day of the experiment, 20 June 1774, the sea cocks were opened but the sloop refused to sink. An additional twenty tons of stone ballast was brought from shore and deposited in the hold. As the vessel started to settle, Day sealed himself in the airtight chamber and the vessel sank. Shortly afterwards there was a large commotion in the water where the ship had gone down.

Although there was a system of signalling buoys, which could be controlled by Day, none appeared. At the designated time the vessel failed to rise and a rescue operation was launched. Very little could be done. No contingency plans had been made; they could not communicate with Day, and there were no ropes or chains connected to the sunken vessel which was lying in about twenty fathoms. After a couple of days, *ad hoc* rescue attempts were abandoned.

It is quite remarkable that Day had such blind faith in his contraption and although he had carried out a successful experiment in Norfolk albeit on a very small scale, no trials or experiments appear to have been carried out at Plymouth. No contingency plans whatever had been made in case there was an accident. One report, in a local paper, even suggested that the area selected for the experiment was: 'full of high pointed rocks' and that in that area soundings had shown variations in depth at low water ranging from fourteen to twenty-two fathoms all within a radius of a few feet. (About six weeks later, when the sloop was located, it was found to be at twenty-two fathoms at low water on a bed of soft clay mud.) As the vessel was never recovered it is only possible to surmise what happened. The large commotion in the water, just shortly after the vessel sank, could have been caused in three ways. It could have been a pocket of air escaping from the hull. If the lid of the airtight chamber had blown off there would perhaps have been a prolonged disturbance as the air escaped from a relatively small aperture but if the chamber had collapsed under the pressure there would have been a sudden commotion in the water. Had it been just a pocket of air which had been trapped in the vessel, for instance under the deck, the vessel might not have surfaced on schedule because when the time came, Day was unable to release the bolts holding the ballast suspended under the hull; if the vessel was not on an even keel or was resting on the ballast this would be quite a strong possibility. As Day failed to send up any signal buoys it would seem that something went wrong from the start and the chamber could well have collapsed under the pressure.

The story of Day does not end here. Nearly a month later a Dr Falk of London offered to salvage the wreck, and it was agreed that he should do this. At Plymouth, on 30 July 1774, Dr Falk started the recovery operation. Slings were dragged under the vessel and twice it was raised sufficiently from the sea bed, using the rise of the tide, so that it could be moved some 100 yards (91 metres). This rescue attempt was eventually abandoned at the end of August because of the weather, wear and tear on the recovery equipment, the time it was taking and possibly also the cost of the operation. The bizarre part of Dr Falk's operation was that it was a rescue attempt. He considered 'that there was a philosophical probability of restoring life to a man whose death he presumed not to be real but a cessation of the animal functions'.

For Day his costly saga ended achieving nothing but serving as a warning to others whose preparation was not sound.

CHAPTER 6

ROBERT FULTON

The French National Archives retained some interesting letters which had been sent to the Minister of the Navy. Presumably such submissions were dutifully read, and filed away for posterity for at the end of the eighteenth century the Government, in common with those of other countries, did not have their own submarine development programme although they probably had a watching brief on developments. Therefore the letters were largely of academic interest to the minister although even he must have admired both the imagination and patriotic fervour of some of those who wrote to him. He could well have been amused by others.

Some proposals were quite serious and put forward new and what could have been workable proposals. For instance those submitted by Sillon de Valmer, who claimed to have been working on his own submarine project for twenty years. Addressed to: 'Citizen Minister for the Navy' his ideas included: oars which had folding blades which worked in a similar way to those of Borelli; he recommended that the submarine hull should terminate at either end in a cone or pyramid shape; he had ideas about ballast tanks which could be evacuated with a syringe; and spherical hull mountings for the oars. Unfortunately, as far as is known, Sillon de Valmer never put his ideas into practice to test them.

Another letter to the minister, this time from a M. Beaugenet, sought assistance to build a submarine which was to be armed with cannon; when necessary it could submerge to hide from the enemy, would surface to use the guns and then submerge again. The vessel would be equipped with sails to make use of favourable winds when out of sight of the enemy. He failed to indicate exactly how the vessel was to be propelled when submerged. Beaugenet went on to say that if he had such a machine with five or six courageous men, or more if the vessel was larger, he could penetrate to the centre of London without an Englishman being a whit the wiser. (It is a shame that he did not say what he was going to do on arrival, one feels that he was not trying to avoid pilotage dues.) His address lacked the right ambience for a serious designer of submarines as it was care of the home of M. Meuniez, the wig maker.

Still another Frenchman wrote a treatise: '*Memoire sur la navigation au-desous de la surface de l'eau et sur l'usage qu'on peut faire par ruiner la Marin Anglaise*'. ('Note on underwater navigation and how it can be used to destroy the English Navy'.) Some Frenchmen did not like the English even before Trafalgar and Waterloo.

Another project was submitted to the Citizen Minister this time by Citizen C. Martner. First of all he warns the minister that he has not had any form of employment linked to ships or naval construction and consequently he may make a number of mistakes. His proposal was for a vessel 200 feet (61 metres) long by 120 feet (36.6 metres) wide and with a depth of 20 to 22 feet (6 to 6.7 metres), with no sails and propelled only by oars. She would carry 4,000 men. Using a form of variable displacement he could submerge the vessel which could be provided with air through a long tube supported on the surface by cork. The tube could also be used as a sort of telescope.

Although these various ideas and theories had been submitted to the Minister for the Navy in good faith they must have been despatched to the archives very rapidly after their receipt. But in France things were about to change and very serious proposals were to be submitted, resubmitted and submitted yet again. Robert Fulton had arrived in France.

Fulton

Robert Fulton (1765–1815) was one of the first truly great engineers. A man of stature, he had many qualities including ability, foresight and business acumen. A very brief account of the man in the *Cambridge Encyclopaedia* highlights that he is best known for his development of the steamboat – but it fails to mention that he also built several submarines.

Around Fulton's first foray into the development of submarines there is a most intricate story. Not, as one would imagine, a straightforward history covering the technical development of his invention but it is more akin to the plot for a political novel with intrigue – manipulation, money, self-interest – all set against a background of war and politics and involving some of the great men of the time. The plot can be further compounded by a quick change of National allegiance by the main character culminating with a handsome pay out by those against whom he had been plotting. Is this really relevant? The answer is that much could be omitted without detriment. However, two ingredients, which are important, are firstly Fulton's submarines *Nautilus I* and *II* and secondly the background of how approval was obtained to build them. It is also relevant to understand the man – the innovator, the brilliant engineer who had such clear foresight and perception, so that he, and his *modus operandi,* can be compared to some of the other submarine builders who came later.

Fulton was born into a poor immigrant Irish family in Pennsylvania. He was apprenticed to a jeweller in Philadelphia, but then he took up painting and became a successful landscape and miniature portrait artist. In 1787 he moved to England to study under the distinguished American painter, Benjamin West, who had settled in London and whose patron was George III. In London, Fulton made the acquaintance of the Duke of Bridgewater and Benjamin Watt the inventor, who were both involved in the development of the English canal system. This completely changed the direction of Fulton's life and he himself started to study engineering. He became involved in canal construction. and later patented a system of using inclined planes, instead of lock gates, as well as writing a treatise on the *Improvement of Canal Navigation.*

France was standing against Europe and in particular her favourite adversary England (who was blockading her ports) when, in 1796, Fulton moved to that country. He offered his services to the French Government indicating that he could not only raise the British blockade but could take the maritime war to the very shores of England. Understandably his offer was not only treated with scepticism but it was ignored. For two years he persevered and then submitted a six-point proposal to the Minister for the Navy: He proposed that his company (Compagnie Nautulus) should build a submarine. His (abbreviated) conditions were:

1 For each British ship he sank the French Government would pay £4,000 per cannon for ships over forty cannon and £2,000 per cannon for smaller ships.
2 Ships and their cargoes captured by the Company would be the property of the Company.
3 Exclusive rights to operate his invention from all French ports. Should the French Government decide to build their own submarines there would be a royalty charge of £100,000 for each boat built.
4 As an American citizen he hoped that it could be stipulated that his invention would not be used against his own country unless it was his country which was the aggressor.
5 There would be a penalty clause (financial), against the French Government should the war end within three months of the agreement being signed.
6 As the crew could be ranked with those of fire ships they would be considered to be pirates and should they be made prisoners-of-war they would be put to death. Therefore Fulton required a 'special commission' specifying that if captured the submarine crews were to be treated as prisoners-of-war and that no violence should be used against them. Should there be violence the French would take reprisals on British prisoners on a 4 : 1 ratio.

The letter was passed to the Minister for the Navy who accepted his ideas in general but with some reservations. In particular the 'special commission' demanded, posed particular difficulties. New and terrible weapons of war invariably posed problems of reprobation; in 1760 Louis XV had been offered 'Greek fire' to use against the British Navy but had refused; in 1789, when offered incendiary bullets, Louis XVI refused and locked the inventor up until the end of the war; 'such means were unworthy to the honour of France'. If men were to be killed, maimed, mutilated and wounded in battle this had to be done in direct confrontation. Similar sentiments had already been expressed by England in connection with Bushnell's *Turtle*, and would continue to prevail, concerning the submarine, into the early part of the twentieth century. The conditions laid down by Fulton were a continual stumbling block. Although they were modified, redrafted and refined several times during the next few years it appeared, in February 1798, that agreement was close, but then Fulton was informed that further consideration of his proposals was to be postponed.

Several months later the Minister for the Navy was replaced and Admiral Bruix took up the appointment. On 24 July 1798 Fulton wrote to the new Citizen Minister. While accepting that his proposal for a completely new type of weapon, on first sight, would appear to be extraordinary, he named some distinguished and well-respected academics who fully supported the feasibility of his project. He recommended that the National Institute should be invited to set up a Commission to examine his plans for a submarine and its method of operation. Less than two weeks later, on 2 August, a Commission, set up by the Minister, convened in Paris. Initially it had four members whose particular disciplines were: chemistry, mechanics, hydrostatics and naval construction; three additional members were co-opted later. The Commission produced its report in just under five weeks.

The report is very detailed; it not only covers a description of the submarine based on drawings and a model but it also includes some of Fulton's arguments, put forward in person, in justification of criticisms and points raised by committee members.

Fulton's submarine was called *Nautilus* and was to be made of copper on iron frames; she was to be 21 feet (6.4 metres) long with a maximum diameter of 6 feet (1.8 metres) (Fig 20). The vessel was to have a small hemispherical conning tower which was to be fitted with a water-tight door, for crew access, and small portholes. At the stern of the vessel there was to be a four-bladed propeller and a combined vertical and horizontal rudder. On the topside of the boat and behind the conning tower there was to be a mast and sail which stowed on top of the hull and which could be raised, set and lowered from within the submarine. This was the first submarine with two methods of motive power. This would be a prerequisite for all submarines one hundred years later.

Inside the vessel there was to be a hemispherical bulkhead at the bow, the forward side of which was open to the sea (free flooding) and would provide external stowage space for the anchor and its winch as well as the mechanism for controlling an explosive charge. In the centre of the interior hull space was the hand-driven main machinery: to drive the pumps for taking on and expelling water ballast; to control both the vertical and horizontal rudders; and to turn the propeller. Above the console was the winch which was not only used to raise and lower the mast but also to set the sail.

Although not illustrated in contemporary drawings the main weapon, the explosive charge, would probably have been stowed on the aft deck with a mechanical release which could be triggered from within the boat.

The crew of the vessel was to be three and it was estimated that they and a candle would have sufficient air for three to four hours once closed down.

This is a very abbreviated description of the vessel. The Commission went into considerable

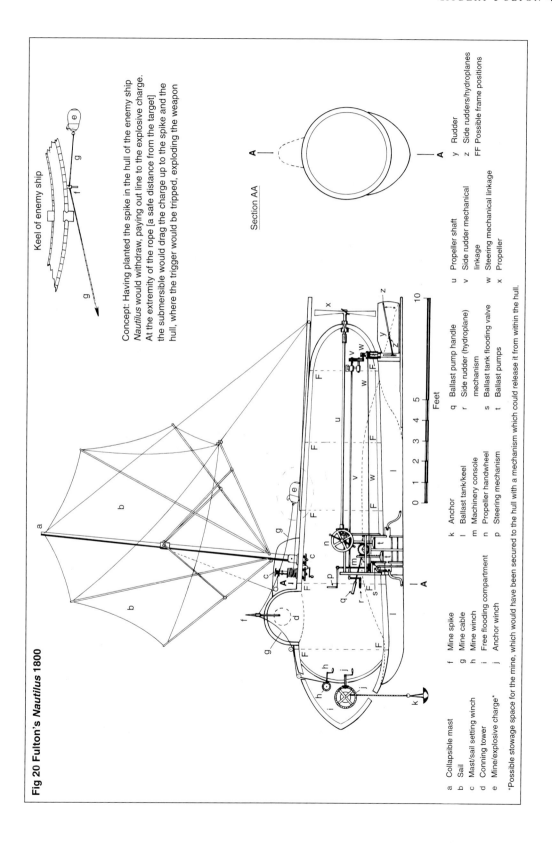

Fig 20 Fulton's *Nautilus* 1800

Keel of enemy ship

Concept: Having planted the spike in the hull of the enemy ship *Nautilus* would withdraw, paying out line to the explosive charge. At the extremity of the rope [a safe distance from the target] the submersible would drag the charge up to the spike and the hull, where the trigger would be tripped, exploding the weapon

Section AA

a	Collapsible mast	f	Mine spike	k	Anchor
b	Sail	g	Mine cable	l	Ballast tank/keel
c	Mast/sail setting winch	h	Mine winch	m	Machinery console
d	Conning tower	i	Free flooding compartment	n	Propeller handwheel
e	Mine/explosive charge*	j	Anchor winch	p	Steering mechanism

q Ballast pump handle
r Side rudder (hydroplane) mechanism
s Ballast tank flooding valve
t Ballast pumps

u Propeller shaft
v Side rudder mechanical linkage
w Steering mechanical linkage
x Propeller

y Rudder
z Side rudders/hydroplanes
FF Possible frame positions

Feet 0 1 2 3 4 5 10

*Possible stowage space for the mine, which would have been secured to the hull with a mechanism which could release it from within the hull.

detail about its construction and three points are highlighted. The innovative propeller was a development of Bushnell's Archimedes screw and most probably was the father of the ship's propeller as we know it today. It was to have four blades each approximately 2 feet (0.61 metres) long and set at thirty degrees and was to be driven by a double crank, which could be turned by either one or two men, through a 2:1 crown and pinnion. It was anticipated that 240 revolutions per minute could be achieved but for sustained power it would be driven at 120 revolutions. The side rudders or hydroplanes were mounted on either face of the rudder and could be elevated or depressed fifteen degrees above and below the horizontal by a mechanism passing through the rudder shaft and controlled with the rudder from the central console. The water ballast appears to have been taken directly into the ballast tanks through a simple, hand-operated valve.

Fulton intended that the vessel, when crewed, would be ballasted down so that only 8 inches (20 cm) of her conning tower would be above the water; to submerge her only 9 to 11 lb (4 to 5 kg) of water ballast would need to be taken on board. Having to move such a relatively small quantity of water would mean that to submerge and surface the vessel could be done very quickly. However, on the surface there would be very little freeboard and there would be the danger of shipping water through the open hatch and even a small quantity could have catastrophic results.

The Commission considered that the vessel had many potential uses but that its primary function, as far as they were concerned, was 'the destruction of the English Navy'. To this end the submarine was to be fitted with the means of destroying a ship. Attached to the top of the conning tower was a sharp, pointed, iron spike which could be released from within the submarine. A rope, controlled from within the submarine, could be let out through the free flooded area of the bow, it passed through a hole in the spike and was connected to an explosive charge in a copper container. The concept was that the submarine would go under an enemy vessel, and rise, so that the spike penetrated her hull; several blows at the bottom of the spike (this could be done from within the conning tower) would set it securely in the hull and it would be released from the submarine. *Nautilus* would withdraw initially paying out rope, the copper-encased explosive charge, carried externally, would be released from the submarine to be drawn to the spike as the submarine moved further away. One of several triggers on the charge would trip when it touched the hull of the enemy ship exploding the device. The Commission considered that if the submarine could get under an enemy ship without being seen, it could cause great damage; however there was no certainty that explosive devices would work and be effective and therefore it should be tested.

Although the Commission considered that the air in the submerged vessel would last longer than Fulton had estimated they had reservations about the buoyancy levels. It was considered that before any breathing vent was opened (there was a valve in the top of the conning tower) it would have to be at least 16 inches (40 cm) above the level of the water.

The Commission had also questioned the speed of the vessel using just the propeller and the consequent effects on steerage in both the vertical and horizontal planes. Fulton successfully used a model to demonstrate his propeller but it was pointed out that it would not be as easy driving a full-size vessel. Fulton had parried this by answering that if it proved to be unsatisfactory either a paddle wheel or oars with collapsing blades could be fitted. Related to this, the Commission was satisfied that if a current was too strong for the vessel to make headway then it could anchor until the tide turned or lessened.

The Commission considered that to effectively and safely use the sail to propel the vessel it would need to have more freeboard. This could be achieved by replacing some of the lead ballast with water ballast although it would take longer and require more effort to pump water into and out of the vessel.

The conclusion reached by the Commission was that France, with a weak Navy, required such a weapon to destroy the British fleet. It also concluded that the proposed submarine was not perfect and that time would be needed to carry out tests and trials and that such trials needed protected waters, with a depth of at least 16½ feet (5 metres).

Although the Commission had not given detailed consideration to the terms proposed to the Government by Fulton, it was considered that it was fair that he should charge for his own capital outlay. The recompense to be paid for the destruction of British ships, considering the uncertainty of success of the project, also appeared to be fair.

The Commission invited the Minister for the Navy to authorise the building of the submarine confident that under Fulton's supervision it would be well constructed and would subsequently develop into an effective warship. It was also recommended that initial trials should be carried out below Rouen; but then the submarine should be moved, 'incognito', to a sea port in the north or west.

The Commission had discussed the security of the project and it was realised that if the British knew that an attack was likely ships could protect themselves with nets. It was recommended that the building of the submarine should be kept secret. Finally, and as a subterfuge to prepare public opinion, it was suggested that information be released that the Commission's findings were that the Government had no confidence in Fulton's concept so that the whole project would be forgotten.

Fulton submitted two modified 'conditions' to the Minister for the Navy a few weeks later. Firstly he proposed that payment for the first British ship sunk by his submarine should be 500,000 francs with which he would undertake to build a flotilla of ten submarines to attack the British fleet. Secondly he produced a new method of establish-

ing how payment was to be made for ships sunk, based on the calibre of weapons.

Fulton must have been rather disappointed, in the light of the very favourable report by the Commission, when he was advised that the project was to be dropped yet again. This was a moral rather than a naval or military decision. He moved to Holland where his efforts to interest the Government of that country in his work, met with the same frigid response that he had received from the French Navy.

The political situation in France was changing and Fulton returned to that country to renew his written assault on the Minister for the Navy. His letter of 6 October 1799 was quite succinct and in it he made three main points:

1 If there were those in the Ministry and Government who were against the submarine the whole matter should be brought out into the open and their arguments examined to see if they were sound.
2 Failing this he would publicise his invention and offer his services to Holland(!) and America.
3 What Fulton really wanted was to serve France.

Attached to the letter was a paper entitled *Observations on the Moral Effects of* Nautilus *should she be Used Successfully*. In a preamble Fulton points out that his project had already been examined three times by different Ministers for the Navy and that little or no progress had been made in some twenty months even though the Commission had recommended that the submarine should be built. He then gets down to the arguments.

If the submarine was used, the British fleet could be destroyed and a blockade of the Thames established. This would be difficult to break because of the difficulty in locating and engaging the submarines. Because of her reliance on overseas trade this would quickly force Britain to submit. He then considered the effects of the British blockade, possibly strengthened by submarines, against France. If France's sea routes were effectively closed she could rely on her own agriculture supplemented with her commercial links with the Continent, and would therefore not be as badly affected as Britain should she be successfully blockaded. His conclusion was that if a successful blockade could be mounted, Britain would have to bend to the will of France and submit to her Republican principles.

He went on to examine the moral issues. The piratical connotation was dismissed using the argument that pirates normally attacked commercial targets to make a profit for themselves and it is they and those who offer them shelter who are in the wrong. (His submarine would be attacking naval targets.) The submarine is purely a logical development of a weapon of war, just like a single-shot pistol being developed to fire several rounds without reloading. He pointed out the use of the *Turtle* in America was a precedent, and smaller, less powerful nations could not be blamed for using such a weapon against a more powerful enemy. Once the smaller nations lead the way, the world would follow; people will not use bows and arrows on principle against guns. Not to use *Nautilus* would be a grave crime against France and Liberty.

Fulton goes on to elaborate the benefits of France becoming the dominant European power and being in a position to bring peace and harmony to Europe. His republicanism is clearly demonstrated in his view that having brought Britain to her knees then she, followed by Ireland, would become republics and the aristocrats who perpetuated the war would be removed from power.

Five days later the new Minister for the Navy ordered that the model of *Nautilus* should be re-examined. In the meantime Fulton continued to submit amendments to his 'conditions'. These included a clause to the effect that *Nautilus* would not be placed under the command of anyone else and he would be free to operate where he wanted. He still expressed concern about the 'special commission'.

At last Fulton was authorised to build *Nautilus* and the submarine was built by Perrier Brothers on the Seine in Paris. Even during construction Fulton continued to press for changes to the 'conditions'. His approach was now slightly different in that he asked for his requests to be put before the First Consul, Napoleon.

Trials were first conducted on the Seine in front of Les Invalides. Fulton, accompanied by a sailor and a candle, submerged completely for eighteen minutes during which time the submarine covered a 'great distance' (unspecified), the submarine submerged again and returned to its starting point. The mast was then raised and the vessel tacked several times across the river.

The submarine was moved to Rouen. In a letter from the Navy Supply and Secretariat officer of Rouen to the Minister of the Navy he reported that Fulton had had a 'sort of boat' made which was about 20 feet (6 metres) long and 6 feet (1.8 metres) wide. Its purpose was to give *Nautilus* the appearance of being a boat when on the surface, and allowed the crew to have somewhere to stand when the submarine was travelling on the surface. The modification did not prevent the submarine from submerging. Quite a vague observation but it is possible that some form of casing had been fitted to the vessel increasing its freeboard when surfaced, however, this would limit what could be observed from within the conning tower.

After two diving tests (the longest lasting 17 minutes) in 25 feet (7.6 metres) of water, with currents running at about 4 km per hour, it was decided to tow the submarine to Le Havre. Here the trials started in earnest. First it was decided to replace the four-bladed propeller with one of two blades and a diameter of 4 feet (1.2 metres). This was followed by an experiment on the surface which showed that driving the boat with the new propeller was nearly four times more effective than driving it using ordinary oars. The second test showed that three men and two candles could remain below the surface for one hour and two minutes with no ill effects. A third test established that the compass could be used for navigation when submerged. A fourth experiment was carried out to test the effectiveness of the hydroplanes; on one occasion, when the boat had not been properly ballasted, they had no effect on the boat, but later, when the vessel was properly ballasted, Fulton found that using the hydroplanes, he could steer the submarine in the vertical plane.

One further experiment was conducted at Le Havre and this did not involve *Nautilus*; it was purely to test the effectiveness of the explosive charges. An ordinary barrel was moored in the harbour. The explosive charge, in a container attached to a long rope, was floated down towards the barrel using the current. Fulton was able to control its direction by adjusting the position of his own vessel, until the rope went under the barrel and snagged the mooring rope, when it was pulled in drawing the explosive charge towards the target. As soon as it hit the barrel it was successfully detonated by one of the triggers mounted on the exterior of the explosive device.

Fulton then sailed down the coast to Growan near Isigny and once logged 1½ leagues (6 km) per hour (there is no indication if this is through the water or over the ground but in this area, with the tide, to cover 6 km in an hour would not be difficult). For the next twenty-five days the weather was bad. However, Fulton later reported that on two occasions British brigs were sighted in the vicinity of the Isigny islands but attempts to get near them failed as they withdrew on sighting *Nautilus'* sail.

Fulton had two very important allies and supporters – Gaspard Monge an academic, past Minister of the Navy and highly decorated by Napoleon and Pierre-Simon Marquis Laplace, also a very distinguished academic. Both these men were highly respected and influential and Fulton constantly kept them informed of his progress. It was at the end of one of his letters to them, written in November 1800, that he advised them that as his vessel was not built for bad

weather conditions and as the winter was approaching he would be returning to Paris to brief the Minister of the Navy. As a result of his various experiments and experiences he had many new ideas to improve his submarine.

One of Fulton's ideas was to fit a propeller on a vertical shaft, on the keel of his boat to help her submerge having established that the hydroplanes did not have as much effect as he had hoped. His plan would involve building a new submarine. *Nautilus* was left abandoned, to rot on a beach not far from Le Havre where she remained for many years. (As events unfolded it did not matter, but this was not good security with a secret weapon, which was supposed to be the ultimate deterrent.)

On his return to Paris, Fulton wrote to his two patrons, reiterating how the British fleet could be destroyed. He also had suggestions on how the operation could be funded by the French Government. His argument was that submarines would be much more cost effective than ordinary ships of the line. Although he had constantly offered his own services to lead the operation he did suggest that if the French Government preferred to use French citizens he would be prepared to stand down and pass on to them all his knowledge relegating his own role to just supervising the construction of the submarine(s). On 27 November his letter was seen by the First Consul and several days after this Fulton was presented to Napoleon by Monge and Laplace who strongly recommended that 60,000 francs should be authorised for the building of a new submarine. Their pleas fell on deaf ears.

By 3 December Fulton was becoming impatient and wrote to the Minister for the Navy with modified proposals (his fifteenth version). The following day, Admiral Decres, who was now the Minister, sent a report to Napoleon. He considered that one of Fulton's proposals, to use an old warship hull as a target, to test the rope controlled floating charge device, was a complete waste of money. He went on to say that 'he had always been an ardent defender of the submarine and it was with sadness that he had to abandon it'.

The influence of Monge and Laplace was considerable and they were able to convince Napoleon that he should support Fulton and not his own Minister for the Navy.

There is no doubt that *Nautilus II* was built but it is not sure whether she was constructed in Paris at the yard of Perrier Brothers or at Brest. In tests carried out with the new boat there is mention that she had a crew of four, this could indicate that she was larger than the first boat. If she was fitted with a vertical lift propeller under the hull another crew member would probably have been necessary. The boat could also have been fitted with a casing if the earlier supposition is correct. But all this is pure conjecture because a drawing of the second submarine has not been found. One report did indicate that in addition to the 'butterfly' sail she also had a jib.

It was at Brest that the new boat was first tested. The vessel was submerged in varying depths up to 25 feet (7.6 metres) and, with a crew of four, remained under water for one hour. Fulton was concerned that the candle was wasting the precious oxygen and had a porthole fitted in the top of the conning tower which allowed in sufficient light for a man to see his watch. A further experiment was then carried out in which a copper vessel, with a capacity of one cubic foot was filled with air, compressed to 200 atmospheres. The air was slowly bled out during a dive, which lasted for four hours and twenty minutes; and the crew suffered no ill effects.

For a time Fulton diverted his attention from *Nautilus II* and arranged to have a 36-foot (11 metres) long boat built. This was driven by paddle-wheels (there could have been two or four on either side) which were turned by twenty-four sailors working four cranks, and the vessel could travel at about 4 knots (7.4 kph). Using the explosive charge attached to a rope technique, Fulton destroyed a small launch. This trial possibly sounded the death knell for his submarine project because he had shown that there was another way

of launching an attack. It also seems strange that if the trial was primarily to test the effectiveness of the charge against a hull, why was it necessary to make a paddle-boat, when he could have conducted the experiment using an available naval rowing pinnace.

Even so he pressed on with his submarine development and in early August sailed along the coast past Coquet to Berthaume where he lay in wait for a British warship to present herself as a target. Although ships were seen their crews were very vigilant, perhaps having been warned of the threat, and no attacks were launched.

Fulton wrote one last letter to Napoleon trying to convince him that a fleet of submarines would be successful. The letter was not answered. Fulton's work on submarine development in France came to an abrupt end either because of an official decree or by his own decision.

Some have criticised Napoleon for not giving Fulton greater support, pointing out that he was too preoccupied with the land battle at the expense of his Navy and that he would have achieved much more had he not ignored the war at sea. But this could be countered by considering what Fulton had produced. Theoretically he had very strong arguments; he had built two submarines which it would appear worked; but he had not managed to carry out an attack on one British ship. Had he managed to carry out one successful engagement the situation would have been completely different. Napoleon, who was reported to have maintained an interest, from afar, of Fulton's activities saw him as a money-grabbing American.

Considering the fifteen or so contracts or conditions that Fulton floated he was certainly a businessman who wanted to look after his own interest. But to be fair to Fulton he appears to have had a great commitment to France and her cause. It could just have been that those with high moral values, who had thwarted Fulton's approaches time and time again, had prevailed in the long term.

Fulton went on to better things via England. A quick change of allegiance and he was able to present his ideas to the British Government. His submarine plans were examined by a committee which declared them to be impractical. However, his floating explosive charge raised a greater interest and two attacks were carried out, unsuccessfully, against the French in Boulogne.

The British were less mean than the French Minister of Marine, Admiral Decres, and provided the brig *Dorothy* as a target. (Perhaps the generosity was not all that great . . . the brig was Danish.) Fulton carried out a demonstration attack, using two boats to control the explosive charge and successfully destroyed the brig.

The supremacy of the British fleet against the French had been amply demonstrated at Aboukir Bay (Battle of the Nile), Copenhagen and more recently at Trafalgar. The Earl St Vincent, First Lord of the Admiralty, was concerned that the Prime Minister was offering Fulton support. He expressed his views quite strongly: 'Pitt was the greatest fool that ever existed to encourage a mode of warfare which those who commanded the seas did not want and which if successful, would deprive them of it'.

However, the Prime Minister, William Pitt, was perhaps not such a fool for he did recognise the danger of Fulton's inventions and to maintain the *status quo*, which was to Britain's advantage, Fulton was bought off with £15,000 to keep his secrets to himself. Fulton returned to New York in 1806, where he was to develop steam ships, and later another but unsuccessful submarine, while Britain continued to rule the waves.

It is difficult to make an assessment of *Nautilus I* and *II* because of the lack of real information that is available. There are a number of short reports or commentaries on the performance of the two submarines, but much of the input is by Fulton himself, and he was hardly going to be too critical. Some observations were made by Naval officers but these were not necessarily based on properly conducted tests designed to evaluate the

vessels. They were generally comments on what the officers had seen Fulton choose to demonstrate under conditions selected by him.

Rather than surmise about the effectiveness of the two boats a number of rhetorical questions and some comments are posed to allow the reader to formulate his own opinion:

1 Various speeds were claimed both on and below the surface; however, there was no indication if this was with or against the current and if so how fast the tide was running. There is no specific comment on the range of the vessel under water or indeed on the surface. *Nautilus I* made several reasonably long passages but these were probably largely under sail and with the tide. A man-powered vessel of this type inevitably has endurance problems. The sail would certainly have been an asset under the right weather conditions but it would also have been a complete giveaway (once the enemy were aware that the submarine used this form of propulsion). With look-outs aloft, the ship would have had an advantage.

2 If the sail was lowered on sighting an enemy ship the crew could have been faced with a very hard task to catch the ship or intercept it.

3 What problems were encountered conning these submarines? Originally Fulton only intended to have a small freeboard of about 8 inches (20 cm) but he would have needed much more than that in the open sea if the boat was to run on the surface because of the danger of flooding through the open hatch.

4 The commander, positioned so that he could see through the ports on surfacing, had no direct physical control over any of the machinery and would have had to issue orders for every variation in course, depth and speed relying on the quick responses of his crew. (As will be seen later, in many small submarines the commander had direct, physical control over the main functions of the vessel which he was not only commanding but driving.)

5 Both submarines carried out submerged runs over several hundred yards, but a straight run in a river or in a harbour, in predetermined and probably advantageous conditions, is one thing but an actual attack on an enemy ship in the open sea is quite a different matter.

6 In an attack, it would have been necessary, periodically, for the submarine to break the surface with the boat's conning tower so that the captain could check his position and course by getting a sight of the enemy through the portholes; he would have needed to gain some height above the water, particularly if there was a sea running, to clear the glass and get an uninterrupted view over the bow wave made by the conning tower. If a form of casing had been fitted, it could have severely limited his view from the conning tower ports unless the height of the conning tower had been raised above the level of the casing.

7 Could the submarine surface and dive both quickly and safely when conducting an attack when the commander only wanted to break surface momentarily?

8 With the water slopping around in the ballast tanks, were these boats stable when submerged or did they have longitudinal stability problems which was so common with later submarines?

9 No record has been found of any form of trial to establish if the spike could be driven into the hull of a ship from below. The small porthole fitted to the lid of the conning tower of *Nautilus II* would have been an asset and at least allowed the captain to discern his target. The French were reluctant to provide suitable hulls for trials (particularly if they were likely to be destroyed) but in this case it would not have been necessary to actually sink the target. As this was the primary function of the vessel it is strange that no such test seems to have taken place. Had one been conducted, it is felt that Fulton would have ensured that the Minister of the Navy was well and truly informed how successfully this had been accomplished.

It is very easy to look back with hindsight and ask questions about submarines, particularly the early ones, and such questions or a variation of them can be posed about many subsequent vessels. Fulton was a brilliant engineer and his submarines a great achievement; they certainly were the most advanced that had yet been developed. Had the French given him their full support and backing from the outset the outcome could have been very different. But Fulton had other special qualities. He persevered and was tenacious, had he not been, he would not have achieved as much as he did in France. He was politically aware and had the ability and foresight to see how the submarine could be used to devastating advantage both tactically and strategically.

Although he was able to present his own case he realised, particularly in the hostile arena in which he had to be involved, that influential and credible allies were necessary, for it was they who opened doors particularly when they had been slammed in his face. He had business acumen and realised that he had an invention which he firmly believed could change history; the market was there – France under siege being blockaded by the most powerful maritime nation in the world; and of course the time was right, for Governments are prepared to spend money on armaments in wartime and at moments of crisis. His business instinct was not affected by loyalty; allegiances could be changed easily and, strangely, at a time when such high moral values reigned in the method of waging war, readily accepted by the other side.

As he was prepared to command his own submarine in an attack against the British and because of his very deep republican feelings, Napoleon's description of Fulton was probably rather harsh: 'this American was a charlatan, a crook who only wanted money'. He may have wanted money, and his own self-interest may have dictated his concern about the 'special commission' but in reality he was a remarkable man and a brilliant engineer.

The course of history cannot be changed but it is interesting to speculate: 'what would have happened if?' For instance, had the French Minister of Marine, when first approached by Fulton in 1796, recognised the potential of what he was being offered and if he had been able to placate the objectors, the development of the submarine could have taken a completely different course. With full Government backing, the submarine could have been developed and there would have been sufficient time, before 1805, to build a small fleet of these vessels, train the crews and deploy them to be carried on men-o-war and launched as a close combat weapon. Although they had a restricted range, and would have had to surface frequently to get their bearings and select a suitable enemy target, they would have been quite difficult to engage as the larger calibre weapons could not be brought to bear as they could not fire with a negative angle of sight. They would have been vulnerable to small-arms fire but this may not have been all that effective. Certainly some account of their potential would have had to be taken into consideration by Lord Nelson at Trafalgar had he known about them; but what would have happened if the French had managed to keep the new weapon secret? Would it have saved the French fleet? Would it have had any effect at all? But of course, they would not have been deployed with the fleet, they would have been used to attack the British blockading ships and home ports trying to establish their own blockade of England. If this had happened what would the consequences have been?

CHAPTER 7

EARLY NINETEENTH CENTURY

While Fulton was busy in France an English engineer called Hodgson was experimenting with a submarine a few miles further north in Folkestone. Very little is known about his vessel except that it was submerged in the sea and remained under water for eight minutes, carried out various manoeuvres and travelled about a quarter of a mile (402 metres). Although nothing more is heard about his invention it is interesting to note that Hodgson spoke to the 'Class of Science, Physics and Mathematics' at the French Institute in Paris about submerging in his submarine in September 1801. Fulton's initial trials on the Seine had been witnessed by many naval officers and engineers as well as passers-by and was far from being secret. Most probably there was an exchange of information amongst those involved and certainly between the academics whose interest was scientific rather than military.

There were no significant submarines developed during the first half of the century, although various theses were written, and both good ideas and wild fantasies were aired. Scientific magazines continued to be a platform from which those with ideas but without the backing or influence to put them into operation could propose them. Some of these ideas were sound like those of Mr B . . . X (writers still liked to maintain an anonymity using just initials) who proposed three interesting ideas: the first was a variation of disposable weights to be jettisoned in an emergency, these were strapped on the side of his vessel; the second was to use two syringes or pistons to make fine tuning adjustments to his equilibrium having taken on water ballast in the normal way; the third idea was to fit his submarine with large wheels so that it could travel on the sea or river bed. These ideas would take shape, but much later.

During the first half of the century there were also fatal accidents in Spain, France and the United States where the inventors submerged in their vessels and failed to return to the surface.

Napoleon became interested in a project proposed by two Frenchmen, the Coessin brothers, and ordered that a submarine, to their design, should be built at Le Havre and evaluated. A commission was set up including academics who had been involved in assessing Fulton's *Nautilus*. Strangely, and possibly with a lack of imagination, the new vessel was also called *Nautilus*.

The submarine was 27 feet (8.2 metres) long, made of wood and shaped like a barrel with cones at either end. She was ballasted with lead. The interior was divided into three compartments the centre of which was the crew space, while those at either end were used as ballast tanks. The vessel was propelled by four rowers with two oars on either side. The speed of the vessel was 2 km per hour but this could be increased by using more rowers. Steering was by rudder and guidance, under water, by compass. Four fins (hydroplanes), two on either flank, were used to submerge the vessel in addition to the water ballast. The submarine was connected to the surface with an umbilical tube to provide air for the crew, but there were problems expelling the foul air. The committee examining the vessel considered that this was an unnecessary fitting as the vessel never remained submerged for more than an hour during which time there was no need to freshen the air.

Although it had many design weaknesses and there was no mention of any weapon system or how an attack was to be carried out, the committee considered that the Coessin boat had potential because it could be made easily and cheaply. Others were less optimistic; the submarine was not as well constructed or thought out as Fulton's. There were also other problems concerning the breathing tube apparatus used by the brothers. Firstly it had been designed by a German called Drieberg and approval to incorporate it in the vessel had not been obtained, and Drieberg was somewhat upset. Secondly, the tube, which in any case was not necessary, slowed the vessel down so much when she was submerged that she would only move at one knot per hour. It is surprising that the committee supported the concept but perhaps not so strange that nothing more was heard of this submarine

A popular fantasy, in some circles, was a project by Captain Johnston, an American. His backers had promised to pay him £40,000 when his 100-foot (30 metres) submarine was ready to set sail to St Helena to 'rescue' Napoleon. Like Fulton, he used a collapsible mast and sail, the vessel was to be armed with an explosive charge with a clockwork timing device and he also compressed oxygen to

freshen the atmosphere in the submarine. It was probably not the most diplomatic move to have the boat built on the Thames, not all that far from where Wellington was currently employed. However, before the submarine was completed, news arrived that Napoleon had died.

His next plan, submitted to the British Government, was to attack the French fleet at Cádiz. This also fell through, so he offered the five submarines he had available (two of which were still under construction) to the French Ambassador in London. These ranged from 20 to 60 feet (6 to 18 metres) in length and they appear to have had no outstanding qualities; this must have been recognised by the Ambassador who did not take up his kind offer. Johnston was from a similar mould to Fulton; having recognised a niche in the market he tried to exploit it. But in his case he produced the hardware first, his timing was wrong and the product not very satisfactory.

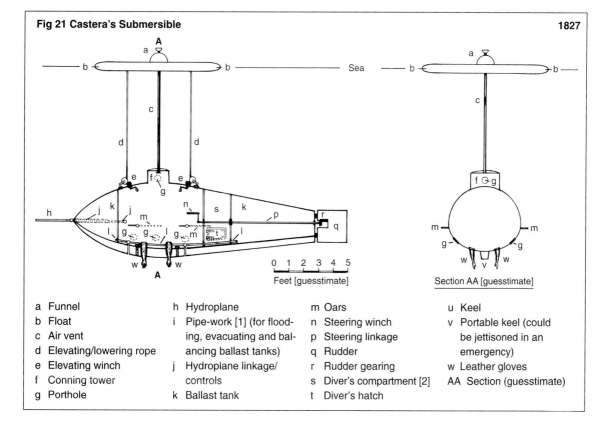

Fig 21 Castera's Submersible 1827

a Funnel
b Float
c Air vent
d Elevating/lowering rope
e Elevating winch
f Conning tower
g Porthole

h Hydroplane
i Pipe-work [1] (for flooding, evacuating and balancing ballast tanks)
j Hydroplane linkage/controls
k Ballast tank

m Oars
n Steering winch
p Steering linkage
q Rudder
r Rudder gearing
s Diver's compartment [2]
t Diver's hatch

u Keel
v Portable keel (could be jettisoned in an emergency)
w Leather gloves
AA Section (guesstimate)

In 1827, a Frenchman named Castera, took out a patent for a submersible which was suspended from a floating platform. The boat had large ballast tanks at either end and negative buoyancy could be achieved. By winching, in or out, the submarine crew could raise or lower their vessel from the mother platform (Fig 21).

Castera's submarine had a detachable keel which could be jettisoned in an emergency. Six portholes were set in the bottom of the hull for viewing the sea bed. To recover small items, a pair of leather gloves extended through the bottom of the hull. There was a door to allow divers to leave the vessel under water but there is no indication whether there was an associated air lock or if it worked on the principle of a diving bell. The vessel was fitted with side 'oars' which appear to have worked like the fins of a fish, and were worked by cranks within the hull. The rudder, at the stern, was also controlled by a crank turning a crown against a pinnion. Fitted immediately forward of the bow, with its linkage passing through the forward ballast tank, was a hydroplane designed to assist in maintaining longitudinal stability.

The vessel was connected to the surface float by 'cords' and a tube which was for fresh air – if it did not collapse, because of the pressure. This could probably also have been used to communicate with the crew on the floating platform. The floating platform did not appear to have any means of propulsion or steering.

Although this was more like a diving bell than a submarine there were a number of new ideas, although many of them would require testing and further development. A later design, which was very similar, had wheels to allow it to travel on the sea bed. Castera's submarine was never built and was purely a paper exercise.

France was still at the forefront of submarine research and development, although her navy had not been armed with one submarine. The commitment or interest at Government level was there. De Montgery, an often quoted and respected critic whose writings had contributed to the develop-ment of submarines, was invited to write a thesis on this new type of warfare by the French Minister for the Navy.

He proposed a new submarine, the *Invincible*, based on well established ship design but made of iron. The length was 112 feet (34 metres), beam 28 feet (8.5 metres) and 16 feet (4.9 metres) draught. On the deck there was a metal dome, for conning the vessel, pierced with viewing ports which closed automatically when the submarine submerged or the dome was hit by a wave.

The motive power of the vessel is glossed over and is rather vague. She was fitted with two masts and a bow sprit complete with a full set of sails. The submarine was equipped with two types of oars and a gas motor to drive the 'principal oar' (which de Montgery declines to describe because it would take too long). The 125-man crew could provide men to row the vessel but the oars could be driven by a steam engine on the surface.

It was the intention that the submarine would be submerged so that only the dome was above water. Penetrating into a harbour or port, at night, the vessel would surface, open her water-tight gun ports and engage the enemy with her twelve carronades. Other weapons were also considered including a form of pump to project 'Greek Fire'.

To end his thesis de Montgery points out that submarines should be able to travel considerable distances. He cites the United States to England, and to do this they must have the necessary means to propel them.

De Montgery produced the design of a second, slightly smaller submarine, called *Invincible II*. This could be made from wood or iron, although the latter was preferred. This vessel was also to be fitted with hinged masts which could be lowered, and a full set of sails. The submarine was to be equipped with a 'martenote' (named after its early eighteenth century inventor) (Fig 22). This was a large mechanical device, prism shaped, and suspended at the stern of the vessel. By oscillating the martenote the vessel would be pushed forward.

Fig 22

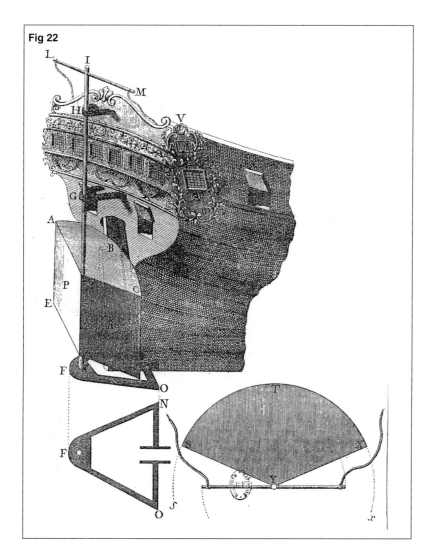

Le Martenote (Illustration published in *La Navigation Sous-Marin* 1906)

working three capstans; the martenote was to be driven by a gas motor when the boat was both on and below the surface. The vessel was to be armed and functioned in a similar way to the first *Invincible*.

De Montgery did not put his theories into practice but he showed that he was a clear thinker and anticipated developments which would be perfected at a later date.

Many engineers built small submarines which could submerge and had very limited manoeuvrability. Some, like Dr Petit in 1834, tested his 12-foot (3.7-metre) long, metal cigar-shaped vessel in the River Somme in front of a large crowd. He circled around on the surface of a lock, momentarily went ashore to take on some ballast, then, with with some panache he waved to the crowd, re-embarked and submerged. He failed to surface and his submarine was recovered intact next day when the lock was drained. Yet again no contingency plan had been made in case of an accident.

However, it was neither possible to go astern nor to steer with this impeller. Therefore three paddle-wheels were to be fitted to either flank of the submarine. These were designed to allow the blades or paddles to feather for the top fifty per cent of the turn. As with his first boat, there were three methods of driving the equipment. The paddle-wheels were driven, when the vessel was on the surface, by a steam engine but when submerged the steam power was replaced by ninety men

Others, like Villeroi, managed to convince the authorities that their boats were worth examination, but support was not forthcoming.

While most inventors were interested in producing submarines to be used for warlike purposes, there were a few who wanted to further science or use their vessel for peaceful purposes. One such was Dr Payerne who, in 1846, built a submarine

Fig 23 Dr Payerne

1846

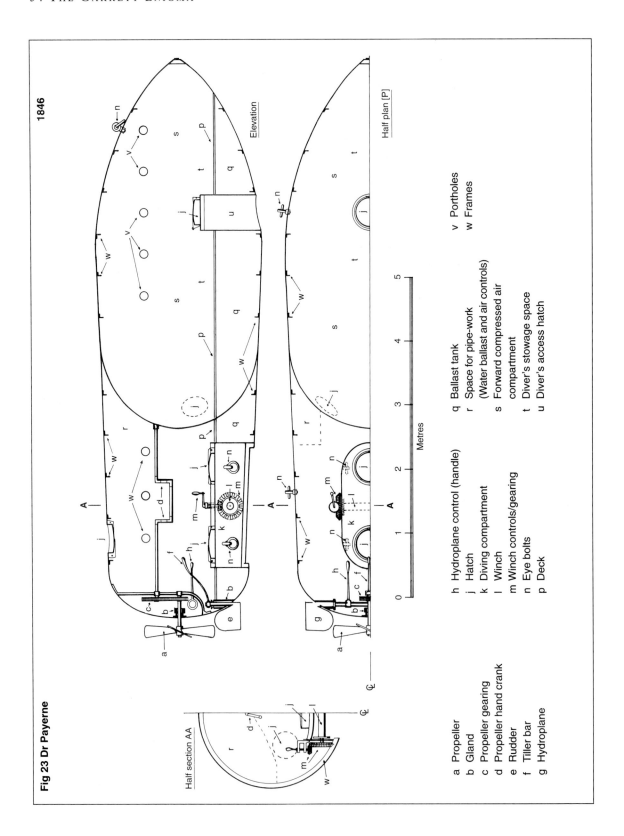

Elevation

Half plan [P]

Half section AA

Metres
0   1   2   3   4   5

a Propeller
b Gland
c Propeller gearing
d Propeller hand crank
e Rudder
f Tiller bar
g Hydroplane

h Hydroplane control (handle)
j Hatch
k Diving compartment
l Winch
m Winch controls/gearing
n Eye bolts
p Deck

q Ballast tank
r Space for pipe-work
   (Water ballast and air controls)
s Forward compressed air
   compartment
t Diver's stowage space
u Diver's access hatch

v Portholes
w Frames

29½ feet by 10 feet (9 by 3 metres) from iron sheet banded with metal rings. (Fig 23) The vessel was designed to transport divers, who could leave the vessel to work under water; the submarine could transport anything recovered from the river or sea bed to the surface.

The interior of the boat was divided into two compartments; the forward one acting as an air reservoir, and that at the stern as a crew working space. The vessel was fitted with a hand-cranked and geared, four-bladed propeller, along with vertical and horizontal rudders at the stern. Under the decks of both compartments were ballast tanks, and through the lower part of the hull were hatches for the divers. There was a watertight access port between the two interior compartments.

Access to the vessel was through the top watertight hatch. The procedure for working the vessel was that once the crew were sealed inside, the vessel would be submerged by taking on water ballast. The boat was propelled in the normal way although navigation could have been difficult with no conning position although there were ports on the sides of the two compartments. Once in position compressed air was bled into the crew compartment building up the pressure until the bottom hatches could be opened without water entering the submarine. Divers could then leave the boat. Any recovered articles could be placed in either the crew compartment or in the diving hatch compartment, below the crew working area, which was equipped with a winch for lifting heavy items. To surface, the lower hatches were closed, the ballast pumped out and the pressure in the crew compartment reduced as necessary.

Although the vessel had the large compressed air chamber and it was possible to refresh the air supply in the working space, this was still a major problem if the vessel was to be submerged for prolonged periods. Dr Payerne, who had been studying the problem of breathing in a confined space, offered the boat to the Scientific Academy (L'Académie de Sciences) so that other scientists could carry out their own experiments. The offer was accepted and numerous scientific experiments were carried out during the next ten years.

CHAPTER 8

WILHELM BAUER

The next inventor of significance was Wilhelm Bauer, a Bavarian. As a soldier he had witnessed the damage caused by the Danish fleet on the German coast and the submarine appeared to be a satisfactory counter-measure. His first boat, built in 1850, was sponsored by the Army of Schleswig-Holstein. Historians give this submarine two names: *Le Plongeur Marin* (Sea Diver) and *Der Brandtauscher* (Fire Diver), although the latter is probably a more fitting name for a submarine which he designed much later (Figs 24–28).

She was built in Kiel where Bauer was given doubtful advice by Dr G. Karsten, a local Professor of Science, who disagreed with Bauer's principles. The dimensions of the vessel, made of sheet metal, were 26 feet (8 metres) long with a 6 foot (1.85 metre) beam. The propeller was driven by a large, double wheel in the centre of the boat and the rudder was controlled from the front of the vessel by the helmsman. He also controlled a heavy weight which was mounted on a threaded rod in the bilges and on the boat's centre line; this could be moved forward and aft to help the submarine submerge by moving her centre of gravity. There were ballast tanks under the interior deck and a hand pump for moving the ballast.

In the starboard side of the vessel were two water-tight doors, which were very low down, indicating that the vessel must have had a considerable free board if the crew were to get in without getting wet and allowing too much water into the submarine. It must also have meant that the submarine had to take on a considerable amount of ballast to submerge.

Once completed the vessel was taken out into the port of Kiel to be tested. She worked satisfactorily on the surface but when it came to diving, the depth at the place selected was 59 feet (18 metres), much deeper than expected. Ballast was taken on board and the weight moved to the forward end of the vessel which suddenly nose-dived to the bottom. It was impossible to pump out sufficient water to make the vessel buoyant and it was only after five hours that Bauer and his crew escaped by allowing water into the submarine to equalise the outside pressure of the sea so that a hatch could be opened. (Bauer had a considerable task to convince his crewmen that the only way to get out was to allow a considerable amount of water to enter the submarine.)

Bauer next tried Austria but the Government of that country showed little interest. However, he was taken under the wing of a lady of wealth and influence in that country who arranged for him to meet the Emperor. A commission was set up to examine his proposal and in due course he was allocated funds to build his submarine. There was considerable opposition to his invention, particularly from the Minister of Commerce, Von Baumgarten, who voiced his concern that Bauer's invention was contrary to natural laws. In due course support was withdrawn and the project abandoned.

England was the next potential customer where, in 1851, he was given financial support by the Prince Consort. For a time he worked with Charles Fox and Brunel. There was some distrust between these men. Bauer failed to take out a patent for his invention feeling that he would part with too many of his secrets which would have to be disclosed publicly if he was to be afforded any protection by the patent. A submarine was built, but during the trials it sank, killing a number of people. Burgoyne, the submarine historian, attributes the failure to modifications of Bauer's design by Lord Palmerston and Scott Russell[1].

Assistance was then sought without success first in the United States and then in Germany, where

---

1 John Scott Russell (1808-1887) a distinguished shipbuilder who constructed the *Great Eastern* was joint designer of the *Warrior* which is now in public display at Portsmouth.

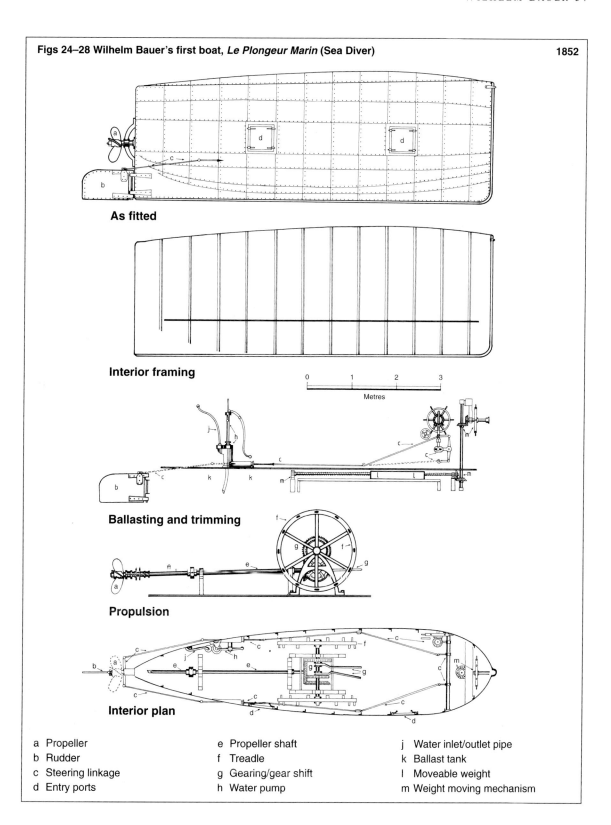

Figs 24–28 Wilhelm Bauer's first boat, *Le Plongeur Marin* (Sea Diver) 1852

As fitted

Interior framing

0 1 2 3

Metres

Ballasting and trimming

Propulsion

Interior plan

a	Propeller	e	Propeller shaft	j	Water inlet/outlet pipe
b	Rudder	f	Treadle	k	Ballast tank
c	Steering linkage	g	Gearing/gear shift	l	Moveable weight
d	Entry ports	h	Water pump	m	Weight moving mechanism

he was considered to be *persona non grata* because he had been consorting with foreign powers. Bauer was a very determined, single-minded man, who was not to be put off by a few failures. So he sought and found support, and financial backing, in Russia. It was there that he built his best known submarine *Le Diable Marin* in 1855 (Fig 29).

Built at St Petersburg, and made of iron sheet on frames, the submarine was 52 feet (15.8 metres) long, with a beam of 12½ feet (3.8 metres) and height of 11 feet (3.35 metres). She had a single propeller driven by four treadmills, two at either end of the boat, each with a diameter of 7 feet (2.13 metres). These were linked and connected to the propeller by a shaft through a gear train at the aft end of the boat. For ballast the vessel was loaded with 47 tons of pig-iron and was fitted with three cylindrical ballast tanks, each measuring 10 feet by 4½ feet (3.05 by 1.4 metres). In addition there was a smaller tank measuring 5 feet by 14 inches (1.52 x 0.35 metres). The ballast capacity of the three large cylinders was about 28 tons; 22.5 tons needed to be taken on board to submerge the submarine. The small cylinder had a capacity of just under 0.3 tons and this was used for trimming. Ballast was taken on and evacuated by pumps.

Fixed to the roof of the interior of the vessel there were long pipes which had been peppered with small holes from which water dripped to cleanse the air.

Fig 29 Bauer's *Le Diable Marin* (Sea Devil). In this early print of Bauer's *Diable Marin* there appears to be no rudder, although it is recorded that after the accident the Grand Duke ordered that the vessel should be sent to the Leuchtemberg yard, for 'repairs to the rudder and propeller'. In the drawing, this omission could have been an artist error but what is interesting is that he did include, slightly forward of and lower than the propeller, what looks like a bow or stern thruster.

The vessel was equipped with an air lock to allow divers to leave and re-enter the submarine; they could handle explosive charges which could be attached to the hulls of enemy vessels using a rubber suction cup. At the bow of the vessel was an observation cupola, fitted with glass ports and waterproof gauntlets, which allowed the operator to attach a charge to the hull of an enemy ship.

Le Diable Marin is shown in most illustrations without a rudder, her stern ending with the propeller, guarded by four iron bars, to prevent it being damaged or snared. Normally, there is mention of the steering and control gear in the descriptions of these vessels by the early historians, but in this case it has been omitted. However, in the engravings of this vessel, low down on the hull and immediately forward of the propeller there is something circular which has the resemblance of a propeller set in a duct. If this was a drawing of a modern vessel, the immediate reaction would be that this was a stern thruster. Had such a novel device been used to replace the rudder surely one of the early historians would have noted it?

The submarine was completed on 2 November 1855 at the Leuchtemberg yard in St Petersburg, but the Russian Admiralty, which was hostile to the whole project, delayed transporting the vessel to Cronstadt for nearly seven months. The Grand Duke Constantine, who was Bauer's main protector and sponsor, only realised what had been going on after returning from the Crimea. Some terse orders were issued and the boat was moved to Cronstadt within twenty-four hours.

Trials of the submarine started on 26 May 1856. The crew consisted of Bauer, Lieutenant Fedorowitch his second-in-command, ten sailors and a blacksmith. To give his crew confidence the first tests in simple manoeuvring, both with full buoyancy and trimmed down, on the surface, were carried out using an animal (presumably a horse/horses) to move the boat. After two weeks, as the crew became confident, the propeller was used. It was found that the vessel could submerge by taking on ballast in the main tanks and then finally taking on a little more ballast in the smaller trim tank. After several practice dives, again to give the crew confidence, various manoeuvres such as diving, surfacing, forward and astern were tried and found to be satisfactory. Bauer, and scientists then conducted various experiments which included:

1 Checking the compass at different depths and finding that it remained constant.
2 Tests with sound under water.
3 Establishing how long a man could exist in a sealed chamber without adverse effects. He also experimented with containers of compressed air to refresh the atmosphere.
4 Readings of the temperature at the surface, in the boat before and during dives, and of the water at different depths, were taken.
5 The submarine had twenty-one portholes and he noted that he could see between 100 to 500 feet (30.5 to 152.4 metres) in clear water but that at a depth of 16 to 18 feet (4.8 to 5.5 metres) there was insufficient light to see things on the sea bed.
6 Adapting a light with a reflector, shining through a porthole so that he could take photographs.
7 Although not an experiment, he did note how silent it was when submerged, although voices from the surface could be heard. Their splendid isolation was duly observed by the fish which were attracted to and peered through the portholes.

Some of his experiments were duplicates of those carried out earlier by his predecessors, while others were quite innovative, particularly taking photographs under water. Bauer, in his approach, was very thorough.

An event, for which he will be long remembered, took place during the coronation ceremony of Alexander II. As the first shot of the salute was fired at Cronstadt, announcing the coronation in Moscow, Bauer submerged in his submarine, with her normal complement plus four musicians. The small band played the National Anthem accompanied by the crew who sang. On the surface their lusty efforts could be heard 220 yards (200 metres) away.

Although Bauer proved his submarine with 134 successful dives, he was generally despised, particularly by the Naval Officers. They thought of him as an artillery corporal, and failed to recognise him for what he was, a brilliant engineer and inventor. Therefore, it must have been at the instigation of Alexander, that he was given the title 'Submarine Engineer' with a brevet and special uniform. Relations between him and his Russian masters were now very strained. He was required to carry out further trials which included passing under a vessel in water which was far too shallow. *Le Diable Marin* fouled the bottom and entangled her propeller. The ballast was discharged, the keel safety weight dropped and the bow broke surface. Shortly after this water started to enter through the hatch, which had been opened, but Bauer managed to escape before the vessel finally sank. Eventually she was recovered only to be lost again later.

Bauer did design another, larger submarine for his Russian masters. She was to be on similar lines to *Le Diable Marin* but was to have had a steam engine for surface running and a compressed air engine to drive her when submerged. The armament of this vessel was to be twenty-four guns. The Admiralty continued to make life very difficult for Bauer and in the absence of Alexander, recommended that he should complete the submarine in Siberia (the submarine was now considered to be a State secret and it would be safe there). But Bauer decided that the time had come to leave Russia and return to Germany.

He contributed much to the development of the submarine; although, not long after leaving Russia he disappeared from public view. Like all the major submarine inventors he not only had vision, ingenuity and determination but also perseverance against heavy odds.

CHAPTER 9

1854–1878

Up to this point the development of submarine boats had been very spasmodic. There are long periods during which there is no record of any development, these were interspersed by sudden flurries of activity when several inventors produced ideas at about the same time.

While Bauer was building and experimenting with his submarines the tempo increased and thereafter new developments appeared nearly every year. Initially this was in Europe as an offshoot of the Crimea War, while the advent of the American Civil War later moved the driving force from Europe to North America. Wars focus the minds of Governments which in turn encourage and finance inventors and innovators, who until then had been conveniently ignored and even derided. Then the technological development speeds up.

As there were so many, it is not the intention to chronicle each and every invention of the next twenty-five years, but to highlight the more important innovations that were introduced or proposed.

In the United States, Lodner D. Phillips designed two submarines using a similar hull configuration; one for peaceful purposes and the other for war. Both vessels were 39 feet (12 metres) long. The armed submarine had a circular cross-section with a diameter of 5 feet (1.5 metres), while the 'peaceful' submarine had a diameter of 4 feet (1.2 metres).

The submarine was fitted with ballast tanks and compressed air tubes. There was a telescopic funnel which allowed fresh air to be drawn into the boat if it was submerged less than 39 inches (1 metre). The propeller was turned by two men on a crank, and the vessel could travel at 4.5 knots. The boat was fitted with two anchors which could be lowered by winch. The naval version was to be armed with an underwater cannon, two methods of launching explosive charges and a form of

rocket, although little detail is known about how these weapons would have functioned.

There were four innovative features about Phillips' boats. Firstly, the longitudinal stability of the vessel was controlled by two pendulums, which controlled ballast being allowed in or forced out of the forward and stern ballast tanks (compressed air must have been used to force the water from the tanks). The second was a spherical joint in the bow which allowed the crew to use such tools as cutters and pincers; portholes had been fitted in the bow so that the operator could see what he was doing. His achievement here was the actual designing and fitting of the attachment rather than its usefulness, which would be somewhat limited. Thirdly, a system, similar to Bauer's, to purify the atmosphere was installed: this pumped the air through tubes, in the ballast tanks, terminating in a spray. On one occasion Phillips, accompanied by his wife and two children, remained submerged for ten hours. Fourthly, the telescopic funnel to allow fresh air into the boat is a variation on other devices that have already been seen. But this was rigid and could be retracted into the hull; so it must have had some form of watertight seal.

No reports have been found about the actual performance of this vessel; it is most likely that it was never submitted to the Government to be evaluated. Its main weakness, like most of its contemporaries, was the lack of motive power, which would have given her a very limited range. It was his intention to fit some form of engine to drive the boat, but unfortunately, Phillips was killed in one of his own submarines before he could further develop his invention.

An important proposal was that of Professor M. Marie-Davy, a Frenchman, in 1854. Although only tested in model form his idea was to use an 'electro magnetic engine' to propel his submarine. The motor was also to be used to turn an auger which would be able to penetrate the hulls of enemy ships. It was many years before the electric motor was reliable enough to be adopted as the standard power unit for running submerged.

The following year several boats were built or designed to be used in the Siege of Sebastopol but they proved to be unsound. One of these, built by Scott Russel, who had helped Bauer while he was in England, and based on Bauer's design, sank, killing the crew. Another Englishman called Babbage drew up plans for a submarine with a triangular cross-section, but no other original features. A Frenchman, and sculptor called Casimir Deschamps, submitted an idea for a one-man submarine to the French Minister of the Navy. This 8½-foot (2.60-metre) long vessel was made of copper; the propeller driven by a hand crank, while the rudder was controlled by the helmsman's feet and ropes. The operator sat with his head in a small conning tower which was fitted with portholes, waterproof leather gloves and an exterior tray on which tools etc could be carried. The operator wore a mask which was connected directly to an air tank

from which he breathed. His exhaled breath was vented through a pipe from the boat. The boat was fitted with a ballast tank but how this was controlled is not known. Elsewhere a Russian officer named Spiridonoff put forward plans for a submarine driven by pistons which were activated by compressed air. But his boat was linked to, and dependent on, another vessel on the surface.

Another proposal to use steam for motive power, for running on the surface, was made by J. Nasmyth who, in 1855, put forward proposals for a submarine mortar. The vessel was 70 feet (21.3 metres) long with a 20 feet (6 metres) beam and its single screw was driven by a steam engine giving her a speed of 10 mph (16.09 kph). The whole vessel was built of wood which in parts was 10 feet (3 metres) thick, providing very adequate protection against the ordnance of the day. She was armed with an explosive charge in the bow which was to be discharged against the hull of the enemy ship. This vessel did not submerge but had a low freeboard (Fig 30).

The next significant step was by a Dutchman, Tetar van Elven, who also proposed to use steam

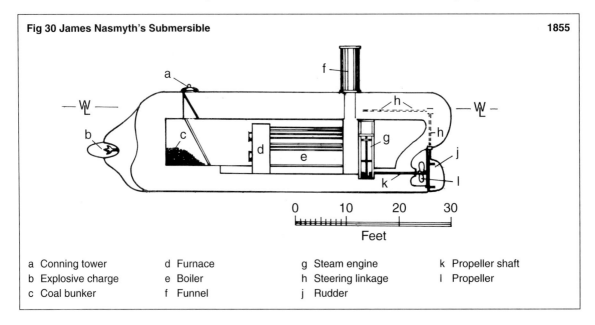

Fig 30 James Nasmyth's Submersible   **1855**

Feet

a Conning tower	d Furnace	g Steam engine	k Propeller shaft
b Explosive charge	e Boiler	h Steering linkage	l Propeller
c Coal bunker	f Funnel	j Rudder	

as the motive power for his vessel. However, his main contribution to the development of submarines was his proposal to fit an 'optical tube' to his boat. This consisted of a tube with two mirrors set at forty-five degrees at either end, the whole of which could be rotated through 360 degrees to obtain a view of the complete horizon. It was many years before this innovation was properly developed by others to become the periscope; an essential piece of submarine equipment.

In 1856 d'Althabegoity built a model of a submarine which, to submerge, not only took on water ballast but also used a vertically-mounted propeller fitted on top of the hull. This, it will be remembered, had first been suggested by Fulton but it was d'Althabegoity who took out a patent (in France) for this idea.

In 1859 a Frenchman, J.M. Masson, proposed to fit a carbonic acid gas engine in his submarine, but purely to clear his ballast tanks. The unique part of Masson's submarine, however, was that his vessel could be connected to the surface for communication using an electric cable. This is probably the first time that this had been proposed.

Also in 1859, a submarine, named *d'Ictineo*, was built in Spain by Narciso Monturiol at Barcelona. She was armed with a vertical firing cannon and a steam-driven auger in the bow; but it is not known if either of these weapons was tested. *D'Ictineo* is reputed to have submerged sixty times, and the design was probably based on one of Bauer's submarines and as such is not remarkable, but it is mentioned to show that the interest in submarines was now expanding.

Oliver Riou designed two submarines with similar hull configurations; the larger one was driven by a steam engine and the smaller by an electric motor. The novel feature of his design was a form of double hull. The vessel was 42 feet (12.8 metres) long with a 12-foot (3.7-metre) beam and consisted of a central cylinder with cones at either end. Within the cylinder was a smaller cylinder of the same length. This had a diameter of about 10 feet (3 metres), which could rotate, independently of the outer shell, on rollers running the length of the boat between the inner and outer hulls. The intervening space was subdivided and used as ballast tanks. Riou's concept was that if the outer hull rolled to the left the inner hull would rotate in the opposite

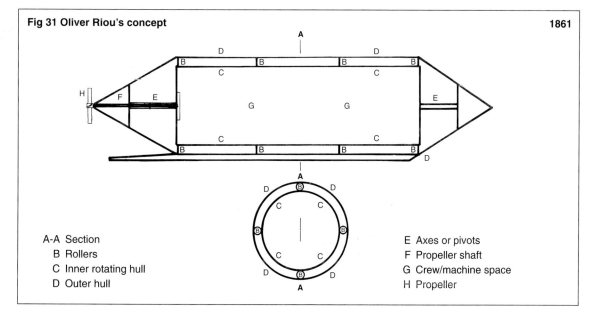

Fig 31 Oliver Riou's concept   **1861**

A-A Section
B Rollers
C Inner rotating hull
D Outer hull

E Axes or pivots
F Propeller shaft
G Crew/machine space
H Propeller

direction to counterbalance the effect. There is no indication on the drawings how the crew entered this vessel nor how she was to be conned or steered; the very simple drawing poses more questions than it answers. There is no record showing if either of the boats was ever built (Fig 31).

Frequently there were reports of submarines that were built and satisfactorily tested before official committees and then nothing more is heard of them. With no bench-mark against which submarine performance could be evaluated, and a lack of knowledge and experience in this type of vessel, it is understandable that committees would express satisfaction with what they had seen. The inventor would no doubt have briefed them, most likely in glowing terms, on what to expect.

One such submarine was built by a French engineer called Villeroi. He had previously built a submarine in France in 1832–35 and an official commission had been set up to evaluate her and she was given a very unfavourable report. Another submarine was put forward in 1855 but again without success. By 1862 Villeroi had moved across the Atlantic where yet another of his submarines was evaluated but this time by the American Government. She was 35 feet (10.7 metres) long with a beam of 3 feet 9 inches (1.1 metres). The hull was constructed from sheets of iron, in ten sections with cones at either end. Propelled by eight pairs of oars with folding blades she was submerged by taking on water

ballast, which could be expelled using a pump, to surface. To maintain a certain depth two buoys were released and theoretically the submarine could winch herself up or lower herself down from them. An air lock was fitted so that a diver could leave and re-enter the submarine. Her armament consisted of two cannon mounted on either side of the conning tower, which had to be loaded before submerging; a spur which could pierce the sides of enemy ships; and a saw on either side of the bow which could be rubbed against an enemy ship. The vessel was tested. Various manoeuvres were carried out which included submerging and allowing the crew to recover some stones and shells from the sea bed. Little else is known about the trial except that the submarine could only manage to achieve 2 knots. The Government lost immediate interest in the project.

As early as 1863 the first submarine appeared with two forms of mechanical motive power: steam and electricity. The vessel was built by an American engineer called Alstitt and from his design a number of lessons could have been learned by those who designed and built submarines at a later date (Fig 32).

The interior of the hull was fitted with a deck below which were ballast tanks at either end, and a coal bunker in the middle. The ballast tanks were sub-divided into compartments which would facilitate the longitudinal trimming of the vessel. Furthermore it would reduce the water-surging

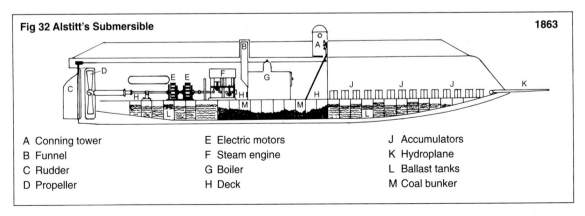

Fig 32 Alstitt's Submersible   1863

A Conning tower   E Electric motors   J Accumulators
B Funnel   F Steam engine   K Hydroplane
C Rudder   G Boiler   L Ballast tanks
D Propeller   H Deck   M Coal bunker

effect, which became very apparent in boats built later by Garrett. To dive, the boiler fire was extinguished, surplus steam blown off and the telescopic funnel withdrawn into the hull and sealed as ballast was taken on and the electric motor engaged. The vessel was fitted with a horizontal rudder or hydroplane at the bow.

The weapon system consisted of barrels of explosive which were carried on the sides of the vessel. On being released (from inside the submarine) they floated. It is believed there could have been different types: some fired electrically from the submarine while others exploded on hitting the target. Or, if the target was moving, a number of barrels could be released in its path, exploding on impact. After the action, it was envisaged that barrels which had not been detonated could be collected and used again. But, if they were the type designed to explode on impact, this could have been a hazardous operation. (This is reminiscent of the actions of Lieutenant-

Commander M. E. Dunbar Nasmith, V.C., R.N. who, during the Dardanelles campaign in World War I, recovered and reloaded torpedoes which had failed to explode on impact or failed to hit their target during operations in the Marmara.)

The next development was a theoretical exercise by Captain Bourgois and Monsieur Brun who designed a submarine which was 134½ feet (41 metres) long, with a 20-foot (6-metre) beam and measuring 13½ feet (4.2 metres) from the keel to the top of the conning tower (Fig 33). The vessel was to be constructed of iron sheets with a strong iron keel. The keel was extendible at the bow by some 15 feet (4.6 metres) to carry an explosive charge; the spar was designed to withstand being driven into an enemy ship at 9 knots. The fore ends were to be filled with material with the same density as water so that should the hull be damaged the longitudinal stability of the vessel would be maintained. The

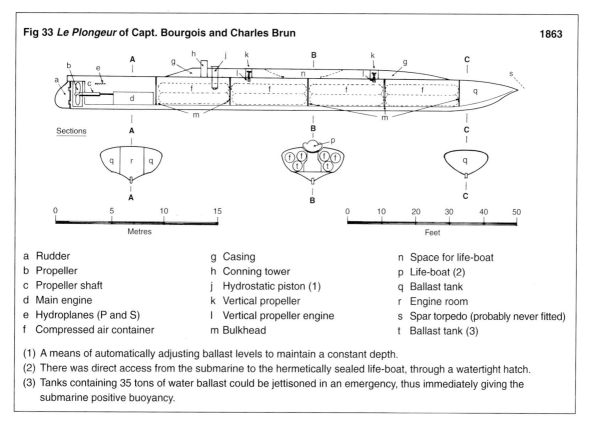

Fig 33 *Le Plongeur* of Capt. Bourgois and Charles Brun 1863

Sections

Metres

Feet

a Rudder
b Propeller
c Propeller shaft
d Main engine
e Hydroplanes (P and S)
f Compressed air container

g Casing
h Conning tower
j Hydrostatic piston (1)
k Vertical propeller
l Vertical propeller engine
m Bulkhead

n Space for life-boat
p Life-boat (2)
q Ballast tank
r Engine room
s Spar torpedo (probably never fitted)
t Ballast tank (3)

(1) A means of automatically adjusting ballast levels to maintain a constant depth.
(2) There was direct access from the submarine to the hermetically sealed life-boat, through a watertight hatch.
(3) Tanks containing 35 tons of water ballast could be jettisoned in an emergency, thus immediately giving the submarine positive buoyancy.

four-bladed, 6½-foot (2-metre) diameter propeller was driven by an 84 hp engine, powered by compressed air, which was stored in a series of air cylinders distributed throughout the boat. The crew of this submarine was twelve men and provisions for forty-eight hours were to be carried. It was estimated that the displacement of the vessel would be 350 tons, which included ninety tons of iron ballast of which thirty-four tons, in the form of cannon-balls, was stowed in compartments at the bottom of the hull and could be jettisoned in an emergency.

This paper exercise was followed by the building of *Le Plongeur* at Rochefort in France, which commenced in June 1860 to the plans of Monsieur Brun. The scantlings were slightly larger than those envisaged in the initial design: the length was 140 feet (42.7 metres), beam 19½ feet (6 metres), and overall height 14 feet (4.35 metres). Her displacement was 453.2 tons, which included 212.35 tons of metal ballast. No bomb spar was fitted as it was agreed that trials to prove the vessel should be completed before the armament was considered. The dorsal fin (or casing) ran forward from the conning tower, which was towards the stern of the vessel. A lifeboat, fitted with air-filled buoyancy containers, was housed in a recess in the casing.

Within the hull there were twenty-three air reservoirs made from sheet steel, which weighed forty-five tons; their designed capacity was 117 cubic metres of air compressed to twelve atmospheres. This fuelled the power plant which consisted of two groups of compound double cylinder engines inclined at forty-five degrees working on the single propeller shaft and driving the four-bladed, 6½-foot (2-metre) diameter propeller. To submerge, 33 tons of water was taken into the ballast tanks, and to surface this could either be pumped out or forced out by using compressed air. A pair of hydroplanes was fitted at the stern forward of the propeller to maintain depth. Two hydrostatic pistons controlled the fine tuning of the water ballast.

Le Plongeur was launched on 16 April 1863 and her trials continued for three years. These were conducted very methodically and thoroughly.

They started with engine trials using only eight air reservoirs, followed by longer surface trials over a 7-mile (11.5km) course, during which the boat was ballasted down leaving only 1.5 feet (0.46 metres) of freeboard. The first submersion tests were carried out in a basin at Rochefort. For safety a large tube containing a ladder was fitted to the top of the submarine. A watertight door, which was only to be opened in an emergency, allowed the crew to escape to the surface should it be necessary On the very first dive the escape route had to be used because one of the porthole lenses cracked allowing water to jet into the submarine. After repairs and more experiments, which were successful, the tube was removed and further trials were conducted both in the basin and then in the open sea. This submarine did work. On a submerged run she logged a speed of 5 knots (9.25kph) over a 1,000-yard (914-metre) course. Later during the trial, because of a fault, it was not possible to close one of the valves which allowed water to enter the ballast tanks and it was necessary to carry out an emergency and successful surfacing by discarding the 34 tons of cannon-ball ballast.

Bourgois and Brun were required for duties elsewhere and the responsibility of continuing the trials was handed over to an engineer called Lebelin de Dionne. To overcome immersion and longitudinal stability problems he had a propeller mounted on a vertical shaft and passing through the deck in the centre of the boat. The diameter of the propeller was 3 feet (0.9 metres) and it was driven by a hand crank. The modification was carried out by September 1864 but trials were not started again for nearly a year. The momentum of the project had been lost.

It was found that the hand-cranked propeller, even combined with the hydrostatic regulators, failed to resolve the problem. Like so many early submarines she had very poor longitudinal stability, and this could not be rectified. The other main limitation was that the range of the vessel was inadequate as there was no means on board of replenishing the compressed air supply. The project was abandoned.

CHAPTER 10

AMERICAN CIVIL WAR

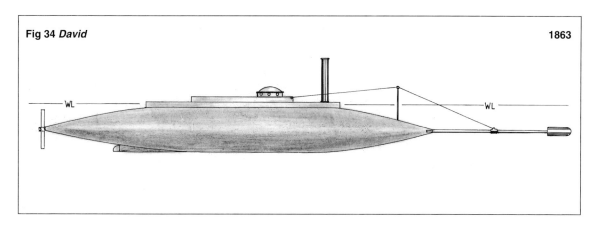

Fig 34 *David*   1863

In America no moral stances were adopted or reservations taken when it came to designing submarines for use in war. A tradition had already been established with Bushnell's *Turtle*, and now America was involved in a Civil War. Inventors had been building submarines in North America but they were not used operationally until 1863, two years after the war had started. It was those who were being blockaded who used the weapon first, and the design used was a submersible rather than a submarine but it was a new concept which worked.

The Confederates' first success came in October 1863 when one of their boats attacked the battleship *Ironsides*. The boat was a submersible which only ran awash and never submerged. Her length was 35 feet (10.7 metres) with a 9-foot (2.7-metre) beam and she was built of iron. The vessel had a single screw which was turned by a small steam engine and her speed was about 7 knots (13kph). The armament was what was known as a 'spar torpedo'; in her case, a 15-foot (4.5-metre) spar, protruding from the bow, at the end of which was a 60-pound (27kg) explosive charge which could be detonated from within the boat. The submersible had a crew of three. She was one of the first of a class of submarine boats known as

Davids, named aptly after the biblical David because of their small size compared to the battleships they would attack.

The first mission was against the blockading fleet at Charleston. The *David* carried out her attack at night, when there was less chance that her small silhouette would be seen. Her target was the very effective and successful battleship *Ironsides* which was the most feared (or respected) ship of the blockading fleet. The *David* was sighted as she approached and in an exchange of fire the officer of the watch, Ensign Howard, was fatally wounded by rifle fire from the *David*. The small vessel was manoeuvred close to the battleship and the torpedo exploded. There was an enormous column of water thrown into the air but the battleship was not damaged. The submersible withdrew under a hail of small-arms fire; boats were deployed to search for the *David* but they failed to locate her.

Subsequently, it was established that the attack had been carried out with the hatch of the *David* open and that when the spar torpedo was exploded the small vessel had shipped so much water, that her crew abandoned boat. An hour later the engineer found himself near the drifting boat, reboarded her, relit the boiler fire and managed to get her back to Charleston. During the remainder of the war the *David* remained there, occasionally operating against the blockading ships.

In the meantime the development of a true submersible was taking place. This was not a Government project but was entirely a civilian initiative. Work had started on the new boat at New Orleans in 1861/62. The boat, called *Pioneer*, had a crew of three and the motive power was a propeller turned using a hand crank. The first trials in early 1862 were successful but to prevent the boat falling into enemy hands she was scuttled by the builders before the fall of New Orleans. She was raised by Union troops who wrote a report on the submersible in which it was noted that she was armed with an explosive charge which was detonated by a clockwork motor. (This would appear to be the same type of device used by Bushnell which had to be attached to the hull of the enemy ship.)

The builder/inventors withdrew to Mobile. Although the Army was supportive, in that a workshop under the command of Lieutenant William Alexander of the 21st Regiment of Alabama Infantry was put at their disposal, they were given no financial backing. By this time James McClintock (part owner of the engineering firm in New Orleans where *Pioneer* had been built) had been joined by H.L.Hunley who probably financed the development and building of the second submersible.

Development included research into replacing man-powered propulsion first with an electric motor and then with a steam engine. Neither solution could be made to work and the new boat *American Diver*, length overall about 25 feet, was fitted with a cranked propeller shaft to be turned by four men. Although the vessel proved to be unsatisfactory she was used operationally. During her final voyage, whilst being towed out to start a patrol, she was swamped in a rough sea and sank, fortunately, without loss of life. The submersible was written off and no attempt was made to raise her.

Although the Government was still keen on the concept it was only prepared to provide the building facilities. Consequently the next boat also had to be built using civilian financial backing of which 33 per cent ($5,000) was put up by Hunley. Work on the next generation of submersible started under the direction of Lieutenant Alexander and McClintock who were later joined by another officer from the 21st Regiment, Lieutenant George Dixon. He was a mechanical engineer with experience on river boats.

The new vessel, which we now know as *Hunley*, was constructed from a boiler measuring 25 feet long with a diameter of 4 feet (7.62 x1.2 metres). The tube was cut in half longitudinally and riveted together with a 12-inch (30cm) iron-plate insert on either side. Castings for the forward and aft ends were fitted and a strengthening 12-inch (30cm) iron plate riveted to the top of the hull. There were two conning towers with portholes, one at either end of the boiler section and these stood about 8 inches above the hull on its centreline. Under, and just aft of the forward conning tower, on the elevation centreline of the hull, hydroplanes or side rudders measuring 8 inches by 5 feet (0.2 x 1.52 metres) were fitted. At the stern, the four-bladed propeller was contained in a shroud on which were mounted the rudder pintles and rudder. Along the keel was a fitted weight which could be detached from within the vessel to give added buoyancy in an emergency (Fig 35).

Within *Hunley* there were two ballast tanks; one at either end of the boat. Unlike the normal ballast tank which is sealed from the interior of the hull by a complete, water-tight bulkhead or is a self contained tank built into the hull, both of which put a finite limit on how much ballast can be taken on, these had only partial bulkheads which were open to the interior of the hull at their tops. Stopcocks governed the flow of water into the tanks which were evacuated by bilge pumps. As the ballast tanks were not sealed they were probably not fitted with vents. If the stopcock was left

Fig 35 *Hunley*

1864

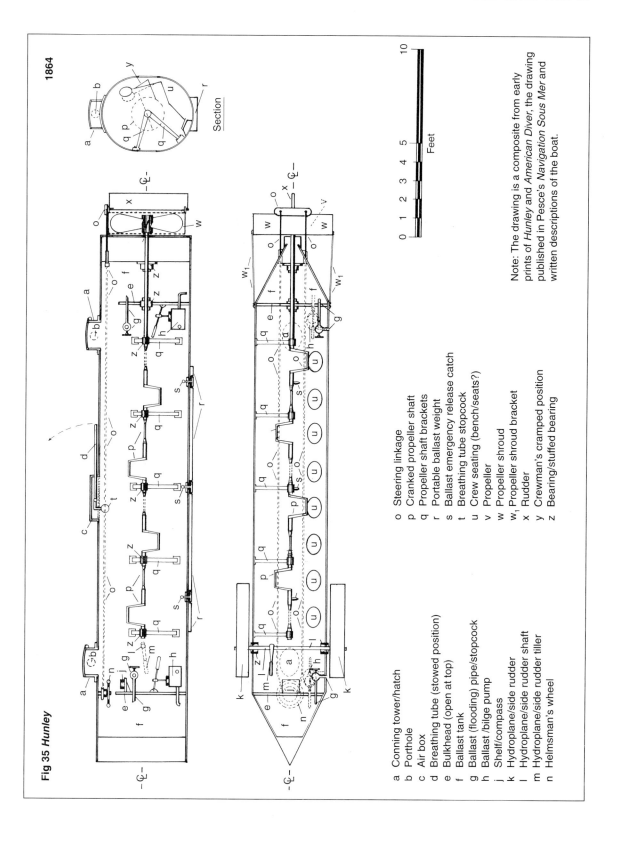

Section

Feet

Note: The drawing is a composite from early prints of *Hunley* and *American Diver*, the drawing published in Pesce's *Navigation Sous Mer* and written descriptions of the boat.

a   Conning tower/hatch
b   Porthole
c   Air box
d   Breathing tube (stowed position)
e   Bulkhead (open at top)
f   Ballast tank
g   Ballast (flooding) pipe/stopcock
h   Ballast /bilge pump
j   Shelf/compass
k   Hydroplane/side rudder
l   Hydroplane/side rudder shaft
m   Hydroplane/side rudder tiller
n   Helmsman's wheel
o   Steering linkage
p   Cranked propeller shaft
q   Propeller shaft brackets
r   Portable ballast weight
s   Ballast emergency release catch
t   Breathing tube stopcock
u   Crew seating (bench/seats?)
v   Propeller
w   Propeller shroud
w₁ Propeller shroud bracket
x   Rudder
y   Crewman's cramped position
z   Bearing/stuffed bearing

open when the submersible was closed down only the build up of air pressure within the hull would limit how much water would flow into the tank and possibly overflow into the crew compartment of the boat. The cranked propeller shaft, which ran nearly the whole length of the hull, was supported by brackets on the starboard side while the eight crewmen who turned the shaft were seated, facing the shaft, on the port side.

An attempt to provide a system to refresh the air in the closed down submersible was made in the form of an air box which was mounted on top of the hull between the two conning towers. A four-foot, pivoted breathing tube was fixed to the box and this could be raised from a stowed horizontal position to the vertical. The box was connected to the interior of the boat by another pipe with a stopcock. The times when the apparatus could be used were probably very limited.

The captain conned the vessel from the forward conning tower. He had a wheel to control the rudder and a lever to move the side rudders. A compass was used to steer when submerged and he had a candle which provided the only real light within the closed down vessel. The captain controlled the forward ballast tank while the crewman in the aft position on the propeller crank was responsible, on orders from the captain, for the operation of the aft tank.

The overall dimensions of the completed submersible were: length 30 feet, beam 4 feet and depth 5 feet (9.1 x 1.2 x 1.5 metres). She was launched in July 1863 and immediately commenced trials culminating with a successful demonstration in which a 'coal hauling flat barge' was destroyed using a towed explosive charge with detonating horns. *Hunley* was then moved by train to Charleston which was being blockaded by the Union fleet. Although McClintock and his team[1] were given priority by the Army to acquire anything that was needed to make the vessel operational still no money was forthcoming from the Government.

For a moment, it is worth considering the posi-tion of the financial backers. As will be seen there are some similarities with another American, Robert Fulton, and his dealings with the French Government just over half a century earlier. Although unprepared to finance research and development the Confederates had agreed to pay Hunley and the other investors a proportion of the value of each enemy ship sunk by the submersible. Furthermore, on arrival in Charleston the business community, whose trade with the outside world had been severed by the blockade and their daily life disrupted by frequent bombardments by ships of the blockading fleet, also offered prize money for the destruction of enemy ships. If the submersible was successful the potential financial return on the original investment was good. Fulton of course had made similar arrangements but had also negotiated payment by the French Government for his research and development. The Confederates were short of shipping but instead of requisitioning and crewing vessels they issued special 'Privateer Commissions' to civilian crewed ships. The *Hunley* would have had such a special 'commission' and furthermore the civilian crew were issued with Confederate Army uniforms. At least, unlike the French who were not prepared to provide a suitable target for a demonstration, the *Hunley* was given the 'coal hauling flat barge' as a target.

During her work-up period *Hunley* was involved in several fatal accidents. These can all be attributed to human error rather than either a structural failure or major design defect in the submersible. Her main fault, like most early submersibles, was that longitudinally she was not very stable.

One accident occurred when a Colonel Charles H. Hasker of Richmond, Virginia, was reputedly on board. He later explained how, apparently, the boat, which had been trimmed down, was under tow and as she gained headway she started to shear. Lieutenant Payne, the captain, tried to release the tow line but in so doing he himself became entangled. The hydroplanes had been set

---

1 Although one of the main backers and protagonists of the submersible concept, Hunley himself was frequently absent on Government business which was in no way connected to the Hunley project.

to hold the bows up and as he struggled to free himself he dislodged the prop holding the hydroplane tiller. Immediately the hydroplanes inclined to the dive position and the boat nose dived taking on water through the open forward hatch. The captain managed to free himself and he, the colonel and two crewmen escaped. The vessel was later recovered from the sea bed where the bows had been embedded in the mud. The integrity of the hull had in no way been damaged.

Another accident occurred while the submersible was under the command of Hunley himself during a routine practice attack against the Confederate Steam Ship *Indian Chief*. The closed down submersible approached in the normal way, probably towing her dummy explosive charge, dived to go under her victim but failed to resurface. The crew, including H.L.Hunley, were all killed. Later when the submersible was recovered it was found that the stop cock on the forward ballast tank was open but again the integrity of the hull was intact. She probably took on too much ballast forward, went into a dive which Hunley was unable to control and the bows again became embedded in the mud.

There are reports of another accident in which the submersible sank after the wash from a passing steamer swamped the boat. On this occasion only the captain, who was positioned in the open forward conning tower, escaped. There is a good possibility that this reported sinking is a garbled account of the sinking of *American Diver* for this submersible was, in appearance, very similar to *Hunley* and the report is taken from an account written some years after the events.

Certainly *Hunley* was involved in two fatal accidents in which at least 15 men lost their lives.

After the last accidental sinking the submersible was raised and prepared for sea. Lieutenant Dixon recruited yet another volunteer crew, this time from the Confederate ship *Indian Chief* which had been used as a target by *Hunley* on many training runs. Dixon's personality, confidence, leadership and ability must have been of the very highest

order to inspire men to join as his crew on *Hunley* which could not have had the best of reputations. The men themselves must have been exceptional and also of the very highest calibre. They must have known about the fatalities, indeed they may well have witnessed the accident when Hunley was in command. Once the boat was ready for sea, training of the new crew started.

Either because it was considered to be unreliable or not powerful enough, the towed explosive charge was replaced with a spar torpedo. This consisted of a long bowsprit on the end of which was carried a 90-lb (40kg) explosive charge in the form of a thimble. The charge was fitted with a spike and was attached to the submersible by a dispensable rope. The concept was that the spike would be driven into the hull of the enemy vessel; the submersible would withdraw extracting the sprit from the thimble and paying out rope connected to the charge; when well clear of the immediate effects of the explosion the charge would be detonated by tightening or pulling on the connecting cord.

The tactics which had been thoroughly practised and tested had to be changed to use the new weapon. Previously the captain had approached his victim, ballasted down, with just the conning towers above the water. He would line up his submersible with the target, dive using the hydroplanes and go under the enemy vessel steering by compass to maintain his course. *Hunley* would surface on the far side, well clear of the target, having towed the explosive charge under the enemy hull where it theoretically exploded. With the new weapon the submersible had to lance the enemy hull with such force that the thimble spike penetrated and held; she then had to withdraw before detonating the explosive charge. To ensure the lance struck the enemy hull at a reasonable depth the *Hunley* would have had to remain very close to the surface. Accurate depth-keeping would have been difficult and there would always be the possibility that she could have either passed below her target or the lance could have struck the curve of the bilge of the enemy ship at an angle which would not have allowed the spike to penetrate and hold. It is therefore likely that attacks with the spar torpedo were carried out when the submersible was awash rather than submerged. Similarly, to guarantee a good chance of penetration, the line of attack would be at right angles to the centreline of the target. This second form of attack would have made the submersible much more prone to detection and particularly vulnerable during the withdrawal stage by which time the crew of the vessel under attack would have been alerted to the presence of the submersible.

The sequence of events would have included a last minute warning for the crew to brace themselves for the collision and stand by to reverse. Once the spike had been set in the enemy hull the submersible would have pulled back to disengage from the thimble. The loss of the 90 lb weight at the end of the spar would give sudden added buoyancy to the bows which should have been immediately compensated. This could only have been done by the captain taking on more ballast in the forward tank. Withdrawal of the submersible would have been very difficult. If he made his withdrawal going astern the captain could have had control problems particularly in maintaining longitudinal equilibrium. Therefore Dixon may have started taking on more ballast as soon as the enemy hull was lanced, then, disengaging from the thimble, while still adjusting the trim, pulled back. As soon as possible he would execute a 180° turn before making a rapid withdrawal. It may also have been considered prudent to submerge as soon as possible and certainly before enemy canon could be brought to bear. Another consideration would be the cord connecting the charge to the submersible: the captain had to avoid becoming entangled while at the same time dispensing rope so that it did not become taught and fire the explosive charge prematurely. Whatever options he chose, during and immediately after the attack, Dixon would have been particularly hard pressed and in the cramped conditions there was no one to whom he could delegate any of his responsibilities.

Should, for any reason, the captain be incapacitated it would be very difficult, in the very confined space, for the leading man on the propeller shaft to take over.

Other experiments were carried out during this period and these included a test to establish how long the vessel could remain submerged. It was found that the candle went out after 25 minutes and the vessel was forced to surface after 2 hours and 35 minutes. It was also established that *Hunley* could operate submerged for 30 minutes.

Although the project was supposed to be secret it would appear to have been common knowledge within the city. Eventually and inevitably word reached the Union forces. In mid January 1864 Vice-Admiral Dahlgren, commanding the fleet blockading Charleston, was personally warned by the Minister for the Navy Department that the Confederates had the ability to attack his fleet with a submersible(s). The warning had been taken seriously and had been passed on to all the ships under his command; this included a description of a submersible in the awash condition.

On 17 February 1864, under cover of darkness, *Hunley*, under the command of Lieutenant Dixon launched an attack on the blockading fleet. As the submersible approached the newly built *Housatonic* she was spotted by the duty watch. Orders were immediately issued to slip anchor chains and her engine was started. By this time the charge had been placed and detonated in the vicinity of the warship's magazine. A large hole was blown in the side of the vessel which immediately started to settle.

A report submitted, on 18 February 1864, to Admiral Dahlgren by Lieutenant F.G. Higginson of the *Housatonic*, on behalf of his captain, who had been grievously wounded by the explosion, gave details of the attack. At 8.45 p.m. 17 February the duty watch had spotted what appeared to be a plank sliding through the water and approaching the *Housatonic*'s starboard side. It was about 100 yards (91 metres) away. Two minutes later it had struck the hull near the magazine by which time the anchor chain had been slipped, the engine started and action stations sounded. It had not been possible to depress the cannon sufficiently to engage the submersible. One minute later there was an explosion and *Housatonic* listed to port and started to sink by the stern. The majority of the crew took to the rigging to save themselves and boats from the *Canandaigua* came to their assistance.

A further contemporary report by Admiral Porter, reiterated what Higginson had stated but gave a little more detail of the actual explosion. 'The ship rocked like an earthquake and seemed to lift out of the water; listing heavily to port she immediately began to sink by the stern. A large proportion of the crew climbed into the rigging to save themselves and there was panic on the *Housatonic*.' The historian Noalhat recorded that the submersible remained alongside the *Housatonic* for as long as a minute immediately before the explosion; bearing in mind all that Dixon had to do it is likely that there was a delay between the *Housatonic* being struck by the spar torpedo and the withdrawal of the submersible.

There is no dispute that the *Hunley* carried out the first successful attack against a warship under operational conditions. However, there is some doubt about the events immediately following the sinking. The traditional scenario is that the explosive charge detonated next to the *Housatonic*'s magazine; the submersible was sucked into the hole made in the warship's hull and sank with her. There was supporting evidence, which came to light three years later, when divers reported that the submersible, with her hatches open, was found fixed in the hole in the side of the *Housatonic*. This certainly seems to be a plausible explanation. As she approached *Hunley* was sighted by the duty watch. She was described as: 'a large flat plank approaching'. This would indicate that the submersible was running awash and it was likely that her hatches were open. Perhaps the charge detonated before she had been able to properly with-

draw and the small vessel could easily have been swamped by the surge of water after the explosion. It would have been necessary for only a relatively small amount of water to be shipped to give the vessel negative buoyancy. If she was still bow on to the *Housatonic* at the moment of detonation water would have probably entered first through the forward conning tower immediately forcing her bow down, as more water flooded in her dive towards the *Housatonic* would have accelerated. Furthermore small-arms fire may have caused injuries or fatalities and the shock of the explosion could have concussed or otherwise injured crew members and consequently they may have been slow to react if indeed they could have reacted under the circumstances.

There is now an alternative scenario which is particularly well explained in Mark Ragan's book.[2] In brief, archival research into the official records of both Union and Confederate forces has revealed that *Hunley* did not necessarily sink immediately after the explosion. Confederate records show that a Lieutenant-Colonel O.M.Dantzler reported that an exchange of pre-arranged signals had been made some time after the attack, between himself and the *Hunley*, which was to alert him to display a light to guide the submersible back to her base. This would indicate that the submersible had withdrawn successfully and was on her return journey although it would not give any indication of the state of the vessel or her crew.

The records of the Union Court of Inquiry into the loss of the *Housatonic* contained eye witness accounts of the survivors. These indicated that the submersible was sighted approaching the *Housatonic* and withdrawing after the explosion during which time she was engaged with small-arms fire. Also that light signals were seen from the sea and the shore (possibly from the submersible and her base). This is a further indication that *Hunley* withdrew after the attack. Presumably any signal would only have been made once Dixon considered that he was out of immediate danger

2 *The Hunley, Submarine, Sacrifice and Success in the Civil War*

from aimed small-arms fire. In fact it may not have been necessary to withdraw all that far before sight of the small boat was lost in the darkness, particularly as the night vision of those on deck had probably been impaired by the flash of the explosion, and there was also some confusion on the deck of the sinking *Housatonic*.

There were contradictory reports from divers who examined the wreck of the *Housatonic* six and nine years after the attack. The first, reported in a newspaper, recorded that divers had been down and the submersible was found lying beside the warship. The second, nearly three years later, was a report, produced after the wreck site, which was a hazard to navigation, had been cleared. This stated that in a survey of the sea bed the *Hunley* had not been found. Perhaps the submersible originally lay embedded or close to the *Housatonic* and she was somehow dislodged and had been moved by currents, the tide or a storm.

Efforts have been made for many years to locate the submersible but armed with the new archival evidence, the search area was reorientated and *Hunley* was found in 1994 by an underwater archaeological team from the University of South Carolina which was supported by NUMA and led by Dr Mark M. Newell. Apparently she was located on or close to the route she would have taken on her return to base.

The successful attack by *Hunley* really heralded the advent of the submersible and submarine as a potent weapon of war although this was not to come to full fruition for many years. The Union had lost a newly constructed warship. Even though they knew of the threat and the duty watch of the *Housatonic* had seen *Hunley* approaching they were unable to do anything to prevent her from laying and detonating her charge. It would not take long to develop and deploy counter-measures, but in the meantime, although the attack had not broken the blockade, it did make the Union Navy more cautious, anchoring further off shore at night. The submersible had become a credible deterrent.

In the light of the archival research that has been carried out in America and the work of the archaeological team it may soon be possible to determine with more certainty what happened to the submersible after the explosion. This is purely of academic interest and in no way should it cloud the heroism of the crew, what was achieved under adverse conditions and the significance of this, the first successful operational attack by a submersible the forerunner of the submarine. When the *Hunley* is raised it is hoped that any remains of her crew can be given a fitting burial.

The Federal Government, not to be outdone, ordered a submarine, from a French engineer. He was paid £10,000 to build the vessel and thereafter would be paid £5,000 for each enemy ship that his submarine sank. The vessel was 36 feet (11 metres) long with a 6-foot (1.82-metre) beam, was made of sheet iron, and her motive power was sixteen oarsmen. This description is very similar to that of Villeroi's submarine, which had been tested and rejected earlier. If it was his design, it is possible that it was the only one available which was remotely suitable for use in the confines of the River Hudson. The alternative may have been to start designing a boat from scratch. On completion, when the submarine was ready to be tested, the designer absented himself, perhaps with the accurate premonition that his boat would be a failure.

By October 1864 the Federals had built their own version of the *David*, based on the design of an engineer called William W. Wood. She was 74 feet (22.5 metres) long, with a beam of 20 feet (6 metres) and a 23-foot (7-metre) draught. Named *Stromboli* she could be ballasted down so that she was almost submerged. Powered by a steam engine her speed was about 8.6 knots (16 kilometres per hour). She was armed with a spar torpedo containing 220 lb (100kg) of explosive. Although she was completed before the end of the war and was despatched to Hampton Roads, under the command of John Lay, it is believed that she was not used operationally.

William Wood and John Lay built a second semi-submersible called *Spuyten Duyvil*. Slightly larger than the *Stromboli* she was 85 feet (26 metres) long, with a beam of 20½ feet (6.3 metres) and a draught of 9¾ feet (3 metres). The vessel displaced 207 tons and could be ballasted down so that only the top of the deck and conning tower was above water. She was fitted with a spar torpedo but this could be withdrawn into the hull when it was not required. She was not completed before the end of the war and her moment of glory came when she carried President Lincoln when he visited Richmond.

Between 1860 and 1864 several submersible monitors were built. One of these, of which there is a good description, was the *Keokuk*. She was 164.5 feet (50 metres) long (including ram) with a 36-foot (10.9-metre) beam and a draught of 14 feet (4.25 metres). She had a ¾-inch (19mm) thick iron hull which was protected on top by 2 inches (50mm) of armour. Fore and aft of the funnel which was in the centre of the boat were two large, non-revolving turrets. She was fitted with two four-cylinder (22 inch by 20 inch stroke (56 x 51cm)) main engines to turn the twin propellers. There were additional engines for ventilation, submersion and other auxiliaries. The hull was fitted with ballast tanks at the bow and stern. It took forty minutes to fill the tanks and fifteen to empty them. When ballasted down only the gun turrets and funnel were above the water line. Mounted in each of the two turrets was an 11 inch (280mm) muzzle-loading gun which fired a 180-lb (81.6kg) shot. Each of the non-traversing turrets had three gun ports which must have severely restricted the ability of the gun crews to quickly and accurately bring their guns to bear on different targets. The crew of this vessel totalled 100.

A brief account of an engagement will give an idea of how this type of vessel was used. *Keokuk*

took part in a bombardment, with other monitors, on Fort Sumter on 7 April 1863. She was positioned between 300 and 600 yards (270 and 550 metres) off shore, where, in thirty minutes, her hull was struck by enemy fire ninety times, some of the rounds penetrating the armour plate and the gun turrets. Although 'riddled like a sieve' she was able to withdraw and remarkably none of her crew had been killed. The bombardment lasted for about an hour during which time neither the fort nor the other monitors, which had participated, were badly damaged.

Submarines, submersibles and semi-submersibles had not previously been used operationally on the scale they were in the American Civil War. Although they did not influence the outcome, they made their presence known and each in their own way posed a threat, which could not be ignored, by either side. In the attacks on *Ironsides* and *Housatonic* alert crews had spotted the attacking vessels but they were not able to do much about it as no suitable weapons could be trained down (with a negative angle of sight) on relatively small targets which were so close. Whenever a new weapon system is introduced, a counter weapon soon follows. The torpedo net was a simple solution to counter the spar torpedo which, to be effective, had to be exploded touching or very close to the hull of its intended victim.

Before leaving this particular phase it is perhaps appropriate to pause for a moment and reflect on the courage shown by those who manned these early submarines. Although the inventors may have had absolute faith in their own inventions they did not necessarily know how or even if their boat would perform as they had predicted; and failure could be fatal. The bravery shown by the last crew of the *Hunley* is extraordinary. The vessel had already sunk at least twice when it was in safe home waters; if it could not survive there what were its chances in a hostile environment? Yet she successfully carried out her attack.

The American Civil War did not contribute significantly to the evolution of the submarine. Production did intensify but there were no major new developments in design or fabrication. There had been earlier steam-driven boats but, unless there was another means of propulsion, these were unable to submerge. This was one of the shortcomings of the steam-powered 'Davids'. It was clearly recognised that the boats needed sustained power; there had been some tentative designs incorporating dual forms of propulsion. But at this time, if a relatively small submarine was to submerge, the best solution was to use a team of men to turn a propeller.

Indirectly, the Americans had consolidated the precedent of using submarines in war and had shown that such a vessel posed a real threat that should be taken seriously. Fulton had realised this at the beginning of the century. The submarine was an effective, cheap option when compared to a capital ship and as such would particularly benefit the weaker side in war. But to be effective the submarine needed much further development.

CHAPTER 11

THE TEN YEARS
PRECEDING GARRETT

In 1866 the next innovative idea that came out of North America was that of Mr Roeber who lived near New York. His first vessel was designed for peaceful purposes. Made of thin iron sheets it was 30 feet (9 metres) long, with a beam of 7.5 feet (2.28 metres) and it had a flattened bottom. A small conning tower was fitted amidships. Before taking on ballast she only had 18 inches (45cm) of freeboard and showed a small deck area measuring 8 feet by 3 feet (2.4 by 0.9 metres). The hull was divided into three compartments; those at the bow and stern were for water ballast whilst that in the centre was for the crew and machinery. It took thirty seconds to fill the ballast tanks and to empty them by pump, with compressed air assistance, took twenty seconds. The three-bladed propeller, which had a diameter of 3 feet (0.9 metres) could be driven by two men but with six men on the crank a speed of 4.4 knots (8km per hour) could be achieved.

The interesting feature of the propeller was that it was mounted on a universal joint so that its axis could be moved both horizontally and vertically, it could therefore also be used to steer the vessel in those directions as well as propelling her forward; Roeber had adapted an idea which had been suggested a few years earlier but had not previously been used in a submarine. The vessel also carried 2 to 3 miles (3 to 5km) of cable so that the vessel could communicate to either a ship or the shore; again this was a development of an earlier idea put forward by Masson in his submarine design of 1859.

Roeber also produced the design for a larger submarine but as far as is known this was never built. This vessel was to be 75 feet (22.8 metres) long with two keels for stability. It would carry

2 inches (50 mm) of armour and a spar torpedo would be fitted in the bow. The spar would be retractable, like that in the *Spuyten Duyvil*, so that the torpedo could be carried in a protective recess in the hull whilst on passage and then projected some 20 feet (6 metres) before going into action.

At about the same time a patent was taken out in France by Merriam. Although his boat was designed to allow divers to work on the sea bed it was more like a submarine than a diving bell because it had limited mobility. It is believed that this was only a design exercise and the vessel was never built. Inventors were becoming increasingly aware of the importance of protecting their designs and inventions, even if they had no intention of developing them, hoping that others would do this for them while paying royalties for the privilege.

The propeller was to be driven by four cranks (although Merriam was thinking about using a motor of some description) and the boat was to be fitted with stern hydroplanes. As in Roeber's boat, the propeller was going to be mounted on a universal joint, but in the horizontal plane only so that it could be used instead of a rudder. The metal on frame construction was to be a double hull, in that the central working area was to be surrounded by tanks; those under the deck for water ballast and those on the flanks for compressed air. Two winches could lower weights for mooring and the boat was to be fitted with a form of moveable spar torpedo, slung under the fore part of the boat. The helmsman's position was to be in a small cupola on the top centre of the boat from where he would be able to steer the vessel.

Over the next few years development continued. Many boats were designed, built, tested, and found to be either impractical or funds ran out before they could be developed. In England, Winan launched a vessel on the Thames with a length of 250 feet (76 metres), steam-powered with a propeller at either end. The concept was: 'that the forward one would cut its way ahead, the stern one to drive the vessel into the vacuum created by the one at the bows'. The inventor himself was satisfied with the performance of his boat, but it did not progress beyond the trial stage. In Russia a 600-ton submarine was built which was crushed by going too deep. But another, designed by Alexandrowsky in 1868, which was of 300 tons, was more successful. It was driven by a compressed air engine and could achieve 6 knots (11km per hour). A trial included an attack on a ship which was sunk; the Russian Government, did not accept Alexandrowsky's suggestion that it should buy the submarine. Elsewhere, the Prussian Government accepted the plans of a German inventor, Otto Vogel, for a heavily armoured submarine which had gun ports through which 'heavy ordnance could be fired in all directions (while on the surface)' as well as a gun which could be fired under water. She was probably never built.

In 1869 an American doctor, Barbour, designed a submarine which was 23 feet (7 metres) long, had a 3¼-foot (1-metre) beam and a draught of 5¼ feet (1.6 metres). She had a double hull, the outer one being made of copper, and the space between them was filled with tubes of air and wood. The propeller was turned by two oscillating carbonic acid gas or ammonia motors. The vessel had ballast tanks and side rudders (hydroplanes) amidships. The armament was a refinement, albeit a rather dangerous one, of that devised by Alsit in 1863; canisters containing nitro-glycerine were held in tubes forward of the central conning tower. The canisters, which were buoyant and connected to the submarine by an electric cable, were released under the enemy ship and detonated. It is not known if this vessel ever progressed beyond the design stage.

Depending on which side you were standing, the English Channel or La Manche has presented a challenge to man for many centuries. It is a barrier to be crossed and we can now look back on the many ways this has been achieved: balloon, airship, glider, aeroplane, surface vessels from large ships to man-powered devices, invasion fleets, swimmers, skimmers, submarines, submersibles and finally by tunnel. In Victorian times the only reliable way to cross was by sea, there were balloons but the wind had to be in the right direction. A tunnel had been considered but this would not materialise for many years. In the meantime Dr Lacomme, a Frenchman, came up with a novel idea: a submarine railway. His concept was, in principle, relatively simple. A standard railway line was to be laid on the sea bed on which a flat-bed rail truck would run carrying a submarine (Fig 36).

The submarine, made of iron, would have propellers at either end, as previously conceived by Winan, and these would be turned by compressed air engines. The vessel would always retain a small reserve of positive buoyancy which would be overcome by attaching her to the heavy flat-bed truck by wires which could be released, if necessary, from within the boat. The design called for a combined weight of the submarine and the flat-bed to provide the minimum level of negative buoyancy necessary to keep the combined vehicle-vessel firmly on the rails but at the same time reducing the friction of the wheels on the railway lines. The flat-bed was to have brakes fitted and there would be communication with the shore using electric cable. The vessel was to be fitted with a diving chamber so that repairs could be carried out to the track, or obstructions removed. Should the propelling machinery fail or in case of some other problem or emergency the vessel could be released from the flat-bed by the crew of the submarine and with her inbuilt positive buoyancy would rise to the surface. Should the release mechanism fail the boat carried a large float which, when

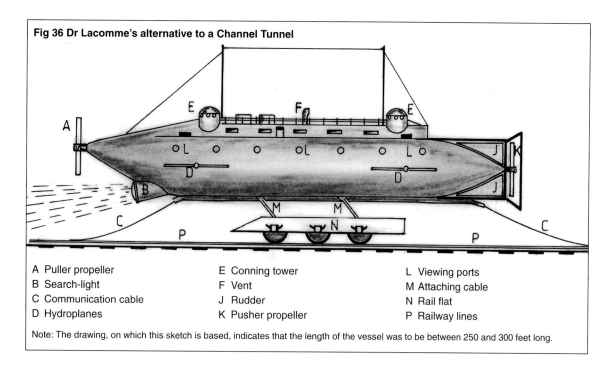

Fig 36 Dr Lacomme's alternative to a Channel Tunnel

A Puller propeller
B Search-light
C Communication cable
D Hydroplanes
E Conning tower
F Vent
J Rudder
K Pusher propeller
L Viewing ports
M Attaching cable
N Rail flat
P Railway lines

Note: The drawing, on which this sketch is based, indicates that the length of the vessel was to be between 250 and 300 feet long.

released, carried a breathing tube to the surface to provide fresh air for the crew and passengers while help was mustered. Had the project ever been launched perhaps the shares in the company would have become a 'Channel Bubble'.

The next invention of note was by a retired French Navy officer Lieutenant Constantin. His proposal, in 1870, was for a variable displacement vessel. His concept was to have large pistons, mounted in tubes, at either end of the submarine. The tube ends would be open to the sea so that as the pistons

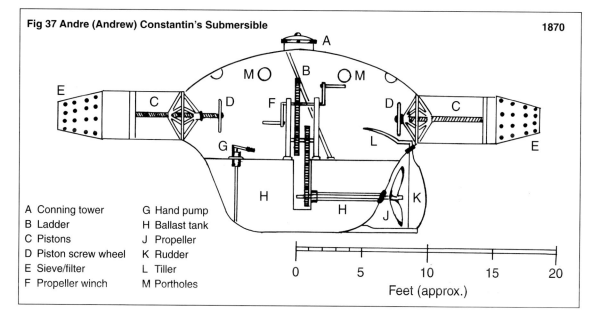

Fig 37 Andre (Andrew) Constantin's Submersible   1870

A Conning tower
B Ladder
C Pistons
D Piston screw wheel
E Sieve/filter
F Propeller winch
G Hand pump
H Ballast tank
J Propeller
K Rudder
L Tiller
M Portholes

Feet (approx.)
0   5   10   15   20

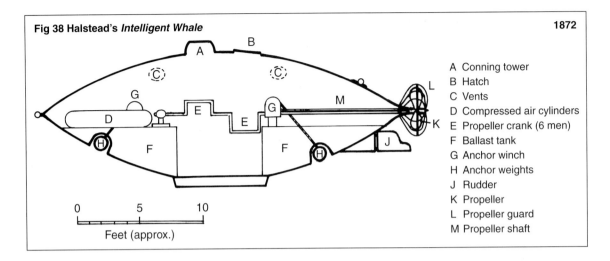

Fig 38 Halstead's *Intelligent Whale* 1872

A Conning tower
B Hatch
C Vents
D Compressed air cylinders
E Propeller crank (6 men)
F Ballast tank
G Anchor winch
H Anchor weights
J Rudder
K Propeller
L Propeller guard
M Propeller shaft

0 5 10

Feet (approx.)

were moved in or out the displacement of the vessel would be either decreased or increased. This principle had been used by many others but by making the adjustment at the extremities of the vessel Constantin was trying to resolve the problem of longitudinal stability. Because she is not what one expects a boat to look like her appearance is rather bizarre (Fig 37).

A submarine called the *Intelligent Whale* (Fig 38) was built in the United States by Halstead. He had previously offered his plans to the French but the plans had been declined. The vessel, ovoid in shape but with more pointed ends, was 29½ feet (9 metres) long and had a diameter of 10 feet (3 metres). She had ballast tanks in the lower half of the hull and at either end of the vessel. The single propeller was driven by a crank which was turned by six of the thirteen-man crew. The rudder was positioned forward of and below the propeller and above it, on either side of the vessel were hydroplanes. Compressed air was carried for the crew. In the bottom of the boat there were two doors so that divers could leave and enter the vessel, and two weights could be lowered by winch so that the submarine could be anchored while the divers were working below. The *Intelligent Whale* was purchased by the American Government in 1866 but remained unused for several years at Brooklyn dockyard.

Trials started in 1872. Halstead appears to have had little faith in his boat and it was attached to a hoist before its first underwater trial. Halstead had in fact been very prudent because the hatch had not been properly sealed, water poured into the vessel and it had to be recovered by the hoist. Fortunately, on this occasion, there were no casualties.

The Government washed their hands of the project although Halstead subsequently tried to renew their interest in his boat, but failed. The *Intelligent Whale* was still used, presumably under Halstead's direction as a an underwater diving platform. One report says that in her various operations thirty-nine, largely inexperienced men, lost their lives.

In 1877 the work of one of the more important submarine designers appeared for the first time. The inventor was Drzewieki, a Russian engineer. His first vessel (Fig 39), made of steel, was just over 13 feet (4 metres) long and was fitted with a ballast tank. She was crewed by one man who turned the single propeller through a gear chain, driven using his feet and bicycle pedals. There was a small conning tower, on each side of which, leather gloves protruded so that the occupant could lay charges. The explosives were to be carried in boxes, on the hull, within easy reach and were to be attached to enemy vessels with rubber suction cups.

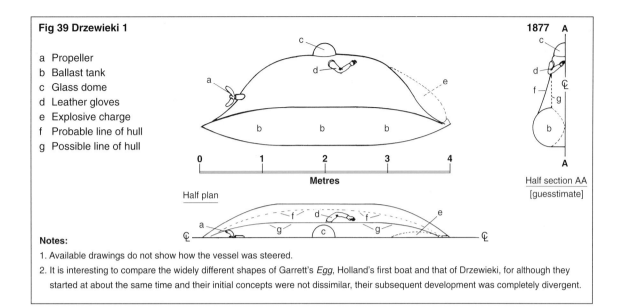

Fig 39 Drzewieki 1   1877

a Propeller
b Ballast tank
c Glass dome
d Leather gloves
e Explosive charge
f Probable line of hull
g Possible line of hull

Metres

Half plan

Half section AA
[guesstimate]

Notes:

1. Available drawings do not show how the vessel was steered.

2. It is interesting to compare the widely different shapes of Garrett's *Egg*, Holland's first boat and that of Drzewieki, for although they started at about the same time and their initial concepts were not dissimilar, their subsequent development was completely divergent.

The Russian Government was most impressed and commissioned Drzewieki to build a larger submarine. His further developments are considered later.

Burgoyne in his book *Submarine Navigation* quotes a scientific paper published in 1875 concerning an invention by Mr Jos. Jones, a shipbuilder of Liverpool. This was a submarine vessel which 'could be made to descend to any required depth in the water – as shown by a working model – to remain stationary at any depth, to move forwards or backwards in a straight line at any level, to go deeper or to rise to the surface'. It was Mr Jones' intention that his submarine would then be able to lodge a torpedo under an enemy vessel. The paper goes on: 'In the model we examined, Mr Jones certainly made out his case, but of course between a model and a perfected apparatus there is a wide gulf, which we fear Mr Jones was unable to bridge, as we never heard any more of his invention. If however it was a step in the right direction, and if it proved successful it would have marked a new era in submarine warfare.' Burgoyne regrets that he has no more information on this invention but points out that it 'is not devoid of interest'. One other thing is known about this proposed vessel: it was Jones' intention to fit a verti-

cally mounted propeller to assist in submerging, maintaining depth and surfacing.

A patent was taken out by A. A. Olivier in 1877 for a submarine which was powered by high explosive. It was quite innovative. The vessel was cigar-shaped with wings or hydroplanes fitted at the bows. These could be folded and retracted into the hull by a system of cranks and they were pivoted so that they could be inclined up and down. Proposed propulsion was by gas, generated by the ignition of high explosives. A tube or gun barrel was fitted so that the muzzle terminated at keel level at the stern. Within the boat the tube was supported by strong bars connecting it to the stem of the vessel. The barrel was rifled to give better direction to the gases and the diameter of the bore increased towards the stern. At the breech, which was in the centre of the boat, was a metal drum which held cartridges, like a revolver. A dovetail, between the drum and the breech, sealed the chamber preventing gases escaping into the submarine when the cartridge was fired. Speed was controlled by the rapidity of firing charges. Although Olivier's proposed 'engine' would appear to be more dangerous to the crew than to

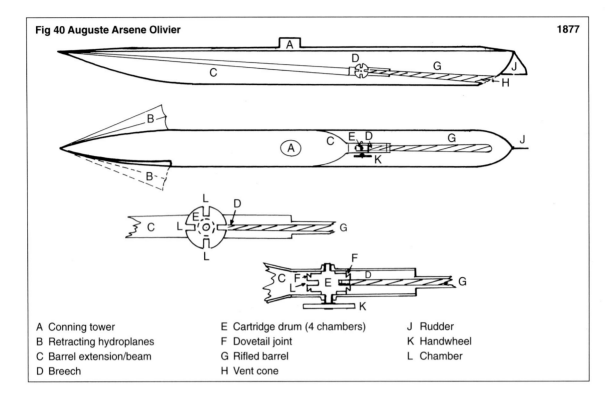

Fig 40 Auguste Arsene Olivier   1877

A Conning tower
B Retracting hydroplanes
C Barrel extension/beam
D Breech
E Cartridge drum (4 chambers)
F Dovetail joint
G Rifled barrel
H Vent cone
J Rudder
K Handwheel
L Chamber

an enemy his ideas were perhaps well in advance of his time (Fig 40).

The concept of retracting the hydroplanes into the hull was used on some submarines in World War I because they were vulnerable to damage when on the surface and docking. Much later, most nuclear-powered submarines were to be fitted with retractable forward hydroplanes. The explosive-powered engine was, looking with hindsight, a crude concept of a jet. It would have been very difficult to surprise an enemy with such a noisy engine; the disturbance of the water would have pin-pointed the position of the boat, it would have had a very limited range; and it would not provide the helmsman with a user-friendly environment in which to work.

Another invention, which was to be adopted and modified over a hundred years later for carrying fuel and exhaust waste was also patented in 1877. E. Thompson fitted his proposed vessel with tubular frames around the hull to use as ballast tanks. Thompson did not, as far as is known, develop his idea any further. The modern version is what is known as a 'toroidal hull', where the hull is made up from circularly formed tubes which are joined laterally; these are used to store fuel and exhaust products from a closed-cycle engine system. When used submerged, the tell-tale hot exhaust is not left in the wake, giving the submerged submarine's position or presence away to an enemy.

The following year, 1878, Messrs Watson and Woodhouse applied for a British patent for 'Submarine Gun-boats' which was divided into two parts: firstly dealing with the vessel and secondly with her armament. The drawings and detail in the patent give no dimensions for the submarine as it was the principle rather than the specific which was to be protected. The shape of the vessel was similar to that of a surface ship except that in the centre of the flat deck a large dome structure was fitted over a lattice-work frame; at the bow there

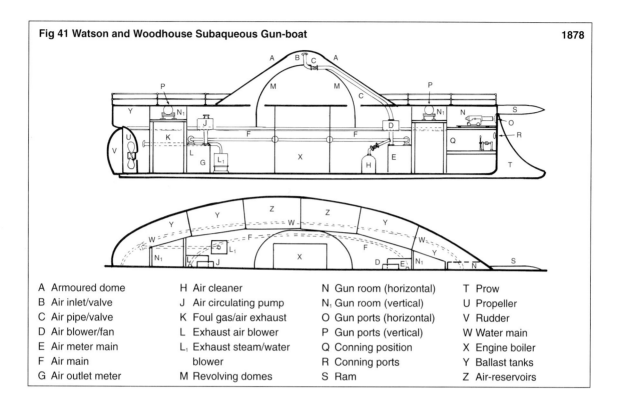

Fig 41 Watson and Woodhouse Subaqueous Gun-boat 1878

A Armoured dome	H Air cleaner	N Gun room (horizontal)	T Prow
B Air inlet/valve	J Air circulating pump	N₁ Gun room (vertical)	U Propeller
C Air pipe/valve	K Foul gas/air exhaust	O Gun ports (horizontal)	V Rudder
D Air blower/fan	L Exhaust air blower	P Gun ports (vertical)	W Water main
E Air meter main	L₁ Exhaust steam/water	Q Conning position	X Engine boiler
F Air main	blower	R Conning ports	Y Ballast tanks
G Air outlet meter	M Revolving domes	S Ram	Z Air-reservoirs

was a prominent prow extending from the keel and a ram, above it, at deck level. The boat was fitted with a conventional rudder and propeller (Fig 41).

The deck of the vessel and the dome were to be sheathed with armoured plate, using a method which had previously been patented by Watson and Woodhouse. The armoured plate would be in two layers between which would be sandwiched a layer of india-rubber. Each embryo laminated armoured plate, would be mounted on a spring loaded pin, which, in turn, passed through a telescopic tube, filled with a packing of cork or rubber, bolted to the main hull plating. The concept was that when the armoured plate was struck the spring and packing would first compress and then expand restoring the armoured plate to its original position. The large dome on the deck was to be watertight and the one under it airtight. The domes were designed to revolve to allow access to the interior of the submarine, but the patent specification is very vague about how this was to work in practice.

Within the hull there was to be a large central crew and machinery space surrounded by air and water ballast tanks. There were to be three deck levels although these did not extend throughout the boat. Most of the machinery illustrated in the drawings is for collecting air through a pipe system from the top of the dome and pumping it into the air tanks through an air main. Various precautions to prevent water entering the vessel through the inlet pipe were considered and before submerging the pipes were to be sealed. The air in the vessel and air tanks was to be gauged and monitored; exhausted air and gases were to be vented by a pumping arrangement at the stern. Consideration was also given to chemical purification of the air. Although space is reserved, in the drawings, for the engine no details are given about the motive power for the vessel, but as boilers are mentioned in the patent it is assumed that it would have been steam.

The helmsman's position was in the bows of the vessel where he was to be provided with two sight holes so that 'the steersman is able to guide the

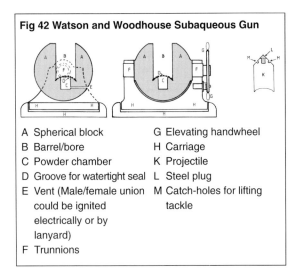

Fig 42 Watson and Woodhouse Subaqueous Gun

A Spherical block
B Barrel/bore
C Powder chamber
D Groove for watertight seal
E Vent (Male/female union
  could be ignited
  electrically or by
  lanyard)
F Trunnions

G Elevating handwheel
H Carriage
K Projectile
L Steel plug
M Catch-holes for lifting
  tackle

course of the vessel with certainty when sub-merged'. Above the conning position there was to be a gun-room in which was mounted a standard 'garrison gun' which could fire through a port (which when closed was watertight), when the vessel was on the surface. There were to be two other gun-rooms under the fore and aft sections of the deck and these were designed to house guns which fired upwards into the hulls of enemy vessels when the submarine was submerged. This was covered in the second part of the Watson and Woodhouse patent (Fig 42).

Firing vertically, these guns would be best described as mortars. The gun was to be wrought or cast in a spherical block, the barrel and chamber bored out, and 'the external surface of the spherical ball or block, forming the gun, turned to a face of the greatest truth and smooth-ness'. Trunnions were to be fitted, one of which was extended to accept an elevating handwheel with suitable gearing to allow the gun to be ele-vated through ninety degrees, fore and aft. In the deck of the submarine there were to be two holes with which the bores of the guns were lined up, and in the gun-rooms, there was to be flexible padding around these apertures. Each gun was to be tightly sandwiched between this padding and the deck; to increase the tightness of fit, cork or

india-rubber matting was to be laid between the gun carriage and mounting. Because of its shape, the inventors' intention was that the gun could be loaded with the barrel in the horizontal position, then elevated to the vertical, the whole time main-taining a watertight seal. During loading a rubber or other watertight seal was to be fitted between the explosive charge and projectile. To increase the penetrative power, the solid shot was to be fitted with 'a chilled steel plug which terminated in a sharp point'. Although the inventors considered that there would be no problems with recoil or damage to the padding around the muzzle, a watertight compartment was to be provided for the gun crew to retire to and from which the gun could be fired remotely.

This vessel was never made but the component parts have been summarised to show the level of detail and thought that was given to such an enter-prise even though the practicality of such a vessel is very doubtful. Finally a direct quote from the 'Provisional Specification' concerning this weapon which would fire into the enemy's soft underbelly:

> For this reason it is therefore necessary that when such gunboats are employed for the purpose of attack that some distinctive mark or sign should be painted or otherwise placed on the hulls of such vessels, as it may be requisite to protect from their attack, as otherwise the greatest disasters and confusion might arise from the destruction of our own vessels or those of other friendly powers.

By 1877 John P. Holland of the United States of America had built two submarines. By the end of the century Holland would be established as one of the most eminent submarine designers in the world. Rather than split his work into two parts, it will be considered as a complete entity later, so that it can be seen in perspective more easily. But at this stage it is sufficient to say that the two, one-manned boats designed by Holland were both under 16 feet (5 metres) in length. The first was driven by a propeller turned by foot pedals oper-

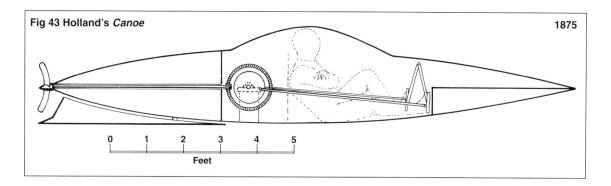

Fig 43 Holland's *Canoe*   1875

0   1   2   3   4   5

Feet

ated by the helmsman who wore a diving suit (Fig 43), while the second was powered by a 4hp petrol engine.

The last submarine design to be examined in this chapter, was patented in August 1878 by John Gilbert Surman. The vessel was about 30 feet (9 metres) long with a beam of 7 feet (2.1 metres) (Fig 44). The interior of the hull was divided into three: the centre section was for the machinery; the forward compart- ment was for the helmsman; and in the stern was an air reservoir. Above the submarine, mounted on a rubber tube was a float connecting the vessel to the surface so that air could be drawn into the boat by a compressing pump, manned by five men, and stored in the air chamber in the stern. A valve closed auto- matically when the air tube went below the water. The engine was powered by compressed air taken from the reservoir and it drove two 'fin propellers'. Exhaust air from the engine would supplement the

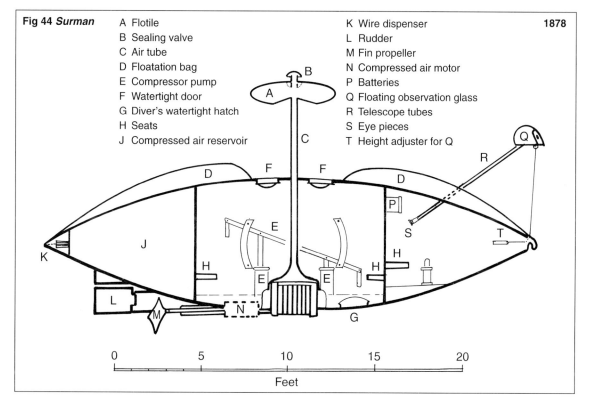

Fig 44 *Surman*

A Flotile
B Sealing valve
C Air tube
D Floatation bag
E Compressor pump
F Watertight door
G Diver's watertight hatch
H Seats
J Compressed air reservoir

K Wire dispenser
L Rudder
M Fin propeller
N Compressed air motor
P Batteries
Q Floating observation glass
R Telescope tubes
S Eye pieces
T Height adjuster for Q

1878

0   5   10   15   20

Feet

air supply in the boat for the crew. The vessel was 'to be about the same specific weight as water when empty' therefore with the crew on board she would have negative buoyancy. Outside the boat was an air bag which could be inflated and deflated by the helmsman to make the submarine surface and submerge. The inventor calculated that his submarine would travel at between 20 and 25mph (32 and 40kph) and could surface in less than two minutes.

The main weakness in Surman's design was that his vessel started with negative buoyancy and this could have been fatal if the floatation bag was damaged, but unlike previous air-powered submarines he was able to compress his own air. The invention did have one interesting idea and that was a floating observation glass for the helmsman. This was a float containing mirrors and lenses connected to the submarine by two tubes which penetrated the hull. The device was pivoted in its mounting in the hull and the floating head was connected through the bow of the submarine by a cable so that the helmsman could adjust its height. The inventor claimed that this allowed 'the commander though many feet under water to see as plainly as though he were on the surface of it'.

This very brief history has covered many of the principal submarines and submersibles which had been built up to the middle of 1878 and which have been documented. Many more were built, but details about them have been lost or never made public. Much of the technology had been discovered and even tried out but it needed to be further developed and adapted to be used efficiently in submarines. There were still two main deficiencies which were holding back progress. The first was suitable motive power to drive a submerged submarine, which did not consume or foul the air supply of the crew, and this needed to be linked with a power plant to drive the surfaced submarine. Once this mutually supporting combination had been found other criteria would need to be introduced like reliability, safety, endurance, economy and so on. The second missing link was also fundamental. Although the development of the submarine had progressed as a weapon of war, it was still largely impotent, and it would remain so until a suitable, reliable weapons system could be developed. But developments in this area were about to progress.

CHAPTER 12

THE TORPEDO

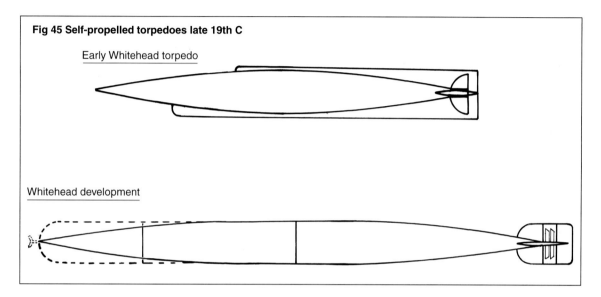

Fig 45 Self-propelled torpedoes late 19th C

Early Whitehead torpedo

Whitehead development

Credible attacks by submarine had been carried out or proposed in three ways: using the spar torpedo; attaching an explosive charge to the hull of an enemy ship and firing it electrically, with a timer or with a trigger; releasing buoyant charges which rose up under a vessel or were laid in its path which were fired electrically or mechanically. Other methods had been considered such as steam-powered augers, cannon and towed charges which either followed in the wake of the attacking vessel or diverged from it so that the submarine was able to stand off from its proposed target. None of these systems was satisfactory. Indeed some were more hazardous to the attacking crew than they were to the enemy.

An Austrian Naval officer, Captain Lupuis, proposed controlling a small self-propelled explosive charge using ropes from the shore. His suggestion was considered unsatisfactory by his Government, unless he could find a satisfactory engine to drive the device. The proposal was taken up by Messrs Whitehead and Co., of Fiume, in Austria. But

initial development and experiments showed that the surface running torpedo controlled by ropes had severe range limitations. After two years of further development a torpedo was developed but it could not be made to keep its depth and frequently broke surface or dived and blew up. The potential of the Whitehead system was recognised by the Austrian Government which gave some limited support to its future development.

The first breakthrough came when Whitehead invented the balance chamber. This worked on hydrostatic pressure, which could be set for any depth. Working in conjunction with a pendulum, any change in depth and posture was transmitted mechanically to horizontal rudders at the stern which compensated for any deviation. The new version of the torpedo was offered for sale to other nations (the Austrian Government had not secured exclusive rights) and Whitehead was invited to take two torpedoes to England for trials.

The torpedoes used for the trials were of the same basic design but one had a 16-inch (40.64cm) and the other a 14-inch (35.56cm) overall diameter. They were fitted with a single propeller and had a fin running the length of the torpedo both on the top and the bottom. The smaller weapon carried an 18-lb (8.17kg) charge while the larger had a 67-lb (30kg) warhead.

The trials were carried out from an old paddle wheel sloop H.M.S. *Oberon*. The torpedoes were mostly fired from a submerged tube from which they were ejected by a rod driven by compressed air; although some were launched from a deck-fitted tube. The torpedoes were tested over 100 runs with an average speed of 8.5 knots (15.8kph) for a distance of 200 yards (182.8 metres), and 7.5 knots (13.9kph) over a distance of 600 yards (548.6 metres). The balance chamber had largely overcome the depth-keeping properties of the weapon and it was concluded that an end on, stationary vessel could be hit at 200 yards (182.8 metres); an anchored ship, broadside on could be hit at 400 yards (365.7 metres); and a vessel moving at a moderate speed could be hit at 200 yards (182.8 metres).

The destructive power of the torpedo was then evaluated. An old corvette, the *Aigle*, was the target and this was protected by thick nets 80 feet (24.38 metres) long and 12 feet (3.65 metres) deep suspended 15 feet (4.57 metres) from the hull of the ship. A large torpedo, 16 inch (40.6cm) diameter carrying 67 lb (30.39kg) of guncotton was fired from a range of 136 yards (124.35 metres). The torpedo passed just outside the net hitting the *Aigle* under the quarter at a depth of 10 feet (3 metres) blowing a hole in the hull 20 feet (6 metres) by 10 feet (3 metres). The second torpedo of 14-inch (35.6cm) diameter with a 18 lb (8kg) dynamite warhead was fired; it hit the net and exploded causing no further damage to the *Aigle*. Very satisfied with the trials the British Government

acquired the rights to manufacture Whitehead torpedoes. Numerous countries adopted this torpedo, although other types were produced during the next few years, such as the Schwartzkopf (Germany), and the Howell (U.S.A.).

After its initial inception, in about 1863, the torpedo was developed fairly quickly in a short time span. The reason for this was that the already established compressed air engine technology could be adapted; hydrostatic pressure was understood and once the depth-keeping problem had been solved it only remained to improve the ability to maintain a straight course and this was achieved by the introduction of contra-rotating propellers and the gyroscope. All the necessary ingredients to make a successful torpedo were available and were quickly and effectively adapted.

Considering what had taken place by the time Garrett started work on his first boat most of the ingredients to build a successful submarine had been tried and tested. Although his father later said that Garrett 'had made a detailed study of submarine developments to date' it is not known what would have been available to him. Many of the earlier experiments were not well documented. Others had been tackled in a cavalier manner without the necessary rigid scientific discipline needed for development. Many letters and documents would have been, and maybe still are, stored in Government archives. With hindsight and the information available today it is very easy to look back and see where mistakes were made or wrong solutions adopted. Much still had to be resolved, but undoubtedly the main problem which still had to be determined was the motive power to drive a submarine when it was submerged and on the surface.

CHAPTER 13

THE EGG

There are a number of imponderables and perhaps the most fundamental is why Garrett was so interested in submarines and underwater breathing equipment. The Victorian period was an innovative age and it could well be surmised that Garrett had identified a niche which he felt he could develop to make his fortune, although this may not have been compatible with his vocation in Holy Orders. This was not the case; his motivation was in fact patriotic which, in Victorian times, is not surprising. Only later did there emerge a humanitarian aspect to his work.

Garrett's father, the Rev. John Garrett, M.A., D.D. justified his son's intentions in a letter to the *Manchester Courier* which was written some years later.[1] An extract from this letter not only defines the motivation but the argument put forward also highlights the Victorian attitude:

> During the recent war between Russia and Turkey two incidents were reported which sent a thrill of deep interest through the public mind, and which combined may be taken as the originating cause of my son's design which he has now brought to a stage of practical demonstration. I refer to the attack which was made by a Russian officer in command of a torpedo boat upon a Turkish ironclad, in which the Russian boat became entangled in certain chains which had been fixed as a barrier round the ship. When reading the account it came to my son's mind, 'Why could not the attack be made safe by going under the chains?' And, about the same time, we were all made intensely anxious by the appearance of a Russian ironclad or other warship, outside the town of Victoria in Vancouver's Island, when for several hours it was felt that such a town and colony must lie almost at the mercy of such an enemy if he came to bombard it. This brought the thought of 'Why some means of defence could not

meet such an enemy underwater, and so render all bombardment of the kind and all landing of hostile troops upon any of our coasts next to an impossibility.' With an accurate knowledge of all previous attempts, especially in America, to bring submarine vessels into use, and also with a clear opinion as to the causes of the entire failure of such attempts, my son concluded that two practical discoveries must be made before such underwater means of defence or attack could become useful and effective. He felt that some handy and effective method for purifying the human breath must be discovered and constructed before any crew could live in the small, shut up space which could be moved and handled under water; and also that some available motive power must be arranged which would not betray the position of such a vessel by giving off any smoke or other evidence of her whereabouts, and which motive power must at the same time be adequate to enable such a craft to work rapidly, and in any desired direction, while immersed in the water. Without such a breathing apparatus, and without such a motive power, it was plain to my son's mind that submarine navigation of the necessary kind could not be effectively carried out. He knew that other mechanical problems would also have to be solved, such as safe means for floating such a body at any required depth, navigating it properly, and any other kindred matters, but the breathing apparatus and the motive power to which I have referred were two discoveries which it became essential for him to make and to apply before the construction of mere machinery could be any good.

It is not known exactly when Garrett seriously started work on his first 'Submarine-Boat'. However, by the spring of 1878 his planning was so far advanced that he was able to submit a Provisional Specification to the Patent Office. It

[1] *Manchester Courier*, 15 December 1879

was this specification which was used as a basis for his first boat. Before considering how that boat was built and developed his early education and career over the proceeding eight years should be examined briefly.

Formative Years

Through the sponsorship of the Baroness Burdett-Coutts and Mr John Abel Smith M.P., he was enrolled in 1863 as a pupil at Rossall School, at Fleetwood in Lancashire and remained there for one year. He then attended Manchester Grammar School which was one of the first schools in England to introduce Science into the curriculum (Clifton was the other) and he studied Physical Science under Dr Marshall Watts. He probably left the Grammar School in 1869. He studied at Trinity College Dublin, entering college on 26 April 1870 as pensioner (i.e. he paid a fixed sum annually). He graduated as a B.A. in the Summer of 1875, after a five year course. He was classed as a respondent (that is he sat the general examination in astronomy, ethics, mathematical physics, experimental science, natural science and classics).

Garrett's father related that 'It was rendered necessary by circumstances that he (Garrett) should begin practical work at an early age. So he entered the University of Dublin, where students pass their courses by examinations, and in the meantime employ themselves in active occupations, if advisable.'[2] During the five year university course Garrett only lived in college for two terms. Academically he made good use of the five years 'at University'; during this period he became an assistant teacher at the Manchester Mechanics' Institution, and attended a chemistry course at the South Kensington Museum under Dr Franklin. He also had gainful employment during the five years, teaching at other schools.

In a brief account of his father's life,[3] Garrett's son wrote:

> He obtained an appointment as Head Master at Pocock College in the County of Kilkenny, famous

for its cats and at that time in the throes of the Fenian riots, which necessitated marching the students to Church on Sunday with guns on their shoulders. On other occasions, when out of the College grounds, they armed themselves with a peculiarly innocent looking but deadly weapon, made by removing the cardboard from the square flat tops of their mortar board caps and inserting a piece of sheet steel in its place. With the addition of a loop to slip over the wrist this made a handy weapon at close quarters.

Having graduated in the summer of 1875 he spent one year travelling around the world during which time he visited New Zealand and Fiji and both taught and practised navigation.

On 17 August 1876 George William Littler Garrett married Jane Parker, at Tallow Parish Church, County Waterford. She was the daughter of William H. Parker a solicitor, and was born on 27 November 1848 making her three and a half years older than her husband.

The newly married couple returned to Manchester where G.W.L.G. embarked on a career in the Church. He was ordained and made deacon, and was appointed as curate to the church of which his father, the Rev. John Garrett, M.A., D.D. was rector. This was recorded in the Manchester Diocesan Registry: 'George William Garrett aged 25 years. B.A. Trinity College Dublin. Ordained Deacon 27 May 1877 to the Curacy of Christ Church Moss Side'. To have been made a deacon he would have needed a theological qualification. There is some consensus that he became deeply interested in theology whilst working at the Science Museum, and that he also unofficially attended some of the University Divinity Course lectures, whilst he was living in college (Trinity Dublin). Many years later his son recorded, in a short paper about his father, that G.W.L.G. had studied at Trinity College, Cambridge where he had obtained his Theological Degree. There is no record of his ever having been at Cambridge (or, indeed, Oxford) or of his having

[2] *Manchester Courier*, 15 December 1879
[3] *An account of the first practical submarine boats*. As told by the son of their inventor and commander, George William Garrett.

obtained a degree at either of these Universities. Even if he had only been admitted by incorporation (being a graduate of Trinity College, Dublin), this would have been noted in the University records. What he probably did was to sit a Cambridge University external examination in theology and this may have been misinterpreted later as his having been to Cambridge University.

As curate he assisted his father at Moss Side. His clerical career, however, was only short-lived and although of interest is not really pertinent to the overall story, therefore it will be dealt with now, although out of sequence. His appointment appeared in the *Manchester Diocesan Directory of Church of England Clergy* until the year 1884 when it was simply crossed out and no note was made as to why he had left the parish, although he also appeared in *Crockfords* as the curate for Moss Side from 1877 to 1892 but this could have been in default of further information. He should have been fully ordained a year after he was made a deacon, but there is no record of this having taken place either in the Diocese of Manchester where he was employed, or in the records at Lambeth Palace. Similarly there is no record that he took formal steps to relinquish the diaconate. It appears that he just allowed his ministry to lapse.

Whilst curate at Moss Side he would have had time to develop his ideas but what is more important is that during the period before the publication of the Provisional Patent Specification, in May 1878, Garrett had worked at the Science Museum and at the Manchester Mechanics Institution both of which would have given him access to research facilities. Certainly during this period he must have been working on both the development of the submarine-boat and an underwater breathing apparatus which he called the 'Pneumatophore'. Indeed, his son recalled, in the paper about his father:

> During his term at the Kensington Museum he had been associated with Professor Watts studying the so called equation of life. (The renewing of the oxygen in the atmosphere by the absorption of carbonic gas by the action of the sun's rays on chlorophyll, the green colouring matter in plants.) During these investigations my Father allowed himself to be enclosed in an hermetically sealed chamber, which contained beside himself, a bird, a rabbit, a guinea-pig, also a lighted candle. He took samples of the air in the chamber every fifteen minutes also working out mathematical problems. He remained under observation until he lost consciousness which was not until the animals had passed out and the candle extinguished.

(In fact 'long after a candle has gone out and it is no longer possible to strike a match through lack of oxygen, human beings can still work and think clearly'. *The British Submarine* by Commander F.W. Lipscomb, OBE, RN)

Breathing Apparatus

It was as a result of his earlier research as an undergraduate that he was able to develop his breathing apparatus. Garrett designed both a diving suit which was not connected by breathing pipes to the surface, and a portable breathing apparatus which could be worn in situations where the air was contaminated. These were described by Garrett's father:[4]

> Next he had a novel diving dress made in London, in which he lived for two hours on the first occasion, sustaining life entirely by the purifying of his own breath, so that the quantity of air contained in the helmet was sufficient for him to use, and this he demonstrated several times by moving about under water, without any tubes supplying him with air from the surface. He also had another dress made, called a 'pneumatophore', with which he entered and continued in chambers filled with sulphur fumes and other deadly gases, proving to himself that he possesses a simple and easily used appliance, with which mines and other places filled with noxious vapours, can be safely and effectively explored for all practical purposes.

[4] *Manchester Courier*, 15 December 1879

Some years later Garrett's brother, by then a doctor (M.D.), also wrote about the pneumatophore, giving just a little more background:[5]

My brother was always dabbling with chemistry and scientific subjects. The starting point of his submarine work was his discovery that caustic potash will absorb carbonic acid gas given off in a man's breath. He made an apparatus which he called the 'pneumatophore' – a sort of diver's helmet with a knapsack attachment. I was a boy of about sixteen at the time and I remember the vivid interest with which I used to follow his experiments. The pneumatophore provided for the absorption of carbonic gas by means of sticks of caustic potash, and then he had an attachment for supplying oxygen.

Having done his research, Garrett probably worked on the practical applications while his first submarine was being developed and built. The pneumatophore was probably further tested and developed during the trials of that boat.

Patent Provisional Specification

G.W.Garrett lodged his Provisional Specification for 'Submarine Boats for Placing Torpedoes, &c' with the Patent Office on 8 May 1878. The Specification, which is reproduced opposite, gives an insight into Garrett's detailed and yet at this stage purely theoretical, preparation. But it must be remembered that he had not been formally trained as a Naval Architect and he was as much a pioneer as those who had developed submarines before him. We are told by his father, that he had conducted his own research into the history of submarines. As we have seen, much had been done in this field, but many of the earlier experiments were not structured and documented and the research he had carried out must have been very difficult and probably quite sparse. He was probably clear, in his own mind, of the weaknesses, strengths and shortcomings of a few of the earlier boats and aware of some of the main problems he would have to overcome, but there were certainly gaps in his own knowledge and understanding of the various issues which would face him.

Some years ago when I made my first model of this boat I affectionately called her *The Egg* as the model was not only egg-shaped but also egg-sized, furthermore the 'egg' shape is mentioned in the Patent. Garrett, with his penchant for Latin, would probably have thought that 'Ovum' would have been more appropriate. Certainly the original germ of his idea had taken on some substance, and G.W.L.G with hindsight, might even have approved of the name and the thought behind it.

It was probably in the late spring of 1878, at about the same time that he applied for the Provisional Patent, that Garrett placed the order to build his first submarine-boat with Messrs Cochran and Co. of Duke Street, Birkenhead. Cochrans only established its general engineering and shipbuilding works in 1878, but it was a fast developing company which specialised in boilers, steam-driven launches, tugs and yachts complete with propelling engines and boilers. By 1881 the firm's catalogue listed twenty-one sizes of boiler and no fewer than four eminent firms were manufacturing Cochran boilers under licence. In an article published in 1922[6] the author states that he had several interviews with Mr Cochran after that gentleman had retired, and he makes the pertinent comment: 'Mr Cochran, a shrewd, farseeing man, accepted the order from Mr Garrett to build the first submarine, the inventor to join in helping with the actual work'. This perhaps indicates that Garrett and Cochran had a good working relationship, and that Garrett actually worked on the boat while it was being built. By doing this it would help to keep the cost down and at this stage this would be important as the project was being financed by Garrett with, most probably, help from his father.

No drawing was submitted with the Provisional Patent Specification. But in Cochran's archives

---

[5] *Manchester (Evening) Chronicle*, Thursday 24 February 1916
[6] *Sea Breezes*, March 1922

A.D. 1878, 8th May. N° 1838.

Submarine Boats for Placing Torpedoes, &c.

LETTERS PATENT to George William Garrett, of 82, Chorlton Road, Manchester, in the County of Lancaster, for the Invention of "IMPROVEMENTS IN AND APPERTAINING TO SUBMARINE OR SUBAQUEOUS BOATS OR VESSELS FOR REMOVING, DESTROYING, LAYING, OR PLACING TORPEDOES IN CHANNELS AND OTHER SITUATIONS, AND FOR OTHER PURPOSES"

Sealed the 29th October 1878, and dated the 8th May 1878.

PROVISIONAL SPECIFICATION left by the said George William Garrett at the Office of the Commissioners of Patents on the 8th May 1878.

GEORGE WILLIAM GARRETT, of 82, Chorlton Road, Manchester, in the County of Lancaster, "IMPROVEMENTS IN AND APPERTAINING TO SUBMARINE OR SUBAQUEOUS BOATS OR VESSELS FOR REMOVING, DESTROYING, LAYING, OR PLACING TORPEDOES IN CHANNELS AND OTHER SITUATIONS, AND FOR OTHER PURPOSES."

This Invention relates to a novel means of constructing boats or vessels for removing or placing torpedoes in channels and like situations, but which may also be employed for diving or submarine surveying purposes.

I generally construct the vessel of small dimensions, a handy size being about 14 feet long (when arranged to contain only one man), so as to be easily lifted by the davits of an ironclad or other ship, or from a pier or other structure.

In shape the hull is elliptical or preferably resembling the shape of an egg, with this difference that both halves are exactly alike. I prefer to construct it of wood, or if of thin iron, or preferably steel plates. The sides can be strengthened with iron stringers well stiffened by gusset plates, so as to resist the pressure to which they will be exposed. I prefer to make the diameter about $1/3$ of the length. Thus, a boat 14 feet long would be about 5 feet at its major axis.

The boat is usually propelled by means of a small gas or vapour engine of suitable construction driving a propeller or screw.

[Price 6d.]

---

2   A.D. 1878.—N° 1838.

Garrett's Improvements in Submarine Boats for Placing Torpedoes, &c.

The gas can be compressed into a suitable tank. I generally use hydrocarbon gas, and add a percentage of oxygen, so that the gas can be exploded under the piston by electricity or otherwise without needing the admixture of air. I can use other explosives for operating the engine instead of hydrocarbon or similar gas.

The exhaust gas passes out into the water through a non-delivery valve, or is otherwise disposed of. On either side of the screw I place a rudder working horizontally. These rudders are preferably of a rectangular shape, and flat, so as to offer little resistance to the water. They can be driven by bevel gearing from the propeller shaft, or otherwise operated.

The vertical movement of the vessel is controlled by means of two other rudders placed in the same horizontal plane as the propeller shaft, and with their axes at right angles thereto; these are of similar form to the lateral rudders, and are operated in the same manner.

To regulate the depth of floatation of the vessel I employ the following means:— At the centre of the vessel, and in the same horizontal plane as the centre line, I place a strong horizontal cylinder communicating with the water by a port or ports at its centre. Inside this cylinder I place two well packed pistons. These pistons are secured to screwed piston rods, each working through screw boxes at the ends of the cylinder. Each screw box is secured to or forms part of a toothed wheel in connection with suitable gearing, so that both wheels may be actuated by handle or otherwise, and thus cause both pistons to approach or recede from each other, preferably evenly and synchronously. When the pistons recede, the water enters, filling the cylinder, thus acting as water ballast.

The handle actuating the gearing is worked till the boat sinks deep enough. By actuating the handle the reverse way, the pistons approach each other, and expel the water from the cylinder, and the boat rises. Several of these cylinders might be used, and could be placed vertically if desired.

The boat could be propelled by manual power if desirable, a man or men sitting on a seat in the centre of the boat working treadles driving the propeller shaft. On the upper side of the boat, and preferably over the centre, I arrange a strong conning tower fitted in the roof with a man-hole for ingress and egress. I place strong glass windows or ports circumferentially round it, and also in the roof so that a person standing or sitting in the boat can observe objects in the water. I arrange two or more openings in this tower fitted with elastic water-tight sleeves, so that a person can get his arms through these to cut the wires of torpedoes, or to place them in position, or operate an anchor or rope.

Below these holes, and in the water, I arrange a box to contain nippers and other tools for cutting wires and for other purposes. I also arrange an electric lamp, so that the occupant of the tower can swing it about in the water in his search for torpedoes and other obstructions. I arrange the roof of the conning tower so that it is easily taken off if anything happens to the boat, so that the occupants can rise to the surface, being aided by life-belts if desired.

Within the boat I arrange apparatus or chemicals for purifying the air, or supplying oxygen to the occupants, or I might supply air by pumps and pipes from a distance, as with divers.

I purpose employing these boats to go before ironclads searching for torpedoes, and when found, cutting the wires connecting them to the shore, or otherwise destroying them.

The boat is easily controlled at any depth by the occupant or occupants, and can be moved about as described.

I might establish telegraphic or telephonic communication with the ironclads or otherwise, so that the occupants of the boat can report progress or issue orders. A supply of insulated wire could easily be carried on a reel and unwound as the boat proceeds.

These boats could also be used for laying or placing torpedoes in various situations, or be used to cut vessels' moorings, or a number of them could tow a

---

A.D. 1878.—N° 1838.   3

Garrett's Improvements in Submarine Boats for Placing Torpedoes, &c.

vessel out of a roadstead by connecting powerful cables to the keel or other part, first taking the precaution (if a steam vessel) to disable the propellor and rudder.

The propellors of these boats should be protected by guards to preclude the possibility of chains and other obstructions fouling them.

The boats can easily be carried on the decks of ironclads, and can be lowered into the water when required.

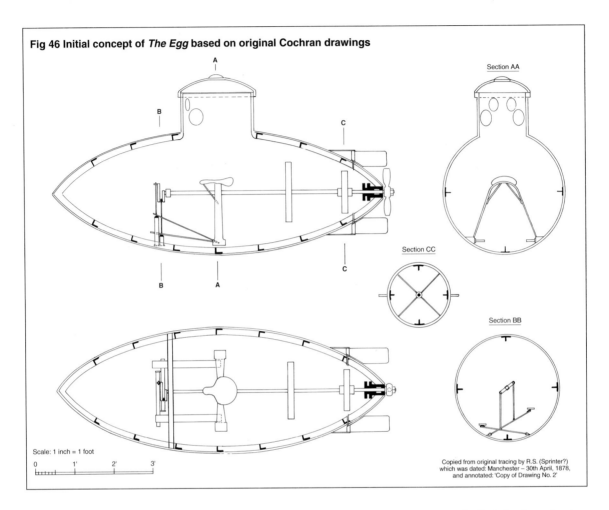

Fig 46 Initial concept of *The Egg* based on original Cochran drawings

Section AA

Section CC

Section BB

Scale: 1 inch = 1 foot

0   1'   2'   3'

Copied from original tracing by R.S. (Sprinter?)
which was dated: Manchester – 30th April, 1878,
and annotated: 'Copy of Drawing No. 2'

there is a blueprint of a boat, similar to *The Egg*, which was originally drawn in Manchester on 30 April 1878 (Fig 46). This submarine is only 8½ feet (2.6 metres) long. The hull has seven transverse frames as well as 'T' section stringers running fore and aft within the boat. It shows the vessel fitted with treadles to drive the two-bladed propeller and that she also had stern hydroplanes and rudders. In the top right corner of the original drawing there is an underlined title: 'Copy of Drawing No 2'. It is only possible to surmise how developments had taken place up to the time this drawing was produced.

Contemporary reports indicate that Garrett's first boat was about 14 feet (4.3 metres) long and although it is possible that a predecessor only 8½

feet (2.6 metres) long was built it is thought that this is not what happened. It is suggested that before approaching Cochran, and whilst still in Manchester, Garrett had had his own rough sketches translated and professionally drawn by a draughtsman. His first attempt was modified, hence the title of the blueprint dated 30 April. This, the second drawing, was used as a basis for initial discussions with Cochran. The 8½ feet (2.6 metres) vessel would have been too small. The helmsman's position would have been very cramped and Garrett would not have been able to sit upright with less than 2½ feet (.76 metres) between the saddle and the inside of the lid of the conning tower. This could well have been identified by Cochran, who was not only familiar

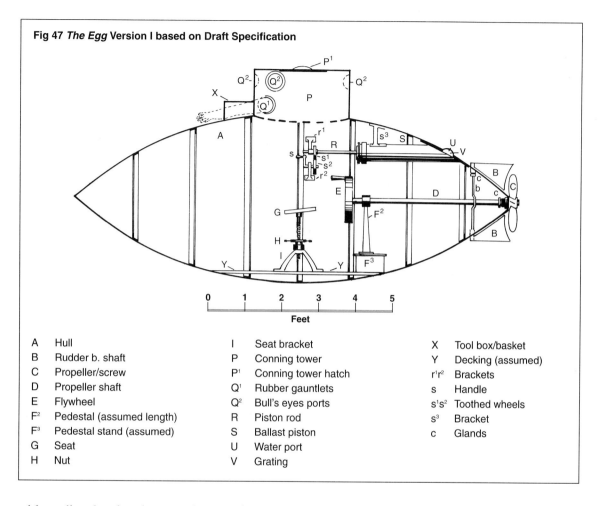

Fig 47 *The Egg* Version I based on Draft Specification

A	Hull	I	Seat bracket	X	Tool box/basket
B	Rudder b. shaft	P	Conning tower	Y	Decking (assumed)
C	Propeller/screw	P¹	Conning tower hatch	r¹r²	Brackets
D	Propeller shaft	Q¹	Rubber gauntlets	s	Handle
E	Flywheel	Q²	Bull's eyes ports	s¹s²	Toothed wheels
F²	Pedestal (assumed length)	R	Piston rod	s³	Bracket
F³	Pedestal stand (assumed)	S	Ballast piston	c	Glands
G	Seat	U	Water port		
H	Nut	V	Grating		

with reading drawings but was also experienced in building boats and ships. Furthermore space would be required for both the ballast cylinder and the small vapour engine that was under consideration. Consequently a decision was taken to build a larger but similarly proportioned boat about 14 feet (4.3 metres) long. Possibly, on the advice of Cochran, the longitudinal stringers were omitted as unnecessary with the proposed framing of the boat and the way in which it was to be constructed.

No drawing or written specification for the first boat ordered from Cochrans is known to exist. But even in the absence of a drawing with the Provisional Specification in May 1878, there is sufficient information to deduce what the first boat was like and this can be supported by drawings produced later and bills raised in the interim by Cochrans.

The configuration of the hull, conning tower and the interior fittings of the boat which was ordered and built was probably very similar to that depicted in the drawing of 'Version I' (Fig 47). The 'Submarine-Boat' was completed during the summer of 1878 and initial tests were most probably conducted during the period June to July. Although no detailed accounts of such trials have come to light, it is possible to make a number of assumptions of how the development of the boat progressed. This will be a little clearer if we move forward in time and examine the Patent Specification, which was registered on 5 November 1878, together with a copy of the drawing of the submarine-boat submitted with it (see Appendix IV).

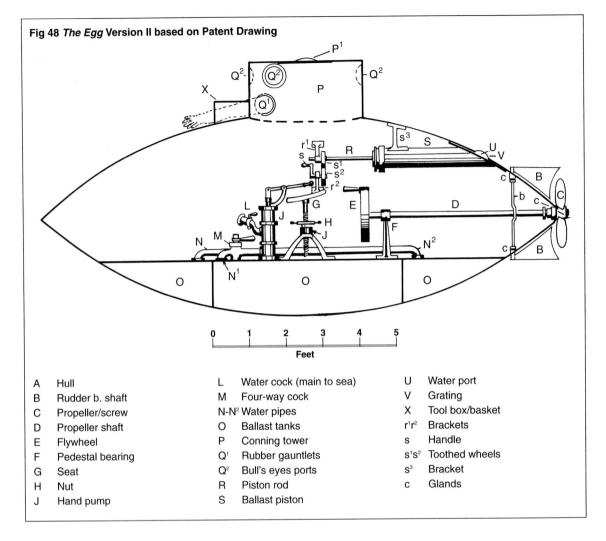

Fig 48 *The Egg* Version II based on Patent Drawing

A	Hull	L	Water cock (main to sea)	U	Water port
B	Rudder b. shaft	M	Four-way cock	V	Grating
C	Propeller/screw	N-N²	Water pipes	X	Tool box/basket
D	Propeller shaft	O	Ballast tanks	r'r²	Brackets
E	Flywheel	P	Conning tower	s	Handle
F	Pedestal bearing	Q¹	Rubber gauntlets	s's²	Toothed wheels
G	Seat	Q²	Bull's eyes ports	s³	Bracket
H	Nut	R	Piston rod	c	Glands
J	Hand pump	S	Ballast piston		

One thing that comes out very clearly in the Specification is that that it is written by a man who had gained practical experience since the Provisional Specification was written. During his initial experiments he must have found that it was not possible to submerge the boat using only the ballast cylinder and that more weight was required. This resulted in a major change which was the introduction of three ballast tanks which would be used to reduce the freeboard before the ballast cylinder was used to regulate the depth. Although he continued to state a preference for a vapour engine this was not included in the Specification drawing (Version II) and there could

well have been problems over its development.

Nearly two months before the publication of the Specification, a bill was raised by Messrs Cochran and Co Ltd,[7] for work carried out in connection with the 'Submarine-Boat' (see opposite). However, not all the work for which Garrett was charged is reflected in the Version II drawing published with the Specification.

From the placing of the order for *The Egg* (Version I) in early 1878 the possible sequence of events could have been that wet trials were conducted as soon as the hull had been completed perhaps as early as May, to test the integrity of the vessel, its stability and its buoyancy. It was found that the ballast cylinder had insufficient capacity to achieve negative buoyancy and the boat could not be forced under the water using the stern side rudders or hydroplanes. The solution was not to enlarge the ballast cylinder or fit more than one in the boat, because of the lack of space within the hull, but to build ballast tanks into the hull. These, fitted in the bottom of the boat, would to a certain extent, improve the stability of the vessel by lowering the centre of gravity when they were used. Much of the interior would then have been stripped out. The three ballast tanks would have been fitted and became an integral part of the hull while conveniently providing a platform or deck for the machinery and fittings.

The drawing submitted to the Patent Office (Fig 48) with the Specification could well show the boat as it was after this refit had been completed which could have been as early as June or July. Further trials would then have taken place. The stability of the craft may still have been poor. To drive, steer, and trim the boat it would be necessary for the helmsman to move his position quite considerably to operate the various controls which were not laid out very ergonomically. This could have had an adverse effect on the overall balance of such a relatively small vessel. Because of the restricted space and the possibility that he was wearing his breathing

apparatus he would not have been able to react very quickly to any change in hull posture. Any stability problem could have been further exaggerated by the ballast tanks. These were probably not fitted with baffles to minimise lateral and longitudinal water movement. If the balance of the boat was upset, for instance if the bow dipped it could be further exacerbated as the water in the ballast tanks surged in the same direction making the bow heavier. There may still have been problems over diving the boat. It may also have been found, during the various trials, that the ballast cylinder was unnecessary or more probably not satisfactory. Certainly, in the position shown in the Specification drawing, the helmsman would have had to duck each time it was extended and in its relatively high position at the stern it would not have improved the stability of the small craft.

The motive power would have been insufficient for prolonged movement particularly against a tide. It would have been very awkward for the helmsman to turn the propeller by hand whilst carrying out his other duties. One can imagine the gymnastics required to do all these tasks (particularly having to turn round, bend down and turn the fly-wheel using its handle): all this very energetic movement would be upsetting the trim and stability of the little vessel demanding even greater gymnastic effort to put it right.

The solutions are covered in the bill raised by Cochrans: five ballast tanks (one of which is subdivided), the machinery was probably for the treadle arrangement, and a lead weight for stability and to make the vessel less buoyant. The interior was stripped out for a second time and the treadle arrangement to drive the propeller was fitted. This gave Garrett the opportunity to re-design the interior. The conditions in the boat must have been very uncomfortable: claustrophobic, cramped space, dimly lit, cold, damp and Garrett may have had to wear his 'pneumatophore' breathing apparatus further restricting his comfort and movement. The six ballast

Messrs Cochran and Co. Ltd, Birkenhead.				
September 11th, 1878.				
Rev. Garrett Submarine-Boat	£	52	11	6
Machinery for same	£	27	10	2
5 Tanks	£	12	3	3
1 pump, cock and pipe connections	£	21	8	4
Rudders and steering gear	£	15	10	5
Sight holes and sundries	£	39	11	5
Raise height of dome	£	17	4	8
Lead keel	£	45	19	6
Total	£	231	19	3

[7] From an old Cochran's (Birkenhead) ledger 'Abstracts of Prime Costs'

tanks were fitted in a configuration to allow space for the treadles which would drive the propeller; this gave the helmsman more space and it was possible to lay-out the controls and machinery in a more ergonomic way. It was probably necessary to raise the height of the conning tower dome because the helmsman would now be sitting with his legs astride the propeller shaft and he needed to be higher. The lead weight could have been added for a number of reasons. It would make craft more stable; it would reduce the freeboard making it easier to achieve negative buoyancy using the ballast tanks; it could have also been a safety device which in an underwater emergency could be released to give the vessel immediate positive buoyancy.

Garrett was very secretive about the work he was doing. Others were building submersibles. In the United States, which had the submarine tradition of Bushnell, Hunley and Fulton, both Simon Lake and John P. Holland were developing their own submersibles. Indeed Holland's first boat was launched in May 1878; while in Russia, which also had a submarine tradition, Drzewieki had a pedal-driven boat working in 1879. By publishing all his secrets in Patents, Garrett would have been presenting his potential rivals with the results of his trials. So it is therefore not surprising that the drawing published in November 1878 probably showed the state of the 'Submarine-Boat' as it was in the middle of the summer, and not as she was after the second refit.

These changes made are reflected in a drawing (Version III) dated 7 March 1879, which was also from the Cochran archives (Fig 49). It clearly shows that the ballast tanks were not an integral part of the hull which would indicate, bearing in mind Garrett's construction philosophy, that they were added later. With the top of the conning tower removed these tanks could have been fitted into the hull without having to cut it open. The layout of the tanks was a great improvement: two tanks forward, two lower and on either side of the helmsman's seat, and one at

the stern which was divided internally, making it two separate tanks. In effect this resulted in having three ballast tanks on either side of the boat's centre line, which would improve her stability. By adopting the use of treadles to drive the propeller it would seem that Garrett had abandoned (possibly as a result of trials) his idea of driving the boat with a small gas or vapour engine. Furthermore the ballast cylinder was omitted because he could achieve better control using his six ballast tanks. The lead weight is not shown in the original drawing but as this is an 'as fitted' drawing of the interior this does not necessarily mean that it was not attached. The final modification was to the stern gear. The propeller size and shape was changed and larger rudders and hydroplanes were fitted.

It is not known how *The Egg* was finally fitted out. It has been established, from contemporary articles, that the propeller was driven by a 'pedalling arrangement' and therefore there must have been modifications to Version II to fit them. The March 1879 drawing, Version III, most likely shows the internal fitting out arrangement of *The Egg* in its final stage of development and is therefore the definitive drawing. Two things appear certain. First, that Garrett progressively developed his 'Submarine-Boat', the final drawing showing vast improvements when compared to the initial blueprint, the original Provisional Specification and the Patent drawing. Second, that the 'Submarine-Boat' did work, albeit with certain dangers involved, as his brother, Dr Garrett, of Princess Road, Moss Side, Manchester, stated in an interview with the *Manchester Chronicle:*[8]

> The next development was to construct a model submarine in which there was just room for himself, and for which he supplied the motive power by a pedalling arrangement. Fitted to it were rubber arms and hands like those attached to a diving dress. His invention enabled him to breathe in the cramped space under water without tubes and by thrusting his arms into the sleeves attached to the

[8] *Manchester (Evening) Chronicle*, Thursday 24 February 1916

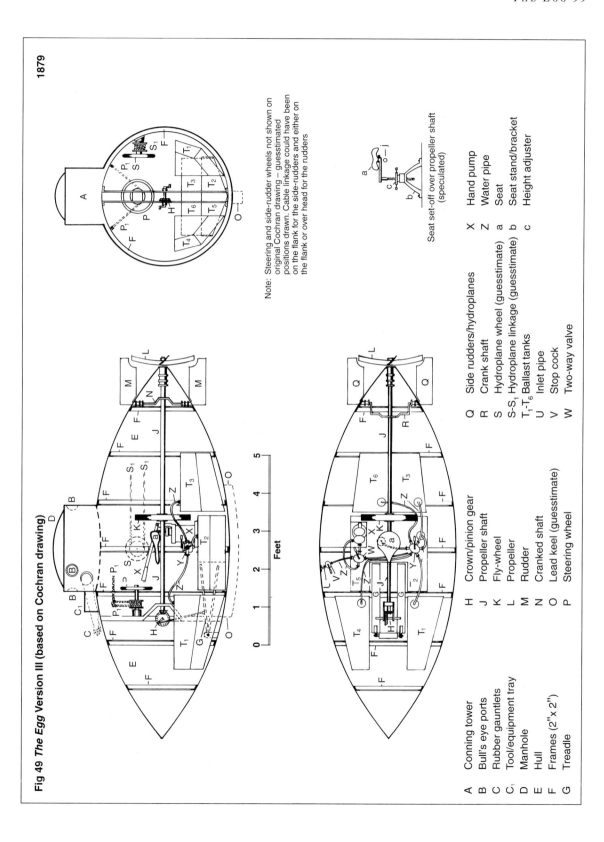

Fig 49 *The Egg* Version III (based on Cochran drawing)

1879

Note: Steering and side-rudder wheels not shown on original Cochran drawing – guesstimated positions drawn. Cable linkage could have been on the flank for the side-rudders and either on the flank or over head for the rudders

Seat set-off over propeller shaft (speculated)

A   Conning tower
B   Bull's eye ports
C   Rubber gauntlets
C₁ Tool/equipment tray
D   Manhole
E   Hull
F   Frames (2"x 2")
G   Treadle
H   Crown/pinion gear
J   Propeller shaft
K   Fly-wheel
L   Propeller
M   Rudder
N   Cranked shaft
O   Lead keel (guesstimate)
P   Steering wheel
Q   Side rudders/hydroplanes
R   Crank shaft
S   Hydroplane wheel (guesstimate)
S-S₁ Hydroplane linkage (guesstimate)
T₁-T₆ Ballast tanks
U   Inlet pipe
V   Stop cock
W   Two-way valve
X   Hand pump
Z   Water pipe
a   Seat
b   Seat stand/bracket
c   Height adjuster

Feet
0   1   2   3   4   5

outside of the 'shell' he was able to perform the sort of work that was accomplished by a diver. This was the primitive beginning of the submarine, and at this time his ideas had not travelled beyond using such an invention for diving and salvage work.[9]

Garrett's brother went on to relate the dangers associated with his brother's work:

> I well remember the trials of the thing (Submarine-boat) in the dock at Birkenhead. By accident or design one of the rubber sleeves had been split and when my brother unscrewed the inside cap there was an inrush of water. He had to pump out his water ballast for dear life in order to rise to the surface and I remember in my excitement, as he got near the surface I fished him up with a boat-hook. However, the damage was repaired.

Other reports indicated that the small vessel did work and Garrett was able to remain submerged for considerable periods of time.

Garrett Submarine Navigation and Pneumatophore Co. Ltd

So far the cost of building and developing *The Egg* must have been financed by the Garretts, father and probably to a much lesser extent the son. The research, theoretical and practical work, and the progress that had been made with both the submarine-boat and the breathing apparatus encouraged Garrett's father to form a limited company to raise sufficient capital to develop his son's inventions. In fact some preliminary and prudent public relations work had been done during the actual trials of *The Egg* and this was noted by Garrett's brother: 'the idea so impressed certain gentlemen who saw it that financial backing to the extent of some thousands of pounds was obtained for a larger venture.' Garrett Submarine Navigation and Pneumatophore Co Ltd, had its Registered Offices at 56 Deansgate, Manchester and was probably formed in the second half of 1878. The chairman was Garrett's father, the Rev. John

Garrett, who had 2,000 one pound shares. Other directors included:

W.A. Sadler, Esq., (a Manchester accountant)
Edward Gabriel, Esq., (an insurance agent from Lymn)
H.W. Clemsha, Esq., (a financial agent)

Other early subscribers included an actuary (John E. Leyland, Esq.) and an advocate (E.F. Monlin, Esq.). A number of one year debentures were also issued. But this was much later, and these were to be repaid with a hundred per cent bonus. This gives a very good indication of the confidence the Company had in Garrett's ability, and the anticipated sales potential.

Dr John Garrett rightly anticipated that there would be some hostile reaction to his and his son's involvement in developing weapons of war and destruction. He was to defend his position vigorously later, but his immediate justification was contained in the preamble to the Company Prospectus: 'As to the invention for murdering people – this is all nonsense. Every contribution by science to improve instruments of war makes war shorter and, in the end, less terrible to human life and human progress.' This quotation was attributed to the Rev. Norman McLeod, Chaplain to H.M. the Queen and previously editor of *Good Words* a widely-known religious publication. In context this was written when the British Empire was all powerful and gun-boat diplomacy was not frowned upon (by the British).

As far as Garrett was concerned the 'Submarine-Boat' project had been a success. He had proved to himself that he could submerge and surface a vessel and survive. He had realised that such a small, man-powered vessel had severe limitations and was not really suitable to either 'go before ironclads searching for torpedoes' or 'for removing, destroying or laying torpedoes'. The size limitation was noted by Garrett in the Patent Specification where the size of the boat was increased from 14 feet (4.3 metres) to 20 feet

---

[9] This was not correct; in both the Patent Specifications Garrett had stated that the submarine-boat had a military potential, indeed it was Garrett's motivation for developing the submersible. The interview was nearly forty years after the event and he may not have seen either of the Patents or he may have forgotten.

(6 metres) in length, although he probably used the original hull for all his 'Submarine-Boat' trials. There had also been the development of his breathing apparatus, the 'Pneumatophore'. The Garrett Submarine Navigation and Pneumatophore Co. Ltd and its investors must have been well satisfied with the progress that had been made. However, it is quite interesting to speculate exactly what this Company hoped to achieve when it was established.

During the previous forty years submarines had been playing a more significant role in war. Wilhelm Bauer's *Le Plongeur Marin* posed a potential threat to the Danish fleet blockading the German coast in 1850; submarines had been used with some success in the American Civil War. Their potential had been recognised by the French who, in 1859, had ordered the *Plongeur* as a coast defence weapon, although this did not prove to be a success. While in 1879, in Russia, Drzewieki, a contemporary rival of Garrett, who had built a one-man submarine was ordered by the Russian Government to develop a two-man submarine which was later ordered in quantity by the Tsar's Navy. The major powers were starting to take a low-key interest in submarines. The exception was Britain, who, with the most powerful navy in the world, still saw no reason to acquire submarines. However, there was a school of thought that such vessels could be used for harbour defence. Perhaps the Company hoped that the submarine-boat could be sold to the Royal Navy for this purpose. On the other hand it may have been Garrett's intention, right from the start, to build a steam-powered submarine, and the development of *The Egg* was just a preliminary step in the evolution process. Garrett had already recognised that an engine was required for his boat; this is covered in the Patent, where the use of the hand-driven fly wheel and treadle is only mentioned in passing. That the treadle was eventually used may indicate

that during trials he had had problems developing a suitable gas engine, and it may have been this that prompted the development of a steam-powered submarine.

Because *The Egg* was, as far as is known, never propelled by a gas or vapour engine this has, so far, been glossed over as it did not appear to figure in the development of this boat. However, the concept put forward by Garrett in the Patent, was a particularly innovative idea. In the Provisional Specification it stated that the boat 'is usually propelled by means of a small gas or vapour engine' whereas in the Specification it says: ' the boat might be propelled by a small gas or vapour engine'. This was written in such a way that it makes it appear that the engine existed and was working when the Provisional Specification was written but it is given less emphasis in the actual Specification as though it had proved to be unsatisfactory. However, in both specifications it explains that he would use: 'hydro-carbon gas with a percentage of oxygen added, so that the gas can be exploded under the piston by electricity or otherwise without needing the admixture of air.' In an article about G.W. Garrett[10] John M. Maber points out: *'The reference to electric ignition is of interest since, in fact, the introduction as a practical means of firing the cylinder charge in an internal combustion engine dates from 1883, some five years after the grant of Garrett's patent.'* Perhaps this was one of the most innovative ideas that Garrett had, but unfortunately he did not follow it up or was unable to make it work.

Whatever the aspirations of the Garrett Submarine and Pneumatophore Co. Ltd were, by 24 March 1879 planning for Garrett's next submarine *Resurgam* was so well advanced that experiments for this project were already being carried out at the yard of Messrs Cochran and Company Limited.

---

[10] *George Garrett! – Who's he? or, The Curate's Submarine* by John M. Maber

Resurgam

CHAPTER 14

RESURGAM

Resurgam, Garrett's second submarine, was also built by Messrs Cochran and Co. Ltd of Birkenhead, and some initial experiments were carried out by the firm in March 1879 several weeks before the draft specification for the boat was discussed and the contract to build the boat was signed. Garrett had decided that the new boat would be steam-powered using a relatively new concept.

The Innovative Power Plant

The steam-propelling machinery fitted in *Resurgam* was based on the general principle of the 'fireless locomotive'. That is, a standard engine, powered by steam which is not being directly generated by a boiler but which has been stored in a reservoir; in other words using latent power. The idea, worked on by Mr Zerah Colburn for the Metropolitan Railway in 1864, showed much promise but nothing practical had been achieved. In 1872 it was successfully revived in the United States for use in tramways, by Dr Lamm of New Orleans. Further development took place in France by M. Leon Francq of Paris, who, in July 1878, had trams, using this system, working regularly between Rueil and Marly le Roi, a return journey of 9½ miles (15.3km). In an article in *Engineering*,[1] M. Leon Francq explained the principle on which the fireless locomotive worked:

In a heated liquid the boiling point rises or falls according to the pressure on its surface increases or diminishes. Hence it follows that if water is heated in a closed and strong vessel by means of a current of steam passing into it, that steam produces in the water an increasing pressure corresponding exactly with the temperature, while it is itself condensed gradually to a corresponding degree.

Instead of having a boiler on board the tram, to generate steam to work the engine, Francq and Lamm had stationary roadside boilers which charged a lagged reservoir on the tram which was connected to its engine. The tram was driven using the saturated steam, which flashed off as the pressure in the vessel reduced, and was able to complete the 9½-mile (15.3km) journey, with stops, at an average speed of just over 11mph (17.7kph). It is of more than passing interest to understand why it was considered necessary to have fireless locomotives for tramways in 1879. M. Leon Francq explains in his article:

The great expense involved in the working of tramways, due first to the nature of the permanent way, and secondly, to the high cost of horse traction, has proved in many cases a serious bar to their success. If mechanical traction be used, it is necessary that the line be kept in better order than it is generally; and the excess of expense thus required by the line must be made up by the greater economy in the motive power. This economy can only be attained by reduction in wages, in consumption of fuel, &., in maintenance and renewal expenses of the road and rolling stock, and in the first cost of the mechanical power.

It is further essential, at least in towns, that the questions of safety and health be taken into consideration. To arrive at that result it is necessary to avoid the use of ordinary engines subject to the chance of explosion, and to the throwing off of sparks. The light of the fire must not be seen and the cinders must not be scattered upon the highway. The noise occasioned by safety valves must be suppressed, as well as that produced by the blast. Lastly, all escape of smoke, soot and noxious gas must be done away with. In resolving the problem of traction under the conditions just established the

[1] *Engineering*, 7 November 1879.

writer had recourse to the practical application of 'the fireless locomotive'.

Garrett adapted this idea for use in *Resurgam*, the fundamental difference being that the boiler would be on board. Once a head of steam had been raised in the boiler the boat could be driven on the surface using the steam engine and boiler in the conventional way. Before it was possible to dive, it would be necessary to charge a steam reservoir; ideally, in Garrett's design, to get maximum underwater range, this would have been to about 150 lb per square inch (about 10 atmospheres). Before diving, the boiler furnace would be damped down and sealed, if fitted, air and smoke vent safety valves closed and the conning tower hatch secured. Under water the engine would be driven drawing on the latent power in the steam boiler and reservoir.

Initial Trials

Extracts from another bill raised by Messrs Cochran and Co. Ltd,[2] itemises various charges for the hull of *Resurgam*, side rudders and wages. One item specifically notes that it was for: '(experiments with 6 Boiler March 24th 1879 £14. 0. 0.)' this was several weeks before the contract to build the boat was signed.

In the absence of other records it is only possible to speculate what boiler experiments were carried out. Although Messrs Cochran and Co. Ltd, specialised in boilers the Lamm system would probably be quite novel to this firm. There may have been a requirement to design a suitable reservoir for the steam and test it, as this was the innovative part of the concept which may have required some new technology. This could be one reason for the specified experiment. It is unlikely that a boiler would have been built before the contract had been drawn up and signed and initial experiments could have been carried out using a standard Cochran boiler, which would probably have been available on site. If the experiments were successful Messrs Cochran and Co. Ltd, with

their expertise in boiler design and manufacture, would have been able to provide Garrett with the detailed specifications for the submarine's power plant. However, if such experiments were necessary it would seem to have been more appropriate for the firm to have done such research and development work.

There is another possibility. In an article about Garrett,[3] the author relates that he had had several interviews with Mr Cochran, who had made various drawings and papers, from the firm, available to him. Although there are a number of questionable statements in the article, his observations about the firm and the activities in the shipyard should be reasonably accurate. He quotes an unnamed newspaper which implies that *Resurgam* had a predecessor:

> The invention (this must refer to *The Egg*) was first submitted to public notice about twelve months ago, but the boat when tried was a sort of working model only, and had been built rather to testify the practicability of the ideas which it embodied than to mark the final part of development. Since the experiments so successfully made with the first boat, Mr Garrett has done a great deal to strengthen the strong, and so do away with the weak parts of his invention. The model constructed a year ago weighed only 4.5 tons but the boat just completed has a total weight of close upon 30 tons, while the experience gained in earlier trials has lead to a number of structural improvements. The boat is cigar-shaped and has a total length of about 40 feet. A small conning tower issues from the centre and is the only object visible when the boat is at its normal level near the surface of the water.

He goes on to say that trials were made in the Great Float, Birkenhead. Finally in this part of the article he writes:

> Next there came the big boat, the *Resurgam*, 40 feet long by 9 feet beam by 30 tons displacement.

[2] Cochran (Birkenhead) Ledger 'Abstracts of Prime Costs' bill dated 29 September 1879
[3] *Sea Breezes*, March 1922.

This is all very tenuous but it is possible that Garrett carried out some form of hull trials early in 1879, before the design of *Resurgam* was finalised. A standard Cochran boiler, suitably modified, could have been used and for this he would have been charged (hence the bill). The beam or diameter of the 40-foot (12-metre) vessel would have been about 6 feet (1.8 metres), if it had displaced 30 tons, as reported in the newspaper article. It is difficult to imagine how the vessel was weighted down to achieve the near negative buoyancy reported in the article. Flooding the hull is a possibility, but it is likely that there would have been problems both with trim and stability; mechanical controls and pumping equipment would have been needed to control the ballast. It is possible to imagine a number of experiments that Garrett would have liked to have carried out with and in such a vessel, particularly bearing in mind the way in which *The Egg* had evolved through a number of major changes to the ballasting (and stability) arrangements as well as its interior lay-out. This lends some plausibility to the idea that some form of trial was not only necessary but was actually carried out, albeit in a very crude way.

The *Resurgam* Specification

A week after these experiments, whatever they were, Garrett was in a position to produce the draft specification for *Resurgam*. He wrote to Messrs Cochran and Co. on 31 March 1879 formally asking for an estimate. His letter (verbatim) accompanied with a rough sketch gives a good insight into Garrett the engineer:

> 82 Chorlton Rd.
> Hulme
> Manchester
> March 31st. 79

Dear Sir.

I leave for Portsmouth this afternoon and if you desire to communicate with me during this week please address me c/o A.J. Durston, HM Dockyard, Portsmouth. I send with this a sketch of the general outline that I propose for the boat and also a short description of the various parts.

You will observe that the boat as sketched by me is 40ft long and 7 feet in Diam with 20ft cylinder and two 10 ft points. I wish that you will make your calculations upon this scale as I am satisfied that these proportions are the best for my purpose.

I think you will see in the sketch and description a mention of all the parts you would have to make but there would be the fitting up of my apparatus, gauges etc, etc which must come after the bulk estimate. I hope you will put as low a price & will pay you upon the bulk estimate as you know there will be many expenses over & above the bulk estimate and I do not want the immediate price to be such as will frighten, and perhaps stop the proper carrying out of my plans. I will call upon you on Monday next and have a chat with you as to the result of your week's consideration before we open the matter of cost to other people.

It is also as necessary for yourself as for me that a good article should be produced.

> Yours faithfully,
> George W. Garrett
>
> Messrs Cochran & Co

The specification sent under cover of this letter shows how far advanced Garrett was:

Boiler

Should be 45 inches in diameter and 144 inches long and capable of standing with perfect safety a pressure of 150 lb per sq in. The fire grate should be as small as possible for efficiently working a 6 horsepower engine (as if it was required to get up steam quickly a stronger blast would effectually do so even on a small grate). The furnace should be of such construction that although a pressure was kept up inside yet it should be possible to supply fuel.

Condenser

Should be of no large or surface as can conveniently be stowed in the boat if it cannot be placed outside as it may be necessary at times to work the engine at more than 6 horsepower. The condenser should be situated between the engine etc and the boiler and should be as close to the boiler as consistent with the efficiency of the condenser.

The boiler and condenser should be considered as one and their centre of gravity should coincide with the centre of the boat (being kept as low as possible).

The engine

Should be situated as near the screw as possible and should be such as would do 6 horsepower at a pressure of from 30 to 40 lb per square inch on the piston.

The blower

Should be situated as near the engine as possible and might possibly be worked by a band round the fly wheel which could be slipped if desired.

The conning tower

Should be 3 feet high and should be 2 feet broad by 3 feet long. It should have a manhole in the top which could be fastened from the inside. The manhole should be 16 inches in diameter and round. There should be lookouts in each of the four cardinal points and a dead light in the top. There should be one pair of sleeves on each side.

The rudders

There are four. Two are situated at the stern of the boat as near the screw as possible which direct the boat either to port or starboard. Two large balanced rudders at the centre of the boat which would raise or lower the level at which the boat would float (within certain limits)

In addition to the above there remains a reservoir for compressed gas which must stand a pressure of 1000 lb and which can be got from Birmingham in the shape of steel tubes which could conveniently be stowed in the boat. These I would provide myself

as also the float which has for its object the minute and rigid variation of the S/s g of the boat.

GWG

The available copy of the drawing sent with the letter has been damaged making it difficult to read so for clarity a copy has been drawn (Fig 50). It was possible to read most of Garrett's comments on the original but that annotated 'J' cannot be read but undoubtedly it refers to the air inlet which was self-sealing to prevent the ingress of water in rough weather or when the boat was submerged. It would appear from the drawing that the smoke exhaust was also fitted with a similar valve although this is not commented upon by Garrett. Neither the engine nor the condenser were shown in the drawing.

Aside from the specifications of *Resurgam*, the letter gives an insight into Garrett's other activities and raises an interesting possibility. His trip to Portsmouth Dockyard to see Mr Durston, who was a chief engineer on the Naval staff, had possibly been set up by an influential patron, but at this stage it is difficult to see what he had to offer the Royal Navy. He only had a draft specification for *Resurgam* and this was in an embryo state. However, a drawing of *The Egg*, in her final form, had been produced, probably by Cochran's draughtsman, a few days earlier, on 3 March 1879. By this time, this small vessel had been fully tested and proved. Perhaps it was in anticipation of this visit that the drawing had been prepared and it was this invention that he was offering to the Royal Navy. This may not be as far fetched as one would imagine. In Russia, in 1877, Drzewieki designed and built his first submarine which was pedal-powered and in principle not unlike *The Egg*; this small vessel attracted the attention of the Russian Government and Drzewieki was ordered to construct an improved and larger submarine which led to an order by the Tsarist Navy. If it was *The Egg* which was being offered, Garrett failed to obtain an order. But the visit may have been used to pave the way to have *Resurgam* evaluated at

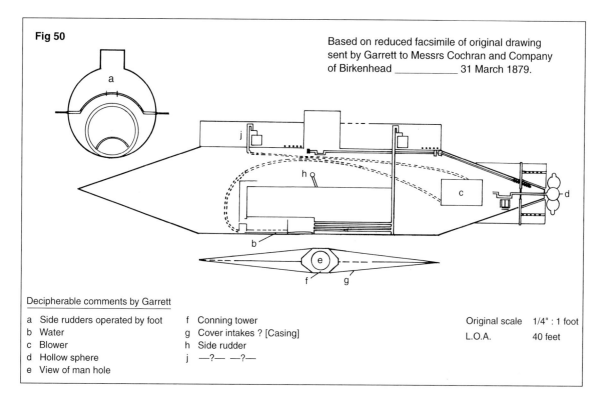

Fig 50

Based on reduced facsimile of original drawing
sent by Garrett to Messrs Cochran and Company
of Birkenhead _____ 31 March 1879.

Decipherable comments by Garrett

a Side rudders operated by foot
b Water
c Blower
d Hollow sphere
e View of man hole

f Conning tower
g Cover intakes ? [Casing]
h Side rudder
j —?— —?—

Original scale   1/4" : 1 foot
L.O.A.   40 feet

Portsmouth when she had been built.

The specifications for *Resurgam*, laid out by Garrett, show that he was well advanced in his concept. His description of the hull and its exterior fittings is quite comprehensive. Before it was drafted he must have already had discussions, possibly with Cochran, about the interior fittings and machinery as he implies that he had been told that the condenser could not be fitted outside the hull. This could have been an outcome of the experiments carried out at Cochrans a week before.

Although the ballast cylinder had been omitted in the final drawing of *The Egg*, Garrett was still considering its use in *Resurgam*. The wheel seems to have turned full circle for in the original concept for *The Egg* there were no ballast tanks but the ballast cylinder was to be used. As the submarine was tested and developed it was found necessary to fit such tanks and three were fitted; later it was modified again and six tanks were installed and the ballast cylinder discarded completely. According to drawings produced

later the ballast cylinder was not eventually fitted to *Resurgam*. But it does not appear, in this case, that its absence was compensated for or replaced by one or more ballast tanks. Garrett's new philosophy was to always retain positive buoyancy in his submarine.

Messrs Cochran and Co. Ltd, produced a rough estimate, based on Garrett's specification:

Hull	Estimated weight of Material 9 tons @ £9	£81
	Labour @ £8	£72
	Charges .. .. ½ labour	£36
		£189

Conning Tower	
1 manhole 5 lights 4 arm holes	£60
Cutwaters or covers for tubes 2 @ £20	£40
Rudders stern including steering gear	£30
Side rudders (not sufficient information)	£45
Bunkersides forming covering for boiler 24cwt including boiler seatings	£25

Engine and Blower seatings		£20
		£409
	33%	£136
		£545
Hull		£545
Boiler		£359
Engine		£340
Blower Handpump		£113
		£1,357
Ballast		£128
		£1,485
Launching		£53
		£1,538

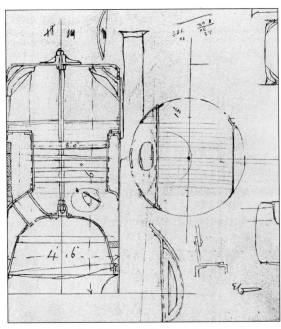

Fig 52 Facsimile of Edward Compton's[4] original sketch of the Cochran boiler circa 1876.

The scheduled meeting took place on Monday 7 April 1879 and undoubtedly Garrett's specification and drawing were discussed at length. A small memento of the meeting still survives: the back of a letter addressed to Messrs Cochran and Co., postmarked (Saturday) 5 April 1879 (which would have been delivered that morning and was probably lying on Mr Cochran's desk), was used as a doodle pad, and the jottings were most likely made during the meeting. One sketch shows what could have been a series of linked tubes; possibly a proposed solution for the steam reservoir, or more likely a water cooled condenser while next to it is a coil arrangement which could also have been a form of condenser. The second series of sketches (by the address) bear a striking resemblance to the original Cochran boiler but with the addition of what could have been reservoirs for the stored steam.

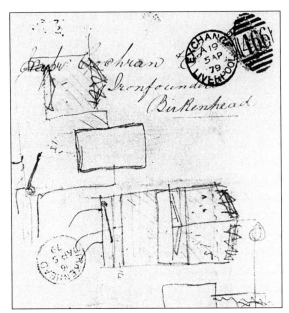

Fig 51 Memento of the meeting – envelope with sketch of boiler.

After the meeting and in the light of the discussions that had been held Cochran produced an 'Approximate Estimate' for the Garrett Submarine Boat (Fig 53).

After further negotiations the order to build *Resurgam* was awarded to Messrs Cochran and Co. Ltd, in mid April.

---

[4] Edward Compton and James Cochran were partners in the newly established firm of Cochran & Co.

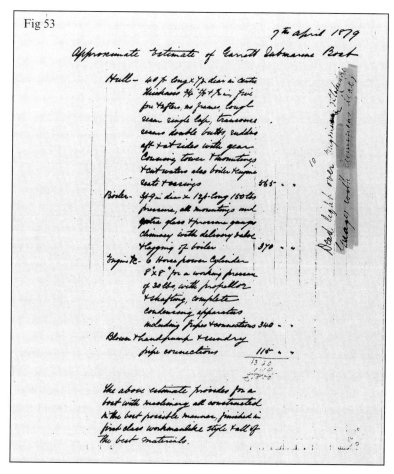

Fig 53

7th April 1879

Approximate Estimate of Garrett Submarine Boat

hydroplanes for diving and maintaining depth) and rudders mounted on both the top and bottom of the hull immediately in front of the screw which had been changed from the original specification for a hollow two-bladed to a standard three-bladed propeller.

In its outward appearance very little had changed to the original specification and rough sketch that Garrett produced at the end of March 1879 (Fig 54).

Within the hull (Figs 55–57), the cylindrical boiler (12 feet 9 inches (3.9 metres) long with a diameter of 3 feet 9 inches (1.14 metres)) which had a water capacity of about three tons, had a wooden insulating jacket. The boiler had the normal mountings: pressure and water gauges, steam stop valve, blow down cock, and the safety valve, which was mounted on top of the boiler. Fitted on top of the boiler was 'the reservoir for compressed gas.' The boiler furnace (5 feet long (1.5 metres) with a diameter of 2 feet (.61 metres)), which was coal fired, was at the forward end of the boiler (boat). The drawing shows five rows of horizontal fire tubes which were 6 feet 6 inches (2 metres) long with a diameter of 1½ inches (3.8cm); these were connected to the smokebox which vented through a self-sealing smoke escape valve located under the casing. Air entered the hull either through the conning tower hatch, or when closed, using a Roots Blower which was connected by pipe to an automatic valve under the forward casing (a form of *snorkel*, an inlet pipe with a simple float arrangement to seal it) (Fig 57). The blower was driven by a belt from the propeller shaft. So that the furnace could be

Resurgam

During the next few months *Resurgam* was built. She was made of iron and was about 40 feet (12 metres) long. The cylindrical centre section had an internal diameter of 6 feet 6 inches (2 metres) and this was sheathed in 18-inch (46cm) wood beams (which were faired at their ends); both ends of the hull were cone-shaped and were fitted with dead-lights on the top centre line immediately after the commencement of taper. Unlike *The Egg* the hull was not framed. The light iron, free-flooding casing (described as 'cut waters'), which covered the air intake and smoke exhaust valve, was fitted amidships. There was a small conning tower with bull's eye lights and a manhole to allow the crew to enter the boat and from which the captain could navigate. The submarine had two side rudders (or

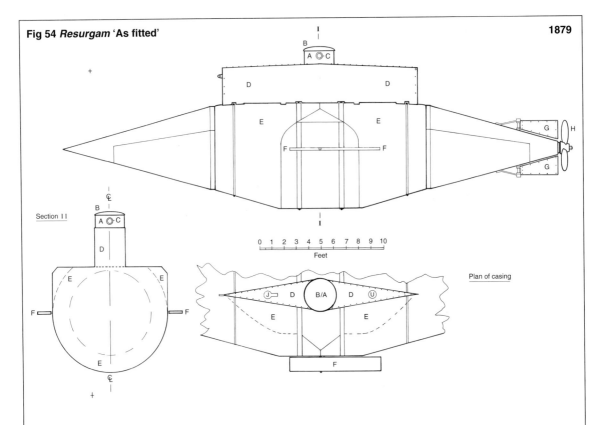

Fig 54 *Resurgam* 'As fitted'

1879

Section II

Plan of casing

0 1 2 3 4 5 6 7 8 9 10
Feet

Key to Figs 54–57

General Steam/Motive Power
A   Conning tower
B   Manhole cover
C   Bull's eye ports
D   Casing
E   Wooden cladding
F   Side rudders/hydroplanes
G   Rudder
H   Propeller

Air Supply
J   Air inlet/snorkel
K   Float
L   Air pipe
M   Roots blower

Boiler Arrangements
N   Coal bunker (assumed)
P   Boiler
a   Pressure gauge
b   Water gauge
c   Furnace air-tight door
d   Ash-pit air-tight door
Q   Furnace
R   Fire tubes
S   Smoke box
T   Smoke pipe
U   Smoke escape valve
V   Wooden insulating jacket
e   Safety valve
f   Blow-off valve
g   Steam reservoir
h   Throttle control valve
j   Steam pipe
k   6 H.P.engine
l   Forward/astern selector/clutch?
m   Propeller shaft
n   Drive for roots blower

Used Steam/Condensate
o   Used steam to condenser
p   Condenser
q   Circulating pumps
r   Cool water for condenser
s   Condensate pipe
t   Hot well
u   Return pipe (to boiler)

Boat Controls
v   Bilge pump (hand)
w   Steering wheel
x   Steering linkage
y   Hydroplane wheel
z   Hydroplane linkage

Probably fitted, but not shown, compass and depth guage.

Fig 55 *Resurgam* interior

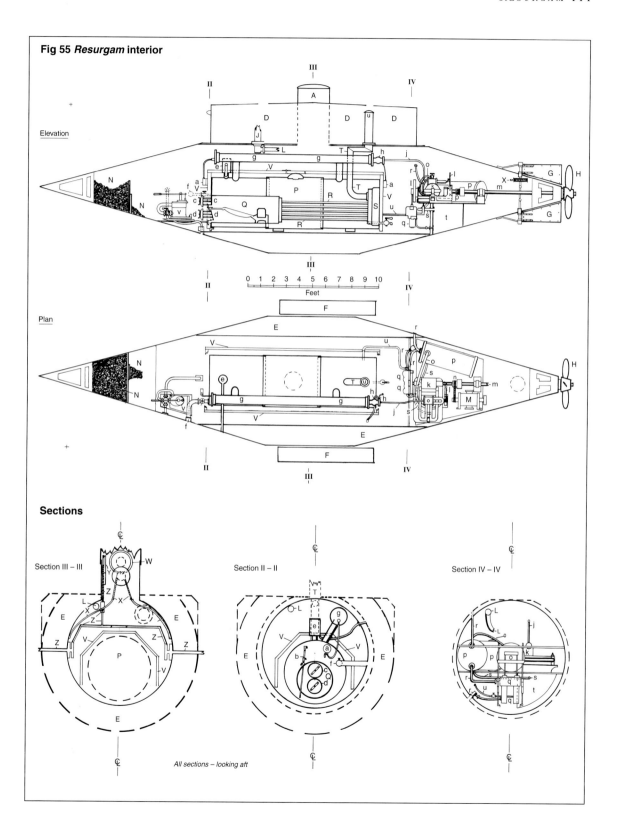

Elevation

Plan

0 1 2 3 4 5 6 7 8 9 10
Feet

Sections

Section III – III

Section II – II

Section IV – IV

All sections – looking aft

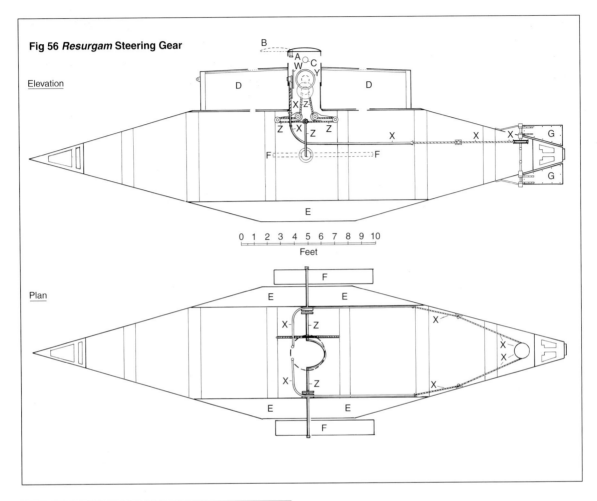

Fig 56 *Resurgam* Steering Gear

Elevation

0 1 2 3 4 5 6 7 8 9 10
Feet

Plan

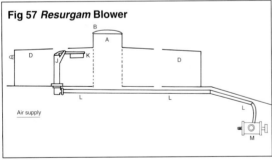

Fig 57 *Resurgam* Blower

Air supply

sealed when diving it was fitted with airtight ash-pit and furnace doors. The fuel bunker must have been at the forward end of the boat and is reported to have had a capacity of about 2.5 tons of coal. To take on a full load of fuel must have been a very tedious and dirty task; it would have had to be taken in through the conning tower, moved through the narrow space above the boiler, lowered and stowed in the bunker at the fore end.

The 6hp engine, with a working pressure of 30 lb (13.6kg), had a horizontal cylinder with an 8 inch (20.3cm) bore and stroke, and was connected directly to the propeller shaft. There were two built-in reciprocating pumps; one to circulate cooling water through the condenser, the other to return the condensate from the hotwell to the boiler. The condenser itself was positioned at engine level on the starboard side of the boat and the hotwell, for the condensate, was under the engine. A bilge pump was fitted at the forward end of the vessel.

The helmsman's position was in the conning tower. He had two wheels: one to control the rudders which worked in tandem, and the other connected to the side rudders (hydroplanes) which were both mounted on the same shaft. Orders to control the engine would have had to be shouted down to the engineer. Most of the time, when at sea, the conning tower hatch would be closed affording the helmsman a very limited view through the four ports, and because of his relatively low position he would not have been able to see very far particularly if a choppy or heavy sea was running.

According to the plans, and unlike *The Egg*, the *Resurgam* had no ballast tanks, and from the drawings it would appear that Garrett had completely abandoned the idea of having ballast cylinders. The boat would have had positive buoyancy but this would have been the barest minimum. The drawings also show that when afloat the top of the hull would have been just awash and only the casing and conning tower would have been above the water.

To work out the submerged displacement of a submarine the volume of the vessel is first established and this is converted into tons (35cu ft (1cu metre) is equivalent to one ton of seawater). The weight of the boat and its contents are then calculated, and this sum is taken from the submerged displacement; the resulting figure is the reserve buoyancy. This can be neutralised or reduced by taking on ballast in the form of pig-iron, or water if ballast tanks are fitted. Messrs Cochran and Co. Ltd, had experience in such calculations with surface ships, where the accuracy is not as critical as it would have been with *Resurgam*, for she was to have only a small margin of positive buoyancy, probably in the order of 100 lb (45kg). The calculations would have to be very accurate, taking into consideration the weight of the vessel including all the fitted equipment, fuel, water (in the boiler), the crew and anything that was to be taken on board. With such a small reserve buoyancy the builders would err on the light side adjusting the trim, (fore and aft, and lateral) and the level of

reserve buoyancy by loading pig-iron when the boat was in the water, fully fuelled and loaded. This would have been done immediately after the boat was initially put in the water; fine tuning may have been necessary and this would have been done after the launch on 10 December. Cochran had anticipated that such additional ballasting would have been necessary as in his first estimate he had costed it at £128 although it was not mentioned in the 'Approximate Estimate'.

Starting from cold it would have taken at least a couple of days to heat the water in the boiler to working temperature. If the Roots Blower, which sucked air into the submarine and through the boiler, was to be used it would have had to be turned manually until there was sufficient steam to drive the propeller shaft from which it could be driven mechanically.

Once a head of steam had been raised (30 to 40 lb psi (2-2.7 atmospheres) the boat could be driven with the engine being powered by steam taken directly from the boiler. Before diving, the steam pressure would have to be raised up to about 150 lb psi (10 atmospheres) and the steam stored in the reservoir on top of the boiler. The best way to achieve this would be to close the conning tower hatch and force air through the furnace using the Roots Blower. (In the original sketch of the boat produced by Garrett the forced air was piped directly from the Roots Blower to the furnace, but this is not reflected in the Cochran 'As Fitted' drawing of the boat. With the conning tower hatch closed and the blower on, the pipe would not be necessary as the only way for the air to get out was through the boiler and smoke exhaust system. By passing through the boat it would have a cooling and refreshing effect for the crew). When sufficient latent power had been stored the furnace would be damped down, its airtight furnace and ash-pit doors sealed and, if they were fitted, any safety cocks on the air and smoke vents closed. With the boat going ahead, the helmsman, using the side rudders, would drive the submarine under the water.

When closed down, either on the surface or submerged, the temperature inside the boat would rise very quickly and it would be unbearably hot, reaching well over 100°F (37.8°C). If the submarine was running, closed down on the surface with the Roots Blower operating, in rough or choppy conditions the air intake could be automatically closed and opened by the sea resulting in air pressure variations within the hull, which would be very uncomfortable for the crew.

Two portholes were fitted on top of the cones of the hull, immediately forward and aft of the casing. During the daytime this would have allowed some light to penetrate into the machinery space and in the stoke-hold area forward of the boiler. Within the vessel most probably there was some form of illumination, either candles or some form of electric light with a limited power supply, either of which would have had to be used economically. Yet it would still have been fairly dark within the boat even when the conning tower hatch was open. This had been anticipated because an after note on the 'Approximate Bill' states the requirement for 'gauges with luminous dials'. There would have been other irritations for the crew: condensation would have been running down the hull walls constantly; the humidity would have been high; it would have been noisy and when closed down for diving, the Roots Blower would not be able to draw in cool, fresh air and the conditions in the boat would soon become very hot and the air foul.

In addition to the heat and discomfort Garrett had three associated technical problems within the hull:

1 The boat would become more buoyant as the coal was burned and water in the boiler was boiled off.
2 The trim of the boat would alter as the weight within the hull was redistributed or lost (coal burned making the fore end lighter, and the build up of condensate in the hot-well weighing down the stern).

3 When dived, he would not want to lower the temperature in the boiler by topping it up with cold sea water.

Had *Resurgam* been fitted with suitable and well-positioned ballast tanks, it would have been very easy to compensate for both the loss and redistribution of weight. Without them, it would be necessary to top the boiler up periodically; the pig-iron ballast, would have to be redistributed to maintain the trim of the boat; and it would have to be accepted that the lost weight of the burnt fuel could not be replaced, resulting in a boat which would progressively become more buoyant. The more buoyant the submarine became the more power would be needed to force her down and keep her under the water reducing the power available for forward momentum thereby reducing her speed and range.

Resurgam was purely a 'test bed' with no frills. Little or no consideration had been given to crew comforts, or indeed 'facilities'; there was little or no space to sit down and, except on the wooden cladding on top of the boiler, nowhere to lie down to rest. And even when the conning tower hatch was open it would have been very dark, claustrophobic and unbearably hot except for the helmsman.

When closed down it was purely a steam plant enclosed in a watertight vessel that could be propelled and steered both on and below the surface of the sea. On the plus side, as positive buoyancy was always maintained, should there be an engine failure, or control breakdown, as long as the integrity of the hull was maintained, she would surface. In all the heat and discomfort it should have been possible to make a quick cup of tea to raise morale.

With the exception of the article published in *Sea Breezes*, mentioned earlier, there is a gap in our knowledge for the eight month period between the placing of the contract to build the boat and the official launching of *Resurgam*. During this time Garrett himself was undoubtedly very busy. *Resurgam* must have undergone some form of seaworthiness trials, possibly in the Great Float, because it is very hard to accept, if you believe the contemporary reports, that Garrett launched the boat on the morning of 10 December 1879 and the same evening started his voyage to Portsmouth in what was an untested, unproven vessel. It must be assumed that *Resurgam* was initially launched some time before she sailed for Portsmouth, complete with steam plant and machinery, and that she underwent hull integrity, flotation and buoyancy trials. Her plant would have also been tested and logically she would have had some form of sea-keeping trial which would have had to be outside the docks. (In his book *Father of the Submarine*, W. S. Murphy states that the boat was completed by 21 November, and was launched on 26 November. This would have allowed time for the initial trials.) She must then have been taken from the water, possibly so that work, modifications or repairs could be carried out on the hull.

Murphy also quotes an extract from *The Liverpool Weekly Mercury* of 29 November 1879, which he implies relates to an early trial of *Resurgam*. A limited archive search, centred on this date, was unable to locate this article in the *Mercury* or any of the other major, local papers. Possibly this is because the date has been corrupted when the book was printed. However, because it is considered to be important, it is quoted in full below. It is thought that it does not refer to *Resurgam* but to *The Egg*; and as such ties in with Garrett's brother's recollections of potential investors being so impressed that 'financial backing to the extent of several thousand pounds was obtained for a larger venture':

> A new submarine vessel, the invention of the Reverend George W. Garrett, of Manchester, was exhibited on Tuesday in the Wallasey Dock, before a large number of scientific and other gentlemen. The object of the boat is to get near to ships of war without being observed. The vessel is pointed at both ends. On top there is a tower provided with windows, and there is a manhole by which the operator gets in or out of the vessel with ease. The Reverend Mr Garrett, who was accompanied by some gentlemen in a steam-launch, began to test his apparatus at one o'clock, and in the first trial, at a depth of 25 feet, he remained under water for an hour and a half, during which time conversation was kept up with him by the telephone. In the second trial the reverend gentleman was under water an hour and ten minutes. The tests appeared to give great satisfaction to the spectators, and no doubt for the purpose intended the vessel will prove valuable in times of war, when ships are liable to be destroyed by torpedoes. We understand that the inventor is in communication with the Government with a view to the purchase of the invention.

The description of the vessel is more likely to be *The Egg* which eventually had the ability to attain a state of negative buoyancy and could have remained under water for sixty and then seventy minutes. With no ballast tanks *Resurgam* could not have submerged without forward momentum forcing herself, and keeping herself below the water with her hydroplanes. This would have required a full head of steam which would surely have been noted and mentioned by the reporter. It is also very unlikely that he (the reporter) would not have mentioned that the submarine had a crew of three had it been *Resurgam*, indeed he specifically reported 'a manhole by which the operator gets in or out of the vessel with ease'. That the submarine was accompanied and seen by 'a number of scientific and other gentlemen' perhaps indicates that this was a way of promoting the interest of potential investors in the Garrett Submarine Navigation and Pneumatophore Co. Ltd, to raise money for the development of *Resurgam*. It is most likely that this is a report of a trial which took place much earlier, even before Garrett travelled down to Portsmouth with his current drawing of *The Egg* in March 1879, with high hopes that he could sell his invention to the Royal Navy.

The Epic Voyage

Contemporary reports state that *Resurgam* was launched, under the supervision of Mr George Price, the boat's engineer, on 10 December 1879 and that she sailed from Birkenhead later that day. Before the launching her boiler must have been brought up to working temperature or very close to it otherwise there would have been a considerable delay while a head of steam was raised from scratch while she was alongside.

It was Garrett's intention to take *Resurgam* to Portsmouth where she was to be evaluated by the Royal Navy. Cochran's advice was to send the vessel over land, but Garrett was determined to use the voyage to prove *Resurgam* while at the same time impressing the Royal Navy with his achievement. During the voyage deep-sea diving trials were to be conducted. What is not known is how he intended to make this journey; he must have planned to complete the voyage in stages, stopping off at regular intervals to take on fuel and allow the crew to rest and eat as this could hardly be done on board. *Resurgam* sailed, unescorted, at 9 p.m. on Wednesday 10 December 1879, on the start her epic voyage. The tide had just started to ebb.

The wisdom of sailing the small boat, on her maiden voyage, through busy shipping lanes during a long December night is questionable. She was displaying navigation lights when she set sail from Birkenhead, but with no mast and a very low silhouette she would have been difficult to see from a ship even if it was expecting such an encounter. It was probably necessary to close the conning tower hatch as soon as possible, particularly if there was a sea running, to avoid water from waves or the wash of a passing ship breaking over the low, short casing and entering the hull through the conning tower hatch. This would have reduced and could have destroyed the small margin of positive buoyancy. There was a bilge pump which could have handled relatively small amounts of water. When closed down the helmsman had a very restricted view through the small portholes which were only just over 3 feet (0.9 metres) above the level of the sea. From this very low position, he would not be able to see far particularly if the water was breaking over the casing and washing over the porthole glass. Undoubtedly Garrett was anxious to start his journey and prove his invention; he may have sailed at night as a security precaution to avoid any possible mishaps being seen and reported by the press.

The maiden voyage is best recorded with extracts from Garrett's own log (*Liverpool Mercury*, 17 December 1879):

Our crew consisted of myself, Captain Jackson, master mariner, and Mr George Price as engineer, and we left the Alfred Dock, Birkenhead on Wednesday night, the 10th December, about nine o'clock. The night was very dark and a little misty, which made it necessary for us to proceed cautiously down the river until clear of the shipping.

However, we reached the Rock Lighthouse without accident of any sort, and entered Rock Channel about ten o'clock. When we started Captain Jackson remained outside on the look-out, whilst I took the helm in the conning tower, but as soon as we were in the Rock Channel Captain Jackson came inside, when we shut ourselves up and fairly started on our way.

We passed down Rock Channel, and safely making Spencer's Spit, we turned into the Horse Channel, which we cleared in due course, and we were then out at sea. We laid our course for the Northwest Lightship, and went very slow, intending to make some experiments in Victoria Deep as soon as daylight should come.

When the morning of Thursday came there was a very thick fog, which prevented our making all the experiments we wished, and necessitated our proceeding very carefully. The fog did not lift all that day, so we moved about, testing various parts of our internal machinery, till the Friday morning, when the sun rose beautiful and clear.

We had now been at sea about 36 hours, a great part of which time we were under water, and we felt desirous of making some port, as sleeping on board was not attended with as much comfort as we wished.

At this time we found the Northwest Lightship close at hand, bearing about North, so we determined to put into the River Foryd, as there is good anchorage there, and she will dry every tide, which is very convenient, as we are going to make a series of further experiments with various propellers. The boat answered splendidly in the sea-way. The seas pass easily over her, and cause hardly any motion, nor do they interfere in any important degree with her way of steering.

The three of us landed at Rhyl in perfect health but rather tired and dirty. However, after a good wash and hot dinner our comfort was entirely restored and we could congratulate ourselves on having passed successfully through as novel and interesting a trip as any sailor could wish to experience. We remain at Rhyl for a few days to perfect a few little matters of some importance to our future comfort.

From Rhyl Garrett telegraphed the *Manchester Courier* advising that paper that he had: 'successfully navigated his vessel from Birkenhead to Rhyl on her first trip. Crew all well.'

In late 1925 and early 1926, forty-six years after the event, another account of the voyage was reported in several newspapers.[5] This was related by the boat's engineer, Mr George Price. There are three discrepancies with Garrett's account but these are not particularly significant:

1 Price related that the submarine was launched on 10 December and went on to say that she sailed the following day; (probably a lapse in Price's memory; the log, written during or immediately after the voyage must be a more accurate record of timings and weather).

2 He stated that the submarine dived to a depth of thirty or forty feet and remained under the surface for thirty hours. This of course cannot possibly be true; with no ballast tanks negative buoyancy could not be established by *Resurgam* and the submerged endurance (claimed by

Garrett himself) using the latent power from a fully charged steam reservoir, was limited to about 10 miles (16km) at 2 to 3 knots (3.7 to 5.5kph). Without forward motion the submarine would have surfaced. What may have happened was that the submarine was closed up for most of the voyage or for long periods to obtain the maximum effect of the Roots Blower on the furnace and possibly to prevent water entering through the conning tower hatch. Those below would not necessarily be aware if the boat was submerged.

3 That the submarine surfaced near a full-rigged ship bound for Liverpool and that Garrett had to ask what his position was. This could well be true as they had been fog-bound all the previous day and perhaps it was not the sort of admission Garrett would have liked to record in his log.

Price's recollections do give an insight into conditions on board the small craft:

... Then Mr Garrett decided to submerge, and we sank to a depth of thirty or forty feet, remaining under water for more than thirty hours. During that time the heat from the boiler was intense, varying from 110° to 115°F (about 45°C) and we experienced great discomfort from the air pressure on the eardrums. We had, owing to the very limited accommodation, to stand all the time, and when we returned to the surface we were all exhausted. The navigator had lost his bearings, and we came up alongside a full-rigged ship, homeward bound for Liverpool. When Mr Garrett threw open the top and shouted, 'Ship ahoy' and inquired where we were, the captain of the ship was terribly surprised, and enquired who we were. We informed him that we were in a submarine torpedo, and had been under his ship two or three hours. The captain almost collapsed at this news, and asked where we had come from, and where we were bound for. Mr Garrett informed him that we had come from Liverpool, and were going to Portsmouth. The captain asked

5 This one was included in the *Rhyl Journal* of 2 January 1926

how many there were in our crew, and when Mr Garrett told him three, he answered: 'Well, you are the three biggest fools I have ever met.'

The ear discomfort reported by Price is a clear indication that the vessel was running on the surface, closed down with the Roots Blower sucking in air but because of the sea conditions the automatic valve on the air inlet pipe was being intermittently closed by the sea. As has been mentioned before this would have produced air pressure fluctuations within the boat. When the submarine was closed down it is understandable that Price was in some discomfort. Theoretically the blower would have been disengaged when the submarine was about to submerge unless it was left on to produce a suction within the inlet pipe to hold the valve on its seat; thereby ensuring no water entered the boat through this system.

The arrival at Rhyl, reported in such a matter of fact way by Garrett, was perhaps more colourful. Mr Price went on:

> The weather was still very thick as we shaped our course for Rhyl, where we arrived at daybreak. There we gave the submarine in charge of a pilot, who took her to the jetty. When the Customs and Coastguard came out, they refused to go below, being frightened by the steam rising from the boiler. When we went ashore we were so dirty and untidy that at first the proprietor of an hotel would not take us in. When Mr Garrett produced his card, however, we were soon enjoying a good meal after a refreshing bath.

Garrett, in his interview with the *Liverpool Mercury*, had indicated that he would 'remain at Rhyl for a few days to perfect a few little matters of some importance to our future comfort'. Garrett certainly would make light of any problems encountered on the maiden voyage. He said in his log that he wanted to experiment with different propellers; it is possible that *Resurgam*'s

propeller may have thrown a blade or that the one fitted was not giving him sufficient thrust. A report in the local paper[6] some years later recalls:

> Many of our present-day readers can remember the submarine at the Foryd. It was an object of great curiosity, but close inspection was denied. During the time it was at the Foryd the owner carried out certain improvements and renewals in the boat, the Rhuddlan Foundry being employed to manufacture the parts which were fitted on by Mr Garrett. When the machine disappeared many were disappointed besides the inventor.

Another modification that could have been carried out was the removal of the casing. An account of the vessel departing from Rhyl, which is mentioned later, described the submarine as 'a huge hippopotamus'. With the casing fitted this would not have been a particularly apt description. Indeed, *Resurgam* would have looked more like a small boat as her casing, which was normally above the water level, sliced through the sea. However, it would be accurate if the casing had been removed; departing from Rhyl, at slow speed and with little wash the submarine could well have looked like a hippopotamus. If, on the maiden voyage, Garrett had experienced problems diving or maintaining the boat's station under water, he may have been very concerned that he was not going to be able to impress his potential customer, the Royal Navy. The propeller modifications and trials may not have been as successful as he had hoped. Therefore, such a modification would at least limit what could be seen of the submarine to the conning tower and the top of the hull, which would be awash. This would present a very small target to an observer or to an enemy particularly in a choppy sea. Such a revised silhouette would be very similar to that of Garrett's next submarine when it was rigged for diving. When *Resurgam* was located in late 1995, preliminary examinations indicated that the casing was missing. After one hundred years of buffeting by the tide it could have been ripped off by the sea, or it could

6 *Rhyl Journal*, 28 November 1925

have been knocked off by a colliding vessel. Should it not be discovered when the wreck site is properly examined, there is the other possibility that it had been deliberately removed as a modification.

Garrett was not without critics, particularly from within the congregation of Christ Church, some of whom considered that his extra clerical activities were unsuited to a man of the cloth. The Chairman of the Garrett Submarine and Pneumatophore Company Limited, his father, always strongly supported him, putting forward the argument that a handful of *Resurgams* could easily defend a coast line from enemy attack and remove the need for large coastal fortresses. By withdrawing to Rhyl, Garrett was well out of sight of any critical parishioners who disapproved of his activities at Cochrans (which was not all that far from the parish in Manchester). This could have also been convenient to the Rev. John Garrett who, although an ardent supporter, could probably do without unnecessary criticism or hostility from his congregation.

It is not known what further sea trials were carried out while the boat was at Rhyl. Something certainly prompted Garrett to return to Liverpool where he purchased the steam yacht *Elphin*. That he did not have an accompanying guard vessel on the maiden voyage shows how confident (or naïve) Garrett and his crew must have been about the reliability and safety of *Resurgam*. Perhaps sea trials were carried out at Rhyl and some incident suggested that it would be prudent to have another vessel in attendance for the voyage to Portsmouth. On the other hand, it may just have been a tender to provide *Resurgam*'s crew with meals and a reasonably comfortable billet. Ironically, had Garrett not purchased this 'guard' ship *Resurgam* might have reached Portsmouth without mishap.

The *Resurgam*, accompanied by the yacht *Elphin* recommenced her voyage to Portsmouth at 10 p.m. on 24 February 1880. She departed 50 minutes before high tide, the weather was fair and there was a full moon although it is not known

what cloud cover there was that night. On this occasion Garrett probably sailed at night so that he would be able to navigate the tricky waters to the north-west of Anglesey and join the busy shipping lanes into Holyhead, some 60 miles away, in daylight. Four days later the local paper[7] reported:

> Torpedo-Boat. The strange and mysterious looking torpedo-boat, which arrived here from Birkenhead early last December, and has remained in the Foryd ever since, undergoing improvements, was successfully towed out to sea last Tuesday night. The queer little craft looked like a huge hippopotamus as it floated down the river. Mr Garrett, the inventor, who was on the torpedo-boat with the engineer, had engaged a steam yacht to tow it to Holyhead, and from thence to Portsmouth, where it will undergo a naval trial.

On the same day there was another account[8] of the departure:

> The Garrett torpedo-boat *Resurgam* which had harboured at Foryd for over two months left her moorings at ten o'clock on Tuesday night, en route for Holyhead and Portsmouth at which latter place the inventor proposed to bring under the notice of the Government authorities, its adaptibility for submarine navigation. While lying up at the Foryd the inventor was engaged in adjusting defects and improving the means of propulsion, and as we have before intoned she was got ready on Tuesday night for the resumption of her journey. The curious torpedo vessel was accompanied on the voyage by a beautiful screw steam yacht belonging to Mr Garrett the inventor, who with his engineer sailed in *Resurgam*. The weather was fine, and with the exception of a slight delay caused by the grounding of the torpedo-boat close to the new sewer outlet both boats were fairly out to sea in a short time.

Early the following morning off Great Orme's Head, some fifteen miles to the west of Rhyl, the yacht *Elphin* developed a problem with her engine.

[7] *Rhyl Journal*, 28 February 1880
[8] *Rhyl Record and Visitor*, 28 February 1880

The captain of the yacht signalled *Resurgam* that *Elphin* was in difficulty being unable to feed her boilers. A boat was sent to the submarine and the crew of three returned to the yacht. Price, the engineer, recalled many years later, that the submarine was then taken in tow (until then she must have been sailing under her own power and was not being towed to Holyhead). While Price worked on the feed pumps the weather deteriorated which prevented Garrett, Price and Jackson from returning to *Resurgam*. At ten o'clock the towing hawser broke and the rough sea 'shattered' *Resurgam*'s hatch and Garrett saw his submarine disappear in the waves.

It could well have been that it was not possible to close and lock the conning tower hatch from the outside and it was this that sealed the fate of the vessel. In his specification for *Resurgam*, Garrett's requirement was: 'It should have a manhole in the top which could be fastened from the inside'. After the near disaster with *The Egg*, when the water flooded into the boat through the ruptured arm sleeve and his brother helped in the rescue with a boathook, it is thought that it would have been prudent, in future designs, to have a hatch which could be locked open and closed from both the inside and the outside of the vessel. As the weather deteriorated and the boat pitched and rolled with the sea, the hatch could have swung to the open position. Waves breaking on the conning tower would splash into the hull and slowly her reserve buoyancy would be destroyed.

When the boat left Rhyl she had probably been fully fuelled etc and her reserve positive buoyancy would have been in the order of 100 lb (45kg). Having been at sea for a few hours some coal would have been burned increasing this figure slightly. When the crew left *Resurgam* to go to the *Elphin* this would have further increased her reserve buoyancy by the weight of the men, their clothing and anything they took with them; say 3 x 14 stone or 588 lb (267kg). Her reserve positive buoyancy, when she was taken under tow, could

have been in the order of about 750 to 800 lb (340 to 363kg). All it would have needed to destroy this buoyancy would be the equivalent of about one and a half domestic baths filled with water.

The *Elphin* then ran to take shelter in the River Dee and dropped anchor off Mostyn. She was sighted as she passed Rhyl and this was reported in the *Rhyl Record*[9]:

> It was expected that the arrival of the vessels (*Resurgam* and *Elphin*) at Holyhead would have been duly made known but nothing transpired till the following day (25 February) when it was reported that a yacht resembling the one which accompanied the torpedo-boat was observed going in the direction of Liverpool without her consort. Various rumours have been circulating pointing to the loss of the boat but nothing reliable has been communicated to us. It is to be hoped, however, that nothing has happened to the boat, its spirited inventor or those who accompanied him.

Elphin remained at anchor that night. There are several accounts of exactly what happened next morning. Either her anchor chain parted or she weighed anchor and attempted to run up the estuary on the flooding tide. There was a strong westerly wind and *Elphin* was still having engine problems and she was soon in serious trouble. A paddle tug, differently reported as *Fire King* or *Iron King*, which was lying with steam up in the harbour came to her assistance for the agreed sum of £10. The next incident is summed up well by Mr George Price: 'unfortunately she rammed us making the *Elphin* a total wreck'.

In his account[10], Price further recalls: 'Garrett returned to Liverpool, by train, the following day, for assistance in search of the submarine. But the weather was still bad, and no vessel was able to venture out, so, unfortunately for us we lost the *Resurgam*'.

The voyage of *Resurgam* had ended disastrously. Both the submarine and *Elphin* were lost; they were uninsured and although Garrett

[9] *Rhyl Record and Visitor*, 28 February 1880
[10] *Rhyl Journal*, 2 January 1926

later sued Messrs Coppack and Co, the owners of the tug, in the Admiralty court; he lost his case. At least there was one blessing: of the five-man crew of *Elphin*, and the three-man crew of *Resurgam* no one was killed or even reported injured.

The *Resurgam* story is swathed in myths and rumours which may have been generated by journalists and writers trying to add mystery and interest to a story which has been regularly resurrected since 1880. The Garrett saga and in particular the disappearance of *Resurgam* is a very emotive subject: when a fisherman caught his nets on what might have been the wreck, a yachtsman struck a sunken obstruction, or a search expedition was planned or launched there would be a flurry of articles published. However, Garrett himself may have been the author of some of the early rumours. For instance it was reported, in the *Rhyl Journal* of 28 February 1880, that financial offers had been made to Garrett for *Resurgam*: £50,000 by the Admiralty and £144,000 by the Russian Government; and there were also some exaggerations about the performance of the vessel. Another elaboration, which made good reading, was that Garrett used his 'ten years old' son (who at the time was actually only a few months old) in the stoke hold of *Resurgam* because of the lack of space. There were other reports that the submarine had been 'stolen' (by Russian agents?) or had parted its mooring chains and had drifted out of the Foryd to be lost at sea. During the epic journey from Birkenhead to Rhyl the vessel they encountered, according to Price, must have been British as it was homeward bound to Liverpool. But other reports have it as an American and a Russian ship; perhaps there were a number of encounters to allow them to verify their position in the fog.

This all has the making of a good yarn worthy of a few column inches of newsprint – but it can be further spiced up by relating a little of Garrett's earlier life and in particular that he had been ordained. That he was a curate adds a sort of respectability and creditability to what he was doing but at the same time incredibility that a man of the cloth should know about such things let alone become involved with them.

Certainly Garrett did not want to advertise the disaster and what could be attributed as a failure. The actual loss of *Resurgam* was not immediately reported in the press although there was some speculation. No record could be found that Garrett had advised the Coastguard that the submarine had been lost and could be a hazard to shipping. There was some conjecture that there had been a mishap, but it would not have been in Garrett's business interests to have broadcast the news, even though he could have argued that *Resurgam* had been a success and that the sinking was not due to either an operating or a serious design fault, but was more an act of God. (Perhaps this would have been a good professional line for the Rev. G.W.L.Garrett to take.)

A veil of secrecy was maintained over the loss of *Resurgam* to such an extent that many years later when Garrett's son and his brother, independently wrote about the events of early 1880 they were both still under the impression that the submarine had just disappeared from its mooring. The son would have been quoting hearsay for he would have been too young, in 1880, to remember what happened. But the brother, as an adult, interested family member who had even been present and helped when *The Egg* was being tested, would surely have tried to find out what had occurred. If Garrett had kept his own council, what was reported to the chairman and the board of Garrett Submarine Navigation and Pneumatophore Co. Ltd?

CHAPTER 15

BREATHING APPARATUS

Before examining the implications of the loss of *Resurgam* and *Elphin* and closing this particular chapter of Garrett's life, it is necessary to move forward three months and travel to Paris. For it was in this city that Garrett demonstrated his breathing apparatus by remaining under water for three-quarters of an hour.

It was noted earlier that Garrett's son had commented[1] on the breathing apparatus and how his father had studied the 'equation of life' whilst studying at the Kensington Museum. This is how he described the equipment:

> This was a chemical device contained in a case to be attached to a regulation diving suit doing away with the air tubes which are a source of discomfort and danger.

Garrett's brother[2] wrote[3] about the pneumatophore:

> My brother was always dabbling with chemistry and scientific subjects. The starting point of his submarine work was his discovery that caustic potash will absorb carbonic acid gas given off in a man's breath. He made an apparatus which he called the pneumataphore – a sort of diver's helmet with a knapsack attachment. I was a boy of about sixteen at the time and I remember the vivid interest with which I used to follow his experiments. The pneumatophore provided for the absorption of carbonic gas by means of sticks of caustic potash, and then he had an attachment for supplying oxygen.

It was this device that Garrett probably used in both his submarines. In *Resurgam* it is probable that only he wore it because the air would be fouler in the conning tower than in the lower parts of the vessel which had the benefit of the air being pumped in by the Roots Blower.

Two extracts from journals printed in Paris were translated and published in Manchester in May 1880[4]. These are quoted, unabridged, as not only do they cover the demonstration but also the unsolicited advertising for *Resurgam* which by then had been resting on the bottom of the sea for two months:

> A very interesting experiment took place on the Seine at Levallois, on Friday, in presence of a committee appointed by the Minister of Marine to assist at the trial of Mr G.W. Garrett's submarine apparatus. The Committee was composed of Captain Landolf, M. Fontaine, the well known chemist, and M. Vidal, an engineer. The apparatus exhibited was an ordinary diving dress, to which the inventor had adapted his system for maintaining air at its normal composition, thereby enabling the diver to dispense with all communication with the surface. Mr Garrett's system appears to be based on the discovery, kept secret for the present, of a certain application of the laws of nature, which enables him to live in a closed space by purifying and renewing, by means of a chemical apparatus, the air necessary for his lungs. Mr Garrett descended into the water and remained there for thirty-seven minutes, and when coming to the surface again was in perfect health and spirits,

[1] *Submarines. An account of the first practical submarine boats.* As told by the son of their inventor and commander, George William Garrett

[2] Both Garrett's brother and son were under the impression that Garrett had taken out a Patent No 1839 to protect his breathing apparatus. In fact this particular Patent was taken out in May 1878 by James Hight of Old Kent Road, in the County of Surrey and was for the invention of 'Improvements in Tumblers or Washing Machines for Washing Hides or Skins, Applicable for washing Other Articles, Materials and Fabrics'. Unfortunately a Patent for the breathing apparatus, taken out by Garrett, could not be located.

[3] *Manchester (Evening) Chronicle*, Thursday 24 February 1916

[4] *Manchester Courier*, 7 May 1880

although the dress employed being one bought in Paris for the purpose, did not fit him comfortably. The use of Mr Garrett's invention is not confined to that of a diving dress, but, what is more important, it will be found the real and so long wanted apparatus necessary for submarine navigation. The inventor has constructed a torpedo-boat of forty tons register, worked by a six horse-power engine, with which he has remained thirty-six hours at sea, going from Birkenhead to Rhyl most of the time completely under water. Mr Garrett attaches the greatest importance to the fact that he has discovered a method by which he is able to keep working an ordinary steam engine without the necessity of giving off the products of combustion. A torpedo-boat fitted with Mr Garrett's system would consequently be able to remain under water without betraying her position and owing to her speed and facility of evolution would be the most dangerous weapon against ironclads or other war vessels. The new invention may be considered as one of the most important steps towards the complete discovery of a method of submarine navigation.

Galigani's Messenger

The second extract was taken from *Republique Française*:

We were yesterday present at an exceedingly interesting trial which took place before a commission designated by the Minister of Marine. The growing importance of torpedoes in warfare is everywhere recognised. These engines of destruction are of two kinds – fixed and moveable. The employment of moveable torpedoes presents great difficulties,

particularly now that men-of-war can by means of electric light search a wide stretch of sea around them. Considerations such as these have induced inventors to turn their attention to submarine torpedo boats. Mr G.W. Garrett of Manchester, is the inventor of such a boat, and he has, it appears, already made several voyages in the boat constructed upon his plans. The trial which he made yesterday was expressly limited to the demonstration that it was practicable to remain for several hours in his boat without the necessity of having to ascend to the surface and without discomfort. That trial took place at the Weir (barrage) in the Seine, near Levallois. Clothed in his diving dress, and furnished with his breathing apparatus, Mr Garrett remained first for twenty minutes, and then for three-quarters of an hour, under the water; when he ascended there was no sign or trace of either suffocation or lassitude in his appearance or movements. A litre of the air which he had been breathing was then secured by one of the members of the commission for analysis, and that done, the results obtained will prove that the inventions of Mr Garrett will resolve one of the numerous problems connected with the employment of submarine torpedo-boats.

It would appear to have been a successful demonstration and publicity exercise. However, it did not result in the placing of orders or, apparently, further interest in either his submarine boat or the breathing apparatus. Garrett had fired his final bolt in this particular phase of his life. But before proceeding with his story the implications of the loss of *Resurgam* should be considered.

CHAPTER 16

IMPLICATIONS OF THE LOSS
OF *RESURGAM*

With the uninsured loss of both *Resurgam* and *Elphin* the Company had suffered a severe if not fatal financial blow. The capital expenditure on research, development and the building of the two boats, together with the running costs, which must include the purchase of *Elphin*, were not recoverable. Even so, nearly a month after the tragedy the Company issued at least one debenture for £25 which was to be paid back after twelve months with one hundred per cent interest, to a Mr George Thompson. In the light of the material losses of the Company the wording of the debenture casts doubt on the integrity of those issuing them for at this time it is probable that the only major asset the Company actually owned was *The Egg*. And this, with no potential customers, had only scrap value. In the debenture the Directors, on behalf of the Company promised: '. . . hereby covenant and declare with and to the said George Thompson Executors, Administrators and Assigns, that all the Property Assets and Effects of the said

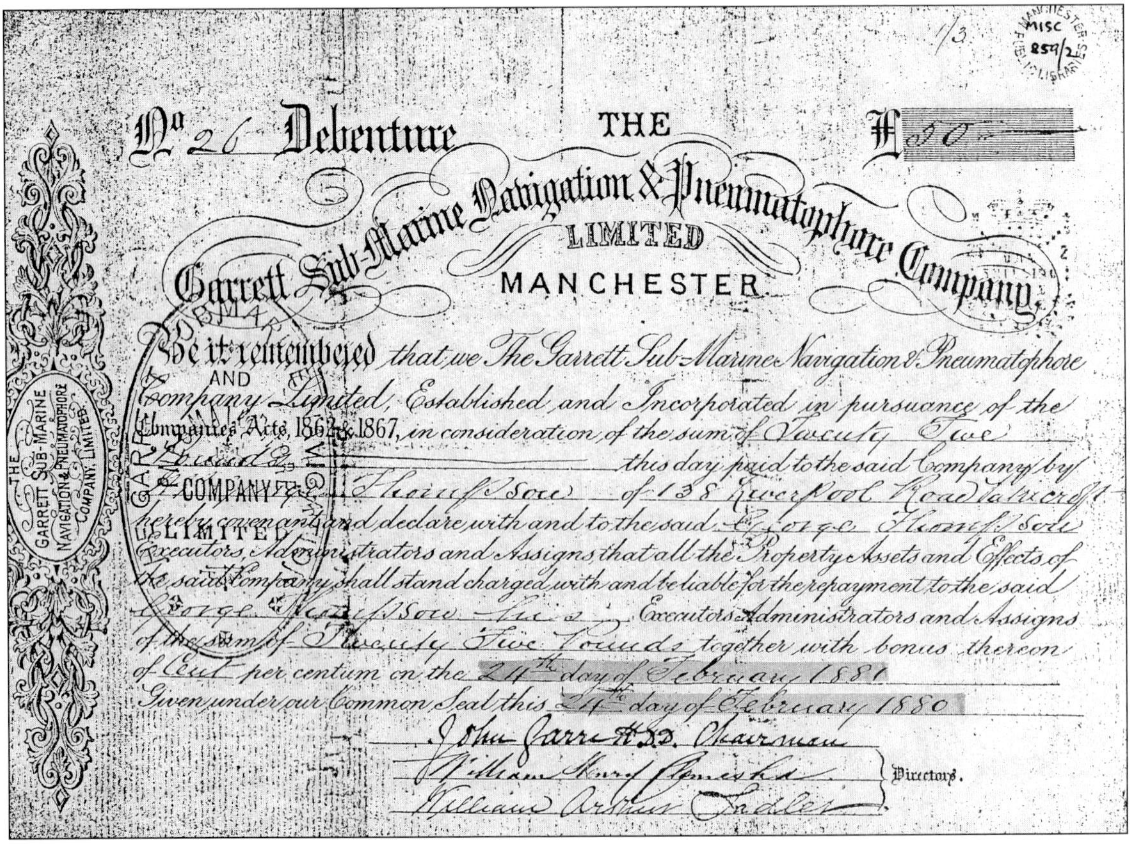

Fig 58 Copy of a Debenture issued in respect of the Garrett Sub-Marine etc., Company

Company shall stand charged with and be liable for the repayment to the said George Thompson Twenty-Five Pounds together with bonus thereon of cent per centum on 17th day of March 1881.' This was duly signed by John Garrett D.D., Chairman, and two of the directors: Clemesha and Gabriel.

Perhaps the Company still considered that it had a saleable commodity. But the reality was that there were no contracts to build submarines and the only way to get one was to have the necessary hardware which would have to be successfully demonstrated to a potential customer. Theoretically, if *Resurgam* had been the success that Garrett claimed, another could be built and offered to the Royal Navy. To do this, with the losses the Company had sustained, more money would have had to be raised. This would have been difficult but probably not impossible; the Submarine Company had been started when Garrett only had *The Egg* and his ideas to convince potential investors.

He was now in a much stronger position having successfully built and tested two submarines. It would be necessary to convince future investors that *Resurgam* was not lost through a structural failure; that the adapted Lamm system worked; that the submarine performed satisfactorily; and that it would sell when completed. In other words that technically *Resurgam* was an unqualified success. His case would have been strengthened if a buyer had already signed a contract to buy a submarine or even the breathing apparatus.

Garrett must have been travelling around trying to find customers. But this must have been a forlorn hope. He no longer had a submarine to offer for trials although he could show potential customers the drawings of *Resurgam*, photographs and his favourable press clippings. Should he have been asked where his submarine was he would have had to admit that it was not readily available for a demonstration.

He was not even equipped to demonstrate his breathing apparatus, in Paris, and had to acquire a diving suit. This is not the image of an organised man going out to sell his wares but has the aura of a rather casual and speculative approach. Unfortunately the Paris demonstration of the Pneumatophore breathing apparatus failed to attract customers or other significant interest.

For the next three years Garrett was not actively involved in building submarines. The Garrett Submarine Navigation and Pneumatophore Co. Ltd, was probably wound up in 1880 having lost most of the money invested in the Company. Garrett's son indicated that his father lost all his own money and £10,000 of his father's. Garrett himself had to find alternative employment to supplement his small income from his work in the church and probably returned, for a time, to the teaching profession.

The important question that has to be asked

There is still a niggling question: 'Why did Garrett, who had devoted so much time and effort to the development of *Resurgam*, just drop the project?' Certainly there was an immediate money problem and more capital was needed. Garrett and the Company may not have been able to convince other potential investors that their money would be safe and in the longer term that there would be a good return on their investment. Perhaps Dr Garrett, the Chairman, and directors had lost faith in him and decided to cut their losses for he had lost all the major assets of the Company in a few short hours and all they had to show for their investment was *The Egg* (if it had not already been disposed of for scrap) and some experience. Maybe Garrett had lost faith in his own invention, but how successful had *Resurgam* really been?

We only have Garrett's word that the voyage from Liverpool to Rhyl, the only time the boat was truly tested, was successful and that the boat performed well. Garrett had written in his log that they had spent much of the voyage under water but is there a possibility that the submarine had only been awash? What modifications and improvements had been carried out necessitating casting work at the Rhuddlan foundry? Garrett himself, on arrival at Rhyl, had said that he wanted to carry out some experiments with different propellers. Perhaps this is the clue; if he was dissatisfied with the propeller it probably was not giving him sufficient thrust. This would be dependent on a series of factors: number, pitch and shape of the propeller blades; propeller diameter; the torque and speed at which the propeller shaft is turned. However, the problem is probably somewhat more profound.

The effective horsepower to drive a submerged submarine can be determined. Firstly it is governed by skin friction which can be established mathematically based on the wetted area of the submerged submarine and the speed of the boat. In the case of *Resurgam*, using the limited data available, in a very simplistic way, it can be shown that the vessel was underpowered and should have been fitted with a 10 to 12hp engine.

However, there are other factors which would have added further demands on the available effective horsepower and these are directly related to the shape of the vessel. There is wave making which is dependent on the hull form and the depth submerged; and there is eddy making or form resistance which is caused by flow separation and *Resurgam* would have had a classic example of this at the junctions between the cones and the cylindrical mid section. Furthermore, when set for diving or holding the submarine under water (to overcome the natural buoyancy of the vessel) the side rudders or hydroplanes, with a combined surface area of about 15 square feet (1.4 square metres), would have a braking effect reducing the speed of the boat; this would be exacerbated as the boat became more buoyant as fuel was expended and more effort was required to hold her under. This is a classic example of the law of diminishing returns; for as more effort was required to hold the buoyant vessel under the water the slower the boat would go making it more difficult to keep her down.

Garrett should have been considering increasing the engine horsepower. But indirectly he was probably quite right when he said that he wanted to experiment with the propeller because today's propellers are typically eighty per cent efficient while his would probably only have been rated at about fifty per cent. The effective power available to drive the boat was probably only just over 3hp. *Resurgam* was seriously underpowered.

It really is a mystery that after experimenting and developing *The Egg*, with the final layout of six ballast tanks, and the ability to remain submerged for relatively long periods (during which he was probably not pedalling or working his controls), that no form of controllable ballasting arrangements were built into *Resurgam*. It is only possible to speculate why this was so. Perhaps the incident when water entered the small vessel when the arm sleeve was ruptured convinced him that for safety reasons future boats should always retain a margin of positive buoyancy. This could have been cancelled out by having a detachable weight that could be jettisoned in an emergency as used by Wilhelm Bauer and others. Fitting internal ballast tanks may have been precluded because of the lack of space within *Resurgam*'s hull; or an envisaged difficulty of evacuating such tanks after they had been flooded. Plus the associated and necessary pipe-work that would have had to be built in (a small steam engine could have been used to drive the pump[s]). Or the cost of fitting such tanks although they were not mentioned in his original specification.

If *Resurgam* had been able to achieve neutral and negative buoyancy, and then maintain equilibrium when submerged, the 6 horsepower engine would have been able to drive her in calm conditions. But she was not designed to do this and consequently to drive the boat effectively she should have been fitted with an engine of 20 to 26hp.

The Victorians were aware of the problems of hull resistance. The leading expert in this field, at this time, was William Froude (1810–1879) who, at the request of Isambard Brunel, on whose staff he had been working, started a study into the laws of ship motion in waves. From 1870 he was employed by the Government. A test tank 250 feet (76 metres) long, 33 feet (10 metres) wide and 10 feet (3 metres) deep was built at the Admiralty Establishment at Torquay in which models were towed through the water from an overhead gantry at different speeds and their resistance measured, using a dynamometer. He also researched power output with different propellers. At this time this science was nowhere near as advanced as it is today. But Froude had published many articles on his experiments, and some of the information would have been readily available to anyone who knew about it. Perhaps one of Garrett's weaknesses was that he had had no formal training as a Naval Architect and was therefore not fully aware of the problems; but in all fairness, the building of submarines was still a black art which was probably only glossed over, if mentioned at all, during such training.

In 1879 technology was changing rapidly and this was well reported in such publications as *The Engineer*. But Garrett, working alone, had to deal with several scientific disciplines; there was no central clearing house. To have kept abreast of the latest thinking and developments in a specialist subject like shipbuilding and development it would have been beneficial to have been a member of the appropriate professional body, in this case the Institute of Naval Architects. Had he not come across Froude's work, membership would at least have made him aware of it.

There was a major, but at this stage of development not a life threatening, design fault linked to the buoyancy of *Resurgam*. Garrett had already identified some of the potential warlike uses of the submarine one of which involved the transportation and placing of torpedoes (explosive charges). If *Resurgam* was required to carry explosive charges, unless they were neutrally buoyant, a compensating weight of pig-iron ballast would have to be removed from the boat to re-establish or maintain the 100 lb (45kg) positive reserve buoy-

ancy. When the charges were deposited or fired the buoyancy of the boat would increase. This could not have been compensated for without ballast tanks and *Resurgam* would have tended to 'pop' to the surface (in a hostile situation not a good thing to do) unless the engine had sufficient reserve power to hold the boat down. This shortcoming should have been appreciated but perhaps it was not. For as will be seen later, it was also a problem with later boats built by Garrett.

Like most innovators, Garrett, with the experience of *Resurgam* behind him, must have known that he could improve on what he had done. Perhaps his appreciation, at that time, was that with the limited resources available to him, the lack of money and the multitude of improvements that were necessary, coupled with a less than enthusiastic potential customer, there was no alternative other than the (temporary) shelving of his project.

It is so easy to criticise with hindsight and in the knowledge of the developments that have taken place during the last century. Garrett, we were told by his father, had researched the development of submarines, most of which had failed. We do not know how thoroughly he had been able to do this and although he had very little proven technology that he could fall back on, we do know, from the brief story of the development of the submarine, related earlier, that most of the principles he had adopted had been tried before.

Like many others, Garrett had been working in isolation. He was particularly secretive about his work, which is understandable as he was developing something new; this would take time and he did not want others to steal his ideas.

During the next few years, throughout Europe and in North America, many submarines were conceived, planned and built (fortunately for their potential crews quite a few never left the theoretical stage of development). Some failed, others were reasonably successful and this culminated in the prototypes for the submarines which were adopted by the navies of the world. Garrett did not have enormous resources, and because of financial restraints he had to produce results quickly. In two years he had progressed from the drawing-board, through a period of research and development with *The Egg* to a steam-driven submarine boat adapting relatively new technology.

Although not to his financial advantage, Garrett had achieved much. He had designed and built the first submarine to be powered by steam both on the surface and under the water; he had probably completed the longest voyage by a submarine; he had adapted the first rudimentary schnorchel to supply air to the engine and crew ever fitted to a submarine; he had developed his underwater breathing apparatus; but, what is probably more important, he had gained two years' experience. Unlike many innovators whose ideas always remain on paper, he had taken that giant step from the drawing-board and produced his invention; what is more the prototype had, within limitations, worked in principle and showed potential for development.

At this time Garrett was well up amongst the world leaders of submarine design and development, if not in the lead. He had partially bridged the gulf between the boats propelled by manpower and the mechanically-powered vessels; that crucial step necessary to make the submarine a feasible proposition. Had it not been for the unfortunate loss of *Resurgam*, or if he had had the immediate, necessary funds and facilities to build a modified boat, the course of submarine development in the United Kingdom could well have been changed. He now needed that sound financial backing, a suitable shipyard, and time to consolidate his ideas and carry out research and development.

CHAPTER 17

THE NORDENFELT LIAISON

It was probably in late 1880 that having failed to interest either the British or French Governments in his underwater breathing apparatus, Garrett obtained a position as one of the engineers working on the construction of the docks at Milford Haven. Early in 1881 he was sent to London to investigate and report on the practicability of using electric arc lighting in the port. According to Garrett's son, it was during this visit to London that he was first introduced to Thorsten Nordenfelt, and the liaison between these two men was first established. Whether this meeting was coincidental or planned is not known. However, there is no doubt that it changed Garrett's life and immediate prospects.

Nordenfelt, a Swede, was born on 1 March 1842 making him ten years older than Garrett. He attended the Institute of Technology in Stockholm and qualified as a civil engineer. As an industrialist he introduced new manufacturing methods throughout Sweden, and his interests ranged from arms to paper. The Nordenfelt Gun and Ammunition Co. Ltd was famous and he had worked with A.B. Palmcrantz, whose company was at Eckensberg near Stockholm and whose machine-gun Nordenfelt improved. By 1880 Nordenfelt had started to deal in arms and the Royal Navy became one of his most important customers.

Nordenfelt recognised the potential of the fast torpedo boat which could not easily be engaged with traditional naval weapons. He also identified the threat imposed by the submarine armed with the torpedo. While he had experience in engineering he knew nothing about submarines. But he had access to engineering works capable of building a boat. As a major international arms supplier he had the right contacts with a market network. With his arms factory and contacts in the arms trade he would be in a position to provide weapons for the submarines. But what was of more immediate importance was that he could provide the necessary financial backing for the research and development that would be necessary to build a successful submarine. Garrett had the practical experience of designing and building two submarines and, according to his son, he had been working on the design of a larger boat while working at Milford Haven.

Theoretically it was an ideal partnership. Nordenfelt undertook to provide financial backing and building facilities; profits would be shared equally but Nordenfelt stipulated that the boats would be called 'Nordenfelt Submarine Boats'. For Garrett it meant that he could pursue the work in which he was most interested without financial limitations, but he would not be in control.

The end product of this liaison was the building of four submarines between 1882 and 1888. Of these one was sold to Greece, two to Turkey and the fourth was damaged beyond economical repair whilst in transit for sale to Russia. Garrett became an international commuter, a submarine salesman, a submarine instructor, a diplomat, blockade runner and was granted a commission in the Turkish Navy. Life for Garrett was never exactly humdrum.

A Provisional Patent Specification for Submarine or Subaqueous Boats or Vessels was published on 17 February 1881 (Appendix 2). The letters of patent were granted to Thorsten Nordenfelt. The provisional specification indicates that the submarine would be powered by steam and although the boiler could be hermetically sealed for diving there was no indication that the Lamm principle was to be used. To dive the vessel, one or more propellers, mounted in tubes, and working in the vertical plane were used. For longitudinal stability the vessel was to be fitted with forward hydroplanes which were controlled automatically. The specification is vague but it could have been the first tangible evidence of the liaison between Nordenfelt and Garrett.

The full and finished specification for the patent was published on 17 August 1881, and this is much more specific. Indeed it gives a clear idea of not only her shape but also how the first Nordenfelt boat worked. Although a full description of the boat is covered later the unabridged Patent is reproduced as Appendix III:

In the patent, Nordenfelt claimed that he had made three improvements in or appertaining to submarines and subaqueous boats or vessels, for which he was claiming the patent.

1 Providing the said vessel with propelling engines and a boiler, the latter being so arranged that after the water has been heated by the combustion of fuel its furnace may be closed gas tight and the steam from the heated water used to drive the engines whilst the vessel is submerged.
2 Providing the said vessel with descending or vertical propelling apparatus, which whilst in motion is capable of sinking the vessel beneath the surface whilst the vessel is lighter than the water which it displaces.
3 Providing the said vessel with automatically acting longitudinal stability rudders controlled by hydraulic or other motor apparatus and plumb weight.

Nordenfelt, the businessman, had acquired for himself rights which could well have been patented earlier by Garrett and Jos. Jones.

The concept or philosophy on which the first and subsequent Nordenfelt submarines were based is quite important as it dictated the way in which they were built, powered and operated:

1 Electric and petrol engines were unreliable and therefore steam would be used.

2 The boat should always be kept horizontal and this would be achieved by using vertical propellers and not hydroplanes only, as in *Resurgam*.
3 The submarine would have a conning tower fitted with ports and observation dome.
4 Steam (from reservoirs) would be used to blow ballast tanks.
5 The shape of the submarine would be designed to reduce underwater loss of speed. The speed of the submarine, with steam power, would be adequate for defending harbours and archipelagoes.
6 Limited underwater range would be accepted.
7 The weapon fit would include one torpedo and machine-guns mounted on deck.

Nordenfelt I was laid down at the works of A.B. Palmcrantz and Co. Ltd of Eckensberg near Stockholm in 1882. (Nordenfelt was a partner of T. Winborg who owned the company which was famous for the manufacture of harvesters and machine-guns.) Some parts of the submarine were made by Boliners and Co. of Stockholm. The submarine was launched in the spring or early summer of 1883, by which time Garrett had moved his family to Sweden.

Nordenfelt I was a direct descendant of *Resurgam* but in outward appearance this would not have been easy to recognise (Fig 59). The Nordenfelt boat was more streamlined with a flowing cigar-shaped hull which was 64 feet (19.5 metres) long. *Resurgam*'s side rudders were replaced by vertical propellers which were housed in sponsons on either flank. The new boat had hydroplanes at the bow; there was no casing but there was a funnel and a conning tower (fitted with a glass dome) both of which could be retracted into the hull. Incongruously there was an 18-foot (5.5-metre) mast, and abaft the conning tower two davits were fitted on the centre line carrying a small dinghy. The submarine worked on the same Lamm fireless locomotive principle as *Resurgam* but it was much more powerful. The interior of the boat housed the 100hp compound engine, the

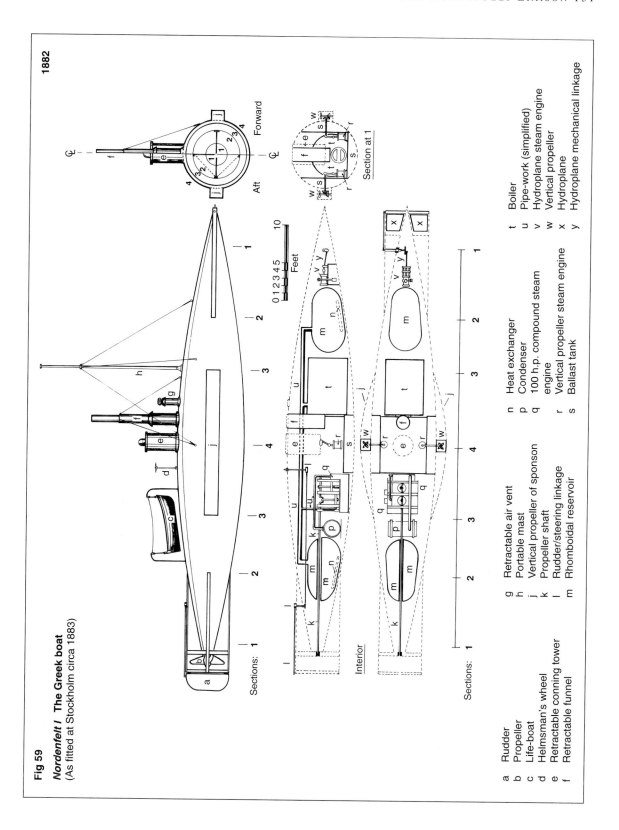

Fig 59
Nordenfelt I **The Greek boat**
(As fitted at Stockholm circa 1883)

1882

Sections: 1   2   3   4   3   2   1

0 1 2 3 4 5   10
Feet

Interior

Sections: 1   2   3   4   3   2   1

Forward / Aft
Section at 1

a Rudder
b Propeller
c Life-boat
d Helmsman's wheel
e Retractable conning tower
f Retractable funnel

g Retractable air vent
h Portable mast
j Vertical propeller of sponson
k Propeller shaft
l Rudder/steering linkage
m Rhomboidal reservoir

n Heat exchanger
p Condenser
q 100 h.p. compound steam engine
r Vertical propeller steam engine
s Ballast tank

t Boiler
u Pipe-work (simplified)
v Hydroplane steam engine
w Vertical propeller
x Hydroplane
y Hydroplane mechanical linkage

boiler, two large reservoirs or cisterns, and engines to control the forward hydroplanes and side propellers. There were three ballast tanks in the centre of the boat, two on either flank and one under the decking. The maximum diameter of the hull was 9 feet (2.74 metres) but because the iron plating was ⅝th inch (15.875mm) thick, and every 20 inches (50.8cm) there was an internal frame made of angle iron 3 inches by 3 inches (76 by 76mm) the available space within the boat was much reduced.

The system employed to store the latent power in the new boat was somewhat different to that used in *Resurgam*. The Nordenfelt boat had two rhomboidal reservoirs which contained about eight tons of water. The boiler, which could provide power for the engine in the normal way for surface running, also heated the water in the two reservoirs. This was achieved by passing steam through heat exchangers in the reservoirs, which heated the water until the pressure in the cisterns reached 150 psi (10 atmospheres). From cold this would have taken about two days.

In surface trim the vessel had 3 feet (.9 metre) of freeboard in the centre of the boat. To dive the boat (assuming the dinghy and mast had been left ashore), the conning tower funnel and air vent would have been retracted and sealed. About four tons of ballast would have been admitted to the three ballast tanks leaving a small reserve positive buoyancy of some 600 to 800 pounds (272 to 363kg). If necessary, to trim the boat fore and aft, water could be shifted from one hot water cistern to the other. The boat would then be driven under the water using the side propellers. The engines for these had a manual overide but were normally controlled automatically. Water pressure, taken from outside the submarine, acted against a weight; this could be adjusted, so that as the submarine went deeper and the pressure increased the throttle was gradually closed. The forward hydroplanes were designed to maintain the longitudinal trim of the boat; they were fitted with a pendulum inside the hull which activated the hydroplane

engine as soon as the vessel's stem dipped below or rose above the horizontal plane. Even so, *Nordenfelt I* lacked longitudinal stability; as the side propellers were positioned in the centre of the vessel they were unable to influence this in any way so, as soon as the boat adopted an uneven keel water in the boiler, two cisterns and ballast tanks would surge, further disrupting the stability, and the hydroplanes had great difficulty in stabilising the vessel.

The submarine was fitted with a four-blade, 5-foot (1.5 metre) diameter propeller; and she was credited later with a surface run of 150 miles (240km) without recoaling, at a maximum speed of slightly more than 8 knots (15kph). Using latent power, with an initial pressure of 150psi (10 atmospheres) she was driven for 16 miles (25.74km) at 7 knots (13kph).

Working-up trials were carried out in the Stockholm area under Garrett's command. The crew consisted of L. Norstrom, an engineer from the Swedish Navy, and Jonsson, a stoker provided by A.B. Palmcrantz and Co. Both the building of the vessel and the trials were conducted in the strictest secrecy. In August 1883 the submarine was sailed, under her own power, to Gothenburg by way of the network of canals and lakes.

Garrett made a log of his journey[1]. He had estimated that with a full fuel bunker (about 150 cubic feet [4.248 cubic metres] of coal) he could steam at between and 6 and 7 knots per hour (11 to 13kph) for 24 hours covering about 150 miles (240km). But as the submarine had just been fitted with new bearings on the high pressure connecting rod, it was considered prudent to travel no faster than 5 knots (9kph). The voyage was uneventful in that there were no disasters and no major mechanical problems. However, there are a few interesting episodes in the log which bring out the discomforts endured and Garrett's panache.

The first part of the journey was from the Palmcrantz yard at Carlsvick, near Stockholm into the Baltic and then south to Soderkoping where he

---

[1] Log of *Nordenfelt* Submarine boat; Stockholm to Goteborg (Gothenburg). Dated 13 September 1883 and signed by G.W. Garrett.

was able to enter the canal to Lake Roxen. Some delays were experienced as he had to pick up three different pilots to guide him down the coast south of Stockholm. Garrett found:

> The canal most troublesome. The boat having no keel steered wretchedly in the very little water we had in the canal and there being no protection whatever to the propeller made the shooting of the bridges and entering the locks an extremely difficult job as they fine you heavily for every time you run against the gates.

Garrett records that there were delays in clearing the canal offices because the officials had never heard of a boat described as 'En Dykeri Pram' (A Diving Boat) particularly as she had no name. So he forthwith christened the submarine *Dykeri Pram En* (Diving Boat No.1).

Sleeping arrangements on the boat consisted of hammocks for Norstrom and Jonsson, but there was no space for the captain. Perhaps this was not a design fault but a considered strategy because when they moored each night Garrett usually retired to a comfortable room at a local hotel. Twice his plan was foiled; on the first occasion he was put up by the captain of a steamer which was also moored for the night and spent the night on a couch. But the second time he had to rest on the sacks in the coal bunker.

The crew were able to prepare food and hot drinks but it proved difficult for the captain to eat ham and potatoes when on watch in pouring rain when 'the plate filled with water the moment it came from under cover'. Eating whilst underway in restricted waters was also a problem for the helmsman standing on the open deck and trying to eat and steer at the same time. Garrett's solution is summed up in his own words:

> Having arrived in sight of the locks which admit one to the Gota Canal and the weather having cleared a little I stopped the engine and let the boat drift while we had some food, as I knew it would be almost impossible to get any food after we entered the canal as the Motala (Gota?) works are close at hand and I knew that crowds would be down to look at the remarkable craft I was in charge of. Whilst eating I was astonished to see quite a number of boats pull off chiefly rowed by women. These came and not daring to come close rowed round and round us.

One can imagine the bearded Garrett proudly standing on the deck of his submarine and inviting the ladies on board to take cognac and coffee but he tells us 'they dared not come aboard'. Their reluctance is not surprising. The crew would not have been a pretty sight with the conditions on board, and Garrett could have been in a bit of a mess if it was the night before when he had had to cuddle up with the coal sacks.

There were two uncomfortable incidents. Whilst crossing Lake Vattern: 'a nasty, choppy cross sea got up which was so high that at times the broken tops of the waves went over my head as I stood on the boat and a little water went down the tower and found its way into the boat'. However, he was able to shelter in the lee of an island although while he was below a sudden wind shift did put the submarine aground momentarily but she suffered no damage. On another occasion, whilst crossing a lake at night, Garrett was nearly run down by a steamer showing no lights, although *Dykeri Pram En* was displaying her mast and side-lights. The position of the steamer straight ahead was apparent because of the sparks from her funnel. The steamer's helmsman must have seen the submarine's navigation lights because he blew the ship's whistle and increased speed. Garrett put his helm to port and the steamer put hers to starboard; with the two vessels still on a collision course Garrett then took immediate evasive action by going full astern with his helm to starboard to bring his stern round. Fortunately the two vessels did not make contact. Without knowing the exact details, the relative positions of the two vessels and the local navigation rules it would be imprudent to apportion blame for this incident. However, the steamer should have been displaying lights – not that this would in itself have prevented the close encounter.

After her safe arrival at Gothenburg a number of modifications were carried out. The funnel was removed and replaced by two pipes, one on either side of the boat, which went under water before re-emerging near the stern; this was to improve the draught for the boiler fire. The davits and dinghy were also removed. Intensive trials were carried out during the next two years and various improvements were made to the submarine.

Before the trials were completed Nordenfelt must have been so confident that the submarine would be successful that he entered into negotiations with the Barrow Shipbuilding Co. Ltd, at Barrow-in-Furness, to build a larger submarine. Neither he nor Garrett realised it at the time, but this was the beginning of the end as far as their liaison was concerned. Doors were opening for Nordenfelt but slowly closing for Garrett.

By the middle of 1885 Nordenfelt and Garrett considered that the submarine was ready to be shown publicly. On 21 September 1885 *Nordenfelt I* was demonstrated at Landscrona (just south of Helsingborg) to thirty-nine distinguished spectators from the main European powers and from Mexico and Japan. These included the Prince and Princess of Wales (later to be King Edward VII and Queen Alexandra), members of the Swedish, Danish and Russian Royal families and Lieutenant-General Sir Andrew Clarke (Inspector-General Fortifications). The demonstration was to show the submarine in three ways:

1 Running on the surface.
2 Running awash.
3 Running submerged.

The submarine performed well on the surface and when running awash with only her small conning tower visible. However, poor results were achieved when running submerged. Apparently the submarine's hydroplane was damaged by a tow rope and there was insufficient time to repair it before the demonstration. A further complication was that Norstrom, the engineer, injured his arm and was unable to go to sea. Even so Garrett, assisted only by the boilerman, Jonsson, managed to pass under the *Edda*, which had the observers on board, but the longest continuous period they were able to keep the submarine submerged was five minutes.

It is inconceivable that Nordenfelt would have jeopardised his standing by arranging a demonstration which could not achieve its laid down aims. There was no way he could have hoped to bluff his way and fudge the demonstration. Garrett must be credited with putting on a good performance considering the limitations of having faulty hydroplanes and no engineer on board. Although the demonstration was not a resounding success, as seen by the spectators, the defensive potential of the boat was recognised by Lieutenant-General Sir Andrew Clarke, who recommended to the British Government and the Royal Navy that a submarine should be purchased for £9,000 for evaluation. This counsel fell on deaf ears.

Some time after the demonstration at Landscrona the submarine returned to the yard of Messrs Palmcrantz and Co. Ltd. However, there is a very remote possibility that before this happened she was transported to Southampton for further trials and demonstrations.

Later in the same year, 1885, the Greek Government decided to purchase a submarine, possibly as a result of the Landscrona demonstration. By this time *Nordenfelt I* had returned to Eckensberg from whence she was sailed to Copenhagen. In his account of his father's life, Garrett's son relates that he has a record of this voyage, written by his father. The submarine, under Garrett's command, under its own power made the voyage of some 400 miles (644km), unescorted. On arrival at Copenhagen she was disassembled at the works of Burmeister and Wains and despatched, by sea to Piraeus, in Greece.

Nordenfelt and Garrett had achieved a couple of records by being the first to construct and export a submarine. Garrett's passage from Stockholm to Copenhagen must have established the first real endurance record for an unaccompanied submarine. This was probably not broken for some considerable time, albeit that it was probably run on the surface.

At Piraeus the submarine was rebuilt under the supervision of Garrett assisted by Jonsson, who had been promoted to engineer. The vessel was then delivered to the Hellenic Naval Base (Salamis) some 25 miles (40km) to the north west where the sea trials were due to take place in April 1886. The submarine was fitted with an external torpedo tube at the bows to fire a Whitehead torpedo. Two Nordenfelt machine-guns of 1 inch (25mm) calibre were mounted on the top of the pressure hull forward and aft of the conning position. No record has been found that a torpedo was ever fired from this submarine.

Garrett's son put a slightly different complexion on the delivery of the submarine. He reported that his father had to run a blockade. This is just possible but if so probably somewhat exaggerated. In April 1886 preparations were being made by Greece with the obvious intention of entering into a war with Turkey. Representatives of Great Britain, Germany, Austro-Hungary, Russia and Italy requested the Greek Government to reduce its land and sea forces to a peacetime establishment. Greece refused. Whereupon on 8 May the five powers declared a blockade of the Greek ports from Cape Malea at the south of the Morea to the Gulf of Aegina.

In the meantime part of the British Mediterranean fleet under Vice-Admiral H.R.H. the Duke of Edinburgh K.G. who was the senior officer (he had the local rank of Admiral and had assumed command on 5 March 1886 in succession to Lord John Hay) was already in the area. On the declaration of the blockade, the fleet under his command and flying his flag in H.M.S. *Temeraire*, proceeded to the Piraeus. Orders were issued for the detention of every vessel under the Greek flag that should attempt to enter or leave the ports on the blockade littoral. The enforcement of this directive soon had its effect. Greece disarmed, the blockade was raised on 7 June and vessels which had been detained were liberated.

Garrett's son's version [2] was:

> When the time came for delivering the boat the British had established what they considered an effective blockade across the mouth of the Bay of Salamis, consisting of three ironclads as they were called in those days. They were equipped with searchlights, and reinforced by patrol or torpedo boats. In spite of all this my father succeeded in running the blockade. He accomplished this by entering at night on the surface with only the glass of the conning tower showing. He passed so close to H.M.S. *Polyphoemis* that he could hear talking aboard her. Admiral Seymour in command of the blockading fleet telegraphed to the Admiralty that the submarine had sunk in the bay, but my father's wire that he was safe in Athens arrived in London before the official report. He later took in two shipments of Nordenfelt guns under the French flag.

The submarine was delivered to Piraeus by sea before the blockade was in place. However, after it had been assembled it had to be delivered to the Hellenic Naval base at Salamis by which time the blockade could well have been established. Although the distance was not great and could be covered in territorial waters by hugging the coast, Garrett could well have encountered blockading ships.

It is documented that H.R.H. the Duke of Edinburgh sent a young officer, Sydney Earley-Wilmot (who was destined to become a distinguished admiral), to investigate the *Nordenfelt I*. On his return he had little to report other than: 'she had some ingenious qualities, one being a

[2] *Submarines. An account of the first practical submarine boats*. As told by the son of their inventor and commander, George William Garrett.

greater difficulty to submerge than to come to the surface'.

Nordenfelt I was never used operationally by the Hellenic Navy, and probably never fired its main armament. The cost was £9,000 for a 66 foot (20 metres) long, steam-powered submarine, for which it was difficult to find a crew, and which certainly performed badly under water. Although it was really a white elephant, Greece had acquired a hidden asset, a secret weapon which they knew did not pose a real threat (except to the boat's crew), but which was of real concern to their traditional enemy. The *Nordenfelt I* was broken up in 1901.

Once Greece had acquired a submarine it was inevitable that her neighbour, Turkey, would also wish to arm herself with such a weapon system and would become more than a potential customer. Indeed on 26 January 1886 the Turkish Government signed an agreement to purchase two Nordenfelt submarines. The negotiations were probably carried out by Nordenfelt's Balkan agent, Basil Zaharof, who was known as Europe's mystery man and was later knighted. In fact he may also have been involved in the negotiations with Greece.

Nordenfelt the businessman was well prepared for such an eventuality having already entered negotiations with the Barrow Shipbuilding Co. Ltd the previous year. In February 1886 he was able to place an order to build one of two Turkish boats with the Barrow Shipbuilding Company Ltd where it was allocated the Yard Number 143 (Fig 60). The new boat was to be of steel, 100 feet (30 metres) long with a 12 feet (3.65 metres) beam and a displacement of 160 tons. Her shape was similar to *Nordenfelt I* but the sponson-mounted vertical propellers, fitted to the previous boat, were replaced by two vertical drive propellers mounted directly on top of the hull (one forward and the other aft). There were to be three ballast tanks: one at either end of the boat and the other in the centre. The weapon fit would include two external Whitehead torpedo tubes at the bow and two

Nordenfelt machine-guns fitted on the hull. The 250hp, twin-cylinder compound engine was to be built by Plenty and Sons Ltd, of Newbury. The vessel was designed to have a crew of six. The order for the second Turkish submarine, built to the same design as the one at Barrow, was awarded to Messrs Des Vignes and Company of Chertsey on the River Thames. Her engine was also to be built at Newbury.

Nordenfelt II was launched at Barrow on 14 April 1886 and was immediately broken down into seven sections. These were shipped to Turkey on the British freighter *Trinidad* (owned by the Coli Company) on 5 May 1886.

Garrett arrived in Turkey when the fourth and fifth sections were being assembled. Satisfied that the work was going well and that his presence was not required he left for Greece to supervise further trials of the Greek boat.

Nordenfelt II was relaunched on 6 September 1886 and later named *Abdul Hamid*, after the Sultan. Initial tests and trials were carried out but these were not satisfactory and after further diving trials, near the Golden Horn in February 1887, Garrett recommended that the boat should be put into dry dock for inspection and repair, while the second boat which had arrived from the Chertsey yard was reassembled. Anticipating that this work would take about three months Garrett returned to the United Kingdom. This also allowed him to be present when a fourth submarine, which by then had been ordered from and built by the Barrow Shipbuilding Company, was launched on 26 March 1887. Garrett's life over the next few months was very hectic with two boats working-up in Turkey and *Nordenfelt IV* working up in England. There is a considerable overlap of his activities with the various vessels and it will be easier to separate the two operations and consider the development of *Nordenfelt IV* later.

He returned to Constantinople on 2 June 1887 to supervise further tests. On arriving he immediately wrote to the A.D.C. of the Sultan:

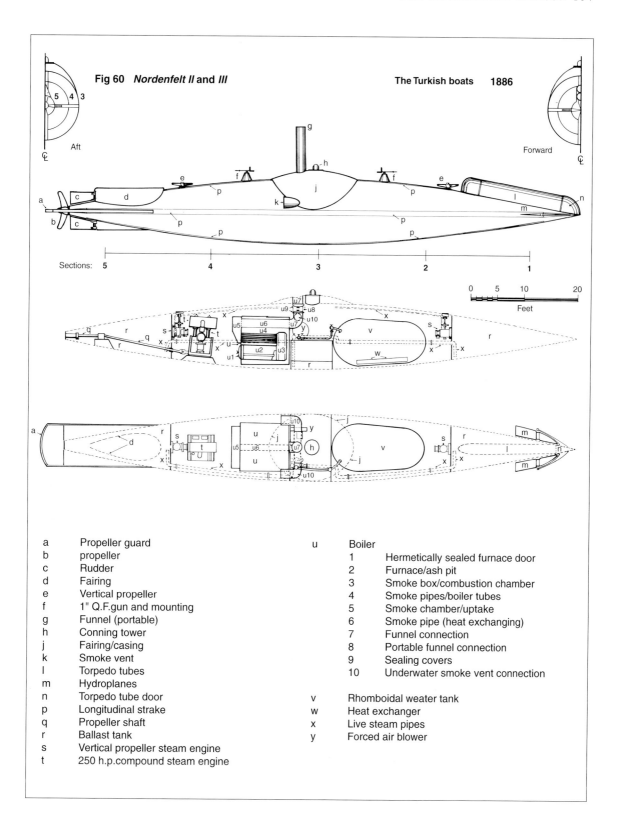

Fig 60 *Nordenfelt II* and *III*   The Turkish boats   1886

a	Propeller guard	u	Boiler
b	propeller	1	Hermetically sealed furnace door
c	Rudder	2	Furnace/ash pit
d	Fairing	3	Smoke box/combustion chamber
e	Vertical propeller	4	Smoke pipes/boiler tubes
f	1" Q.F.gun and mounting	5	Smoke chamber/uptake
g	Funnel (portable)	6	Smoke pipe (heat exchanging)
h	Conning tower	7	Funnel connection
j	Fairing/casing	8	Portable funnel connection
k	Smoke vent	9	Sealing covers
l	Torpedo tubes	10	Underwater smoke vent connection
m	Hydroplanes		
n	Torpedo tube door	v	Rhomboidal weater tank
p	Longitudinal strake	w	Heat exchanger
q	Propeller shaft	x	Live steam pipes
r	Ballast tank	y	Forced air blower
s	Vertical propeller steam engine		
t	250 h.p.compound steam engine		

NORDENFELT
Submarine Torpedo-Boats

Hotel Byzance,
Constantinople
2/6/87

His Excellency
Hakki Pasha
A.D.C. to His Majesty
The Sultan
Dear Sir

I have this day arrived for the purpose of obeying the order His Majesty was pleased to give to me namely that the Nordenfelt Submarine Boat should be experimented with on the 15th day of Ramajan.

I am extremely anxious that His Majesty should see with his own eyes that he has not been deceived by Mr Nordenfelt but that he really is in possession of the best Submarine Torpedo-Boat in the World. Can you give me any idea when and where His Majesty would like to see the boat go?

I am

Your Excellency's Obdt Servt.

George Wm. Garrett

The submarine which was to be demonstrated had a number of improvements and innovations over the previous vessels. The vessel was larger than its predecessor and had a much more powerful engine rated at 250hp at 100psi (6.8 atmospheres). The circulating and air pumps were worked by a separate cylinder which could be operated independently from the main engine. Therefore a vacuum could be maintained which was designed to make the engines in the boat more efficient by allowing them to take power from the latent steam below normal atmospheric pressure. The boiler had two furnaces with a heating surface of 750 square feet (69.67 square metres). The submarine was fitted with a fan, located under the conning tower, which drew air into the boat, when on the surface, which was forced to travel through the furnace and out through the funnel in a similar way to *Resurgam*. The boiler

heating pipes were connected to the smoke box in the normal way. The funnel, in an attempt to reduce the temperature within the boat, was routed through the boiler, where the heat was conducted to the water, before exiting the hull. The funnel vented on either side of the hull just behind the conning tower.

The Turkish boats had only one hot water cistern which, together with the boiler, contained about 30 tons of water. As in the *Nordenfelt I* boat, this was heated by passing live steam through a heat exchanger, which was positioned in the bottom of the cistern and then recirculating it to the boiler. The heat exchanger had a surface area of about 500 square feet (46.45 square metres). The cistern and the boiler were both heated to 150psi (10 atmospheres) and this gave a theoretical range, using only latent power, of 30 to 40 miles (48 to 64km).

Each of the vertically-operating propellers had a three cylinder engine which ensured there was no dead centre and, as soon as the steam was switched on, the engine responded. Control of these two engines was exercised by the captain in the conning tower. Using steam valves he controlled the speed of the propellers which could be operated independently of each other, thereby governing the depth of the vessel. The submarine was fitted with bow hydroplanes which had a similar pendulum control to that used in the Greek boat. They could also be controlled from the conning tower by the captain.

The submarine was fitted with three ballast tanks. One at either end of the boat with a fifteen-ton capacity and the third in the bottom centre of the boat which could take seven tons. This allowed the crew to compensate for changes in weight distribution as the eight tons of coal briquettes were used up. This made it easier to trim the vessel.

Before diving the vessel, the funnel tube inside the hull would be disconnected and sealed, the furnace doors hermetically closed, the conning tower hatch locked and water allowed to flow into the ballast tanks. The boat would flood down until only the conning tower remained above water and possibly a small section of the top of the hull at the foot of the tower. The vertical screws would then be used to force the boat, which had retained positive buoyancy, under the water. In the same way as her predecessors, once submerged all her steam engines and machinery would draw their power from the stored latent energy. Within the boat there was no equipment for cleansing or purifying the air as it was considered by Nordenfelt that this was unnecessary.

The *Abdul Hamid* was demonstrated to her namesake the Sultan in the Golden Horn. She started by making a run down the waterway 'threading her way dexterously through the lighters and caiques'. As the submarine progressed there was very little visible above the surface – her small conning tower, the hump of the hull immediately under it and the top of the torpedo tube. She was immediately nicknamed the 'Whale Ship' by the onlookers. Garrett was then ordered by the Sultan, who was controlling the demonstration from the shore, to stem the tide where it was strongest, off Seraglio Point. The submarine had no difficulty in complying with this order and maintained her position for fifteen minutes, although the accompanying vessels were unable to stem the tide. During this particular manoeuvre a lighter passed too close to the submarine and was struck by her propeller and holed. She was able to reach the shore and no serious damage was done to the submarine.

Garrett was then ordered to carry out a surface attack against a steamer lying off the Seutari. The submarine was turned towards the target and crossed the current. Tail on to the spectators she was very difficult to see both because of the small amount of the boat above the water and her pale colouring. Furthermore the bow wave made a trough in which the vessel moved making it more difficult to pick her out. Garrett simulated the attack by opening the bow caps of the torpedo tubes which allowed the tubes to flood suddenly sending a spray of water into the air through the vents at ther rear of the tubes. This emphasised the similarity to a whale.

The next test was to run, on the surface against the current, again at Seraglio Point. The submarine soon left her attending escorts behind and she was recorded as having covered eight knots over the ground against a five knot current which is equivalent to 13 knots, or just under 15mph (24kph).

The Sultan then ordered Garrett to carry out a submerged attack against the steamer which had been the first target. The submarine was steamed slow ahead while she closed up and took on ballast until only the conning tower and the very top of the hump could be seen. She was turned towards the target and stern on she was even more difficult to see than earlier with so little showing above the surface. She then disappeared completely to emerge shortly afterwards on the far side of the target, having passed under her.

The trial lasted for five hours during which the submarine ran off stored power for two hours. Although the Sultan expressed his satisfaction with the trial, further trials had to be carried out. In the meantime Garrett himself returned to the United Kingdom to command *Nordenfelt IV* in various trials and demonstrations in the Solent at Southampton.

The second Turkish submarine, *Abdul Mecid*, named after the Sultan's brother, was eventually launched on 4 August 1887. That it took over a year longer than the first boat to reconstruct indicates that there must have been unusual delays. Apparently there had been problems rebuilding this boat in Turkey – possibly because she had not been completely assembled, as had the Barrow boat, before being packed up in segments and exported from England. Difficulty was experienced in joining the different sections. Furthermore various fittings were either never despatched or subsequently lost and had to be replaced.

Both submarines underwent sea trials and torpedo firing tests at Izmit in the Sea of Marmara. Turkish records show that both submarines failed

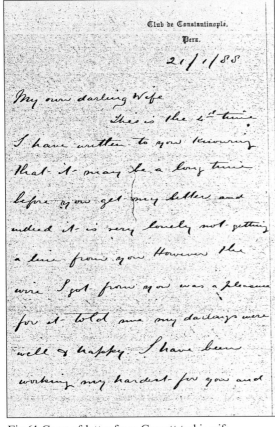

Fig 61 Copy of letter from Garrett to his wife

part of their diving tests in 1887 and further sea trials were started in early 1888. At their conclusion it was found that the submarines were satisfactory on the surface but 'underwater navigation was unsatisfactory'.

A letter from Garrett to his wife gives an insight into the lonely existence of the International Submarine Designer/Salesman/Instructor/Commuter:

While he was in Turkey, Garrett's two assistants were Captain P.W.D'Alton and Mr Lawrie. It was not until 1901 that Captain D'Alton made his comments about the Nordenfelt submarines public. This is reminiscent of the delay in publishing details of the last voyage of *Resurgam*, some of which were critical, by George Price. In the late nineteenth century 'cheque-book' journalism was not rampant and perhaps the public were less

interested in failure than success. On the other hand, perchance both Garrett and Nordenfelt put pressure on their employees not to speak to the press. D'Alton eventually became Chief Engineer to the Central London Railway, and so long after the event would hardly be in a position to harm Nordenfelt or Garrett but his comments on his own practical experience contribute to the story:[3]

> She had the fault of all submarine boats, viz., a total lack of longitudinal stability. All submarines are practically devoid of weight when under water. The Nordenfelt, for example, weighed by a couple of hundredweights less than nothing when submerged, and had to be kept down by screw propellers provided for the purpose. The Turkish boat was submerged by admitting water to tanks aided by horizontal propellers, and raised by blowing the

---

[3] *Submarine Warfare* by Herbert C. Fyfe. Also published in *The Engineer* in 1901.

ballast out again and reversing the propellers. Nothing could be imagined more unstable than the Turkish boat. The moment she left the horizontal position the water in her boiler and the tanks surged forwards and backwards and increased the angle of inclination. She was perpetually working up and down like a scale beam, and no human vigilance could keep her on an even keel for half a minute at a time. Once, and we believe only once, she fired a torpedo, with the result that she as nearly as possible stood up vertically on her tail and proceeded to plunge to the bottom stern first. On another occasion all hands were nearly lost. Mr Garrett was in the little conning tower. The boat was being slowly submerged – an operation of the utmost delicacy – before a committee of Ottoman officers, when a boat came alongside without warning. Her wash sent a considerable quantity of water down the conning tower, the lid of which was not closed, and the submarine boat instantly began to sink like a stone. Fortunately Mr Garrett got the lid closed just in time, and Mr Lawrie, the engineer, without waiting for orders, blew some water ballast out. It was an exceedingly narrow escape.

D'Alton only confirms much of which is already known about the Turkish boats: the most important fault was that they lacked longitudinal stability. Water in the boiler, cistern and ballast tanks would surge as soon as the boat departed from the horizontal plane further exacerbating the problem, and making it very difficult to keep the boat on an even keel. The submarines were vulnerable to swamping through the conning tower.

This was the downfall of *Resurgam* off Great Ormes Head. At least, when crewed, *Resurgam* could be sailed closed down inducting air through the primitive schnorchel. The Turkish boats did not have such a system; the fan (or blower) sucked air in through the open conning tower hatch making the boat vulnerable to the heavy wash of passing ships, or to waves in a heavy sea. Indeed, the boat would have been particularly susceptible, in a prolonged storm, when it periodically needed

air for the furnace and the crew. Finally the inevitable effects on the boat of firing a torpedo are described by D'Alton:

> The sudden discharge of a heavy weight from one extremity of the submarine, the bow, is going to make her stern heavy. Unless immediately compensated, and the vessel was not equipped for this, she would go down by the stern, the water in the various tanks would surge further compounding the problem. The loss of weight of the torpedo would add to the positive buoyancy already established in the submarine and she would surface, or at least the bow would surface, which in an attack on an enemy ship may be rather imprudent.

No wonder the Turkish authorities were not satisfied with the underwater performance of the two boats. They could not do what they were supposed to do.

Garrett wrote to the Defence Minister at the conclusion of the trials:

NORDENFELT
Submarine Torpedo-Boats

Hotel Byzance,
Constantinople
22/2/88

His Excellency Hassam Pasha
Dear Sir,

I write to confirm that at an interview which your Excellency kindly granted me at your private residence last evening you promised me that if I wrote to you a letter stating the result of the aforesaid interview you would never allow anyone to either see it or know of its existence except His Imperial Majesty the Sultan.

This is the letter you promised to keep secret. Having explained to your Excellency the great advantages the Nordenfelt Torpedo-Boats have over the ordinary Surface Boats I admitted that the contract had been drawn up most ambiguously and by persons ignorant of the subject and that it was quite possible that His Majesty had been led to expect that the boats would perform more than they have done.

And therefore although at this moment there is not any profit on these boats yet if His Majesty will accept in all honor (sic) these two boats and will contemplate the purchase of one more Mr Nordenfelt will on his side be content to allow one half of the balance now due to him by Article XII of the Contract to remain unpaid until after the settlement of the contract for the new boat and that if a new boat be bought the sum so left unpaid shall be deducted from the price of the new boat.

I have agreed to the above because I am extremely anxious that the Nordenfelt Submarine Torpedo-Boats should form part of the Ottoman Navy because the defence of Constantinople and the Mediterranean of the Ottoman Empire in its integrity is to the interest of England and further because I believe that the defence of some Turkish harbour, Strait or Sea will play an important role in the coming war and if the Nordenfelt Submarine Torpedo-Boats render good service in such a defence it will cause them to be adopted by the whole world.

I repeat that Mr Nordenfelt does not want to make money in Turkey nor has he done so but he wishes to be Patronised by His Majesty and allowed to show the value of the Submarine Boats in the defence of the rights of the King who has up to this done much to assist him to the success and fortune which he enjoys.

For my own part if His Majesty adopts as part of his Navy the Nordenfelt Submarine Boats I will do all that lays in my power to make them thoroughly effective and maintain them in good order and I would propose as the best means of guarding the interests of His Majesty in this matter.

That Turkish Captains and crews should be appointed to each of the Submarine boats but that I should hold a commission in the Turkish service with a rank sufficient to enable me to override the captains of the boats. I could not of course give my whole time to the Turkish service in time of peace but I could give one month each year during which

I would examine and exercise the boats and their crews. I would of course ask no salary for my services. For the first year it would be advisable that two of my trained engineers should remain in Turkey to keep the boats in order and to instruct the Turks in the maintenance of their machinery. These men would have to be paid by His Majesty.

By giving me the command of His Submarine Torpedo-Boats His Majesty would have the advantage of my experience which will be continually increasing and should have the advantage of knowing that the boats were kept in good order and ready for use should they be wanted to fight.

In conclusion I would wish to assure your Excellency that should I have the honor (sic) to serve under you either in peace or war I will do my utmost to carry out your wishes for the guarding of the interests of His Majesty the Sultan.

I have the honour to be
Your Exellency's Obdt Servt
George William Garrett.

As a result of the letter on 15 March 1888 a five article protocol was signed by the Navy Minister, Hasan Pasha and the Nordenfelt representative, G.W. Garrett. Two of the articles are particularly interesting:

4th Article of Protocol. Garrett was given the honorary rank of Lieutenant-Commander (Binbasi). He would go to Constantinople for one month each year to supervise and train officers in operating the submarines, without payment.
5th Article of Protocol. It was agreed that in time of war Garrett had guaranteed he would serve the Turkish Government.

On 22 March 1888 the two submarines were officially accepted by the Turkish Navy and Garrett received his honorary rank from the Sultan.

Exactly how much was paid for the submarines by the Turkish Government has not been established but there still remains a facimile of a cheque to the value of £2,000 made out to Mr T. Nordenfelt and dated Constantinople, 20 March 1888.

There has been implied criticism that Garrett wheedled a commission from the Turkish Establishment. It may have been in his self-interest to improve his social status but as a civilian with a naval crew under instruction, and for all intents and purposes under command, in the confined space of the submarine he could have been in an invidious position. Although he probably had more 'hands-on experience' of commanding a submarine successfully than anyone else in the world there could well have been resentment by a professional naval crew who did not like being told what to do by a mere civilian and foreigner to boot. Delay in reacting to an order, which could have been rather terse particularly with the language barrier, in an emergency could have had fatal consequences. A commission would at least have given him 'authority'.

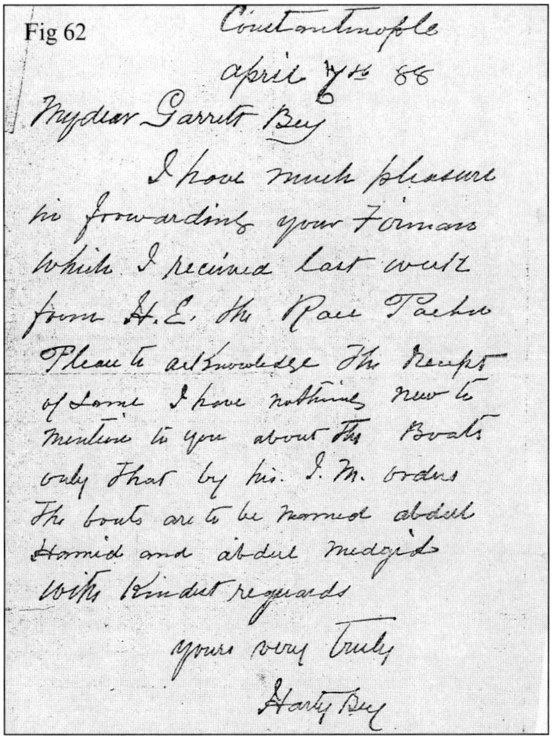

The Turkish boats, like the Greek boat, were never used operationally. Indeed there were even problems finding crews for them. In 1909 the two submarines were stored in a weather-beaten shed with grass knee deep growing around them. They were neglected, rusting hulks and efforts to sell

Copy of letter from Marty Bey with cheque

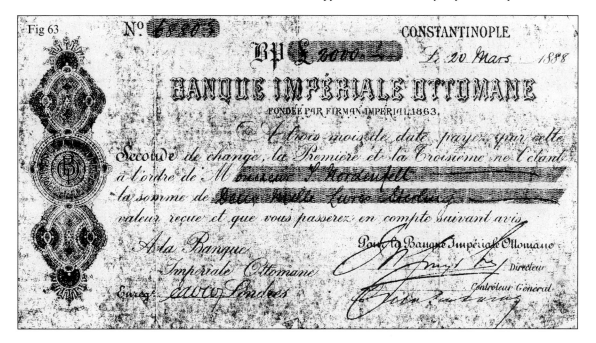

Fig 62

Fig 63

them failed. In 1914 the two boats were rediscovered by the German Military Mission to Turkey, but by this time they were beyond repair.

Nordenfelt and Garrett could claim some success. Three submarines had been sold even though they were not particularly successful boats. The Greeks really had little to complain of in that the vessel they purchased had been experimented with for several years and had been publicly displayed so they should have known what they were purchasing. Perhaps the scales were literally upset by the addition of a torpedo tube, which had been thought about but its addition to the hull had not been fully tested. The Turkish boats had a number of improvements, based on the experience gained in the *Nordenfelt I* trials; these were incorporated on the drawing-board. The boats were built fairly quickly and immediately despatched to Turkey without the detailed evaluation that the first boat had had. Nordenfelt and Garrett had failed to design and build a prototype vessel which worked satisfactorily, which could be successfully demonstrated, and then copies of it ordered. They were selling experimental boats which it was hoped Garrett and his team could make work at the delivery site and convince the customer that he was acquiring a proven vessel. Even so no other firm or individual was in a position to build and sell a submarine boat. Indeed with foresight, Nordenfelt had cornered the market. He and Garrett were ahead of the rest of the field although the product was far from perfect. But Nordenfelt was first and foremost an arms dealer and not a philanthropist. Submarines were a very small part of his business and the cost of research and development was hardly offset by sales while the attitude to submarines by the major Governments and potential market was not favourable.

CHAPTER 18

NORDENFELT IV (THE SOUTHAMPTON OR RUSSIAN BOAT)

The last of the submarines built by Nordenfelt and Garrett was the *Nordenfelt IV*. She was laid down in late 1886 at the Barrow Shipbuilding Co., where it was designated Yard No. 149. This was to be a larger boat of a radically different design; it was a speculative venture although Turkey did have an option to buy her when completed and this is reflected in the 1887 edition of *The Naval Annual* (Brassey) which includes her under Turkish Ships. This submarine was being built while the Turkish boats were undergoing their initial trials and the time frame of the main events, although mainly covered earlier, is relevant and worth summarising:

1886

January	Turkey ordered two submarines
February	Order placed to build *Nordenfelt II* (Barrow)
Spring?	Order placed to build *Nordenfelt III* (Chertsey)
April 14	*Nordenfelt II* launched
April	Sea trials of Greek boat scheduled at Salamis
May 5	*Nordenfelt II* shipped to Turkey
September	*Nordenfelt II* (*Abdul Hamid*) relaunched, Turkey
Autumn	*Nordenfelt IV* laid down, Barrow

1887

February	*Nordenfelt II* (*Abdul Hamid*) trials, Turkey
	Nordenfelt II (*Abdul Hamid*) dry dock, Turkey
	Nordenfelt III (*Abdul Mejid*) rebuilding, Turkey
March	*Nordenfelt IV* launched, Barrow-in-Furness
June	*Nordenfelt II* (*Abdul Hamid*) demonstration and further trials, Turkey
August	*Nordenfelt III* (*Abdul Mejid*) launched

1888

March	*Nordenfelt II* and *III* accepted by Turkish Navy.

The design of the two Turkish boats had been based on the first *Nordenfelt* and improvements which were made to her as a result of the various trials carried out between the summer of 1883 and winter 1885. *Nordenfelt II*, which had significant changes, was launched on 14 April 1886 and shipped to Turkey on 5 May. It is hard to believe that during the eighteen days available there would be sufficient time to: finally fit her out; check the integrity of the hull; get the boiler to working temperature; prove the equipment, conduct any significant tests and trials; make any changes or modifications that were necessary; retest; close all the systems down including draining the boilers etc.; disassemble the vessel and box it ready for transit. Trials with a new boat would have been essential to evaluate and check the changes that had been made. An added complication could well have been that Garrett, the expert and driving force, should have been in Greece at about this time where the sea trials of *Nordenfelt I* were due to be taking place. No one is indispensable but as it is unlikely that anyone else had the required experience to conduct the necessary tests at Barrow it could be assumed that the scheduled trials in Greece were delayed and Garrett was available to evaluate the new boat.

In Turkey, having been reassembled, *Nordenfelt II* was relaunched on 6 September 1886. Trials were conducted between then and February 1887 and this must have been the first real opportunity to thoroughly test the submarine, which incorporated the latest thinking. The actual date *Nordenfelt IV* was laid down has not been established but it is thought to have been in the autumn of 1886. Therefore there was a gap of only a few weeks in which to carry out the evaluation of the latest hardware and the planning of the new submarine. This presented an interesting time and space problem, particularly for Garrett who would have had to travel back to the UK to liaise with both Nordenfelt and the Barrow Shipbuilding Company. The new drawings were produced and the new boat laid down.

Although *Nordenfelt IV* was much larger than her predecessors the drawings produced for her must have been based, to a certain extent, on the design of the Turkish boats and where necessary adapted to take into consideration any modifications that had had already been made to the first Turkish boat. But at this stage, having completed trials over a period of several months, the first Turkish boat had been deemed to be unsatisfactory and she was put into dry dock so that further modifications could be carried out to rectify the faults which had been found. These unproven modifications could also have been incorporated in the plans for the new boat. The Turkish boat was then in dry dock for several months and therefore it is assumed that the work carried out was significant (unless Garrett put her there as an excuse to absent himself so that he could be in England to supervise the building of the new vessel at Barrow). Without details of the early trials and of what modifications had to be made, it is only possible to speculate that development was going ahead rather too fast. It is unlikely that further trials had been carried out with *Nordenfelt II* in time to influence any other changes to the plans. It could well have been the influence of Nordenfelt the businessman forging ahead to consolidate on the apparent success of selling two boats to Turkey, rather than the engineer waiting to test, prove and then develop before going ahead.

The new submarine was launched on 26 March 1887. Due to a serious miscalculation she settled by the stern taking some 9 feet (2.74 metres) of water while at the bow she was only drawing 4½ (1.37 metres). The fault was rectified but there is a report that Garrett suffered 'a kind of seizure'. However, he must have recovered fairly quickly as he was soon as deeply involved in events as he was before.

Nordenfelt IV was registered with the Board of Trade as a Merchant Ship. She was built of steel, and was 125 feet (38 metres) long with a beam of 12 feet (3.65 metres) (Fig 64). The cigar shape of the earlier boats was abandoned for a hull with a circular cross-section amidships tapering fore and aft, in plan view, with sections formed from two arcs of a circle. The frame spacing was 20 inches (50cm) and the plating was about $^5/_{16}$th inch (8mm) thick except on the turtle-deck where it was 1 inch (25mm) thick. Two conning towers with glass domes were fitted fore and aft, and amidships there were two portable funnels which could be stowed for diving. The vessel was propelled by a single screw with a diameter of about 7 feet (2 metres) and there were two vertical propellers mounted immediately below the centre-line of the vessel at the bow and at the stern. Unlike any of her predecessors *Nordenfelt IV* was fitted with hydroplanes at both the bow and the stern. The surface displacement was 160 tons and when submerged 243 tons.

A pair of two-cylinder compound engines were made by Plenty and Co. of Newbury, and these were collectively rated at 1,000hp at a pressure of 150psi working directly onto a four-throw crank shaft directly coupled to the propeller shaft. The high pressure cylinders were 15½ inches (39cm) diameter and the low pressure cylinders 27½ inches (69.9cm) with a stroke of 16 inches (40.6cm). The vertical propellers had independent engines and there were additionally seven more

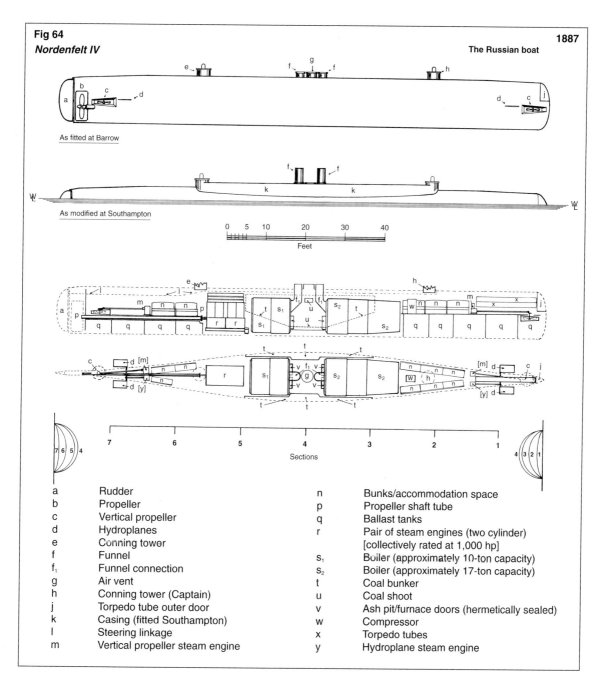

Fig 64
Nordenfelt IV

As fitted at Barrow

As modified at Southampton

Feet

Sections

1887

The Russian boat

a	Rudder	n	Bunks/accommodation space
b	Propeller	p	Propeller shaft tube
c	Vertical propeller	q	Ballast tanks
d	Hydroplanes	r	Pair of steam engines (two cylinder)
e	Conning tower		[collectively rated at 1,000 hp]
f	Funnel	s_1	Boiler (approximately 10-ton capacity)
f_1	Funnel connection	s_2	Boiler (approximately 17-ton capacity)
g	Air vent	t	Coal bunker
h	Conning tower (Captain)	u	Coal shoot
j	Torpedo tube outer door	v	Ash pit/furnace doors (hermetically sealed)
k	Casing (fitted Southampton)	w	Compressor
l	Steering linkage	x	Torpedo tubes
m	Vertical propeller steam engine	y	Hydroplane steam engine

engines to drive: pumps for the circulation of water in the condensers, steering, forced draught fans, and both ballast and bilge pumps. Unlike the earlier boats there were no cisterns as such to store the steam and a modified system was used in the new boat. There were two cylindrical locomotive boilers each with two furnaces, the smaller, fitted aft of centre contained about ten tons of water and the larger, positioned just forward of the centre of the vessel, held about seventeen tons. To raise steam for diving, all four furnaces would be fired up; as soon as a head of steam had been raised in the smaller, aft boiler, steam was fed into the bottom of the forward boiler to accelerate heating. As soon as 150psi (10 atmospheres) was reached the boiler was segregated and its fires banked. For surface running the aft boiler provided steam for the main and auxiliary engines. Under water when all the furnaces had been damped down and sealed, steam would be flashed from the forward boiler to the aft boiler as it had been from the reservoirs in the earlier boats. Normally eight tons of coal, sufficient for 1,000 miles (1,600km) at 8 knots (15kph), was carried. If necessary, a further twenty tons could be stowed by requisitioning ballast tanks, if they were not to be used for their primary purpose, for example on a long passage run on the surface, thereby increasing her range to about 2,500 miles (4,000km). There was no electric lighting within the boat and the crew of nine had to rely on candles or oil lamps.

The submarine was fitted with nine ballast tanks; five forward of the larger boiler, and four aft of the main engines. Their combined capacity was about thirty-five tons of sea water. Unlike her predecessors the water was pumped out. The pumping rate was about one and a half tons per minute.

The main armament of the boat consisted of two Whitehead torpedo tubes mounted one above the other in the stem. The tubes had a bow door, which could be controlled from within the submarine. It was the intention to carry four torpedoes. Two Nordenfelt two-pounder guns were to be fitted to the turtle back, but these were probably never shipped.

From his position in the forward conning tower the captain had direct control of the machinery which was driving the main engines, the vertical propellers, the fans and steering. He could control the taking on and pumping out of ballast and finally he could 'discharge the torpedoes'. The vertical screws were governed by hydrostatic pressure, as in the previous boats, which slowed them down as the submarine approached the set depth. If it went below this it would reverse them forcing the submarine to rise; this control could be overridden by the helmsman in the forward conning tower.

The initial work-up trials were probably carried out at Barrow where Nordenfelt had access to various engineering establishments. She was then sailed from Barrow to Southampton; the 500-mile (805km) voyage would have established yet another world record as it was slightly longer than the journey from Stockholm to Copenhagen in 1886. On arrival at Southampton, having experienced some bad weather en route, it was decided to fit a casing between the two conning towers and this work was undertaken by Messrs Oswald Mordaunt and Co. of Woolston. Further trials were conducted in the following few days in Southampton Outer Dock (now the Princess Alexandra Dock) and then in the Solent in the area of Mother Bank.

Nordenfelt IV was unofficially and affectionately referred to as 'The Southampton Boat' and later as 'The Russian Boat'.

Satisfied that the submarine was ready, Nordenfelt organised a demonstration which was held on 26 May 1887. This was essentially for the Armed Services of the United Kingdom, although some colonial representatives attended. To start with the visitors were allowed to tour the vessel. But this took some considerable time as they had to go round in small groups because of the general lack of space.

The official guests then boarded the steamer *Alexandra*. The submarine, probably under command of Garrett who was in the United Kingdom at the time, trimmed right down until only her conning towers and the casing were visible. With the funnels stowed and everything sealed she ran, using the latent power, against a lively breeze, up to Netley Hospital. She maintained a speed of 5 knots (9kph), although she did run for a short while at 8 knots (14.8kph). Painted grey, emitting no smoke or noise and showing only the two conning towers, she presented a very indistinct target which was difficult to see at ranges over 200 yards (183 metres). This part of the demonstration culminated by her circumnavigating the ironclad, H.M.S. *Invincible*, which was lying at anchor.

Next the funnels were erected, her furnace stoked up and she made a surface run as far as Calshot Castle and back, a distance of 13 miles (21km). She achieved a maximum speed of 14 knots (26kph). Like the Turkish boats her bow wave tended to hide the casing from view so that all that could be seen was a pair of small conning towers and the funnels streaking through the water. During the run she was accompanied by Torpedo-Boat No.23. Compared to this vessel the submarine presented a target which it would have been difficult to see, let alone engage.

Not to miss a chance of free publicity, the submarine was presented to public (and even Royal) gaze at Queen Victoria's Golden Jubilee Naval Review at Spithead on 23 July 1887. The date happened to coincide with one of Garrett's commuting trips from Turkey. There is an account of this in the *Illustrated Naval and Military Magazine* of January 1888:

> Those who witnessed the great Jubilee Naval Review at Portsmouth from the great Indian Trooper *Tamar* saw that she was steadily followed from Southampton Docks by a craft which, looked on from the great height of *Tamar's* taffrail, more resembled in hue and shape, but certainly not in speed, a huge slug than anything else. This was the submarine torpedo boat, the *Nordenfelt*. The *Tamar* got out of dock late, as she had to give way to the *Orontes* and *Himalaya*, and she did not waste time in steaming to Portsmouth. She is a fast ship, too, and returning to Southampton in the evening she very easily and handsomely beat the *Orontes*. But on the run down to Portsmouth the *Nordenfelt* just kept the position with regard the troopship that she liked best. She was not nearly submerged; yet the target she presented was extremely small. Coming bows-on 200 yards (182 metres) or so in the wake of the *Tamar*, little could be seen but an upheaved mass of water. Unlike torpedo boats, which, when going at speed, lift their bows out of

the sea, the *Nordenfelt* keeps on an even keel, and raises in front of her a curious wave, which is proof against machine-guns, because the solid mass of water deflects bullets upwards at such an angle that they clear the hull. The *Nordenfelt* appeared to be the very incarnation of destructive power. There was not one of the magnificent and costly men-of-war reviewed by Her Majesty that could do anything to avert destruction by the *Nordenfelt*, if that destruction were contemplated, save take to her screws as fast as she could. At a distance of a mile (1.6km) the boat, when *à fleur d'eau* – that is to say, with only her little conning-towers out of the water – is invisible; when within a couple of hundred yards (182 metres) she would not be detected, save by chance, if there was a little sea on; at night, the chances of her being found by torpedo guard-boats would be extremely small. She could thus run quite close up to a ship without availing herself fully of her submarine powers, and her chances of getting away unhurt, after discharging her torpedoes, would be very good. But she could approach within a mile of an ironclad at anchor; take her bearings accurately and then go down, and proceed under water until she had run the requisite distance – she could, if in any doubt, come nearly to the top for a moment to permit the steersman to see where he was precisely, and then go down without being detected, or, if detected, injured – and immediately afterwards deliver a blow which would send a great ironclad to the bottom. The *Nordenfelt* has rendered naval operations against forts and harbours nearly impossible. No commander dare lie near a harbour from which a submarine boat could be despatched to blow up his ship, whether just off the shore or 50 to 100 miles (80 to 160km) out to sea. The one chance remaining is that ships may be rendered torpedo proof, and how that is to be done is the problem of the future.

The surface trials had been relatively impressive. But the submarine had the Nordenfelt/Garrett characteristic: it was prone to lack of longitudinal stability; even though the ballast tanks were smaller and more evenly distributed, the water still surged, particularly in the larger boiler. Trials continued throughout the remainder of 1887 although Garrett was absent for much of the time in Turkey.

Having failed to sell *Nordenfelt IV* after the first demonstration, a second was arranged to include representatives from abroad. The United Kingdom representatives were led by an Army officer, General Sir Gerald Graham, while the Royal Navy was represented by two Captains and the Director of Naval Construction, showing how unimportant the Royal Navy (and Establishment) considered the event and the submarine to be. Naval attachés from Austria, Germany, Italy, Japan, Spain, Turkey and the United States attended. Most of the party travelled by train to Southampton on 19 December where they boarded the steamer *Alexandra*. The first demonstration was in surface trim, with funnels raised and the submarine travelled at about 15 knots (28kph). The *Alexandra* then steamed up Southampton Water from Calshot Castle until the two vessels were separated by about 3,000 yards (2.75km). The *Nordenfelt* then approached at full speed and, because of her low hull silhouette and the overcast conditions, she was difficult to see. It was noted that she ran quietly with no smoke emission, which favourably impressed the visitors.

The second trial and demonstration was held at night. This was also described in the *Illustrated Naval and Military Magazine* of January 1888:

> The second trial was devoted to a night attack. It was known that Captain Garrett would submerge the boat; but as it was supposed that he might attempt a surprise from some unknown point of the compass, a long watch was kept up on board from 5 o'clock until near upon 8. The moon came out and cast a shimmer of light upon the water, and it was thought that the enemy would be certain to be detected in crossing the ray. Presently, however, a nimbus cloud came floating over the scene from the north-west, and rain began to fall, followed by total obscuration. To make matters worse, a large German mail steamer anchored close at hand, and a number of tenders, with coloured and mast head lights, began to move about. The *Alexandra's* headlight, on the other hand, was of indifferent brilliancy: and just as those on board had made up their minds that Captain Garrett had lost his bearings, or that he had delivered his attack in some other direction by mistake, or that he had met with an accident, a whistle at some distance to windward aroused the spirits of the watchers, as this was the signal agreed upon when the boat had arrived at 400 yards (365 metres) from the steamer, ready for discharging her Whiteheads. The *Nordenfelt* carries two torpedoes in the tubes, which can be discharged simultaneously or one after the other, and two spare torpedoes. This was at 10 minutes to 8, and nothing further occurred until after the lapse of 8 minutes, when a grampus-like blowing was heard about a hundred yards away on the port bow, which was afterwards ascertained to have been caused by an attempt to free the whistle from water on the boat emerging from below the surface. Some imagined they could perceive the outline of the *Nordenfelt* near at hand but the majority were sceptical: and it was not until the captain blew a loud blast from his whistle, and exhibited a light to signify that the attack had succeeded, that the spectators had really any tangible evidence of the presence of the enemy, who then was only some 80 yards (75 metres) off. It appeared that Captain Garrett had begun his approach on a slack tide about 7 o'clock, at a cautious speed of not more than 4 knots (7.4kph), and at a depth of 5 feet (1.5 metres) below the surface. The lights of the many craft on the water, and the arrival of a fleet of fishing vessels under sail which showed no lights at all, somewhat confused him. Apprehensive of being run into, he deemed it necessary to rise for observation at every 50 or 60 yards (45 or 55 metres). The attack was very cleverly conducted under great disadvantages, and proved a genuine surprise. Of course, it is quite possible that the electric searchlight might have succeeded in discover-

ing the boat during one of its look-rounds if the sea had been absolutely calm, but it would have disappeared long before any gun could be brought to bear upon it. And even if this were not the case, as only the forward cupola – which is nothing more than a helmet large enough to contain a man's head – would have been visible, the chance of a hit would be exceedingly remote. On the other hand, as the position of the opposing vessel would itself have been clearly defined by the light, the balance of advantage would be on the side of the attack.

The following day the officers were allowed to go over the submarine while it was in dock. As the submerged simulated attacks had been carried out in the dark and they had not seen the vessel submerge this was demonstrated. All vents and hatches were secured and ballast water was admitted to the tanks until the turtle back was under water. All that could then be seen was the casing with the conning towers at either end, and these protruded for about 30 inches (76cm) which included the small glass dome. Garrett started the vertical drive propellers and the submarine submerged by the stern. As soon as the propellers were stopped the submarine 'came up like a cork'. This experiment was carried out several times successfully.

The demonstration was applauded in the *Engineer* which, in its issue of 23 December 1887, suggested: 'We may – we hope we shall – have quite a little fleet of *Nordenfelts* when Christmas comes round again. When once Columbus had shown the way to America, the water was freely traversed.'

The *Army and Navy Gazette* was also very supportive: '. . . a great and assured future before it, that with a gun or two on her turtle back and working as an above water torpedo boat she certainly possessed many advantages over the ordinary first-class torpedo boat, and that her powers of submerging should make her the more valuable craft . . .'

A few weeks after the demonstration Garrett returned to Turkey. At one stage that country had expressed an interest in acquiring a third submarine. Garrett followed this up in his letter to the Turkish Naval Minister Hassam Pasha by offering the Sultan what was a discounted price for the new submarine. However, Turkey had had first-hand experience with the two Nordenfelt submarines that were eventually purchased and although they were about to accept them there were serious misgivings about their underwater performance. It was a true case of *caveat emptor*. Turkey did not follow up the 'special offer'.

Garrett returned to England in due course where trials continued but without a customer there was little enthusiasm.

In the business world an amalgam of firms was about to be formed into a major company. The Barrow Shipbuilding Co. changed its name to The Naval Construction and Armamament Co. in 1887 and in the same year Nordenfelt agreed that Basil Zaharoff could act as their agent. A year later he also became the agent of Vickers. The Nordenfelt Guns and Ammunition Co., which had been formed in 1886, was amalgamated with the Maxim Co. in 1888. The new firm, Maxim Nordenfelt Guns and Ammunition Co., would be able to exploit and combine development of their respective machine-guns. Nordenfelt joined the board of The Naval Construction and Armament Co. in 1888. It was inevitable that Vickers, whose main product was steel and particularly armoured steel, would want to obtain a captive market. This was achieved by acquiring first The Naval Construction and Armament Co. followed by the Maxim Nordenfelt Guns and Ammunition Co. It is ironic that both the original Maxim and Nordenfelt companies were established to develop their own machine-guns; that both deviated, unsuccessfully, to build aircraft and submarines respectively. But later the new Vickers Co. not only built very successful aircraft, but became the lead company for submarines in the UK, and also developed and produced the Vickers machine-gun, which was standard equipment in the British Army for many years.

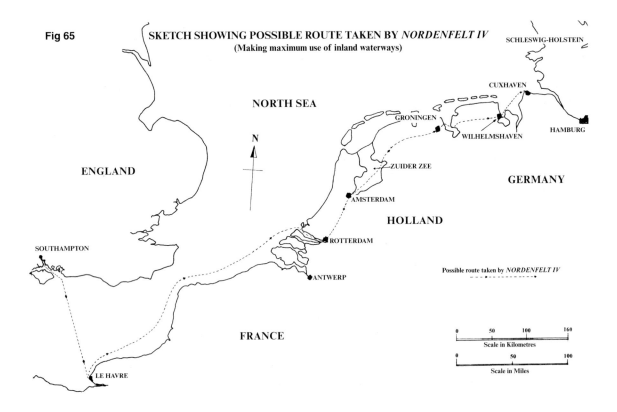

Fig 65

SKETCH SHOWING POSSIBLE ROUTE TAKEN BY *NORDENFELT IV*
(Making maximum use of inland waterways)

Russia was not represented at the Southampton demonstration in December 1887, but *Nordenfelt IV* may well have been seen by the Czar at the Jubilee review. In any case, *Nordenfelt IV* was far from being a secret and the various demonstrations had been well covered by the press. Russia was already developing its own submarines, and she would be well aware that both Turkey and Greece had submarines on her own back doorstep. It is therefore not surprising that this country showed some interest in *Nordenfelt IV*, and a demonstration was duly arranged, for a group of Russian naval officers, in June. In the late summer of 1888 a notice appeared in *The Times* from the Russian Embassy stating that Russia had no intention of purchasing the Nordenfelt submarine. Whether this was to scotch rumours which were perhaps generated by Nordenfelt or a negotiation ploy is not known. However, negotiations did take place and it was agreed that the submarine would be taken to Kronstadt where it would be assessed

and, if it was found to be satisfactory, purchased. Garrett, accompanied by his young son, sailed from Southampton at the end of October accompanied by the yacht *Loadstar*. They went first to Le Havre,

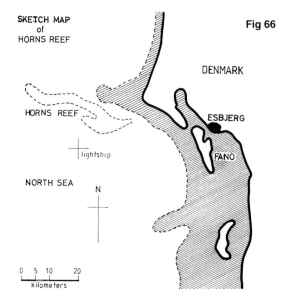

then along the French coast to Holland and through the North Sea Canal to Amsterdam. His son recounted, years later[1], 'that they then passed through the Zuider Zee and on to the German port of Cuxhaven where some engine maintenance was carried out'. By this time the submarine had travelled some 500 odd miles (800km) since leaving Southampton. The son goes on to say: 'we sailed down the Elbe and safely reached the old town of Schleswig-Holstein'.[2] This is very vague. Schleswig is a port on the Baltic, the eastern seaboard of the southern and German part of the Jutland peninsula, which is known as Schleswig-Holstein. As the Kiel canal, giving access to the Baltic, was not opened until 1895, Garrett would have had to travel north/north-east from Cuxhaven over the Elbe estuary and thence up the west coast of Schleswig-Holstein and Denmark so that he could pass through the Skagerrak and Kattegat and thence into the Baltic. Unfortunately he did not get this far.

It is worth recording the son's version of the events which followed.

At one am the following morning both boats grounded on the dreaded Horn Reefs off Blauvans Hook on the coast of Jutland. It was blowing a gale of wind and after futile efforts to kedge the *Loadstar* and navigate the *Nordenfelt* out of the maze of sand banks, at two pm the next day we were forced to abandon them as the bottom of the *Loadstar* had crashed in and the *Nordenfelt* showed signs of rolling over which would have trapped the crew. There was no wireless in those days and no hope of obtaining assistance in time to do any good. We loaded the crews of both vessels in the life boat and dinghy from the *Loadstar* and a Berthen collapsible carried on the submarine. In spite of the heavy sea we reached the little port of Esbierg (*sic*) (Esbjerg) next morning at two am. Next morning we drove overland in carts to the wrecks and found that the natives had stripped them of everything moveable, even the piano from the saloon of the *Loadstar*. With some difficulty and

the payment of a considerable sum we recovered most of our personal belongings.

Although, over the years, much has been made of what Garrett's son went on to say it is repeated to show how the seeds of a myth are sown.

It developed that these people lived by wrecking and helped the good cause along by changing the light on shore to appear the same as the lightship stationed off the reefs. This was brought out in the suit to recover insurance.

The truth is less romantic. The Danish Embassy in London confirmed that wrecking was not practised on this coast at this time, and that the Horns Reef was well marked. Indeed, a lightship was put in position that summer and this is confirmed in the Danish official *Notice to Mariners* covering the period January to 1 May 1888. There it was announced that a lightship would be positioned 'four quarter miles South West of Grunden Vyl on the Horns Reef'. The *Notice* also gave a description of the lightship: 'The vessel is painted red with a white cross and has two masts. From the forward mast – marked with a red hourglass-shaped top mark – a flashing light will appear 30 feet (9 metres) above water with two short flashes every half minute. In fog a foghorn will give two short blasts every two minutes.' In the next issue of the *Notice*, May to September 1888, it was confirmed that the lightship had been positioned at 55 degrees 23.6 North, 7 degrees 45 East.

The tragic loss of *Nordenfelt IV* is germane to the story only because as a consequence she was not purchased by Russia. The cause was most probably human error as there has been no suggestion that there was either a structual or mechanical problem.

The available facts, provided by the son, indicate that the grounding took place at night and it was, or became, windy. The vessels were not finally

---

[1] *Submarines. An account of the first practical submarine boats.* As told by the son of their inventor and commander, William George Garrett

[2] It should be remembered that Garrett's son would have been only about ten years old when he made this voyage and it is was written years after the events. Therefore it is understandable that there are a number of what would appear to be inaccuracies. Even so it is an important historical record in the absence of other material.

abandoned for some thirteen hours and it took a further twelve hours to reach Esbjerg. Neither the exact time of grounding nor, consequently, the state of the tide at the time, have been established, but by remaining with the vessels for thirteen hours this would have allowed the tide to pass through a complete cycle, thus allowing the crews to try and float the two vessels off, at high water.

Garrett's original intention is not known. If he had been going straight for the Skaggerak it would, with hindsight, have been more prudent to have given the reef a wide berth, leaving Blaavands Huk some 25 miles (40 kilometres) to his east. But because of the prevailing conditions he may not have wanted to be so far out to sea. He may have been trying to navigate through the channel to the east of the reef, but the passage was to be made during darkness and navigation, particularly at night, would have been quite difficult. The reef itself does not dry out at low water but in parts it may be covered by less than 10 feet (3 metres) of water. It is also quite shallow along the coast and the shaded area on the sketch map shows those parts which, at low water, may be covered by less than 14¾ feet (4.5 metres) or in some places less than 10 feet (3 metres). The draught of *Nordenfelt IV* would have been about 10 feet (3 metres). Because they were able to go overland by cart to recover their chattels indicates that the submarine had gone aground close to the shoreline rather than on the reef proper, and this in turn suggests that Garrett was either heading for Esbjerg or was attempting to use the inshore passage. The tragedy was probably a straightforward navigational error, possibly because the charts being used did not show the position of the newly-positioned lightship or because of a human error. That two vessels were grounded may indicate that one was blindly following the other.

Nordenfelt IV was recovered and taken to Esbjerg where, because she was beyond economic repair, she was broken up.

Nordenfelt in the meantime was trying to drum up business elsewhere. The United States Government had suddenly taken an interest in the development of submarines and sponsored an open competition to find a suitable submarine for the United States Navy. Exacting criteria had been laid down about both the submarine required and also about funding its building. Nordenfelt submitted a tender, but his proposal was not accepted and the contract was awarded to John Holland. This will be covered in more detail later.

Garrett returned to England and, in January 1889, produced a complete Specification for an 'Apparatus for Generating Vapour for use in Vapour Engines', which was accepted by the Patent Office in April 1889. The Provisional Specification had been lodged with the Patents Office in May 1888. He must have been working on this new idea spasmodically for nine months. This was the last significant work that he did in Europe for the demand for Nordenfelt-Garrett submarines was non-existent and no further development work on submarine boats was carried out by the partnership.

CHAPTER 19

PRE-MORTEM, POST-MORTEM OF THE LIAISON

Before concluding Garrett's working partnership with Nordenfelt it would be appropriate to examine Nordenfelt's submarine philosophy about which he spoke frequently, and once, in particular, at the Institute of Naval Architects. The occasion was a presentation, delivered by Lieutenant G.W. Hovgaard, Royal Danish Navy[1], which was based on his own concept for a submarine. Although covered later it is appropriate to give a brief description of Hovgaard's submersible to set the scene.

Hovgaard's designs were well thought out and, as he is one of those whose work should be considered, it is convenient to examine his proposals now as they are also relevant to Nordenfelt's remarks and will put them into context.

Although he had had no practical experience in constructing either a surface vessel or submarine, Hovgaard had completed a three-year course in Naval Architecture at Greenwich. The theme of his lecture was on the lines that torpedo boats were no longer as effective as they had been because of the development of countermeasures against them which included the searchlight, the machine-gun and anti-torpedo nets. He proposed two solutions. The first was a surface vessel which was made less visible and less vulnerable to the enemy. He discounted putting armour on the existing boats as they would become unstable while still remaining visible. His proposal was that reducing the freeboard would make them less visible. Progressing a stage further, his second solution, was that the boat should be able to submerge.

His presentation then covered proposals for a torpedo boat which could alter its displacement allowing it to run awash thereby offering a very small target to the enemy.

The second part of his presentation consisted of his proposals for a submarine torpedo boat. The criteria he used for his design had been laid down, in late 1887, by the United States Navy Department in a circular inviting proposals for the construction of a submarine for that country. (The American requirements will be considered later, and only selected, salient criteria mentioned by Hovgaard are considered below.) The vessel was to have three conditions:

1 Fully submerged.
2 The covered condition where the boat was to be protected by at least 3 feet (.9 metre) of water but could observe the object of the attack through air.
3 The light condition where she had some freeboard.

Hovgaard's proposed submarine was to be 122 feet (37 metres) long over all, with an 11 foot 9 inches (3.6 metres) beam (Fig 67). There was to be a light metal, free flooding casing with a height of 3 feet (.9 metre). The free flooding openings were designed to have watertight doors which could be closed after the water had drained from the casing on surfacing thereby increasing the positive buoyancy of the surfaced vessel by 8.5 tons. The hull was to be framed internally with 'Z' frames spaced 12 inches (30cm) apart which, with steel plating tapering from 5 to 3 eighths of an inch (16 to 9mm), would give a diving depth of up to 150 feet (45.7 metres). The submarine was to be fitted with a conning tower, stern hydroplanes and a vertical lift propeller fitted amidships. Internally the main power plant would be a vertical compound

[1] A Paper: *Proposed Designs for Surface-Boats and Diving-Boats* by Lieutenant G.W. Hovgaard, Royal Danish Navy, read at the twenty-ninth Session of the Institute of Naval Architects on 23 March 1888 and minutes of the discussion which took place after the presentation.

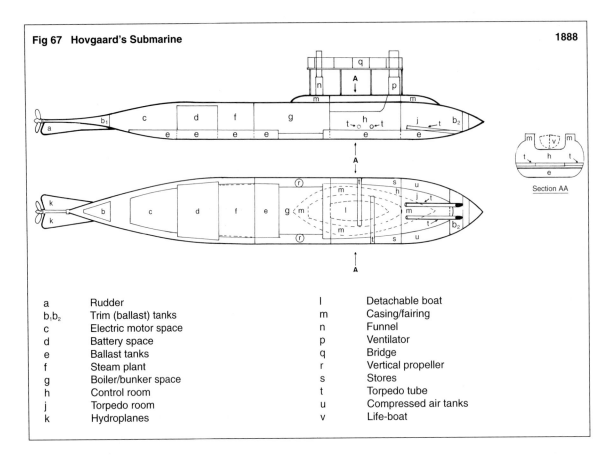

Fig 67 Hovgaard's Submarine   **1888**

Section AA

a	Rudder	l	Detachable boat
b,b₂	Trim (ballast) tanks	m	Casing/fairing
c	Electric motor space	n	Funnel
d	Battery space	p	Ventilator
e	Ballast tanks	q	Bridge
f	Steam plant	r	Vertical propeller
g	Boiler/bunker space	s	Stores
h	Control room	t	Torpedo tube
j	Torpedo room	u	Compressed air tanks
k	Hydroplanes	v	Life-boat

surface-condensing engine developing 600hp at 315 revolutions with a boiler pressure of 125psi (8.5 atmospheres); the speed at full power was estimated to be 14 knots (26kph). Steam propulsion would be used only for surface running. With a bunker capacity of 13.5 tons of coal this would give an endurance of nineteen hours and a range of about 250 miles (400kms). The main propulsion, when submerged, would be an electric motor taking power from 540 electric cells, which would give a submerged endurance of six hours at 5.5 knots (10kph). A smaller electric motor would drive the vertical propeller and, like the Nordenfelt boats, this was automatically controlled by a preset hydrostatic pressure switch. On the surface the electric motor would be used as a dynamo to charge the electric cells.

The ballast tanks would have a capacity of thirty-one tons and their centre of gravity would be well forward. The tanks would be filled in about half a minute and they could be evacuated by electric pump (thirty minutes), steam (twenty minutes), or hand pump (two hours). It was intended that the boat should always retain a small level of positive buoyancy.

The submarine would be armed with two torpedo tubes forward, each containing a 15-inch (381mm) Whitehead torpedo. No spare torpedoes would be carried.

Air purifying equipment was also to be fitted in the submarine. Stale air would be pumped through a solution of caustic soda by a small electric motor, and oxygen would then be added before the air was recirculated through the boat.

Hovgaard admitted that his design could not meet all the criteria which had recently been laid down in the U.S. Navy Specification, which was by then, the new standard for submarines.

Nordenfelt's Philosophy

At the conclusion of the presentation there was a discussion. The first to speak was a visitor to the Institute, Mr T. Nordenfelt, who started by saying:

> I am perfectly unprepared to say anything upon this paper, as it has only been put into my hands at this moment; and I have not seen the drawings or the description.

He went on to say that as a Dane, Hovgaard was a sort of second cousin to the Swedes, and he wished him well in his venture. He acknowledged, as did Hovgaard, that changes may have to be made in the light of practical experience to the various proposals. Nordenfelt then explained his own philosophy:

> I am not quite with Lieutenant Hovgaard in the proposal of having electro-motive power for this reason. Lieutenant Hovgaard admits that when you are on the surface steam power is the most convenient; when you go below, if you keep up your steam pressure you have a certain amount of power stored which, under ordinary circumstances, should be sufficient for the time that you wish to remain below. You must make up your mind, for a boat of this kind, whether you want it only to work inside a port, or whether you want it to work as a sea-going boat. Given that you want it to work as a sea-going boat, and that you wish to go below for a certain given time, you naturally require a certain amount of stored power; but if the boiler power, with the assistance that can conveniently be carried, be not enough for the length of time you require to be below water, I do not for a moment believe that his electric power would fulfil the desired object, because, in the first place, if the water storage is not enough, I would simply add to it a little or build the boat a little bigger; and weight for weight for the given time required, the weight of electrical accumulators with the accessories must become larger than the weight of the water. The weight of the electrical power has the advantage, that if you make arrangements for lying at the bottom of the sea say for twenty-four hours and then to come up, of course most of your store of steam is gone, but I fancy that practically you would never intend to lie fallow for a longer time than a couple of hours. I further believe in a submarine boat being on the surface, but meant now and then to go below water, simplicity is everything, or almost everything. I believe that if you require an electrical engine of Lieutenant Hovgaard's type for certain things, or some other type for other things, with electricians on board, and with the possibility of electrical apparatus getting into trouble through short circuiting and otherwise, I think most men would prefer steam power, and would limit their requirements to what steam power would do. But on this point, as Lieutenant Hovgaard says, we are advancing every day in electricity, and it is possible, though today I cannot admit it, that the accumulators may yet be relied upon even for this purpose. I may be considered too biased to speak about the general use of this kind of boat, but I believe in its usefulness if properly constructed, and I feel fully satisfied that the different powers will be bound to have vessels which, when running as surface boats, present a very small target, and which, when going below, can avoid for a given time the destructive power of the enemy. All the powers in Europe except England and Germany are now studying this subject exceedingly seriously and the United States, as Lieutenant Hovgaard has stated, has issued an invitation tending in that direction. England is under the impression that she does not require them, because she has such a very powerful navy to rely upon for all purposes. I humbly suggest that we have some few outlying stations, and some ports in England and our Colonies, in which, in case of sudden war, perhaps we might not have a powerful man-of-war or an ironclad, or the means of supporting her, in which case a submarine boat might for a time be a warning to the enemy who might suddenly attack us.

Lieutenant Hovgaard did not reply immediately as there was then some discussion on the proposed scantlings and registration of the proposed vessel. When he spoke again Lieutenant Hovgaard's reply was illuminating:

> With respect to the remarks of Mr Nordenfelt as regards electric power compared to steam power, I would just say that I think Mr Nordenfelt is not quite correct in his statement that the weight of the electrical power compares unfavourably with the weight of steam power, because in the boat which Mr Nordenfelt has now just completed, I think I have been given the weight of the hot water cistern as 25 tons. Mr Nordenfelt will be able to tell us whether this figure is correct. The weight of the accumulators and electric machinery put together is 22.5 tons in my design. Moreover the power of endurance of the electric machinery is 5.5 knots (10.1kph) in 6 hours. With the steam machinery in Mr Nordenfelt's boat I understand it to be 5 knots (9.25kph) in 4 hours. As regards the use of electricity in general I feel convinced that in a few years you will see Mr Nordenfelt build a boat with electrical machinery, but that of course is a matter of opinion.

When this presentation was made Nordenfelt had not sold *Nordenfelt IV* to Russia, and therefore he was still fully committed to the steam-only propulsion system as that was all he had to offer. It is understandable therefore that he argued strongly against the use of electric propulsion although some of his arguments were rather thin. He vented some of his frustration when he pointed out that many of the major powers were considering the submarine option very seriously but the United Kingdom was showing no interest whatsoever.

The End of the Garrett – Nordenfelt Liaison

Although much had been going on elsewhere while Garrett and Nordenfelt were building their own submarines the pace of development speeded up during the last decade of the century. Unfortunately they themselves were not destined to play major roles in the submarine success story that was now unfolding. Indeed, they did not even have walk-on parts. Their liaison died, but it seems to have been a rather slow and lingering death because no real submarine development took place after *Nordenfelt IV* had been launched in 1887 and thereafter their efforts were concentrated on selling that vessel.

There are a number of possible reasons which prompted Nordenfelt to terminate the liaison. He was, first and foremost, a business man and the speculative building of *Nordenfelt IV* had not been a success. Generally there was very little international interest by Governments to purchase submarines. Only the French, and, to a lesser extent, the United States and Russia, were officially intent on incorporating submarines into their navies and they were largely using their own internal development and building resources. Efforts to break into these markets had not been successful.

There is also a very strong probability that Nordenfelt was 'warned off' by the British Establishment which considered that the Royal Navy did not need submarines and that other nations, particularly the less powerful, should not be encouraged to have them because of the danger they posed. This could have been in the form of an ultimatum by the Admiralty advising him that if he persisted with his interests in developing, designing and building submarines, which were not in the interest of the UK, his position as supplier of arms and ammunition to the British fleet and to the British colonies would be jeopardised. As far as he was concerned, it was as an arms manufacturer that he had made his money. Presented with such an ultimatum, it would have been most unlikely that he would have deserted that part of the business which had a well-established market, and still had a good potential. Nordenfelt had probably made very little profit from his deviation into the manufacture of submarines. He did not actually have a very satisfactory product and there did not appear to be any more potential customers. To have persisted in it would have necessitated designing and building another 'speculative' boat;

this would have been costly with the possibility that, like *Nordenfelt IV*, it would be difficult to sell. If an ultimatum was issued it was probably unnecessary. With the given situation it made good business sense to pull out.

Another factor was the business amalgamations that had taken place or were about to take place in the near future at Barrow. When running his own company, Nordenfelt would have had a free hand to follow his whims and instincts. But this changed as the companies were amalgamated and others started to dictate what would happen within the new firms. Certainly the new arms consortium which was about to evolve and would be supplying the British Government with warships, steel, and weapons, did not want to jeopardise its relationship with its main customer by not toeing the official line, particularly as the production of submarines was, at this time, not a profitable venture. But things would change at Barrow-in-Furness during the next few years.

What had gone wrong? Or perhaps it would be better to ask what had not gone right? In the beginning there was *The Egg* and the initial experiments and subsequent modifications appear to have developed logically until the vessel worked. Although others had built similar vessels, achieving similar results these were not well documented and therefore it was a sound base from which Garrett could develop his larger, steam-powered boat. *Resurgam* was less successful; she was underpowered and probably very unstable when submerged. Garrett had proved, as had many others before him, that ballast tanks were essential but these had been omitted from the *Resurgam* design. Probably Garrett realised that even had *Resurgam* not been lost, without major changes she really had no future.

The liaison with Nordenfelt was a necessity in that Garrett needed both the financial support and building facilities that Nordenfelt could provide. However, Nordenfelt as the backer presumably had the final say in any decision making and with his aversion to the use of electrical propulsion he could have stifled development in this direction.

Perhaps this is not fair to Nordenfelt; it may well have been Garrett, who strongly supported his own adaptation of the Lamm engine, who was not prepared to switch to another, newer technology. In either case this limited development.

It is interesting that two men, who had been closely associated with Garrett while he was building *Resurgam* and *Nordenfelt I*, designed and built their own submarines (both of which are covered later). James Waddington, who had worked at Cochrans, set up his own business and took out a patent for a submarine-boat in 1885. Suffice to say at this point, that the submarine incorporated some very novel ideas and worked. L. E. Enroth worked at the Palmcrantz yard in Sweden during the construction of *Nordenfelt I* and his design 'attracted special attention' in a French submarine competition in 1896. Both these men were very capable and it is interesting to speculate whether or not Garrett used their talents.

The main problem, as far as both Garrett and Nordenfelt were concerned, was that they were ten years too early. In the early eighties they had produced a credible power pack which drove the submarine both on the surface and under the water, in a vessel which carried its own fuel. This had not been done effectively before. The steam engine they used was an innovative adaptation of an established, tried principle (albeit on tramways). Compressed air engines had been used before in submarines, but the boats had a very limited range and did not carry the machinery required to recharge the compressed air supply on board. At that time they were perhaps right not to use the petrol engine as it was as yet unreliable and in a submarine could be dangerous. Others had used the electric motor and, although it was in its infancy, it did work. Simply put, Nordenfelt did have an aversion to this form of power. In any case the combination of steam and electricity would not have been as ideal as the petrol engine and electric motor which gave instant power in either mode and was not dependent on raising a head of steam if the boat had been submerged for some time. In 1885–88 Nordenfelt and Garrett were well abreast or even ahead of their main rivals and other inventors. But they failed to maintain their lead by refining and further developing their product.

The Nordenfelt boats had not evolved or developed in the true sense in that although they were made larger they were not better and they retained the same major faults.

Without Nordenfelt's backing and ability to promote the submarines Garrett may have achieved much less than he did. Together their PR was good and Nordenfelt had the right contacts although this did not do them very much good. Certainly all the available press reports on the performance of the various boats are quite favourable. This is understandable. The reporters writing the articles had no criteria against which the *Nordenfelts* could be properly compared and they were undoubtedly impressed as the boats surged through the water and at times disappeared. They would have been given, in most cases, an enthusiastic and very favourable briefing by Nordenfelt or Garrett who, quite naturally, would have extolled their product. This was then reflected in most of the subsequent articles. The press was on their side and tried to encourage the Government to buy Nordenfelt submarines. For instance, after one of the demonstrations of *Nordenfelt IV* there was the glowing report, already mentioned, in a reputable periodical which went on to suggest: 'We may – we hope we shall – have quite a little fleet of *Nordenfelts* when Christmas comes round again'.

There is a general lack of official assessments of these boats. As far as is known only three men ever travelled in *Resurgam* and for many years it was only Garrett's press interview and later his log which told the world how successful this boat had been on its one and only significant voyage. What else could be expected? He was hardly going to criticise his own invention and thereby jeopardise its future. By the time Price wrote his story nearly fifty years had elapsed and much had been forgotten. In any case he was telling a yarn rather than assessing the boat.

There are a couple of comments on *Nordenfelt IV* which most probably were based on the official report by the United States Naval Attaché who attended one of the demonstrations at Southampton[2]:

> In an exhibition of one of these boats (*Nordenfelt IV*) given last month, the main features accentuated by the exhibitors were that the boat awash was more difficult to make out than another boat of greater freeboard – a fact that would seem to need no very extensive proof – that she was always buoyant, a property that, as has been shown, is common to all submarine boats worthy of the name, and which she possesses in a much less degree than she might were she constructed on common sense principles for real submerged work, for which she showed less capacity than the small American boats. The showing of submerging qualities consisted of hauling the boat down to the bottom of a dock by means of her down haul propellers, and then allowing her to rise by her own small buoyancy, thus exhibiting the application of a general principle that could have been just as well shown, and with just as much bearing on real submarine boat work, by pushing a cork under the surface of the water and then allowing it to bob up ... and the Nordenfelts are apparently failures in all respects save surface speed and fuel endurance, and their trials show nothing of practical use.

These comments in no way reflect the glowing press accounts which had been published. But if this is the damning view of professional sailors it is no wonder that there were no buyers for *Nordenfelt IV*.

It is not really surprising that the Nordenfelt – Garrett liaison was terminated. Had the British Establishment shown some interest there would have been a reason to continue. However, had they continued, there would have had to be a reassessment of what they were producing. Moreover, unless they could have been more flexible in their approach they still would have failed to succeed.

In 1890 Garrett, accompanied by his family, emigrated to the United States of America, to start a new life.

---

[2] *Proceedings of the United States Naval Institute*, Vol XIV of 1888.

CHAPTER 20

MINOR DEVELOPMENTS
UP TO 1900

While Garrett was building *The Egg* and *Resurgam*, and later when he was working with Nordenfelt, other inventors were building submarines or writing theses about them. There were many ideas and proposals put forward which contributed in some way to man's knowledge and ability to construct a better submarine. But with very few exceptions, which are highlighted below, there were no major breakthroughs until the end of the century. There were of course a few, to say the least, impractical proposals. The major advances took place on the international stage in those countries where inventors were encouraged and or financially supported by Governments and Navies which recognised the importance of the submarine. Inevitably there were a few sound proposals which, had they had the necessary financial support and official backing, could have been developed successfully.

Although between 1879 and 1900 many individuals, from all parts of the world, came forward with new ideas and designs, the character of development was changing. Several Governments were becoming interested in submarines. Some had even started to encourage research and development. During the first part of the period, submarines were a domestic national consideration. But this was about to alter and become more international, although the national self-interest would dominate. But perhaps the greatest change was that, during this period, several eminent inventor-designers had emerged and they dominated the scene from the United States to Russia. It is easier to consider their work as a whole rather than dealing with overall developments chronologically, and this will be done on a national basis. Before doing this, however, some of the miscellaneous inventions, for that is now what they are, will be considered.

In 1878 Mortensen, an American engineer, designed a vessel with no new innovations except that he proposed to have a torpedo tube in the bows of his vessel. In 1879 Mr Leggo resurrected an idea proposed by Bauer in his first boat. This was the use of a weight which could be moved backwards and forwards within the hull: first the weight would be moved towards the bow, which was consequently forced down and the vessel would dive. Then, by feeding gas into a flotation bag, the vessel would rise towards the surface. The process would be repeated after ascending by allowing the gas to escape and again moving the weight forward. Theoretically the vessel would progress like a dolphin or a porpoise.

A proposal put forward by Messrs Berkley and Hotchkiss of Paris was for a submersible which was driven by a steam engine. The design of the hull was not remarkable, but attached to it, on either side, were two long cork floats (Fig 68). These were mounted on a davit-type arrangement. By lowering them the hull would rise and by raising them above the submersible the hull would be suspended below water and the cork would afford some protection from enemy fire. This vessel was also armed with an internal bow torpedo tube. The submersible was never built and Hotchkiss is probably better remembered for the machine-gun which he designed.

Old ideas were still being resurrected, adapted, modified, and developed. One such was the variable displacement submersible designed by Andrew Campbell and James Ash in 1885 (Fig 69). These innovative ideas and designs kept emerging but few of them added anything significant to the

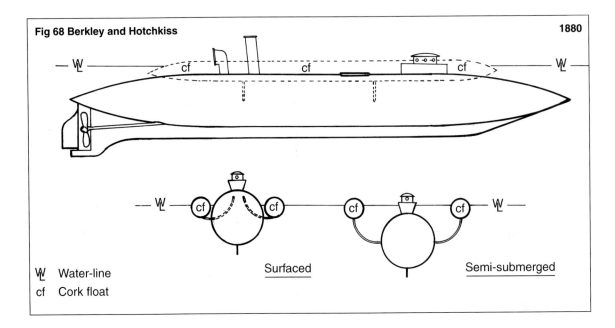

Fig 68 Berkley and Hotchkiss   1880

Surfaced   Semi-submerged

W̲   Water-line
cf   Cork float

development of the submarine. They are of interest, simply to show how inventive and even imaginative the Victorian engineer was.

Frequently patents were taken out for the proverbial 'all singing all dancing machine' which could also perform miraculously. For example in 1881 Mr S.J. Woodhouse took out a patent for a submarine driven by compressed air engines and submerged using ballast tanks at the bow and stern. The shape of the vessel was somewhat different than those seen before in that it was a cylinder with a cone at the bow but blunt at the stern. Along its top there was a casing mounted in which was a conventional naval cannon. A torpedo tube was mounted in the bow. The vessel was fitted with two engines, one turning a conventional propeller at the stern and the other working two paddle-wheels towards the front of the boat. The submarine carried a diving bell which could be lowered through folding doors in the bottom of the boat. The conning tower also doubled

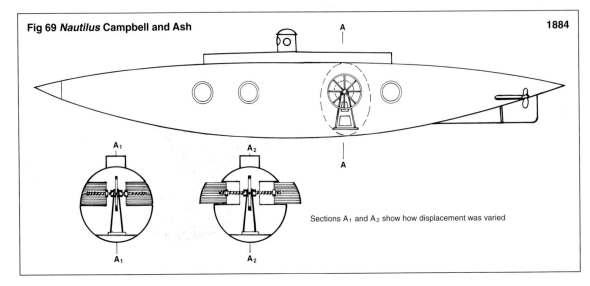

Fig 69 *Nautilus* Campbell and Ash   1884

A

A

A₁   A₂

A₁   A₂

Sections A₁ and A₂ show how displacement was varied

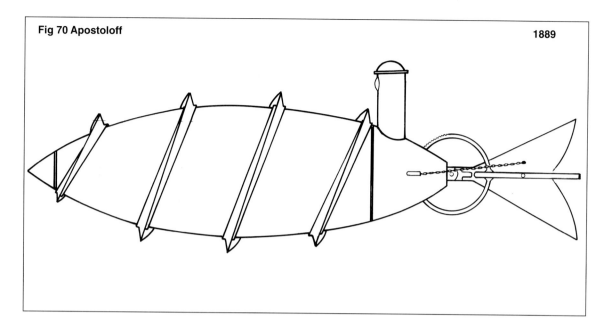

Fig 70 Apostoloff

1889

up as a lift between the upper and lower decks.

Other ideas were tried. Possibly inspired by the vessel designed by Berkley and Hotchkiss, a French engineer, Lagane, designed a submersible 91 feet (28 metres) long. The crew's accommodation and machinery space were contained in a steel hull which was supported in the water by a very solid wooden hull on top which was also to provide a form of 'armoured' protection. The boat, which was to be powered by a conventional steam engine and stern propeller, was armed with a torpedo tube and also a spare torpedo.

Very elaborate theories were aired. For example, that put forward by Mr T. Todorasco from Moldavia, for maintaining a constant depth. His system consisted of a series of plungers, working on hydrostatic pressure, controlling the level of water ballast using compressed air. A further refinement was the use of mercury to regulate the load on the plungers so that the vessel could be kept at a constant depth. To maintain stability or equilibrium four of these devices would be fitted to the submarine. It was complicated. The fittings would have had to be very precisely engineered, and it is possible that it would have been susceptible to jamming from even the smallest particles picked up in the sea water.

Ingenious but perhaps not very practical designs still kept appearing. One was the Apostoloff 'submarine with the turning body' (Fig 70). The rudder and hydroplanes, fitted at the stern of the submarine, were shaped like a fish's tail, giving the boat a fish-like appearance. Between the extremities of the hull, and within the boat was an axle on which the central part, the outside of which was fitted with an Archimedes screw, turned. The compressed-air engine, which turned the hull, was housed in the central part of the boat. The helmsman's position was in the conning tower which was at the stern of the vessel. Above it the vessel could carry a boat-like structure supported from the extremities of the vessel. This was for carrying passengers and in an emergency could be released to float to the surface. The inventor claimed that his boat would cross the Atlantic in twenty-eight hours; perhaps it was this claim that encouraged some entrepreneurs to register a company to exploit the potential of the submarine; 'The Lightning Express Submarine Navigation Syndicate Ltd'. In this case there was no potential to exploit.

Five years later, a Venezuelan, Sebastien Lacavalerie, designed a similar submarine, which

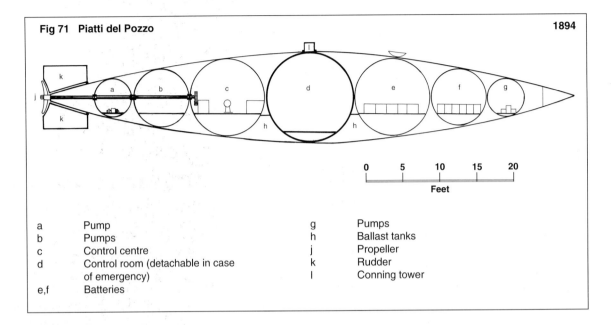

Fig 71 Piatti del Pozzo 1894

a	Pump	g	Pumps
b	Pumps	h	Ballast tanks
c	Control centre	j	Propeller
d	Control room (detachable in case	k	Rudder
	of emergency)	l	Conning tower
e,f	Batteries		

looked even more like a fish. His vessel was equipped with an electric motor and had a series of fins at the stern to steer the boat both vertically and horizontally. The conning tower was also positioned at the stern but in a fin.

An interesting design was put forward by Piatti del Pozzo in 1894. The exterior shape of his vessel, which was 74 feet (22.5 metres) long, was quite ordinary but it housed a series of spheres (Fig 71). These were all self-contained and it was not possible for the crew to move from one to the other. The spheres housed the pumps (a and b), the compressed-air engine, compressed-air containers, and steering gear (c), batteries and accumulators (e and f), pumps (g). The control room and crew quarters were in (d), which, in case of an emergency, could be released from the vessel, to float to the surface. The ballast tanks were in the lower part of the boat at (h). The vessel had a conventional propeller (j) and rudders (k). The spherical compartments gave the submarine the potential to dive deeper than the normally-designed contemporary submarines.

Two other engineers, F. Forrest of France, and Degli Abbati of Italy, independently produced designs for submarines with an elliptical cross-section. While Messrs Freese and Gawn from the United States developed a hose which could be deployed from a reel in the submarine to collect air from the surface. An Englishman, called Watkins, proposed a submarine with telescopic ends which could be adjusted hydraulically to alter the displacement of the vessel.

Although inventions, or resurrected inventions, were still being announced, important patents were also being taken out for fittings and attachments for submarines. Andrew Campbell designed a water lock to allow men to leave and enter the submarine under water. By using water from the ballast tanks, or the bilges to flood the chamber rather than directly from the sea he hoped that the equilibrium of the vessel would not be upset. Stenhouse and Fenoulhet designed, and patented, a propeller guard. At the other end of the spectrum, patents were being taken out for high-speed submarines which all promised considerable endurance. The criteria for this always seems to have been the ability to cross the Atlantic in forty-eight hours; these rapidly disappeared into obscurity!

CHAPTER 21

MORE SIGNIFICANT
DEVELOPMENTS UP TO 1900

In Sweden L.E. Enroth, who had worked at the A.B. Palmcrantz and Co. yard when *Nordenfelt I* was being constructed, designed his own submarine. His boat was 82 feet (25 metres) long with a 13-foot (4-metre) beam, a surfaced displacement of 142 tons and a submerged displacement of 146 tons (Fig 72). She had twin propellers, each driven by a triple expansion engine of 100hp. Power was derived from two oil-fired boilers; submerged, latent energy was used, but without having large reservoirs like the Nordenfelt boat. When the steam stored in the boilers was exhausted, hot compressed air was used. The funnel was mounted horizontally and the fumes were forced out by a screw arrangement; two air funnels or vents, which could be retracted into the hull, were fitted immediately behind the second conning cupola. There were two cylindrical fuel tanks in line amidships in the bilge; each of these cylinders was fitted with a piston which pushed the fuel out and at the same time drew in sea water to compensate for the loss of weight.

The four ballast tanks, which had a combined four-ton capacity, were positioned on the flanks of the oil fuel tanks. At either end of the vessel there were large air reservoirs into which air was compressed by a pump when on the surface. The sub-

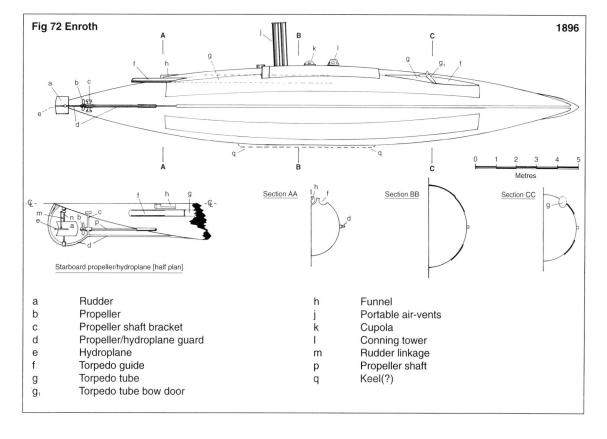

a	Rudder	h	Funnel
b	Propeller	j	Portable air-vents
c	Propeller shaft bracket	k	Cupola
d	Propeller/hydroplane guard	l	Conning tower
e	Hydroplane	m	Rudder linkage
f	Torpedo guide	p	Propeller shaft
g	Torpedo tube	q	Keel(?)
g₁	Torpedo tube bow door		

Fig 72 Enroth   1896

Starboard propeller/hydroplane [half plan]

Section AA   Section BB   Section CC

Metres

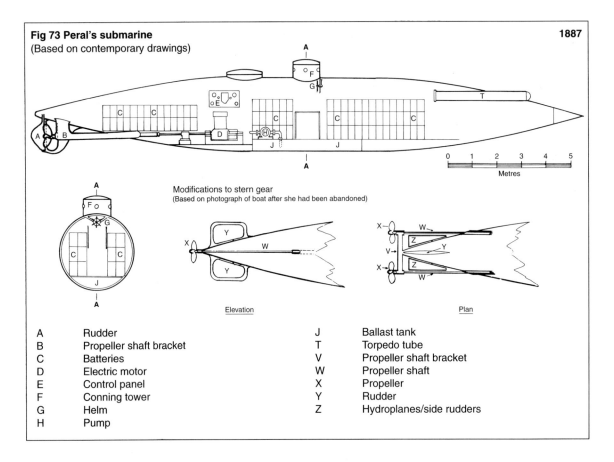

Fig 73 Peral's submarine
(Based on contemporary drawings)

1887

Modifications to stern gear
(Based on photograph of boat after she had been abandoned)

Elevation

Plan

A	Rudder	J	Ballast tank
B	Propeller shaft bracket	T	Torpedo tube
C	Batteries	V	Propeller shaft bracket
D	Electric motor	W	Propeller shaft
E	Control panel	X	Propeller
F	Conning tower	Y	Rudder
G	Helm	Z	Hydroplanes/side rudders
H	Pump		

marine was armed with four torpedoes mounted in tubes (two forward and two astern) on top of the hull. Enroth calculated that the surface speed was 12 knots (22kph) and submerged 10.5 knots (19kph). This vessel certainly had some interesting features. The design was offered to and rejected by the Swedish Government. In 1896, it was entered in a 'French Submarine Competition', where according to the *Engineer*, 'it attracted special attention'. In the light of this international acclaim the design was accepted by the Swedish Government and the submarine was built and launched in 1902. But by this time Enroth's boat was dated.

In Germany, whilst publicly ridiculing the submarine, a quiet interest was being taken in the development of this new weapon. In 1890 two submarines were built and these were based on the earlier Nordenfelt boats. Like their forebears they

also proved to be unsatisfactory.

Another German boat, which is accredited to Karl Leps, was built at Kiel in 1897. She was about 46 feet (14 metres) long and was powered by an electric motor driving a four-bladed propeller. She was equipped with stern hydroplanes and a single rudder mounted forward of the single screw. Compressed air was carried to evacuate the ballast tanks, but this had to be replenished from a shore base. The submarine was armed with one forward, internal torpedo tube. There was no conning tower as such, but a diver's helmet was fitted to the top centre of the hull to afford the captain a very limited view of the outside world. The vessel did not have much potential for development and was scrapped in 1902.

Germany's main concern was the build-up of her surface fleet and she did not want to squander her resources on the development of vessels which had not yet proved their worth.

In Spain, with Government support, Lieutenant Isaac Luis Peral built a twin-screw electric boat fitted with a bow torpedo tube which fired the Schwartzkopf torpedo. The vessel was launched in 1887 and, although reports indicate that the trials were satisfactory, Peral failed to obtain further Government funds to build an improved version of his submarine (Fig 73). It is interesting to note that a few years later an American military observer stated that had such vessels been deployed during the Puerto Rico war they would have posed an enormous threat to the U.S. fleet and could have influenced events.

In England, the latest Nordenfelt-Garrett boat, *Nordenfelt IV*, was no longer worth considering. It had been demonstrated to the world, but had been rejected. Only one other important submarine was built but without the required support, sponsorship and financial backing it ended up as a rusting hulk when possibly, with the right encouragement, it could have put the United Kingdom on par with developments in France and possibly the United States.

In his wake Garrett had left a flurry of activity. After leaving Birkenhead, James Franklin Waddington, who had been employed at Cochrans during the building of *Resurgam*, took out a patent on his own submarine in 1885. His boat was 37 feet (11.25 metres) long with a 6-foot 6 inch (2-metre) beam and was made of steel (Fig 74). In shape it was similar to the early Nordenfelt boats but the hydroplanes were at the stern. Inside there were two bulkheads dividing the interior into three compartments; the central one containing the machinery etc while those fore and aft stored air. The single propeller was driven by an electric motor which drew its power from batteries stored below the deck. The submarine was also fitted with propellers to move the boat in the vertical plane; these were housed in two tubular shafts, on the centre line, on the inboard side of the air reservoirs. The vertical propellers were driven by small electric motors

which, like the aft hydroplanes, could be controlled by a pendulum arrangement to maintain the trim of the vessel. Additionally there were 'side rudders', similar to those fitted to *Resurgam*, and these were operated manually by the helmsman. There was a mid-ship ballast tank which could be evacuated by a pump driven from the propeller shaft or by a hand pump. The submarine was designed to always retain an element of positive buoyancy.

As a safety measure, a weight was attached to the bottom of the boat which, in the case of an emergency, could be released from within the boat immediately giving her a surplus of positive buoyancy. The submarine was also fitted with a depth gauge, an electric searchlight, a patent log, and a camera obscura. An air lock so that articles could be passed to and from the submarine when submerged was positioned forward of the conning tower. It was envisaged that on a larger boat this could be adapted to be used by a man. It was the intention that two Whitehead torpedoes should be carried in brackets, between the conning tower and central side rudders, which could be launched from within the vessel.

In the *Complete Specification*, Waddington claimed that he was patenting four ideas in relation to a submarine actuated and controlled by electric power:

1 The vessel, as described in the patent, with storage cells, accumulators or batteries and additional 'dynamic machines or electo motors' to drive the propeller and other mechanism.
2 The combination of the stern hydroplanes, pendulum control and electric power to maintain a horizontal course.
3 The combination of the watertight compartments, the ballast tanks, and the side rudders to control the vessel under water.
4 The vessel, as described in the patent, less the tubular mounted vertical screws and the torpedo brackets and firing gear.

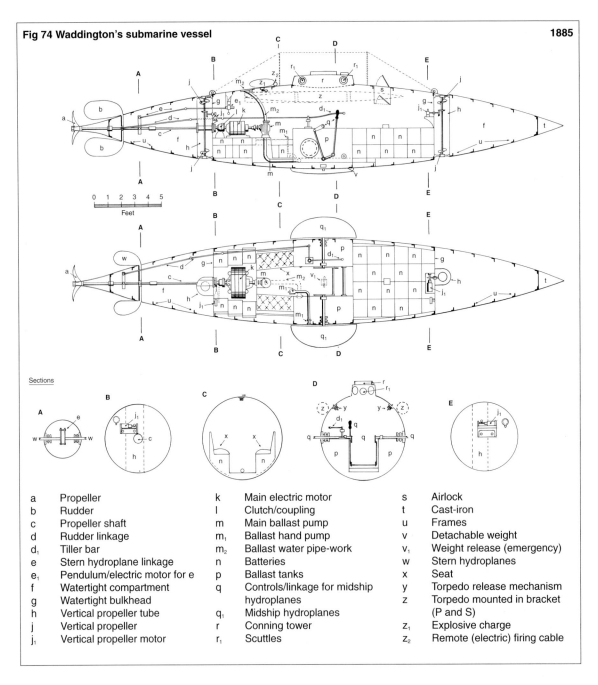

Fig 74 Waddington's submarine vessel　　　　　　　　　　　　　　　　　　1885

Sections

a	Propeller	k	Main electric motor
b	Rudder	l	Clutch/coupling
c	Propeller shaft	m	Main ballast pump
d	Rudder linkage	m_1	Ballast hand pump
d_1	Tiller bar	m_2	Ballast water pipe-work
e	Stern hydroplane linkage	n	Batteries
e_1	Pendulum/electric motor for e	p	Ballast tanks
f	Watertight compartment	q	Controls/linkage for midship
g	Watertight bulkhead		hydroplanes
h	Vertical propeller tube	q_1	Midship hydroplanes
j	Vertical propeller	r	Conning tower
j_1	Vertical propeller motor	r_1	Scuttles

s	Airlock
t	Cast-iron
u	Frames
v	Detachable weight
v_1	Weight release (emergency)
w	Stern hydroplanes
x	Seat
y	Torpedo release mechanism
z	Torpedo mounted in bracket
	(P and S)
z_1	Explosive charge
z_2	Remote (electric) firing cable

Waddington had replaced the steam engine with the electric motor; except that his were electrically controlled, most of the systems he used had been tried before. There was no need to concede that Garrett had used side rudders in *Resurgam* because this idea had never been patented. In any case they had been used by others much earlier. He did acknowledge that the vertical propellers, mounted in tubes, had been used before; these had been introduced by Jos. Jones of Liverpool in about 1887, when he designed a submarine, which apparently never got beyond the working model stage. But the concept of the vertical propeller could be traced back to Bushnell.

Waddington, who by this time had his own yard at Seacombe, built his submarine after patenting it. It was launched the following year (1886) and named *Porpoise*. She was very advanced. Regrettably there do not appear to be any reports of trials and very few comments about her in the press.

Fortunately A.H. Burgoyne wrote about her in his book *Submarine Navigation Past and Present*. The submarine was credited with a range of 250 miles (400km) at 'moderate speed'; at full power the speed was 8 knots (15kph) and this could be maintained for ten hours. The combination of stern and central hydroplanes, tube mounted vertical propellers, relatively small ballast tank amidships and the centrally positioned working area for the two-man crew probably gave the boat reasonable longitudinal stability. The helmsman controlled the vessel from the conning tower where he had 'steering apparatus, speed and course indicators'. Unfortunately Burgoyne does not describe the course indicator but it was probably some form of compass. The helmsman also had a camera obscura which allowed him to see the surface of the sea above him.

The weapon fit consisted of two torpedoes, carried externally on either side of the conning tower. The releasing mechanism automatically started their engines. A high explosive mine was carried immediately behind the conning tower; this could be released under an enemy ship and detonated on contact or electrically when the submarine had withdrawn to a safe distance. The second crewman was responsible for the machinery, ballast tanks and air supply. The air was purified by passing it over caustic alkali or other absorbent chemicals and additional fresh air could be taken from the fore and aft air compartments where it was stored under pressure. This compressed air could also be used to evacuate the ballast tank if the pump failed.

There is an eyewitness report which records sightings of the vessel around Liverpool docks[1]. The author of the article about Garrett was searching for people who had a personal experience of *Resurgam* and he found a tugboat man who had some memories but these transpired to be of *Porpoise*:

> I was then working on a vessel lying near the Victoria Wharf, Birkenhead and saw the first submarine going through some of her trials in the East Float. Her favourite run was from the Grain Warehouse to the entrance to the Egerton Dock. Her movements were slow and how she was propelled I cannot say. But on her trials I saw her being submerged. By the ripples made on the surface you could always tell where she was, and now and then would see her diver-shaped helmet come to the surface. I suppose that was to fix her position. I heard that she was the invention of a clergyman, and thought that he was probably a relative of Mr Waddington, for after the trials she was put into his yard at Seacombe.

The author of the article, who interviewed the tugboat man, acknowledged that this was not *Resurgam* but *Porpoise*. This conclusion makes sense. The way the tugboat man refers to '. . . her favourite run was from. . .' implies that she did this often or certainly on several occasions. *Resurgam* was not in the water at Birkenhead long enough to have 'regular runs' and her trials would have been very limited. In any case, when *Resurgam* was undergoing her very brief trials Waddington was still working at Cochrans and had not established his own yard at Seacombe, therefore the sightings must have been later than *Resurgam*'s departure from Liverpool.

A contemporary news item[2] stated that the *Porpoise* had been 'tried at Liverpool with success' and then goes on to describe the boat. This adds little to the Patent Specification but it goes on to say that vessel had been fitted with: 'the most powerful installation of electrical power ever fitted to a boat.

[1] *Sea Breezes*, March 1922
[2] *Broad Arrow*, 3 April 1886

This work had been carried out by Messrs Perry and Cox of Liverpool, and the electric batteries and cells had been provided by the Electrical Storage Company of London.' It also noted one of the advantages of the submarine which was: 'that it could be carried on davits on a warship, where its batteries could be charged by the ship's dynamo, and it would be always ready for instant action'. At least the Press tried to help the early inventors and builders but unfortunately the right people either were not reading their articles or if they were, were taking them with a pinch of salt.

The design of *Porpoise* was well thought out. Without any authoritative comment on her detailed performance, her two main faults would appear to be that she used the two vertical propellers and that there was no means of charging the batteries on board. Although she did have a good range of operation without a re-charge, and there was the option of carrying her on a 'mother' warship.

Waddington, like both Garrett and Nordenfelt, failed to raise any interest in the Establishment or the Royal Navy for his invention. It is not known if he tried to raise capital in any other way or whether he himself funded the building of *Porpoise*. In some ways *Porpoise* could be considered to be a second generation development, in that Waddington was at Cochrans during the building and trials of *The Egg* and had, most probably, witnessed the initial runs of *Resurgam* before she left Liverpool. It is a great shame that Waddington's first and only, submarine was not developed, as it showed much promise and that he did not have the opportunity to develop his talent. After rusting away on the shore at Waddington's yard *Porpoise* was eventually broken up and sold for scrap. Waddington himself eventually emigrated to the United States.

As will be seen presently, the development of a submarine which was acceptable to be commissioned as a naval vessel, was a slow, painstaking business, progressing through many different stages some of which may not be successful. The inventor needed to be rich or have financial backing and the ability to further develop, adapt, and modify his own ideas while maintaining an open mind on the use of other technologies. To do this the inventor first had to establish himself by producing some hardware which worked. Or, failing this, to get himself into a position where he could convince others that his proposals were sound and warranted support for further development. Certainly in England, at this time, such support was difficult to find.

In Russia, Drzewieki, having been told to develop his first invention by the Russian Government, produced his first four-man submersible in 1879.[3] This was larger than his first boat, measuring nearly 20 feet 6 inches (6.3 metres) in length and crewed by four men sitting two abreast and back to back. With pedals they turned the two propellers (one at either end of the boat). The propellers were moveable; the forward one in the vertical plane to help the boat submerge and surface, and that in the stern in the horizontal plane which was also used to steer the small vessel. The boat was fitted with ballast tanks which were filled and emptied by a pump driven off one of the propeller shafts. There was also a moveable weight which was used to overcome longitudinal instability. Compressed air was carried to replace stale air and there was a second pump, again driven off a propeller shaft, for air circulation. The submarine was also fitted with a conning tower with ports and a tube through which the surface could be observed when submerged. Two explosive charges were carried and these were a form of limpet mine which could be attached to the hulls of enemy ships with rubber devices. The Russian Government was so impressed with the progress made by Drzewieki that fifty similar submarines were ordered.

Three years later a modified version, *Drzewieki*

---

[3] For their own convenience early historians often allocated numbers to a builder's submersibles to differentiate between different versions or developments. Theoretically this submersible should have been called *No II* as Drzewieki's first boat, *No I*, was built in 1877. However, in early records this boat did not appear to be allocated a number and the next two models are shown as *II* and *III*. To avoid confusing the situation further this convention, in respect of the subsequent Drzewieki boats will continue to be followed and they will be referred to as *II* and *III* and this boat as the first four-man boat.

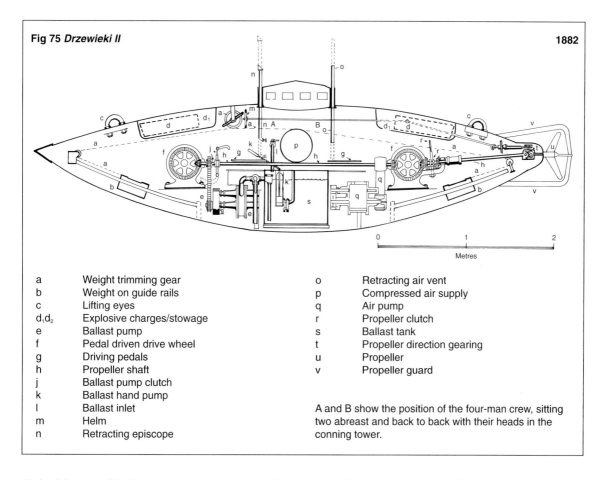

Fig 75 *Drzewieki II*   1882

a	Weight trimming gear	o	Retracting air vent
b	Weight on guide rails	p	Compressed air supply
c	Lifting eyes	q	Air pump
$d_1 d_2$	Explosive charges/stowage	r	Propeller clutch
e	Ballast pump	s	Ballast tank
f	Pedal driven drive wheel	t	Propeller direction gearing
g	Driving pedals	u	Propeller
h	Propeller shaft	v	Propeller guard
j	Ballast pump clutch		
k	Ballast hand pump		
l	Ballast inlet	A and B show the position of the four-man crew, sitting	
m	Helm	two abreast and back to back with their heads in the	
n	Retracting episcope	conning tower.	

II, had been built. It was very similar to the first four-man boat but the forward propeller was omitted and the stern propeller could be moved in both the horizontal and vertical planes (Fig 75).

By 1884 the inventor had recognised that man-power to drive the submarine was inadequate and he fitted his next boat, *Drzewieki III*, with an electric motor and accumulators (Fig 76). Thus powered, the vessel could achieve 4 knots (7.4kph). In outward appearance the vessel was the same as the second version except that she was fitted with a conventional propeller as well as a rudder. It was possible to reduce the crew to two, which was in fact necessary because of the extra weight of the accumulators that had to be carried. Eventually, with a change of minister, it was decided that these small submarines would

serve little purpose and Drzewieki went on to design a larger boat.

France was making much more progress because her Government had recognised the significance of the submarine and its potential. Research was officially sanctioned and financially supported. In 1885 Monsieur Goubet built an electric submarine which was 16.4 feet (5 metres) long, with a beam of 3.2 feet (1 metre) and a height of 5.8 feet (1.76 metres) (Fig 77). Stability of the vessel was achieved with a pendulum arrangement which controlled the movement of water between the ballast tanks at the bow and stern. Under the boat was a large weight which could be dropped in an emergency restoring positive buoyancy to the vessel. This weight contributed to the stability of the boat when submerged. The single propeller was

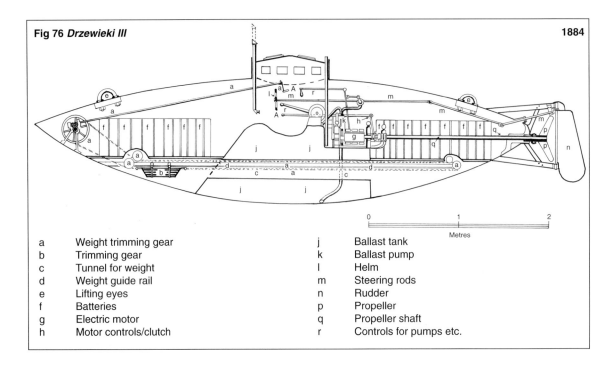

Fig 76 *Drzewieki III*   **1884**

a	Weight trimming gear		j	Ballast tank
b	Trimming gear		k	Ballast pump
c	Tunnel for weight		l	Helm
d	Weight guide rail		m	Steering rods
e	Lifting eyes		n	Rudder
f	Batteries		p	Propeller
g	Electric motor		q	Propeller shaft
h	Motor controls/clutch		r	Controls for pumps etc.

moveable in both planes and consequently the vessel was not fitted with either a rudder or hydroplanes.

The submarine carried an explosive charge which could be attached to the hull of an enemy ship and exploded electrically from a safe distance. *Goubet I* had a crew of two who sat back to back under the small conning tower. This submarine had difficulty in maintaining a constant depth.

A second submarine was ordered by the French Navy in September 1886 and was built at Cherbourg where she was launched in 1889. Made in bronze, she was 26.2 feet (8 metres) long, with a 6 feet (1.8 metres) beam and was powered by an electric motor (Fig 78). The hull of this vessel weighed 5 tons and the detachable keel was 1.5 tons. Her range was about 25 miles (40km) and her speed 5.5 knots (10kph). Although she also had problems with her depth keeping she was very stable because in addition to the safety weight there was, centrally placed in the lower part of the hull, another half ton of lead ballast. The result of the combined weights allowed men to move in the vessel without having to adjust longitudinal trim the whole time. However, the boat was slow and

although armed with two Whitehead torpedoes carried in brackets externally, it was not a suitable naval submarine for the late nineteenth century.

At the same time work had been progressing on the *Gymnote*, a submarine designed by a famous French marine engineer, Dupuy de Lome. Unfortunately he died before the submarine could be built. A close friend, a naval engineer Gustave Zede, became interested in the project and started work on the drawings adding some of his own ideas. He presented the revised plans to the French Minister for the Navy and was immediately given official backing. The submarine was launched in September 1888. Her shape was similar to *Nordenfelt II/III*, but only about half her size, with a length of 56.4 feet (17 metres), and a beam of 5.9 feet (1.8 metres) (Fig 79). Made of steel plate 6mm thick in the centre she had additional lead ballast stowed on either side of the keel. There were three ballast tanks: one at either end and the other in the centre of the boat. In front of the single propeller there were vertical and horizontal rudders. Steering a straight course was assisted by using a

Fig 77 *Goubet I*

1885

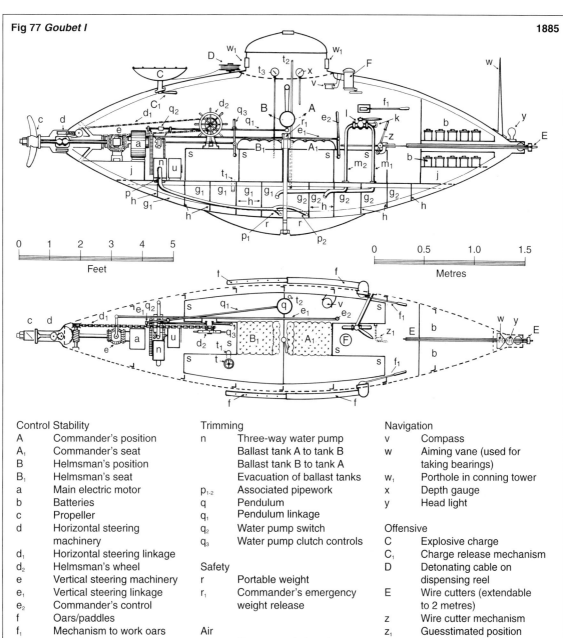

0 1 2 3 4 5
Feet

0 0.5 1.0 1.5
Metres

Control Stability

A	Commander's position
A_1	Commander's seat
B	Helmsman's position
B_1	Helmsman's seat
a	Main electric motor
b	Batteries
c	Propeller
d	Horizontal steering machinery
d_1	Horizontal steering linkage
d_2	Helmsman's wheel
e	Vertical steering machinery
e_1	Vertical steering linkage
e_2	Commander's control
f	Oars/paddles
f_1	Mechanism to work oars

Ballasting

g_1	Ballast tank A
g_2	Ballast tank B
h	Baffle plates
j	Trim tank
k	Main ballast water inlet
l	Two-way valve
m_1	Ballast tank pipework
m_2	Ballast tank pipework

Trimming

n	Three-way water pump
	Ballast tank A to tank B
	Ballast tank B to tank A
	Evacuation of ballast tanks
$p_{1\text{-}2}$	Associated pipework
q	Pendulum
q_1	Pendulum linkage
q_2	Water pump switch
q_3	Water pump clutch controls

Safety

r	Portable weight
r_1	Commander's emergency weight release

Air

s	Compressed air tanks
t	Compressed air valve
t_1	Compressed air pipe
t_2	Compressed air hull vent
t_3	Pressure gauge
u	Air pump

Navigation

v	Compass
w	Aiming vane (used for taking bearings)
w_1	Porthole in conning tower
x	Depth gauge
y	Head light

Offensive

C	Explosive charge
C_1	Charge release mechanism
D	Detonating cable on dispensing reel
E	Wire cutters (extendable to 2 metres)
z	Wire cutter mechanism
z_1	Guesstimated position of cutter controls

Communications

F	Message container through which items could be floated to the surface

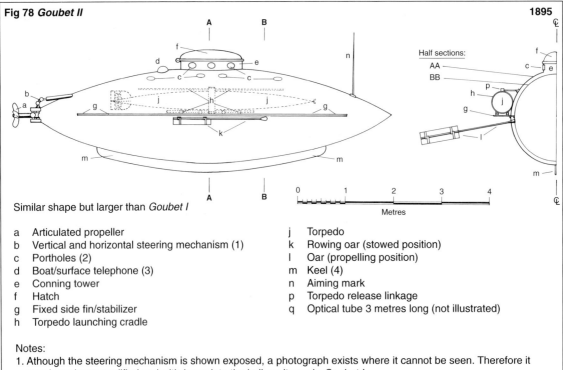

Fig 78 Goubet II 1895

Half sections:
AA
BB

Similar shape but larger than *Goubet I*

a	Articulated propeller
b	Vertical and horizontal steering mechanism (1)
c	Portholes (2)
d	Boat/surface telephone (3)
e	Conning tower
f	Hatch
g	Fixed side fin/stabilizer
h	Torpedo launching cradle

j	Torpedo
k	Rowing oar (stowed position)
l	Oar (propelling position)
m	Keel (4)
n	Aiming mark
p	Torpedo release linkage
q	Optical tube 3 metres long (not illustrated)

Notes:
1. Athough the steering mechanism is shown exposed, a photograph exists where it cannot be seen. Therefore it may have been modified and withdrawn into the hull, as it was in *Goubet I*.
2. Different photographs show the ports in various positions which could indicate that more than one hull was built.
3. In an emergency the telephone could be floated to the surface. There was also a method of launching an explosive charge which also floated and then exploded to indicate the position of the submarine.
4. In an emergency it was possible to to drop 1,200 kilograms of keel to give the submersible immediate positive buoyancy.
5. **Method of Attack**. On sighting an enemy ship the commander would take a bearing using his compass and the aiming mark (n). The vessel would be submerged to 4 metres and would approach on a compass bearing, using the electric motor. Progress would be monitored through the optical tube and when 'close enough' final manoeuvring would be carried out using the oars to avoid 'alerting the enemy'. The torpedo would be launched and the submersible would withdraw rapidly (oars and electric motor?).

gyroscope because the metal hull and all the electrical equipment adversely effected the reliability of the compass under water. The submarine was fitted with both a twin-mirror optical tube and a periscope. Of the two the former was better.

The submarine was used both for training crews and as a test bed. Many changes and modifications were made to her during her career and her performance varied. But at one stage she could run at 8 knots (14.8kph) for 32 miles (51km) or 4 knots (7.4kph) for 100 miles (160km). Bourgoyne comments: 'The French Naval Officers as a whole were at once favourably impressed with the result of the experiments carried out by this vessel and are today keener on submarine boats than our British juniors are on commanding torpedo boats and destroyers'. In 1890 the French Minister of Marine placed an order for another submarine designed by the engineer Romazotti (who had supervised the building of *Gymnote*). During the construction of this submarine, which was the largest in the world with a length of 159 feet (48 metres), Gustave Zede died and the new boat was named after him. Although she was not very successful, subsequent boats were and France was well in the lead as far as submarines were concerned.

Yet another distinguished designer was at work in France. Maxime Laubeuf designed a submarine called the *Narval*, which was 112 feet (34 metres) long, had a beam of 12 feet 5 inches (3.8 metres) and a draught of 5 feet 3 inches (1.6 metres). She had a surface displacement of 116 tons and submerged she displaced 200 tons. Her motive power was a steam engine with an oil-fired boiler and an electric motor. She was fitted with a standard propeller and hydroplanes at the bow and stern. Her range of action was 250 miles (400km) at 12 knots (22kph) or 620 miles (1,000km) at 8 knots (14.8kph). Submerged she could cover 25 miles (40km) at 8 knots (14.8kph) or 71½ miles (115km) at 5 knots (9.2kph). Four torpedoes were carried in brackets on the top of the hull. *Narval* was launched on 24 October 1899. She was an improvement on the other submarines which had been built in France to date, but had one major fault: it took twenty minutes to submerge.

In the United States of America there were three major submarine designers: G.C. Baker, Simon Lake and John P. Holland, who all entered an open Government competition for the design of a submarine-boat for the United States Navy.

In 1884 Professor J.H.L. Tuck, of San Francisco, built his first submarine which was equipped with an electric motor. His submarine was 30 feet (9 metres) long with two propellers, one conventionally placed at the stern and the other on the keel to force the boat under water (Fig 80). The vessel was fitted with ballast tanks and hydroplanes as well as tubes which could be floated to the surface to gather air should this be necessary. Instead of having a conning tower the vessel was fitted with a diving

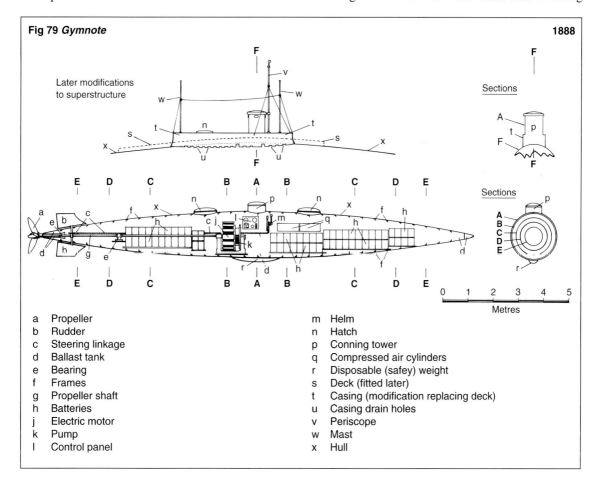

Fig 79 *Gymnote* 1888

a	Propeller	m	Helm
b	Rudder	n	Hatch
c	Steering linkage	p	Conning tower
d	Ballast tank	q	Compressed air cylinders
e	Bearing	r	Disposable (safey) weight
f	Frames	s	Deck (fitted later)
g	Propeller shaft	t	Casing (modification replacing deck)
h	Batteries	u	Casing drain holes
j	Electric motor	v	Periscope
k	Pump	w	Mast
l	Control panel	x	Hull

dress for the helmsman who had a small compartment, which was open to the sea, from which he controlled the vessel. There was an air-lock so that he could disrobe and enter the submarine. She carried two buoyant charges which were attached to her hull by electro-magnets. When released they floated and attached themselves magnetically to the hull of a ship where they were detonated using an electric cable fixed to the charge and linked to the submarine. On trials the submarine performed well.

In the following year, 1885, Professor Tuck developed a second submarine called the *Peacemaker*.

Made of iron this vessel was also 30 feet (9 metres) long, with a 7.5 feet (2.25 metres) beam and a draught of 6 feet (1.8 metres). She was fitted with a small conning tower with glass ports, a conventional hanging rudder, single propeller and hydroplanes at both the bow and stern. Perhaps too much was expected from the electric motor particularly when it was the only source of power. In his next boat it was replaced by a 'fireless engine' which generated steam using a solution of caustic soda as the heat source. In trials, the submarine ran a distance of 2½ miles (4km) without break-

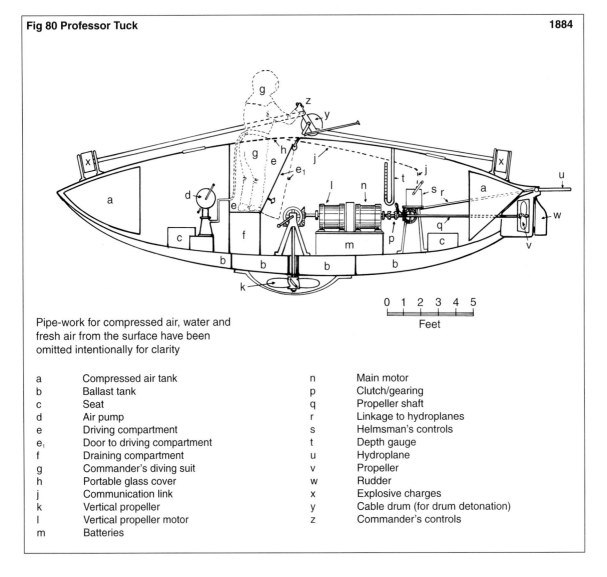

Fig 80 Professor Tuck   **1884**

0 1 2 3 4 5
Feet

Pipe-work for compressed air, water and fresh air from the surface have been omitted intentionally for clarity

a	Compressed air tank	n	Main motor
b	Ballast tank	p	Clutch/gearing
c	Seat	q	Propeller shaft
d	Air pump	r	Linkage to hydroplanes
e	Driving compartment	s	Helmsman's controls
e_1	Door to driving compartment	t	Depth gauge
f	Draining compartment	u	Hydroplane
g	Commander's diving suit	v	Propeller
h	Portable glass cover	w	Rudder
j	Communication link	x	Explosive charges
k	Vertical propeller	y	Cable drum (for drum detonation)
l	Vertical propeller motor	z	Commander's controls
m	Batteries		

ing surface although the boat had problems in maintaining a constant depth.

Baker's design resembled, in outward appearance, Garrett's *Egg* with a small conning tower (Fig 81). The vessel was 46 feet (14 metres) long, with a 9 feet (2.75 metres) beam and a depth of 13 feet (4 metres). She was powered by a steam engine and an electric motor. On either side of the hull in the middle of the boat, were propellers which could be rotated through 360 degrees and could be used to drive the vessel forward, astern, up and down. These were powered by a 60hp steam engine, which was also connected to the dynamo which charged the accumulators. To submerge the funnel was lowered into

the hull and sealed, the furnace damped down and closed up, ballast taken on and the electric motor connected to drive the propellers. Baker built his boat in 1892 and she performed reasonably well, although depth keeping proved to be a problem.

Simon Lake was interested in submarine navigation from the age of ten when he was introduced to Jules Verne's book *Twenty Thousand Leagues Under the Sea*. His approach was not completely novel, as it had been proposed before, but completely different to that of his contemporaries. His vessel was designed to travel on the sea or river bed using wheels. The original plans were for a vessel 80 feet long (24 metres), but he was unable to raise the estimated $75,000 required to build her. Not to

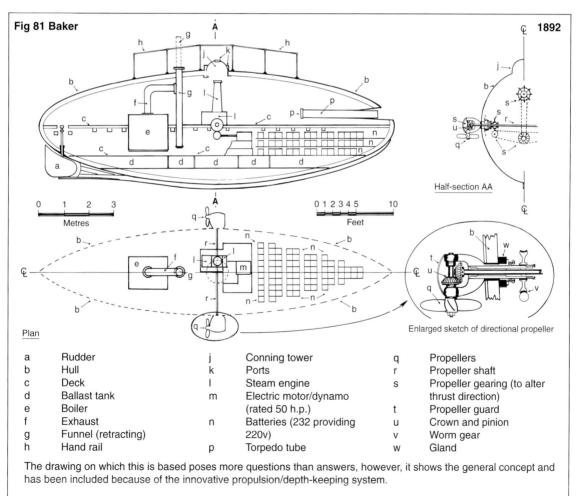

Fig 81 Baker   **1892**

Half-section AA

Metres

Feet

Plan

Enlarged sketch of directional propeller

a	Rudder	j	Conning tower	q	Propellers
b	Hull	k	Ports	r	Propeller shaft
c	Deck	l	Steam engine	s	Propeller gearing (to alter
d	Ballast tank	m	Electric motor/dynamo		thrust direction)
e	Boiler		(rated 50 h.p.)	t	Propeller guard
f	Exhaust	n	Batteries (232 providing	u	Crown and pinion
g	Funnel (retracting)		220v)	v	Worm gear
h	Hand rail	p	Torpedo tube	w	Gland

The drawing on which this is based poses more questions than answers, however, it shows the general concept and has been included because of the innovative propulsion/depth-keeping system.

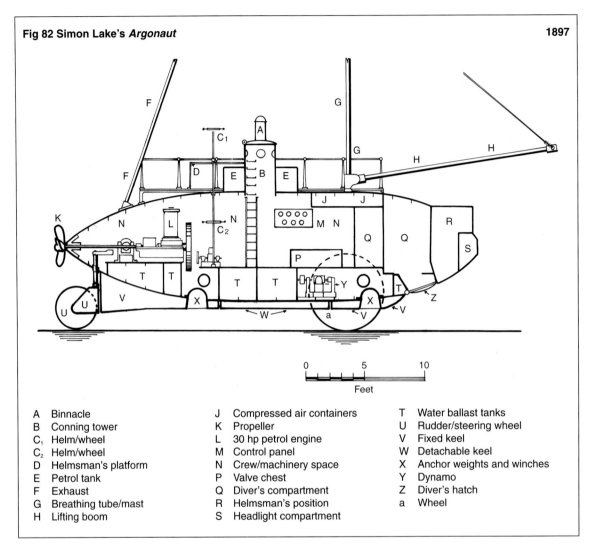

Fig 82 Simon Lake's *Argonaut* 1897

A	Binnacle	J	Compressed air containers	T	Water ballast tanks
B	Conning tower	K	Propeller	U	Rudder/steering wheel
C_1	Helm/wheel	L	30 hp petrol engine	V	Fixed keel
C_2	Helm/wheel	M	Control panel	W	Detachable keel
D	Helmsman's platform	N	Crew/machinery space	X	Anchor weights and winches
E	Petrol tank	P	Valve chest	Y	Dynamo
F	Exhaust	Q	Diver's compartment	Z	Diver's hatch
G	Breathing tube/mast	R	Helmsman's position	a	Wheel
H	Lifting boom	S	Headlight compartment		

be deterred, at his own expense he managed to build a smaller vessel himself. Made of wood, she was 14 feet long (4.26 metres) with a 4.5-foot (1.4-metre) beam and a height of 5 feet (1.5 metres). Fitted with wheels, she was propelled by turning a crank inside the hull.

Lake made himself a diving suit; the helmet was shaped from iron and reached down to his breast, and the window was an old deadlight from a yacht. The lower part of the helmet was covered with painted canvas and lead weights were attached to his legs to keep him down when walking on the river bed. Air was compressed with a plumber's hand pump and stored in a converted soda water fountain tank. The suit was connected to the air supply with a piece of garden hose strengthened with binding wire. The small vessel worked and Lake was able to demonstrate it.

Still unable to raise sufficient funds to build his planned 80-foot long (24-metre) vessel, Lake designed a smaller boat which measured 36 feet (11 metres) long with a 9-foot (2.75-metre) beam. She was fitted with a 30hp petrol engine (which was used both on the surface and when the vessel was submerged, drawing air originally through a hose pipe connected to the surface but later through a rigid pipe) (Fig 82). The vessel also had a dynamo, an air compressor, and water ballast pumps. The vessel had a standard propeller and like the original *Argonaut Junior*, wheels. Extensively tested this vessel proved to be very successful. Later modifications to improve her performance were made which included enlarging the small vessel which originally had a crew of five so she could accommodate eight. Lake went on to develop more sophisticated submersibles.

John P. Holland, who was to become one of the most eminent submarine designers, was born in south west Ireland in February 1841. As a young man he designed a submarine but could get no one interested in providing financial backing. The project was shelved and not resurrected until he had emigrated to the United States where he revised his drawings during a period of convalescence while recuperating from a broken leg. His first submarine was very basic and has been likened to a canoe. It was driven by a single propeller which was turned by foot pedals. The sole occupant wore a diving helmet and was provided with air from compartments at the bow and stern and a water ballast tank.

In 1875 Holland tried to get the United States interested in his work but to no avail. It was not until 1876, nearly four years after arriving in America, that $6,000 was raised to build his first powered submarine. His financial backers were the trustees of the Fenian Skirmishing Fund; and some historians suggest that Holland's aim was to build submarines that could be transported across the Atlantic to use against the British. The boat was built in 1877 at the Albany City Iron Works in New York. Her length was 10 feet (3 metres), beam 3.5 feet (1 metre) and depth 3 feet (0.9 metres), and she was propelled by a single propeller driven by a 4hp petrol engine. Originally fitted with hydroplanes in the centre of the hull, experiments showed that it was best to have them near the stern rudder. The vessel was thoroughly tested, stripped of her equipment and sunk.

Holland's next boat, again financed by the Fenians, was also built at the Albany City Ironworks, but was a much larger vessel (Fig 83). Her overall length was 31 feet (9.4 metres), her beam 6 feet (1.8 metres) and her depth 6 feet (1.8 metres). The engine was a 15hp petrol engine and she had a crew of three. Compressed air was used both for the crew and to expel water from the ballast tanks.

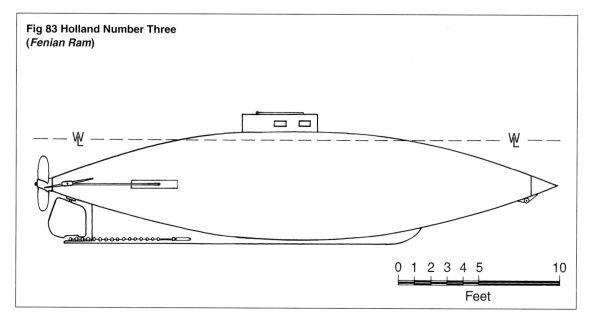

Fig 83 Holland Number Three (*Fenian Ram*)

0 1 2 3 4 5   10

Feet

The vessel was also fitted with an underwater gun. This was a 9-inch (228.5mm) tube on the central axis of the boat with a bow cap and within the boat a breech. It was Holland's intention to design some projectiles, but another inventor allowed him to copy 'torpedoes' that he was about to use. In two experimental firings from the submarine the 'torpedo' was ejected with compressed air and after running a few yards in the sea became airborne, one going up some 60 feet (18 metres)

then nose-diving into the dock where it buried itself in the mud. The second only rose 15 feet (4.5 metres) and struck a pile. Other more successful trials were carried out with the gun which could project a missile about 130 feet (40 metres) in a straight line. Extensive and methodical trials were carried out with this vessel.

Her fate, like that of so many early submarines but in this case for different reasons, was that she became a rusting hulk on the shore. Apparently

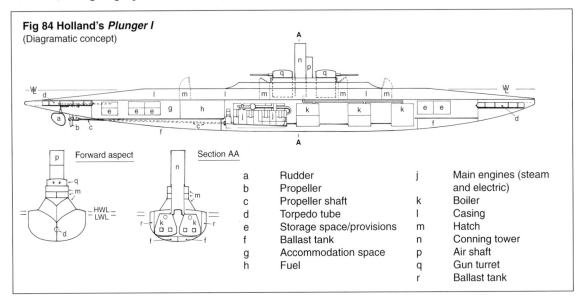

Fig 84 Holland's *Plunger I* (Diagramatic concept)

a	Rudder	j	Main engines (steam and electric)
b	Propeller		
c	Propeller shaft	k	Boiler
d	Torpedo tube	l	Casing
e	Storage space/provisions	m	Hatch
f	Ballast tank	n	Conning tower
g	Accommodation space	p	Air shaft
h	Fuel	q	Gun turret
		r	Ballast tank

Forward aspect   Section AA

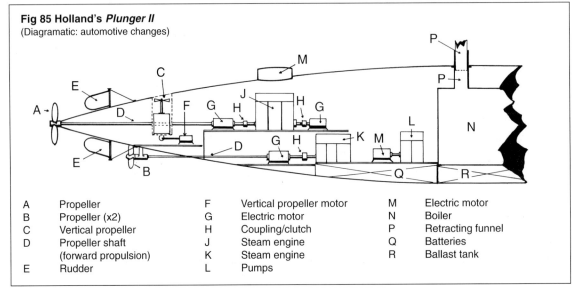

Fig 85 Holland's *Plunger II* (Diagramatic: automotive changes)

A	Propeller	F	Vertical propeller motor	M	Electric motor
B	Propeller (x2)	G	Electric motor	N	Boiler
C	Vertical propeller	H	Coupling/clutch	P	Retracting funnel
D	Propeller shaft (forward propulsion)	J	Steam engine	Q	Batteries
		K	Steam engine	R	Ballast tank
E	Rudder	L	Pumps		

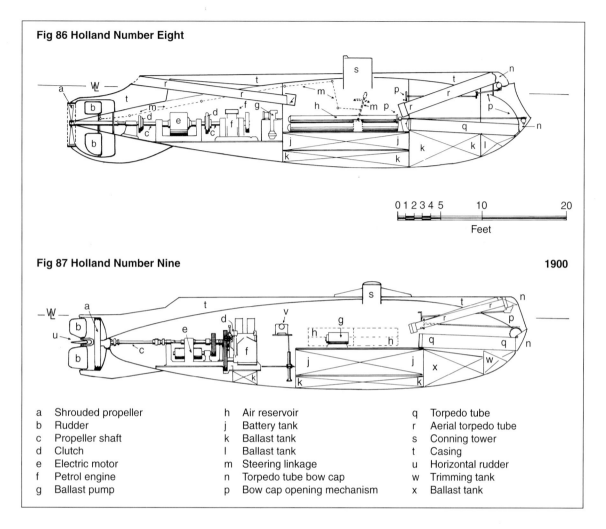

Fig 86 Holland Number Eight

0 1 2 3 4 5   10   20
Feet

Fig 87 Holland Number Nine   1900

a	Shrouded propeller	h	Air reservoir	q	Torpedo tube
b	Rudder	j	Battery tank	r	Aerial torpedo tube
c	Propeller shaft	k	Ballast tank	s	Conning tower
d	Clutch	l	Ballast tank	t	Casing
e	Electric motor	m	Steering linkage	u	Horizontal rudder
f	Petrol engine	n	Torpedo tube bow cap	w	Trimming tank
g	Ballast pump	p	Bow cap opening mechanism	x	Ballast tank

she was removed from her mooring one night by one of the Fenian backers, who unsuccessfully tried to dive her. Having been warned by a harbour master that he was a danger to shipping, the submarine was hauled from the water onto the property of another member of the Fenian committee. There was a rumour that an attempt had been made to sell her to Russia but this had failed because there was no proof of ownership. As far as Holland was concerned the trials conducted with the *Fenian Ram* had been very successful and her loss did not pose a problem.

Holland then built a small submarine which was propelled by explosive charges, but the experiments were curtailed when the boat sank because

the hatch had not been properly secured.

He took up employment with the Pneumatic Gun Company as a draughtsman, and while there interested members of the company and others in a new design drawn up after the *Fenian Ram* had been taken. While the company was being formed, Holland met Captain Zalinski, a serving officer in the United States Army. The next boat was built under the supervision of this officer and thereafter was known as the Zalinski boat. The boat was 50 feet (15 metres) long with a 6-foot (1.8-metre) beam and was built of wood. It was launched in 1886, but as she was about to enter the water the boat crashed into some pillars. The damage was so great that there was insufficient money left in the company to effect repairs and the vessel was broken up.

Holland 6, the next design, was purely a paper exercise and was the basis for *Holland 7* which was built for the United States Navy. The submarine was 85 feet (26 metres) long, with an 11.5 feet (3.5 metres) beam and a similar depth (Fig 84). On the surface she was to be driven by two independent sets of triple expansion steam engines with a 1,625 I.H.P. giving a speed of 15 knots (28kph) on the surface. There were to be five tubular boilers to provide the steam and these were to be oil fired. For running submerged there were two electric motors each with a rating of 100 I.H.P. The submarine was armed with three torpedo tubes, two in the bow and one in the stern. In addition there were turrets, fore and aft of the funnel, with quick-firing guns. The boat was launched in August 1897 and although the engines were replaced by petrol engines (Fig 85) she was never completed because she was considered to be inferior to the *Holland* and *New Holland* which had been developed while she was being built.

The new No. 8 boat was modified and the No. 9 boat became the prototype of a generation of submarines. She was 53 feet 10 inches (16.4 metres) long, with a 10-foot 3 inch (3.12 metre) beam and a height of 10 feet 7 inches (3.2 metres) (Figs 86 & 87). There was a small conning tower and a single propeller behind which was cruciform supporting two vertical and two horizontal rudders. The main engine was a 45hp petrol engine and the main motor was a 50hp (nominal) electric motor. The submarine was fitted with a bow torpedo tube to fire an 8-inch (203mm) Whitehead torpedo, as well as a fixed elevation bow gun. Exhaustive trials were carried out with *Holland 9* and the United States Government purchased the boat in April 1900.

CHAPTER 22

U.S. NAVY DEPARTMENT ADVERTISEMENT FOR TENDERS TO BUILD A SUBMARINE

Bearing in mind that the only operational attacks which had been carried out by submarines had taken place in American waters it is not so remarkable that the United States Government was the first to officially recognise that submarines were going to play an important role in any future wars. On 26 November 1887, the United States Navy published an advertisement for tenders to build a submarine for the United States Navy.

In the United States Navy Department Circular or Advertisement[1] very clear parameters were laid down and this document was certainly the bench-mark for the submarines of the United States Navy and the Royal Navy, and was probably used as a set standard for other countries and navies which were doing their own research and development. The United States had probably been considering its position from much earlier as a notice of 'An Act making appropriations for the Naval Service for the fiscal year 30 June 1888 and for other purposes,' was approved on 3 March 1887, and was reported in *Proceedings of the United States Naval Institute* in January 1888. That Act called for proposals for the construction of a submarine torpedo boat, and gave design requirements.

The covering paper of the advertisement, signed by the Secretary of the Navy, William C. Whitney, covered the general procedures for submitting proposals. These had to be submitted by 1 March 1888 for 'the construction, by contract, of one submarine torpedo boat, complete with torpedo appendages – such a vessel to be of the best and most modern design to be constructed of steel, of domestic manufacture, having a tensile strength of

not less than 60,000 lb per square inch'. The contractor had to furnish, at his own expense, all working drawings necessary to the complete construction of the vessel; the expense of trials, before final acceptance of the vessel under contract, were also to be borne by the contractor. Furthermore proposals had to be accompanied by a certified cheque for an amount equal to five per cent of the bid. This was returnable. For the successful bidder, who entered a contract with the Navy, there was a penalty clause amounting to sixty per cent of the bid price.

The specifications laid down by the United States Navy are reproduced unabridged in Appendix I. Briefly the General Requirements specified that the most desirable qualities to be possessed by the submarine while approaching a hostile ship under way, were speed, certainty of direction, invisibility, and safety from the enemy's fire. Concern was expressed about the 'certainty of approach' when dealing with a moving target which was not on a constant course. That visual contact had to be maintained, even intermittently, was clearly recognised.

The United States Navy envisaged that the boat would be used in three different conditions:

1 Surfaced with freeboard (casing) awash.
2 Covered with at least 3 feet (.9 metre) of water covering the hull of the submarine (the pressure hull) but not necessarily over the conning tower.
3 Submerged at any safe depth, cut off from communicating with the atmosphere and no view of the target other than through water.

---

[1] *Proceedings of the United States Navy Institute* Vol XIV 1888

Specific parameters were laid down for: speed, power endurance, ease of manoeuvre, stability, structural strength and offensive power. The endurance requirements also required that power for submerged runs should be 'maintained at maximum efficiency for instant use', and that the recovery rate, to reachieve this state, should be no longer than twice the duration of a submerged run. The boat was also to have air-purifying equipment to allow it to remain submerged for twelve hours, and a lesson possibly learnt from the Nordenfelt boats was that the interior temperature was to be kept down to 100°F (37°C). The requirement set was very high and could not have been met by some of the submarines which entered naval service fifteen years later.

This document had been prepared by professional naval officers who had defined the operational requirement of the United States Navy. Previously no one in authority had said what was required. Excluding the drawing-board builders, who often made outrageous claims concerning the potential of their boats, the inventor-builders had tended to construct and then tell the world about the capabilities of their vessel. Now a very strict set of criteria had been laid down which would be very difficult to achieve, but there was no point in setting the sights too low.

It is interesting to speculate what prompted the United States Government to act when it did. In 1877 *Nordenfelt IV* was probably the most advanced submarine and she was being demonstrated to the world; in France, *Gymnote* and *Goubet I* had been built and were undergoing trials. In Spain, Peral launched his submarine in October and the Americans would have known about this vessel. Drzwieki was making a name for himself in Russia while in America, Holland, Baker, Lake and Tuck were building their reputations. None of these developments would have posed a threat to the United States. However, it could be foreseen that in the future they could be developed, completely changing the situation.

With one exception, the developments were being kept in the countries of origin, but Nordenfelt was prepared, indeed he was trying very hard, to sell his submarine to anyone who was willing to buy. This may have been the spur which influenced the Secretary of State for the U.S. Navy.

Having reached this conclusion, it is only fair to register some of the observations which were being made in the United States, at the time, concerning the submarine generally and its development. *Proceedings of the United States Naval Institute* of 1888 recorded some of these views: 'The proposals put forward by Lt Hovgaard were considered to be interesting. It was considered that the prospects of getting a serviceable boat (in response to the advertisement) was not very good.' In the United States the *Peacemaker* was considered to be inadequate, while the Holland boats lacked speed, endurance and carrying capacity. As far as European boats were concerned it was thought that the Goubet boats 'lacked power in all directions' while the Nordenfelts were 'apparently failures in all respects save surface speed and endurance as their trials showed nothing of practical use.'

Looking on the positive side, the proceedings continue to record:

> On the other hand, in looking over the field of possibilities for the immediate future it is apparent that there are plenty of practical devices extant to make a submarine boat successful, plenty of experience to apply them and plenty of money to pay the expenses of construction; and therefore it only remains to be seen whether or not the owners of the devices, experience and money will have the wisdom to comprehend that in combining to give the Navy Department the boat it requires they will be working to their own advantage as well as that of the Government.

Finally the conclusion reached, as recorded in the same proceedings:

Even if the Department fails in its first attempt to obtain a practical construction of the kind, the submarine boat, as such, must soon appear as a factor in Naval warfare – for just as rapidity and range of aimed fire have forced the use of earth cover ashore, so will the same causes force the use of water cover afloat – and unless 'we the people of the United States,' choose to continue to be as stupid as we have been for the last score of years concerning everything that floats, we are in our own interests bound to lead in its development. When it comes it will not, like every new warlike device conceived in the brain of a cranky inventor, 'entirely revolutionise warfare,' but it will assume the well defined place and duties awaiting it – place and duties that will urgently require to be filled and done if there is to be even a faint attempt at placing this country in a condition of partial defence.

The Open Competition

Many designs were entered for the competition including one from Thorsten Nordenfelt. Baker submitted a design for a boat of 60 feet (18 metres) length and Lake entered the plans for a twin screw boat of 80 feet (24.5 metres) length, while Holland submitted his design for *Holland No. 7*. It was the Holland design which was accepted. Because of delays in drawing up the contract it was not signed, as was the original intention, in 1888. The following year, when the details of the contract had been finalised there was a change in the Administration and the whole project was put on hold. It was not until 1893 that Congress authorised the building of a submarine and another two years passed before a contract was eventually signed. *Holland No. 7*, which had been called the *Plunger* was laid down but never completed. During building she was being modified, and while this was going on, Holland had designed a superior submarine, *Holland No. 9*. In due course, it was agreed that the

Holland Torpedo Boat Co. would refund to the United States Government, all the money connected with the *Plunger* contract, on the understanding that the Government placed an order for the new submarine with the company. This was agreed and two of the new boats were ordered. *Holland No. 9* was built, tested and purchased by the Government on 11 April 1900. Three months before this the Secretary for the Navy had been authorised to order a further five improved Holland boats and this order was later increased to six submarines. The USS *Holland* was commissioned, into the Navy of the United States, on 25 June 1900, under the command of Lieutenant H.H. Caldwell, U.S.N. This was the foundation of the United States Submarine Service.

In the decade since Nordenfelt and Garrett had parted company, submarine development in Europe and North America had suddenly accelerated to produce the prototypes which would be used as the foundations for the national submarine fleets which were to be constructed in time to participate in World War I. If it had been a race, of the main four contenders, France would have been in the lead. The United States Government had recognised the importance of the submarine as early as 1887. But because of a change of Administration, had failed to become involved as early as she could have done. Thanks to private enterprise, however, she was not all that far behind France. Germany was still watching the situation from the sideline and had made very little progress. While Great Britain had maintained its aloof position and was only now realising that the submarine had been invented and would not go away. To participate in the race, like Germany, she would first have to acquire a foreign design, because there was nothing suitable in the home market. Then, these two countries could go to the starting blocks and participate in the race.

CHAPTER 23

GARRETT THE IMMIGRANT

In November 1890 the Garrett family arrived in New York. They moved to Florida where they purchased a 150 acre (60ha) farm on the shore of East Lake, Tohopekaliga, some 16 miles (25km) east of Kissimmee in an English settlement. His interest in farming lasted only two years, and the family moved back to New York in 1892.

Perhaps it was the wanderlust or just the necessity of getting a job, but on 1 September 1893 Garrett joined the United States Revenue Service. He was 'shipped' as O.S. and rated as seaman, on board the Revenue Steamship *Galveston*, at Galveston, Texas.[1] His name appeared in the log again on Wednesday 6 September with a two line comment: 'Disrated from 1st inst inclusive, Geo. W. Garrett Seaman to Ord. Sea., for incompetency'. The *Galveston* was a disciplined ship and this is reflected in an extract from the same log: 'At 3.30 p.m. placed Thos. N. Thomas and John Freeling, Seamen, in double irons and confinement for insubordination to officer of the deck. At 8.15 p.m. released Seaman Thomas from irons and confinement and for continued insolence placed Seaman Freeling upon bread and water.' The log finishes: 'Day ends, gentle N'ly breeze and clear'.

The log of Saturday 9 September records that Garrett was sent to the Marine Hospital in Galveston.

The Muster Roll for September 1893 tells us a little more about this episode. It records Garrett's enlistment in which he declared that he was born in London, England, that his age was thirty-eight. and his occupation was seaman. His physical record showed that his eyes were blue, hair black that he had a fair complexion, and that his height was 5 feet 10 inches (1.77 metres). It also reveals that he remained in hospital for the remainder of the month. The Roll for October confirms that he was still in hospital and remained there until 6 October.

On 27 September 1893 the First Lieutenant of the Steamer *Galveston* wrote to the Hon. Secretary of the Treasury, in Washington D.C., requesting authority to discharge Garrett. Apparently George William had been sick from the day after his enlistment: *'Shipped on the 1st instant, the latter (Garrett) was taken sick next day and continued off duty until the 9th inst, when sent to the hospital upon the vessel's return from a cruise. His disease is not incident to his service upon this vessel and his usefulness, as a seaman, for several weeks, is gone. He was carefully examined by the M.H. Surgeon before enlistment.'* He was discharged from the Revenue Service on 6 October 1893, on the same day he was released from the hospital.

It is very difficult to visualise Garrett working 'before the mast' with all his command and sea experience, particularly in Texas for his family were still in New York and therefore he was a long way from home. It is pure speculation, but possibly, it could have been one of several reasons why Garrett ended up so far South. He may have been scouring sea ports hoping that he might again be able to become involved with submarine development. Finding no such work, circumstances may have dictated that he had to accept what was on offer, for he had to support his family whilst searching for employment. He had a wealth of experience, was educated and well travelled, but he did not have the sort of qualifications and expertise that a normal employer would expect a man of his age to have. Another possibility, bearing in mind that he went sick immediately after joining the Steamer *Galveston*, was that he may have wanted or been advised to get a job in the fresh air because of a weak chest brought about by inhaling fumes in the various submarines in which he had worked.

At some time Garrett returned to Europe and made contact with Thorsten Nordenfelt in the

---

[1] Extracts from the Log and Muster Roll of the Revenue Steamer *Galveston* for the months of September and October 1893.

hope that he could help in some way. This did not materialise, Nordenfelt had long lost interest in the building of submarines. Garrett may have tried elsewhere. Because development was advancing so rapidly and his own work had been so insular, he probably did not have sufficient to offer a potential employer, who in any case already had his own well established team, and was working on a very tight budget.

Five years after his short spell with the Revenue Service Garrett enrolled[2] into the 1st Regiment United States Volunteer Engineers for the 'Spanish War'. In his enlistment papers he declared his age as thirty-nine years eleven months, born at London, in England. His previous occupation is shown as rigger, with previous military service in the Turkish Army. His physical description had not changed much since he joined the Revenue Service. He had gained 0.25 inches (6.35mm) in height, and his hair was now described as sandy. His chest measurement was 33/36.5 inches (838/927mm), his weight 150lb (68kg) and except for a slight hearing problem he was deemed fit by the examining surgeon. At the time of enlistment the family had been living at 466 Lenox Avenue, New York for at least two years.

On 29 June he arrived at a camp near Peekskill, N.Y. having been given accelerated promotion to corporal. From the available records it would appear that he was granted only three days leave before the Regiment moved to a camp west of Ponce, in Puerto Rico. For four days in late September he was detained in hospital under observation for muscular neuralgia, but was returned to his company, which was then at Coamo, for drunkenness. He reported sick again on 3 October and three days later was transferred to the Regimental hospital at Ponce. This time he had a chest problem which was was attributed to 'line of duty'. On 18 October Garrett was on the road to recovery and there was a celebration, which unfortunately got out of hand. He was charged with being drunk and acting in a dis-

orderly manner, in violation of the 62nd Article of War. The charge was not particularly specific. It stated that he was intoxicated and acted in a disorderly manner, while in the convalescent tent, attached to the Regimental hospital at 2.30 p.m. 15 October 1898. He was found guilty at a Summary Court and was reduced to the rank of 2nd Class Private and forfeited $2.00. The findings of the court were confirmed by the Regimental Commanding Officer.

In the meantime action was being taken to have Garrett discharged because of his muscular neuralgia, which made him unfit for duty. This was backdated to the date it was first diagnosed, 18 September, although it was now noted that this 'disability was not incurred in line of duty'. It took several months for the paperwork to be cleared. In a preliminary medical Garrett signed a declaration that he had no reason to believe that at the present time he was suffering from the effects of any wound, injury or disease or that he had any disability or impairment of health, whether incurred in the military service or otherwise. The examining surgeon, Major Ezra Woodruff, in his very brief report, indicated that 'he had thoroughly examined Garrett and that he did not have any disability, whether incurred in the military service or not'.

G.W.G. was discharged on 25 January 1899 in the rank of Private First Class.

During the next three years he did work, at least for a time, as a fireman. Apparently there were relatives who worked for the railroad and they possibly helped him to get a job.

Garrett died at the Metropolitan Hospital, New York on 26 February 1902. His death was from a chronic respiratory problem and exhaustion.

The land of promise or opportunity did not live up to its reputation for G.W.L.G. His decade or so in the United States could not have been the happiest part of his life, indeed, it was probably the most miserable. He seemed to be unable to settle down. This could have been a combination of his age and his lack of experience in the everyday world in

[2] Record of Enlistment for the 1st Regt. U.S. Vol. Engrs showing that Garrett enrolled on 23 June 1898.

which most people live. He was well educated with a good degree but the only real work qualification he had was that he had been made (ordained) deacon; there was no record that this had been relinquished but had just been allowed to lapse. Had he been inclined, he could have returned to the Ministry but initially only as a deacon for he was not priested whilst in the diocese of Manchester. As a young man he had done some teaching and one of his visiting cards from the time he was living in Lenox Avenue in New York, describes him as a 'Visiting Tutor' in Classics, Mathematics and Science. This was probably pursued after the *Galveston* adventure.

In some ways he seems to have squandered his talent and it is not really clear why he joined the *Galveston* or whether it was really necessary to join the Army. He certainly had a very strong sense of adventure and a desire to travel. These two hallmarks of his earlier life would have been difficult to discard. Perhaps it was just too much to expect a man who needed a challenge to settle down.

CHAPTER 24

TWENTIETH CENTURY

Having seen how the submarine was developed to the stage that it was a viable weapon system it would be illogical not to consider how it progressed, once it was taken over officially by the various navies. Irrespective of the developments and achievements which had taken place in many countries during the previous centuries, those best prepared to move forward at the turn of the century were France, the United States of America and Russia, as these were the only countries which had encouraged and supported development officially during the latter part of the nineteenth century. But there were two other countries which had had a lacklustre performance as far as development was concerned, and these were Great Britain and Germany. But they were destined to play an important part in the future development of the submarine.

Once development was started by the major powers, others would follow. The submarine had been truly invented and, regardless of the wishes of any nation, there was no way it could be un-invented or ignored.

While some countries developed their fleets from one basic source, others used two or more prototypes and consequently there were many 'development paths' or national family trees as each proceeded in its own way. An attempt to cover even the most important would end up as a very long catalogue of hull and performance statistics. Therefore, as so many countries started to build submarines, only the principal nations will be considered and it will be limited to show the boats they chose as the foundations for their future submarine fleet development. These initial and important decisions were all taken during the first few years of the century.

Around 1890 the individual inventor-designer-builder started to be phased out. His demise was heralded by the tender for designs issued by the United States Department of the Navy, which at long last showed that a serious interest was being taken in submarines. His death knell was sounded when Governments realised that they could no longer hold out against what was progress, even if they did not like it or agree with it. They placed their first orders for submarines and took control.

This removed some of the panache associated with much of the early submarine development; an element of the romance had gone. Development would be more disciplined and co-ordinated. It would speed up and be generated by the professional sailors who were to drive and crew the submarines, which, on their insistence, would become increasingly reliable and at the same time more lethal.

France

The French Republic was in a unique position as their building programme had already started at the turn of the century. There had been twenty-nine entries for the open competition, sponsored by France in 1896. The winner was Laubeuf, and his submarine, *Narval*, was built (Fig 88). In 1900 four more Laubeuf submarines were launched and these were very successful in exercises conducted in the Mediterranean, even though they took twenty minutes to submerge. On a wave of enthusiasm more boats were ordered and built and in the 1900 Government Estimates provision was made for thirty-eight submarines.

The French submarine-building programme was ambitious and they were in many respects more advanced than anyone else. But there was still a dependence on steam in the larger submarines. The internal combustion engine was introduced in boats designed by Romazzotti, Maugas and Bertin but they continued to have trouble with this form of power.

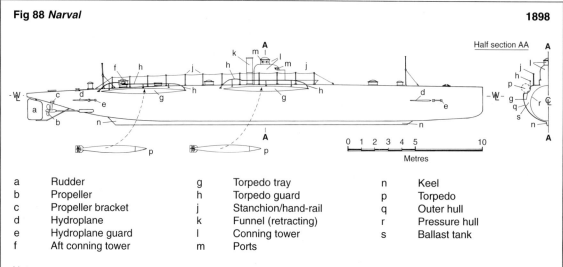

Fig 88 *Narval* 1898

Half section AA

0 1 2 3 4 5 10
Metres

a	Rudder	g	Torpedo tray	n	Keel
b	Propeller	h	Torpedo guard	p	Torpedo
c	Propeller bracket	j	Stanchion/hand-rail	q	Outer hull
d	Hydroplane	k	Funnel (retracting)	r	Pressure hull
e	Hydroplane guard	l	Conning tower	s	Ballast tank
f	Aft conning tower	m	Ports		

Notes:
1. Like many French submarines of this period *Narval* was used extensively for trials. Although the vessel was subjected to various modifications to overcome a longitudinal stability problem, it was not possible to eradicate the excessively long time taken to dive the boat.
2. In later submarines the more practical internal combustion engine was adopted and the Drzewieki torpedo drop collar launching system was soon to be universally replaced by the incorporation of internal, reloadable torpedo tubes.
3. *Narval* was a very important step forward. The general configuration of this boat with its double hull was to be used for many future generations of submarines particularly those built in Germany.

A large proportion of the French boats were fairly small and were best suited for coastal waters. Flotillas were established at Rochefort, Dunkirk, Toulon and Cherbourg, and the submarine was given the role of harbour defence.

United States of America

Although the United States had issued its invitation for tenders years before the French had their open competition and theoretically should have been in the lead, changes in the Administration had slowed progress. USS *Holland* was commissioned on 25 June 1900, just after the second boat, the *Fulton*, had been launched and by which time six additional Holland class submarines had been ordered. Four of these were launched in 1901 and the other two in 1903. Extensive trials were carried out with these boats.

In the meantime Simon Lake's *Protector* was launched in November 1902. She was 65 feet 7 inches (20 metres) long with a 13-foot 9 inches (4.2-metre) beam and her submerged displacement was 174 tons. She was powered by two gas motors and was fitted with various electric motors to drive the ancillary machinery and equipment. There was a double compartment for divers and the vessel was fitted with wheels for work on the sea bed. Lake fitted his boat with side rudders and actually called them hydroplanes. In October 1904 Lake launched his next submarine the *Argonaut* which was 68 feet (20.7 metres) long and equipped with a petrol engine and two electric motors for submerged work. This vessel was also fitted out with a diving chamber for divers.

Russia

Although Russia had taken an active interest in submarine development, designs from abroad had to be acquired. Fourteen boats of the 'Holland' design were built, six at Newsky and eight at

Sevastopol, as well as four of Simon Lake's *Protector* (450 tons). In 1904 a Russian delegation visiting Germany purchased a submarine, called *Trout* or *Forelle*, which had been built at Kiel by the Spanish engineer Raymondo d'Equevilley-Montjustin. At the same time they ordered three submarines of 250 ton displacement by the same designer from the Germaniawerst shipyard which was owned by Krupps.

At St Petersburg seven submarines designed by Boubnoff and Beklemissscheff were built. They were somewhat like the Hollands, measuring 77 feet (23.5 metres) in length with a 14-foot (4.25 metre) beam and displaced 175 tons. They were fitted with a petrol engine and electric motor and had a crew of twelve. Unlike the Hollands these boats were fitted with both forward and stern hydroplanes and the torpedoes were carried externally in Drzewieki brackets.

Drzewieki, had, by then, been established as a submarine designer in Russia for about two decades. He was well respected and had come second to Laubeuf in the French open submarine competition. Two boats one of 130 tons and the other of 550 tons were built at St Petersburg, but little is known of them.

Other Nations

Several other countries had purchased the Holland design and these included Norway and Japan. Italy and Sweden were developing their own boats in 1900 and others such as Austria, the Netherlands, Portugal and Peru were showing interest.

The Way Ahead

Some of those who had developed the very early, primitive submarines considered how 'fleets of them' could be employed but they could not possibly have envisaged how they would eventually be used. Even now the submarine is still evolving and it would be pure conjecture to say how it will be used in the future. However, it is possible to move forward from 1900, just a few years, to see how

things were starting to develop. This can best be illustrated by looking in more detail, at the progress made by two countries: Great Britain and Germany. In 1900, for different reasons, neither country was ready to build its own submarine force based on its own design of boat.

Up to the turn of the century the British had continued to refuse to have anything to do with submarines. They were not required. Realisation eventually dawned: the United States had ordered submarines and France not only had started to build submarines but also had appropriated funds to develop a large submarine fleet. Progress would not stand still. Something would have to be done.

In Germany there was also doubt about the submarine but the reasons were different. Admiral von Tirpitz was not prepared to sacrifice development of his High Seas Fleet by squandering valuable resources on the unproven submarine. After all, the two Nordenfelt-type submarines had been built, evaluated and found to be unsatisfactory. The German Navy considered that steam was not suitable for the propulsion of a submarine, but they also had severe reservations about the petrol engine which was considered unsafe.

United Kingdom

At the beginning of the chapter it was pointed out that progress was to become faster once the professional sailors became involved. This is very clearly exemplified by developments in Great Britain, where during the first few years of the twentieth century enormous progress was made. But it must be remembered, that had it been a race in 1900, Great Britain would still have been in the starting blocks and not even straining to go.

Although, at this time, the submarine was not a good counter-measure against submarines, at least to have them meant that they could be studied. But the British had a major problem. There were no 'off the shelf' submarines available in the country. The Nordenfelt boats were way out of date and the only other contender was Waddington, who had

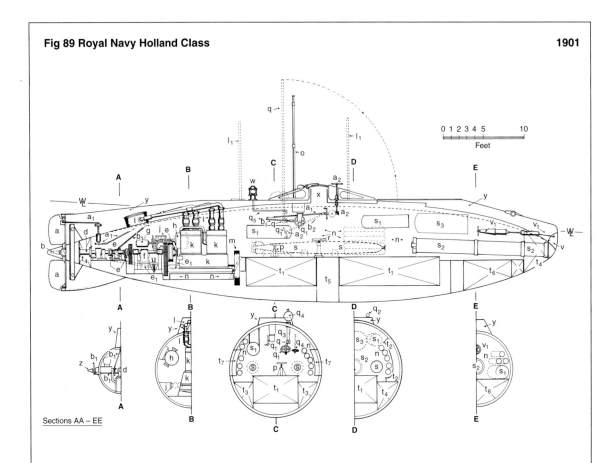

Fig 89 Royal Navy Holland Class   **1901**

Sections AA – EE

a	Rudder	q_4	Periscope training gear
a_1	Steering linkage	q_5	Compass periscopic tube
a_2	Steering gear	q_6	Other instruments/gauges not shown
b	Hydroplane	r	Commander's stand (for conning tower)
b_1	Hydroplane linkage	s	Torpedo
b_2	Hydroplane diving controls	s_1	Torpedo compensation tank
c	Propeller guard	s_2	Torpedo tube
d	Propeller shaft	s_3	Torpedo firing tank
e	Clutch	t	Tanks
e_1	Clutch linkage/controls	t_1	Battery tank
f	Electric motor	t_2	Main ballast tank
g	Air compressor	t_3	Auxiliary ballast tank
h	Main bilge pump	t_4	Trimming/compensating tank
j	Compressor/bilge pump drive	t_5	Ballast buoyancy tank
k	Petrol engine	t_6	Fuel (petrol) tank
l	Exhaust system	t_7	Oil tank
m	Flywheel	u	Main sea valve
n	Air bottles	v v_1	Bow cap, and opening mechanism
o	Mast	w	Compass
p	Helmsman's seat	x	Conning tower
q	Periscope	y	Casing
q_1	Helmsman's wheels	z	Stabilising fin
q_2	Periscope stowed position		

been given no support and his invention, by then, had been overtaken by developments elsewhere.

The only satisfactory submarine available was the improved Holland type, which had been ordered by the United States Navy. Arrangements were put in hand for five boats to be built by Vickers Sons and Maxim under licence from the Holland Torpedo Boat Company (Fig 89). At least Vickers had had the experience of building two Nordenfelt boats a few years previously. The Admiralty appointed Captain R. Bacon, Royal Navy, as the Inspecting Captain Submarines. He was given a free hand to oversee the development.

Initially Vickers had problems because the drawings which had been provided had many discrepancies and errors. However, building continued, but after a boat had nearly turned turtle during a flotation test in a dock, modifications were carried out. In the meantime, Bacon had realised that the submarines under construction had serious deficiencies. Because of their size and profile they would lack the sea-keeping qualities that would be necessary around the British coast. Moreover they did not have either the speed or the endurance that would be needed.

A second class of submarine was designed by Bacon working closely with Vickers, and this was given the designation 'A Class' (Fig 90). The boat was 40 feet (12 metres) longer than the Holland boats with a submerged displacement of 205.5 tons compared to 122 tons. On the surface, the A class could make about 11 knots (20kph) while the Holland could only manage 7.5 knots (14kph) and the respective ranges of the two submarines were A Class 600 miles (965km) and the Holland 355 miles (571km). The first boat of the Class, *A 1*, was fitted with only one bow torpedo tube, but it was decided that subsequent boats in the class would have two bow tubes, side by side, with two re-loads. The Holland had only one tube with two re-loads.

The new class of boat was larger, faster, and more heavily armed than the Holland. For surface work the boat had been fitted with an enlarged casing, which slightly improved her sea-keeping qualities, and a conning tower making it easier to handle the vessel while giving the crew increased visibility.

Holland No. 1 was launched in 1901, *Nos. 2 to 5* and *A1* in 1902. In all, fourteen A Class boats were built and launched during the period 1901 to 1905. But these were not identical because modifications and improvements were being made constantly during the building programme. *A14*, became *B1* on completion.

The B Class followed on quite quickly (Fig 91) and was 40 feet (12 metres) longer, a 10-inch (25-cm) increase in the beam, 2 knots (3.7kph) faster, and fitted with a more substantial casing. Surface performance was better than the A Class and the submarine's range had been doubled, but there had not been much improvement over the submerged performance of the Holland. Eleven of this class were built between 1903 and 1906.

Next came the C Class (Fig 92) and these boats were very similar to those of the B Class. Development, which was now slightly slower, was still being done jointly with Vickers, and improvements continued to be made. Thirty-eight C Class boats were launched between 1906 and 1910, but the monopoly had been taken away from Vickers as six of these were built at H.M. Dockyard at Chatham. Later, two major improvements were made to the boats when they returned for refit; they were equipped with a second periscope and a wireless receiver.

Serious development had started. Feed-back was now coming from the broad base of the boats which had been commissioned and were operational. This was so unlike the early days when individual designers had to rely on their own personal experiments and experiences. Although the hardware was being developed and produced in relatively large numbers, the role of the submarine had not been decided. There was still a large element of the Royal Navy which still subscribed to the views of the Earl St Vincent expressed in 1804. It will be remembered that as First Lord of the Admiralty he had said about the Prime Minister, who at that

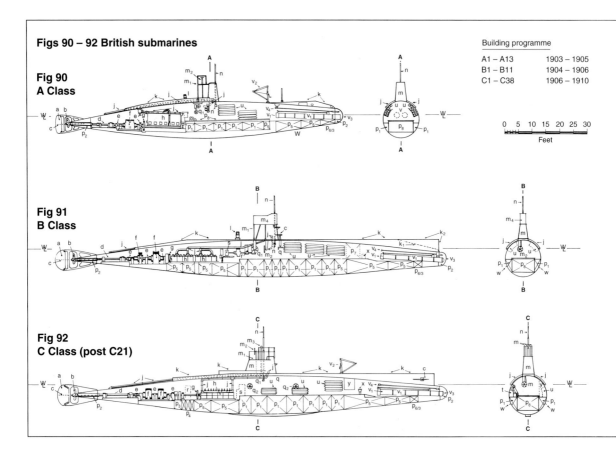

Figs 90 – 92 British submarines

Fig 90
A Class

Fig 91
B Class

Fig 92
C Class (post C21)

Building programme

A1 – A13	1903 – 1905
B1 – B11	1904 – 1906
C1 – C38	1906 – 1910

0 5 10 15 20 25 30
Feet

time was interested in the work of Robert Fulton: 'Pitt was the greatest fool that ever existed to encourage the mode of warfare which those who commanded the seas did not want and which if successful, would deprive them of it'. In any case its use was considered by many to be 'a damned un-English weapon'.

Fortunately a champion arrived on the scene in the form of the First Sea Lord, Sir John Fisher. He had become aware of the potential offensive capability of the submarine whilst he was Commander-in-Chief at Portsmouth. To quote his own words from a letter from Admiralty House, Portsmouth dated 20 April 1904 to a 'high official' quoted by Commander F.W. Lipscomb in his book *The British Submarine*: 'It is astounding to me, perfectly astounding, how the very best amongst us fail to realise the vast impending revolution in Naval warfare and Naval strategy that the subma-

rine will accomplish.' In the same letter he wrote: 'In all seriousness I do not think it is even faintly realised the immense, impending revolution which the submarine will effect as offensive weapons of war.' It was with his full support that the submarine fleet flourished.

The new First Sea Lord considered that the submarine could be used in a port defensive role. More flexible than static minefields and able to operate at a greater range than shore batteries, it could patrol during the day while torpedo boats covered the area by night. Accordingly, flotillas were established at Dundee, Harwich, Dover and Portsmouth, much in the way the French were deploying their boats.

The development of the next group, the D Class, was taken over by the Admiralty (Fig 93). For the first time the submarine was to be developed in exactly the same way as other warships.

Key to Figs 90 – 92
Royal Navy, A, B and C Classes

a	Rudder	m_2	Wheel	q_1	Helmsman's position
b	Propeller	m_3	Vents	q_2	Planesman's position
c	Hydroplanes	m_4	Canvas dodger	r	Air compressor
d	Propeller shaft	n	Periscope	s	Bilge pump
e	Clutch	p_1	Ballast tank	t	Battery ventilation equipment
f	Electric motor	p_2	Trimming or	u	Air bottles
g	Flywheel		compensation tank	v	Torpedo
h	Petrol engine	p_3	Compensating tank	v_1	Torpedo tubes (18" x 2)
j	Exhaust position	p_4	Oil	v_2	Torpedo derrick
k_1	Casing as fitted	p_5	Fuel tank	v_3	Torpedo bow door
k_2	Modified casing	p_6	Water tank	w	Bilge keel
l	Compass	p_7	Torpedo firing tank	x	W.C.
m	Conning tower	p_8	Battery tank	y	Storage space
m_1	Helmsman's platform	q	Control room		

Notes:
1. There were many variations in the shape and size of the conning tower in the early boats.
2. The forward casing, in some of the A class, was raised and extended back to the conning tower to improve the sea-keeping qualities.
3. The original 16-cylinder petrol engines fitted to A5 – A13 were built by Wolsey. Vickers started making the engine, thence known as the Vicker's engine, and these were fitted to B1 – C18. The remainder of the C Class were fitted with a 12-cylinder variant.
4. Forward hydroplanes were fitted to the B Class immediately in front of the conning tower. The 'planes were moved to the bows in the C Class.
5. The complements of the three classes were: A Class 11, B Class 15, C Class 16. In addition, three mice were mustered in each crew to detect any escape of petrol fumes.
6. Sections are all drawn looking forward.

The D Class, designed to overcome the limitations of the earlier boats, was approved by the Admiralty Board in 1906. Eight boats were to be built – two at H.M. Dockyard, Chatham and the remaining six by Vickers at Barrow-in-Furness. The development of the D Class was one of the most significant in the evolution of the British submarine in that the design of this class was to continue to be the basic type for the next forty years. The overall length was 164 feet 7 inches (50 metres), the beam 13 feet 11 inches (4.24 metres), and submerged displacement was 620 tons. In outward appearance the conning tower was larger than those of previous classes, and the boat was fitted with the deeper casing, which later housed a retracting, twelve-pounder gun. The submarines were fitted with external saddle (ballast) tanks, on either side of the hull which resulted in additional inboard space. All the boats in the class were fitted with twin propellers, and after *D1*, these were each driven by a diesel engine. The submarine was equipped with three, 18-inch (457mm) torpedo tubes, two in the bow and one in the stern.

Although previous boats were being retrofitted with wireless receivers, the D Class was equipped with a transmitter/receiver. The aerial was rigged from a mast which had to be lowered by hand and stowed along the side of the casing before diving.

The surface range of the class was 2,500 miles (4,000km) at 11.5 knots (21kph). While submerged she could cover 70 miles (112km) at 5 knots (9kph) before it was necessary to surface and recharge batteries. These submarines also had the battery capacity to remain submerged during daylight hours, giving them much greater potential.

The characteristics of the D Class submarines showed a dramatic improvement over earlier boats

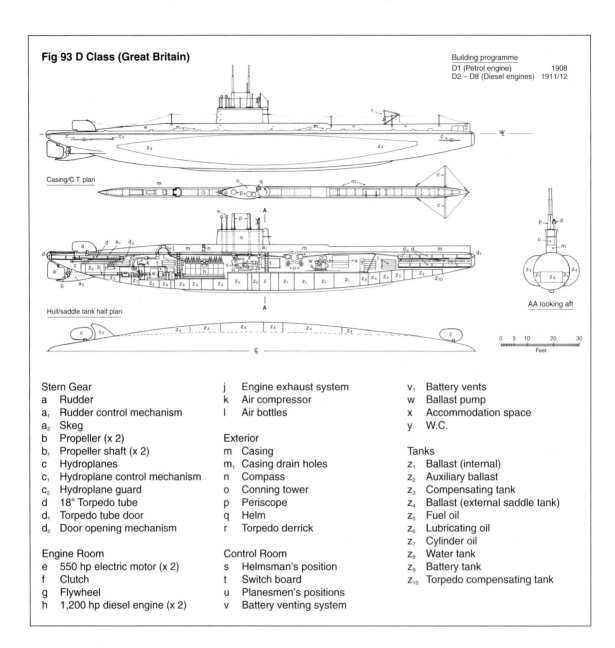

Fig 93 D Class (Great Britain)

Building programme
D1 (Petrol engine)   1908
D2 – D8 (Diesel engines)   1911/12

Casing/C.T. plan

Hull/saddle tank half plan

AA looking aft

0 5 10   20   30
Feet

Stern Gear	j Engine exhaust system	v_1 Battery vents
a Rudder	k Air compressor	w Ballast pump
a_1 Rudder control mechanism	l Air bottles	x Accommodation space
a_2 Skeg		y W.C.
b Propeller (x 2)	**Exterior**	
b_1 Propeller shaft (x 2)	m Casing	**Tanks**
c Hydroplanes	m_1 Casing drain holes	z_1 Ballast (internal)
c_1 Hydroplane control mechanism	n Compass	z_2 Auxiliary ballast
c_2 Hydroplane guard	o Conning tower	z_3 Compensating tank
d 18" Torpedo tube	p Periscope	z_4 Ballast (external saddle tank)
d_1 Torpedo tube door	q Helm	z_5 Fuel oil
d_2 Door opening mechanism	r Torpedo derrick	z_6 Lubricating oil
		z_7 Cylinder oil
Engine Room	**Control Room**	z_8 Water tank
e 550 hp electric motor (x 2)	s Helmsman's position	z_9 Battery tank
f Clutch	t Switch board	z_{10} Torpedo compensating tank
g Flywheel	u Planesmen's positions	
h 1,200 hp diesel engine (x 2)	v Battery venting system	

and although, at this stage, the submarine was still considered to be a defensive weapon for guarding British ports, it now had a greater aggressive potential than ever before. These submarines not only had a greater range, but with twin screws they were more reliable, and the diesel engine was much safer than its petrol predecessor. They had greater fire power and when surfaced had a rudimentary means of communication.

In the defensive role, the submarine could extend the defensive perimeter of a harbour denying the enemy the ability to set up a close blockade. Blockading an enemy was one of the ways to establish and maintain command of the seas, and if the submarine was to preclude battle fleets from doing this, some thought the blockading role could be taken over by the submarine. Although the D Class would be well suited for this, it would take time for the true role of the submarine to develop.

Before war was declared in 1914, eleven E Class submarines, the next class, had already been launched (Fig 94). These boats were slightly larger, with a greater range than the D Class. Initially they were fitted with four torpedo tubes, two in the bow and two in the beam, below the conning tower, one on either flank firing at right angles to the hull. After *E6* a stern tube was added. This class provided the backbone of the British submarine fleet during World War I and fifty-six of them had been built by 1917.

At the outbreak of war in 1914, Great Britain had seventy-seven submarines. This had not been achieved without accidents and losses, but these contributed to the development as hard lessons

were learned. It was a remarkable achievement in that Britain had produced many very capable submarine designers and builders in the past, but when the development programme started there was no one with in-house experience or a submarine design which could be used. This was the fault of the Government and Admiralty who lacked foresight and failed to invest in the future by encouraging those like Garrett and Waddington. It was fortunate that Britain was not put at a great disadvantage in 1914, and that development had progressed rapidly and fairly smoothly once it was decided to go ahead with the Holland submarines.

This is to the credit of the professional approach of the Royal Navy and in particular Captain Bacon, with the help of Vickers Son and Maxim.

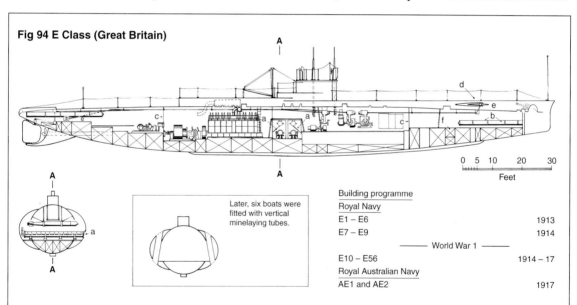

Fig 94 E Class (Great Britain)

Later, six boats were fitted with vertical minelaying tubes.

0 5 10   20   30
Feet

Building programme
Royal Navy
E1 – E6   1913
E7 – E9   1914
———— World War 1 ————
E10 – E56   1914 – 17
Royal Australian Navy
AE1 and AE2   1917

Although 16 feet longer, the E Class was very similar to the earlier D boats; only the major changes are highlighted in the drawing:
a. Two beam torpedo tubes with re-loads.
b. Forward torpedo tubes fitted side-by-side.
c. Watertight bulkheads were fitted, thereby increasing hull strength and giving a greater diving depth (200 feet compared to 100 feet in the D Class).
d. Forward hydroplanes were normally fitted to the pressure hull below the waterline, but in some boats retracting 'planes were fitted to the forward casing.
e. During the war, substantial guards were fitted to protect the hydroplanes.
f. A variety of guns were fitted to the class, mostly forward of the conning tower.

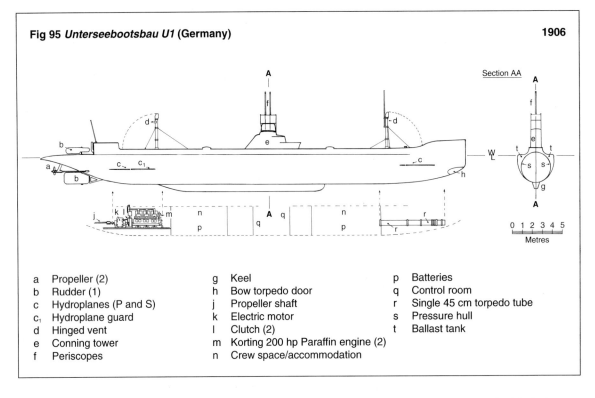

Fig 95 *Unterseebootsbau U1 (Germany)*   **1906**

Section AA

W L

0 1 2 3 4 5
Metres

a	Propeller (2)	g	Keel	p	Batteries
b	Rudder (1)	h	Bow torpedo door	q	Control room
c	Hydroplanes (P and S)	j	Propeller shaft	r	Single 45 cm torpedo tube
c₁	Hydroplane guard	k	Electric motor	s	Pressure hull
d	Hinged vent	l	Clutch (2)	t	Ballast tank
e	Conning tower	m	Korting 200 hp Paraffin engine (2)		
f	Periscopes	n	Crew space/accommodation		

It should also not be forgotten that the crews for this fleet of submarines had to be trained and the administrative support needed for training, maintaining and supplying the submarine fleet also had to be developed and put in place. In twelve (and to those involved it must have seemed twelve very, very short) years the Royal Navy had produced an effective submarine branch from scratch.

In 1914 the Royal Navy had the submarines, the crews and the necessary supporting services. The next stage of the evolution would be to develop the strategic and tactical role of the submarine.

Germany

In 1900, Germany like Britain, was not in a position to launch her own domestic-building programme without outside assistance. A licence to build one Holland type submarine was obtained and this was built at Kiel.

Raymondo Lorenzo d'Equevilley-Montjustin, a Spanish naval engineer, who had been trained in Paris and had worked there with Laubeuf, offered

his designs to Germany. It was decided that an experimental boat would be built by Krupps at Kiel. The submarine, later called *Forelle* or *Trout*, was 43 feet (13 metres) long and displaced 15.5 tons. She was powered by a one-speed, non reversible, electric motor and fitted with a variable pitch propeller to control speed and direction (forward and astern). The weapon system consisted of two external torpedo tubes, one on either flank of the submarine. The boat, after some initial problems, generally handled well and had a range of 25 miles (40km) at 4 knots (7.4kph). There were problems. For instance, on firing a torpedo the vessel took on a heavy list. The severest limitation was that her batteries had to be recharged either at a shore base or by a depot or mother ship. Compared to her American (and now also British) contemporary *Forelle* was quite inadequate.

In 1904 Russia was at war with Japan. A Russian delegation, with the task of building up the Russian Navy, visited Kiel. After a demonstration of *Forelle*, that submarine was purchased by the Russians and they also placed an order for three submarines 131 feet (39.9 metres) long with a displacement of 250 tons. These boats were to be built by Germaniawerst (Krupps) at Kiel and fitted with 200hp Korting paraffin engines. They were to be of a double hull construction.

In Germany the situation was the exact opposite to that in Great Britain. In Britain, the First Sea Lord was the champion of the submarine while there was a strong anti-submarine lobby elsewhere in the Royal Navy. In Germany von Tirpitz was against the submarine while there were others who very much favoured its development. The turning point came in May 1904; von Tirpitz was asked by a Deputy of the *Reichstag* why no submarines were being built for the German Navy. His answer was that until then he had considered the submarine to be unreliable and inadequate. It was not long after this that the German Submarine Research and Development Programme was initiated.

Gustav Berling, a naval engineer, was appointed to supervise the construction of the first German boat. He was seconded to the Torpedo Inspectorate which had overall responsibility for submarine development. A modest development programme was announced which provided for the construction of eight boats over several years and the first of these was ordered from Germaniawerst in December 1904.

This was most convenient because the design of the German boat was based on that being used for the three Russian submarines and the experience already gained in their construction could be used to good advantage. However, there were considerable delays because of changes to the original specification. The diameter of the pressure hull was increased and the positioning of the forward, single torpedo tube was altered necessitating a change to the forward profile of the vessel. There were also problems with the development of the diesel engines.

On 6 August 1906, twelve months after the expected delivery date, the submarine, designated U1, was launched (Fig 95). She was 131 feet (39.9 metres) long and of double hull construction. She had twin screws driven by electric motors and two Korting paraffin engines each of 225hp. Her armament was a single internal, forward torpedo tube and three torpedoes were carried. This boat, like the three Russian submarines, was to the designs of d'Equevilley-Montjustin and their French ancestry was very apparent.

After the initial hull integrity tests, sea trials were carried out. She was handed over to the German Navy in December 1906. Two days later the Navy announced that U1 met their requirements.

Von Tirpitz was still not in favour of the submarine. This was reflected in the Naval Estimates of 1907 to 09, which allowed for only four submarines.

U2 was ordered from the Kaiserliche Werst in Danzig in the spring of 1906. This submarine was to be larger than U1 and was to be fitted with Daimler-Benz paraffin engines as Kortings were having development problems. The submarine was to have four torpedo tubes: two internal at the bows and two external at the stern. Like the first boat there were delays because changes were made to the specification. The promised engines did not materialise and two Korting 300hp engines were fitted. U2 was launched in June 1908. Underpowered, the boat did not perform as well as expected. In 1909 the Korting engines were removed and the Daimler-Benz engines were fitted, but a few days later one suffered a failed crankshaft. Even after this had been rectified the boat continued to have dynamo problems. U2 was not a very successful boat.

The next two boats (U3 and U4) built by Kaiserliche Werst were fitted with more powerful Korting engines and proved to be more reliable (Fig 96).

In the meantime Germaniawerst had accepted orders for two submarines from Austria-Hungary and another for Norway. The Torpedo Directorate was concerned about placing further orders with this firm not only because of the foreign sales but because by then (a foreigner) d'Equevilley-Montjustin was in a senior position in the firm.

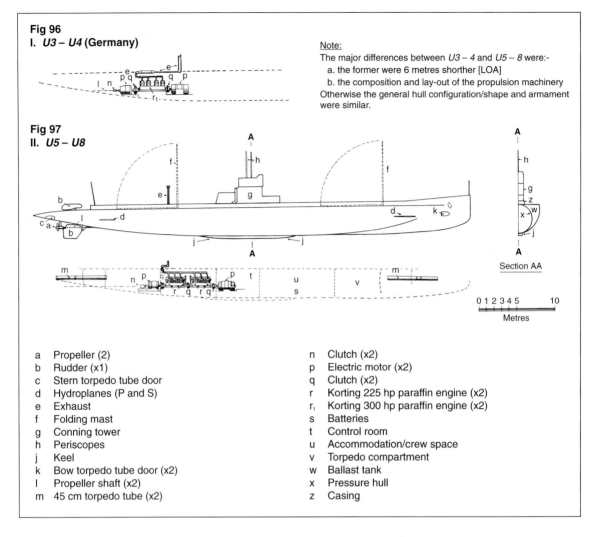

Fig 96
I. *U3 – U4* (Germany)

Note:
The major differences between *U3 – 4* and *U5 – 8* were:-
   a. the former were 6 metres shorther [LOA]
   b. the composition and lay-out of the propulsion machinery
Otherwise the general hull configuration/shape and armament
were similar.

Fig 97
II. *U5 – U8*

Section AA

0 1 2 3 4 5   10
Metres

a	Propeller (2)	n	Clutch (x2)
b	Rudder (x1)	p	Electric motor (x2)
c	Stern torpedo tube door	q	Clutch (x2)
d	Hydroplanes (P and S)	r	Korting 225 hp paraffin engine (x2)
e	Exhaust	r_1	Korting 300 hp paraffin engine (x2)
f	Folding mast	s	Batteries
g	Conning tower	t	Control room
h	Periscopes	u	Accommodation/crew space
j	Keel	v	Torpedo compartment
k	Bow torpedo tube door (x2)	w	Ballast tank
l	Propeller shaft (x2)	x	Pressure hull
m	45 cm torpedo tube (x2)	z	Casing

The situation was resolved by easing the Spaniard out and appointing, at the recommendation of Gustav Berling, Hans Techel as head of submarine development in the firm. Techel was destined to play an important role in future submarine development in Germany.

During the next three years orders were placed for fourteen more submarines:

1908	April	*U5 – U8*	Germaniawerst
1908	July	*U9 – U12*	Kaiserliche Werst
1909	February	*U13 – U15*	Kaiserliche Werst
1909	August	*U16*	Germaniawerst
1910	April	*U17 – U18*	Kaiserliche Werst

(Figs 97 – 100)

As new boats had been ordered, improvements had been incorporated although the hull shape and profile had remained much the same. They were all of the double hull construction. Progressively they had increased in length from 139 feet (42.4 metres) (*U1*) to 205 feet (62.4 metres) (*U18*). From *U2* onwards the armament consisted of two forward and two stern tubes and six torpedoes were carried. But a long-awaited lightweight diesel engine had still not materialised. Indeed, all boats up to *U18* were fitted with either six- or eight-cylinder Korting paraffin engines with the exception of *U2* which was eventually fitted out with Daimler-Benz engines.

These engines had three disadvantages. Firstly they lacked power, and from *U5* onwards, to increase the rating it was necessary to have two engines in tandem on each shaft. Secondly, the paraffin engines had little speed adjustment and could not be reversed. Consequently, to overcome these problems, there was a complicated in-line arrangement of motors and engines (which differed between groups of boats), on each propeller shaft. Thirdly, the paraffin engines emitted clouds of white exhaust smoke which was visible for miles. This was partly remedied with the introduction of a new but costly paraffin, which, for economy was used sparingly in peacetime.

The development programme was not without accident. In 1911 at Kiel, *U3* on her maiden voyage took on water through an open ventilation valve during her first dive, and sank. The Captain immediately ordered the crew and passengers (the normal complement was twenty-two and thirty-two were on board) to move to the forward compartment of the boat; he, another officer and the helmsman remained in the conning tower. After twenty-seven hours and one abortive attempt to raise the bows, twenty-nine of the crew were finally rescued through the bow torpedo tubes, but the captain and two others, who had remained in the conning tower, were later found dead. Those in the bows were only just able to survive because caustic-potash air purifiers were positioned in that part of the boat.

The cause of the accident was that an indicator showed that the ventilation valve was closed but it had been incorrectly fitted. The Torpedo Inspectorate immediately introduced new safety measures in the crew drills and design modifications were later incorporated to improve safety.

In 1908 several firms had been invited, by the Inspectorate, to develop a suitable, lightweight diesel engine of 850hp. Germaniawerst had already produced the smaller engine of 300hp which was fitted to the submarine *Atropo* which was being built for the Italian Navy. The development time was lengthy but in due course the MAN test engine was accepted after trials. In November 1910,

having established that a suitable engine could be made, four diesel boats (*U19* to *U22*) were ordered from Kaiserliche Werst and these were to be fitted with MAN engines (Fig 101). A further four (*U23* to *U26*) were ordered from Germaniawerst and these were to be fitted with diesels made by that firm, although they had not yet been fully developed and tested. This was not a good decision because the engine, when it was finally produced, was not reliable.

The German Navy had been adamant from the start that on safety grounds the petrol engine would not be fitted to German boats and steam propulsion was considered unsatisfactory for a submarine. But the long delays in developing a suitably powerful diesel engine undoubtedly encouraged the Torpedo Inspectorate to consider other forms of propulsion. These included closed cycle engines one of which used exhaust gas enriched with oxygen. Experiments were carried out with some success and although an engine was adapted, the technology at that time was insufficiently advanced to properly (safely) regulate the fuel supply and the project was abandoned.

Looking back with hindsight perhaps the most interesting proposal was to revert to steam, using a steam-caustic soda system. Compared to an internal combustion engine arrangement the proposed steam system had the advantages of being lighter although bulkier; able to raise steam more quickly than batteries could be recharged; and it provided a better performance both on the surface and submerged. One of the protagonists was d'Equevilley-Montjustin who had produced a design for a submarine incorporating the proposed steam system.

Two boats were ordered by the German Navy so that they could be evaluated. The first was d'Equevilley-Montjustin's steam-driven boat. Although it was clearly recognised by the German Navy that steam propulsion was not really the way forward this system did have some advantages particularly bearing in mind the delays experienced in developing the diesel. The second was a

Diagramatic layout U9-U22 (Germany)

Fig 98 I *U9–U12*

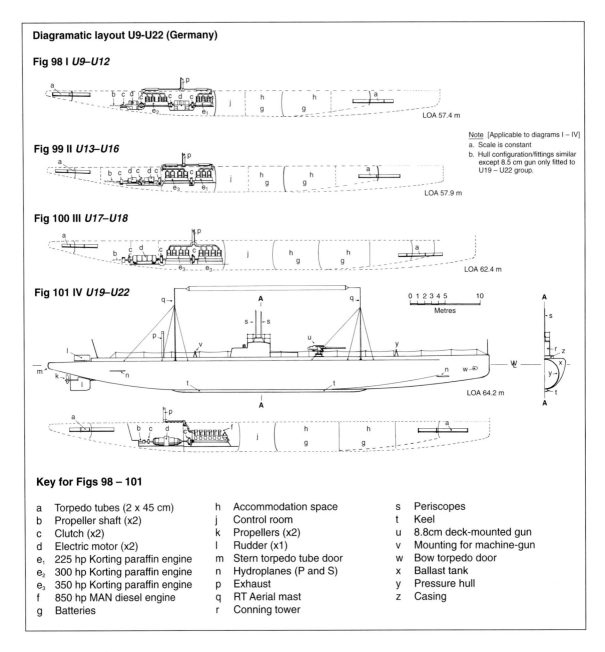

LOA 57.4 m

Note [Applicable to diagrams I – IV]
a. Scale is constant
b. Hull configuration/fittings similar except 8.5 cm gun only fitted to U19 – U22 group.

Fig 99 II *U13–U16*

LOA 57.9 m

Fig 100 III *U17–U18*

LOA 62.4 m

Fig 101 IV *U19–U22*

0 1 2 3 4 5   10
Metres

LOA 64.2 m

Key for Figs 98 – 101

a	Torpedo tubes (2 x 45 cm)	h	Accommodation space	s	Periscopes
b	Propeller shaft (x2)	j	Control room	t	Keel
c	Clutch (x2)	k	Propellers (x2)	u	8.8cm deck-mounted gun
d	Electric motor (x2)	l	Rudder (x1)	v	Mounting for machine-gun
e_1	225 hp Korting paraffin engine	m	Stern torpedo tube door	w	Bow torpedo door
e_2	300 hp Korting paraffin engine	n	Hydroplanes (P and S)	x	Ballast tank
e_3	350 hp Korting paraffin engine	p	Exhaust	y	Pressure hull
f	850 hp MAN diesel engine	q	RT Aerial mast	z	Casing
g	Batteries	r	Conning tower		

diesel-powered boat by the Italian designer Laurenti. Having exported a submarine (*Atropo*) to Italy, Germany now wanted to see what progress that country was making.

Germaniawerst had gained experience by building boats for foreign powers. Four submarines were built for Norway, three for Russia and one for Italy. Efforts were made to sell submarines to Turkey and

Greece although nothing came of them because of the outbreak of the war in 1914.

The Inspectorate was also evolving both tactical and strategic policy. As early as 1909 exercises had been carried out with three boats (*U1*, *U3* and *U4*) to evaluate the feasibility of submarines working together. The possibility of collision between boats and the inability to communicate dictated that boats would have to work in clearly defined areas or formations.

In January 1912 the Torpedo Inspectorate produced draft proposals for the future operational deployment of submarines. The main part of the force, consisting of thirty-six submarines, would provide a permanent defensive screen to cover the German Bight and approaches to Kiel. Twelve boats would be kept available for offensive operations; and an operational reserve of twelve boats would be maintained. Based on the experience of the mechanical reliability, already gained, it was assumed that at any one time one boat in six would be non-operational. In addition to the operational boats there would be a requirement for a small training flotilla which would consist of four submarines (*U1* to *U4*). The Inspectorate's plan gave the submarine force a largely defensive role. To meet this requirement it was recommended that a fleet of seventy operational submarines were required plus four training boats. This was an ambitious programme which, in addition to the boats already ordered, would necessitate the placing of orders for thirty-three more boats at a cost of about one hundred million marks.

These official proposals did not meet with approval throughout the Navy. Unlike the Royal Navy where there was still opposition to the introduction of the submarine, in the German Navy there was a strong school of thought that the submarine was being wasted in a defensive role. It was considered that the boats should be larger, with an increased radius of action. This would allow the submarines to attack the vital merchant shipping on which Great Britain depended.

The Inspectorate's proposals were accepted and the Naval Estimates for the next five years were substantially increased.

By the end of 1912 it became clear that there were problems with the Germaniawerst diesels fitted to *U23* to *U26*. There were continuous development delays and when eventually fitted in the boats they proved to be unreliable. To further exacerbate the problem a further eleven boats had been ordered. Recriminations followed and a number of changes

were made in the Torpedo Inspectorate which included the removal of Berling. He was blamed for ordering the Germaniawerst engines before they had been developed and proved. Eventually these diesels were brought up to the standard of the MAN engines.

The significance of the submarine arm had grown rapidly since Berling had started working on *U1* in 1904 and it was decided, in late 1913, to establish an independent U-Boat Inspectorate. Although he was eventually moved, credit must be given to Berling for the way the German submarine arm had developed in the ten years before World War I.

A detailed comparison of the German and British boats is beyond the scope of this book. However, it is interesting to compare the vital statistics:

Type	L.O.A. Metres	Torpedo Tubes	Range N. Miles	At (Kts)
BRITAIN				
Holland	19.4	1 x 14"	500	8
A Class	30.48	1 x 18"	310	10
B Class	41.15	2 x 18"	1,000	8.5
C Class	49.37	3 x 18"	1,500	8.5
D Class	49.37	3 x 18"	2,500	10
E Class	55.16	5 x 18"	3,000	10
GERMANY				
U1	42.4	1 x 45 cm	1,500	10
U2	45.4	4 x 45 cm	1,600	13
U3-U4	51.3	4 x 45 cm	1,800	12
U5-U8	57.3	4 x 45 cm	1,900	13
U9-U12	57.4	4 x 45 cm	1,800	14
U13-U15	57.9	4 x 45 cm	2,000	14
U16	57.8	4 x 45 cm	2,100	15
U17-U18	62.4	4 x 45 cm	6,700	8
U19-U22	64.2	4 x 45 cm	7,600	8
U23-U26	64.7	4 x 45 cm	7,620	8
U27-U30	64.7	4 x 50 cm	9,770	8
U31-U41	64.7	4 x 50 cm	8,790	8
U43-U50	64.7	4 x 50 cm	11,400	8

At the outbreak of World War II the German

Navy had an operational fleet of twenty-nine boats with a further sixteen under construction. One of the operational boats was *U9*, the boat with which the story was started. In Germany, and in particular within the U-Boat Inspectorate, as a result of Weddigen's success in September 1914, the submarine was seen in a completely different light and its role was to be completely reappraised.

CHAPTER 25

LEGACY

It is very difficult to pick out individuals who have made a specific and significant contribution to the development of the submarine. Much had been thought out and tried before 1800 and thereafter designers incorporated, modified, improved and adapted what had been used previously. There are exceptions. John Holland experimented with and combined the right component parts to build a submarine which was the first to meet the requirements of a number of nations. What is more, the design of this submarine had the potential to be further developed. Rudolph Diesel contributed to submarine development indirectly with his diesel engine. Whitehead will be remembered for his torpedo which was a breakthrough using and developing known technology. Others will be remembered for what they achieved, rather than what they contributed: Bushnell, Hunley, Day, Bauer, Fulton, etc.

Garrett is also one of the exceptions. Although there was nothing ingenious in the method of operating *The Egg* – every system had been used previously – *Resurgam* was different. Although steam had been used many years before in submersibles, the adaptation of the Lamm system allowed a submarine to submerge, but still use the steam engine. *Resurgam* was the first self-contained submarine, with a reasonable operational range, to bridge the very wide gap between a manpowered submarine and one driven by an engine. This was the giant step that needed to be taken before the submarine would become a viable proposition. He had recognised the possibility and done something about it.

Unfortunately *Resurgam* was not a successful boat because it was underpowered and there was a lack of control over the diving ability and stability of the craft. The steam engine, although cleverly adapted, was not a satisfactory power plant; nor were the boats he built with Nordenfelt a resounding success but at the time they were the best commercially-built submarines in the world.

In the wings were other builders with immediate but undeveloped potential like Peral and Waddington. As the leaders Garrett and Nordenfelt probably acted as a spur, warning the USA and France that a reliable submarine would be invented in the near future and if they were not to be left behind something should be done about it immediately. Other nations were slower to take heed.

At the end of the nineteenth century steam was not a real option. Although reliable in surface vessels, in submarines there were too many problems associated with this form of power. Garrett was too early. Had he been a little later he may have used the new technology that was harnessed by Holland and others. Even so he does have a place in history, as do all his predecessors. In the development of the submarine nothing can be specifically attributed to him, but then there are very few who can lay claim to such a distinction, but without such men as Garrett no progress would have been made.

It has been necessary to be critical. How easy this task is, particularly with hindsight. What should be remembered is well summed up in the words of President Theodore Roosevelt[1]:

> It is not the critic who counts, nor the man who points out how the strong man stumbled, or where the doer of deeds could have done better, the credit belongs to the man who is actually in the arena, whose face is marred by dust and sweat and blood; who strives valiantly; who errs and comes short again and again; who knows the great enthusiasms, the great devotions and spends himself in a worthy cause; who at the best, knows in the end the triumph of high achievement; and who at the worst, if he fails, at least fails while daring greatly, so that his place shall never be with those cold and timid souls, who know neither victory or defeat.
>
> President Theodore Roosevelt
> 1858–1919

[1] *Warriors' Words* A Quotation Book by Peter G. Tsouras

APPENDIX I

General Requirements for Submarine Torpedo Boats for the United States Navy

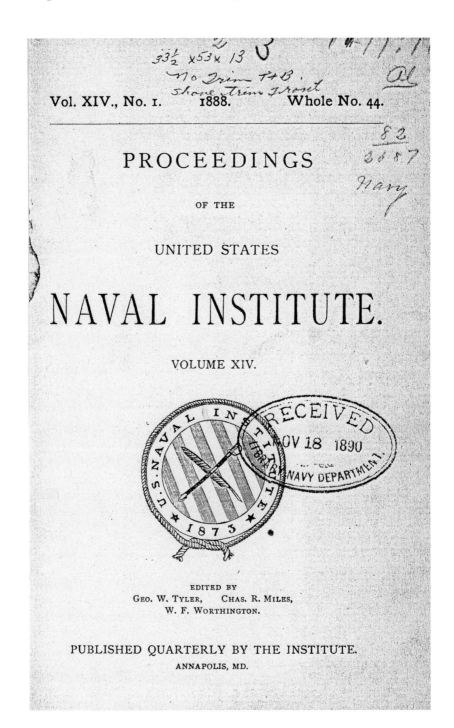

Vol. XIV., No. 1.   1888.   Whole No. 44.

PROCEEDINGS

OF THE

UNITED STATES

NAVAL INSTITUTE.

VOLUME XIV.

EDITED BY
GEO. W. TYLER,   CHAS. R. MILES,
W. F. WORTHINGTON.

PUBLISHED QUARTERLY BY THE INSTITUTE.
ANNAPOLIS, MD.

In an exhibition of one of these boats given last month the main features accentuated by the exhibitors were that the boat awash was more difficult to make out than another boat of greater freeboard—a fact that would seem to need no very extensive proof—and that she was always buoyant, a property that, as has been shown, is common to all submarine boats worthy of the name, and which she possesses in a much less degree than she might were she constructed on common sense principles for real submerged work, for which she showed less capacity than the small American boats. The showing of submerging qualities consisted in hauling the boat down to the bottom of a dock by means of her down haul propellers, and then allowing her to rise by her own small buoyancy, thus exhibiting the application of a general principle that could have been just as well shown, and with just as much bearing on real submarine boat work, by pushing a cork under the surface of the water and then allowing it to bob up.

On the other hand, in looking over the field of possibilities for the immediate future it is apparent that there are plenty of practical devices extant to make a submarine boat successful, plenty of experience to apply them, and plenty of money to pay the expenses of construction ; and therefore it only remains to be seen whether or not the owners of the devices, experience, and money will have the wisdom to comprehend that in combining to give the Navy Department the boat it requires they will be working to their own advantage as well to that of the Government.

Even if the Department fail in its first attempt to obtain a practical construction of the kind, the submarine boat, as such, must soon appear as a factor in naval warfare—for just as rapidity and range of aimed fire have forced the use of earth cover ashore, so will the same causes force the use of water cover afloat—and unless " we, the people of the United States," choose to continue to be as stupid as we have been for the last score of years concerning everything that floats, we are in our own interests bound to lead in its development. When it comes it will not, like every new warlike device conceived in the brain of a cranky inventor, " entirely revolutionize warfare," but it will assume the well defined place and duties awaiting it—place and duties that will urgently require to be filled and done if there is to be even a faint attempt at placing this country in a condition of partial defense.

SUBMARINE TORPEDO BOAT FOR THE UNITED STATES NAVY.

[Reprint of circular showing the general requirements desired to be fulfilled in the design and trial of a steel submarine torpedo boat for the United States Navy.]

NAVY DEPARTMENT,
WASHINGTON, D. C., *November 26*, 1887.

Under authority conferred by the act of Congress, entitled " An Act making appropriations for the Naval Service for the fiscal year ending June 30, 1888, and for other purposes," approved March 3, 1887, to which reference is made as a part of this advertisement, sealed proposals are hereby invited and will be received at this Department until 12 o'clock noon, on the first day of March, 1888, for the construction, by contract, of one submarine torpedo boat, complete, with torpedo appendages—such vessel to be of the best and most modern design ; to be constructed of steel, of domestic manufacture, having a tensile strength of not less than 60,000 pounds per square inch and an elongation in eight inches of not less than 25 per cent, and to have the highest attainable speed.

254   PROFESSIONAL NOTES.

For information as to the conditions desired by the Department, reference is made to the "circular showing the general requirements desired to be fulfilled in the design and performance of a steel submarine torpedo boat," approved by the Secretary of the Navy, copies of which can be obtained on application to the Bureau of Ordnance, Navy Department.

Each proposal must be accompanied by drawings and specifications of the vessel which the bidder proposes to build. The drawings must be drawn correctly to a convenient scale, and must show clearly all the essential requisites of the vessel. The space and weight allowed for torpedoes and their appendages must also be shown in the design, and the fittings for the same are to be furnished or installed by the contractor.

A statement, in detail, of the weights in the vessel and their distribution, and full particulars and explanation concerning the kind, power, and economy of the engines, power generators, and propelling devices, and all other mechanism, must accompany the proposal.

In order that the Department may be prepared to act intelligently in making a selection, it must be clearly shown by the drawings, specifications, and statement or statements accompanying the proposal, that the displacement and stability are sufficient, and that the balance of qualities is such that everything will be carried properly and safely ; and such additional information must be included as may be necessary to enable the Department to readily determine the character of the proposed vessel and the correctness of the calculations upon which the design is based.

The contractor must furnish, at his own expense, all working drawings necessary to the complete construction of the vessel, and the expense of all trials, before final acceptance of the vessel under the contract, must also be borne by the contractor.

Proposals must be made in accordance with forms which will be furnished on application to the Bureau of Ordnance, and must state the time within which the bidder will complete, for delivery, the vessel which he proposes to construct.

Each proposal must be accompanied by a certified check, payable to the order of the Secretary of the Navy, for an amount equal to five per cent of the bid. The check received from the successful bidder will be returned to him on his entering into a formal contract for the due performance of the work and giving bond for the same, with security to the satisfaction of the Secretary of the Navy, in a penal sum equal to sixty per cent of the amount of his bid ; but in case he shall fail to enter into such contract and to give such bond within thirty days after notice of the acceptance of his proposal, the check accompanying such proposal shall become the property of the United States.

All checks accompanying proposals which are not accepted will be returned immediately after the award shall have been made.

Payments under the contract will be made in five equal instalments, as the work progresses, upon bills duly certified. The last payment will be made upon the acceptance of the boat after trial. Twenty-five per cent of each instalment will be reserved until the final acceptance of the boat by the Department.

Proposals must be made in duplicate, inclosed in envelopes marked "Proposals for a submarine torpedo boat," and addressed to the Secretary of the Navy, Navy Department, Washington, D. C.

The Secretary of the Navy reserves the right to reject any or all bids, as, in his judgment, the interests of the Government may require.

(Signed) WILLIAM C. WHITNEY,
Secretary of the Navy.

GENERAL REQUIREMENTS.

The design for a submarine or diving boat, to be acceptable to the Department, should show the manner in which it is proposed the vessel shall be manœuvred under all conditions, but more especially how she is to be brought into action from a distance.

PROFESSIONAL NOTES. 255

The most desirable qualities to be possessed by such a vessel while approaching a hostile ship under way, are speed, certainty of direction, invisibility, and safety from the enemy's fire ; the design and description should plainly show the amount of each of these qualities that the boat would possess, and the advantage that results from diminishing any one for the purpose of increasing any other.

The Department has no knowledge of any method by which certainty of approach to an object constantly moving and constantly changing its direction of motion can be secured, unless the object is kept constantly in view or lost sight of for brief intervals only ; consequently, if no novel method for insuring certainty of approach (when submerged) be devised, a design, showing, at the expense of invisibility, great speed for use outside the range of effective hostile fire would be desirable ; providing always that submergence to a safety depth can be quickly secured, and certainty of approach still be retained when coming within the danger zone. Within the danger zone a part of the speed of approach may be given up for the sake of obtaining water cover, provided certainty of approach can be still maintained until the object of attack is so near that this certainty is virtually secure even when the boat is deeply submerged for the purpose of obtaining total invisibility or for delivering the attack at a vulnerable point.

The following definitions are adopted for convenience in describing the conditions under which submarine boats generally move :

"*Surface*"—*i. e.* with freeboard or awash.

"*Covered*"—*i. e.* protected by at least three feet of water over the highest point of the shell, not necessarily cut off from connection with the atmosphere, and furnishing a view of the object of attack through air.

"*Submerged*"—*i. e.* at any safe depth, cut off from communication with the atmosphere, and affording no view of the object of attack other than one through water.

Any boat not designed for running "submerged" cannot be considered submarine ; and she should be able to run in at least one of the other ways mentioned in order to be satisfactorily effective.

The features essential to the usefulness of a submarine boat designed for offensive warlike purposes are in general terms held to be :

Great safety, facility and certainty of action when "submerged," fair speed when "covered," good speed when running on the "surface," a fair endurance of power and stores, great ease of manœuvring under all conditions, sufficient stability, great structural strength, and fair power of offense.

The Department would particularize as to these qualities about as follows :

I. *Speed.*—The boat should be capable of making at least fifteen knots per hour when running on the "surface," and at least twelve knots per hour when running "covered." When running "submerged" she should have a mean speed of at least eight knots per hour.

II. *Power endurance.*—She should be able to run for about thirty hours at full power, on the surface or "covered," while at the same time she should maintain at its greatest efficiency the power that is to be used for "submerged" running. When "submerged" she should be capable of running at least two hours at 8 knots mean speed. If intended for "covered" and "submerged" work *only* (without using air draught), she should be capable of running in that condition about thirty hours at full power.

She should carry about ninety hours provisions and water for the crew.

III. *Ease of manœuvring.*—When running on the surface, "covered" or "submerged," the boat should be able, when working at full power, to turn in a circle of a diameter not greater than four times her length, and this without reversing her engines.

If designed to run part of the time on the surface, she should be able to pass from the surface to the covered plane in 30 seconds.

When below the surface, she should be able to make very quickly a minimum change of 10 degrees in direction in the vertical plane.

The conditions necessary for furnishing power for "submerged" runs must at *all* times during the working endurance be maintained at their maximum efficiency and ready for *instant use* until the first "submerged" run is commenced. After the boat has again made communication with the air, the time of renewing that part of the power that was used while "submerged," or re-arranging the conditions for submerged running, which were altered during submergence, should not be longer than twice the period of the submerged run.

While lying still the boat must be able to maintain any desired depth within the limits of safety from crushing pressure upon the shell. It is not considered that this requirement can be fulfilled simply by varying the specific gravity of the boat.

IV. *Stability.*—This quality must be possessed in good measure when the boat is on the "surface"; and when "covered" or "submerged" the stability must in great part depend upon "normal buoyancy"—*i. e.*, a certain amount of buoyancy normally remaining in the boat and never given up, unless it should be necessary to sacrifice buoyancy in order to sink from under an obstruction or to lie upon the bottom for the purpose of conserving power.

The amount of this normal buoyancy and consequent stability must be sufficient to allow the necessary movement of the crew in working the machinery and torpedo appliances while the boat is "submerged" and lying still, but not on the bottom; and it is thought that this amount of buoyancy will be more than sufficient for the purpose of successful and convenient navigation when the boat is "submerged" and moving at moderate speeds.

V. *Structural strength.*—The shell should be sufficiently strong to withstand an exterior water pressure due to a submergence of at least 150 feet.

VI. *Power of offense.*—Against any part of the bottom of a ship running at speed the boat must be able to deliver, with reasonable certainty, torpedoes carrying charges equal in minimum effect to 100 pounds of gun-cotton. The mode in which this requirement is to be met is left entirely to the designer; but it is to be remarked that the method which gives the greatest under-water range, with accuracy, will be preferred. Rapidity of rate of delivery, extension of angle through which torpedoes can be delivered, number of torpedoes that can be carried, and effective over-water delivery, are all important factors for determining the power of offense.

Besides the foregoing principal requirements, the boat must be provided with means for the attainment of the following objects: Enabling the commander to see the object of attack when running "covered," and an all-around view should also be provided, if practicable; compensating or otherwise *insuring the accuracy of the compass*, when "submerged," and under all conditions; purifying the air for the crew so as to allow at least 12 hours submersion; keeping the temperature within the boat down to 100 degrees Fahr.; getting away from obstructions—above, below, or lateral; pulling out of mud; automatically preventing a dive below a predetermined depth; preventing the fouling by lines or other obstructions of any working parts exterior to the shell proper; lighting the interior, and for the escape of the crew in case of disaster.

These qualities are expected by the Department both because, in its opinion, they are necessary, and because they have already been attained with more or less success in submarine structures now extant. But as the bids are to be made upon the basis of guaranteed results, bidders are at liberty, in their proposals, to modify or omit, as they may think proper, any of the qualities mentioned herein, always excepting qualities of workmanship and material used in the construction of the hull, engines, power generators, and other mechanism.

Any valuable qualities not enumerated by the Department (which limits itself to pointing out those that appear to be the most useful) will be fully considered and given due weight in deciding upon the design to be adopted.

As the Department does not define the means by which results are to be attained, it will accept no responsibility as to the efficiency of the methods proposed to be used.

PROFESSIONAL NOTES. 257

Designs must be accompanied by written explanations fully setting forth the operation of the boat and appendages, and stating all the advantages of the proposed vessel.

The bidder to whom the award is made will furnish detailed drawings and specifications of his boat, and the contract will be based on these. They must not differ in any important way from the general design and explanation submitted with the proposal.

QUALITY AND WORKMANSHIP.

All material is to be of the best quality, of domestic manufacture, and subject to the tests and inspection laid down in the appended instructions concerning tests to be applied to steel for use in the construction of the hull and machinery of a torpedo boat, approved by the Secretary of the Navy, July 15, 1887.

The workmanship shall be of the highest class, and subject to the inspection of officers designated for the duty. Such inspectors shall have free access to the works of the builders at all times, for the purpose of witnessing and examining the progress of the vessel and machinery, and they are to be afforded every facility and assistance for inspecting and for ascertaining that the work is done in accordance with the terms of the contract.

GENERAL REMARKS.

Conditions will be inserted in the contract requiring, upon the completion of the boat, trial sufficient to test her efficient operation, and to insure that the contract has been properly performed, and that the guarantees assumed by the contractor have been complied with.

A boat rejected under the contract may have exhibited certain important qualities in a much greater degree than was contemplated by the contract, or she may embody devices and improvements novel and very valuable but not called for by the contract.

In such a case the Department might possibly be disposed to purchase the boat, but such a course will not be pursued unless the advantages to the Department are of the most obvious character.

The Department limits the maximum displacement to two hundred (200) tons when the vessel is "submerged," and it puts the displacement at so large a figure in order that designers may not be hampered in attaining good speeds by lack of space for motors; but it is thought that designs showing about ninety (90) tons displacement will give the best results. No bidder is limited to the submission of a single design, but each is invited to submit as many as he may see fit. Independent drawings and explanations, and a separate proposal for building the vessel shown, must accompany each design.

The foregoing statement of "general requirements" is intended only as suggestive, and as embodying for the benefit of bidders the views of the Department as to what ought to be accomplished by any person assuming to offer a plan for an effective submarine torpedo boat; but the Department is of the opinion that results already attained justify the purchase of a submarine boat though the exact requirements of the circular may not be guaranteed. Bidders are therefore invited to submit their designs even though these may show qualities less desirable or less difficult to attain than those hereinbefore described: they should be careful to state what matters are guaranteed.

All bids will be considered without regard to the residence of the bidder, but the boat must be of domestic manufacture.

No bid will be accepted that does not offer guarantees of results approximating to those stated in this circular, nor unless accompanied by plans justifying, in the opinion of the Department, a reasonable expectation that results guaranteed will be attained.

All other bids will be rejected.   (Signed) WILLIAM C. WHITNEY,
                                            Secretary of the Navy.

Appendix II

Provisional Patent Specification for Submarine or Subaqueous Boats or Vessels taken out by Thorsten Nordenfelt – February 1881

A.D. 1881, 17th February. N° 693.

Submarine or Subaqueous Boats or Vessels.

LETTERS PATENT to Thorsten Nordenfelt, of No. 1, Saint Swithin's Lane, in the City of London, Civil Engineer, for an Invention of "IMPROVEMENTS IN OR APPERTAINING TO SUBMARINE OR SUBAQUEOUS BOATS OR VESSELS."

PROVISIONAL SPECIFICATION left by the said Thorsten Nordenfelt at the Office of the Commissioners of Patents on the 17th February 1881.

THORSTEN NORDENFELT, of No. 1, Saint Swithin's Lane, in the City of London, Civil Engineer. "IMPROVEMENTS IN OR APPERTAINING TO SUBMARINE OR
5 SUBAQUEOUS BOATS OR VESSELS."

This Invention has for its object improvements in or appertaining to submarine or subaqueous boats or vessels.

I construct the hull of my vessel to withstand the pressure of the water and to pass readily through the water and attain as much speed as the engine power
10 admits. Preferably I construct the hull of such proportions that laterally its section is a perfect circle, and a line drawn from bow to stern through the centre forms a chord to any longitudinal section of the skin.

The boat is propelled by an ordinary screw propeller, which is actuated by a steam engine. The boiler is so constructed that although the fire door, ash pit
15 door, and funnel can be hermetically closed yet it continues for a limited time to supply the engine with the steam necessary to keep it in motion.

For the purpose of causing the descent of such boats or vessels below the surface of the water I do not rely upon vertical steering apparatus, nor do I cause the vessel to descend by gravity, as has been done heretofore, but I effect the descent
20 by the direct application of power to that end.

The descending apparatus which I employ consists of an upright tube or tubes passing through the vessel and containing a screw or screws which can be driven by shafting passing through stuffing boxes from the interior of the vessel. The boat or vessel has a small amount of buoyancy, and consequently rises to the
25 surface whenever the rotation of the screws and the application of power is suspended.

[*Price 8d.*]

Nordenfelt's Improvements in Submarine or Subaqueous Boats or Vessels.

To prevent the boat or vessel from deviating far from an horizontal position when afloat I provide automatic steering gear, which corrects any deviation from the horizontal by steering the nose of the boat or vessel upwards or downwards. I arrange in the bow two side rudders upon an axle which runs horizontally through the skin of the boat or vessel. Upon the shaft within the boat or vessel 5 there is an arm which is controlled by a piston working in a cylinder. Water or fluid under pressure is admitted to the cylinder either on one or other side of the piston as may be required by a valve governed by a plumb weight. When the boat or vessel is upon an even keel the plumb weight holds the valve in a middle position, in which it closes both of the passages leading to the cylinder ends, but a 10 deviation of the boat or vessel from the horizontal position causes the valve to uncover one of the cylinder ports to the supply and the other to the exhaust, and the vertical rudders are thus moved to steer the nose of the boat or vessel upwards or downwards, as may be required, to correct the previous deviation.

APPENDIX III

Patent Specification for Submarine or Subaqueous Boats or Vessels taken out by Thorsten Nordenfelt – 17 August 1881

Nordenfelt's Improvements in Submarine or Subaqueous Boats or Vessels.

SPECIFICATION in pursuance of the conditions of the Letters Patent filed by the said Thorsten Nordenfelt in the Great Seal Patent Office on the 17th August 1881.

THORSTEN NORDENFELT, of No. 1, Saint Swithin's Lane, in the City of
5   London, Civil Engineer. "IMPROVEMENTS IN OR APPERTAINING TO SUBMARINE OR SUBAQUEOUS BOATS OR VESSELS."

This Invention has for its object improvements in or appertaining to submarine or subaqueous boats or vessels.

I construct the hull of my vessel to withstand the pressure of the water and to
10   pass readily through the water and attain as much speed as the engine power admits. Preferably I construct the hull of such proportions that laterally its section is a perfect circle, and a line drawn from bow to stern through the centre forms a chord to any longitudinal section of the skin.

The boat is propelled by an ordinary screw propeller, which is actuated by a
15   steam engine. The boiler is so constructed that although the fire door, ashpit door, and funnel can be hermetically closed, yet it continues for a limited time to supply the engine with the steam necessary to keep it in motion.

For the purpose of causing the descent of such boats or vessels below the surface of the water I do not rely upon vertical steering apparatus, nor do I cause the vessel
20   to descend by gravity, as has been done heretofore, but I effect the descent by the direct application of power to that end.

The descending apparatus which I employ consists of an upright tube or tubes and containing a screw or screws which can be driven by shafting passing through stuffing boxes from the interior of the vessel. The boat or vessel has a small amount
25   of buoyancy and consequently rises to the surface whenever the rotation of the screws or the application of power is suspended.

To prevent the boat or vessel from deviating far from an horizontal position when afloat I provide automatic steering gear which corrects any deviation from the horizontal by steering the nose of the boat or vessel upwards or downwards. I
30   arrange in the bow two side rudders upon an axle which runs horizontally through the skin of the boat or vessel. Upon the shaft within the boat or vessel there is an arm which is controlled by a piston working in a cylinder. Water or fluid under pressure is admitted to the cylinder either on one or other side of the piston as may be required by a valve governed by a plumb weight. When the boat or
35   vessel is upon an even keel the plumb weight holds the valve in a middle position, in which it closes both of the passages leading to the cylinder ends, but a deviation of the boat or vessel from the horizontal position causes the valve to uncover one of the cylinder ports to the supply and the other to the exhaust, and the vertical rudders are thus moved to steer the nose of the boat or vessel upwards or down-
40   wards as may be required to correct the previous deviation.

In order that the said Invention may be most fully understood and readily carried into effect, I will proceed to describe the Drawings hereunto annexed.

DESCRIPTION OF THE DRAWINGS.

On Sheet 1 of the Drawings the general construction of the boat is shewn in 6
45   views. Figure 1 is a sectional elevation. Within the boat are two hot water tanks A and A¹ and the boiler B. F is its telescope funnel; E is the condenser; and e the main engines driving the stern screw for propelling either when at the surface or submerged. They are provided with surface condensers and all necessary parts usual in marine engines. e¹ is one of the cylinders of an engine for working the

Nordenfelt's Improvements in Submarine or Subaqueous Boats or Vessels.

side screws. K¹ is a tank at the sides and bottom, into which sea water can be taken for the purpose of regulating the amount of buoyancy to be overcome by the action of the side screws. e^{11} is the engine which operates the longitudinal stability rudders R; T is the moveable conning tower.

Figure 2 is a plan of the boat with such parts of the skin or shell removed as to 5 show the two hot water tanks A and A¹, the boiler B, the condenser E, the main engine e, the side screws or descending apparatus s, s, and the engine e^{11} for working the longitudinal stability rudders R. The hot water tank A¹ is represented in section. This figure also shows the pumps P¹, P², P³. The duty of these pumps is as follows :—P¹ takes from the hot water tank A and discharges into boiler B; 10 P² takes from the boiler B and discharges into the hot water tank A¹; P³ takes from A¹ and discharges into A.

The object of these pumps is that there shall be a complete circulation of the water over the heating surface of the boiler B, whilst a perfect control of the quantity of water in each of these reservoirs is always maintained.   15

Figure 3 is a transverse section taken amidships and looking towards the bow of the boat. It shews the side sinking or vertical propelling apparatus s, s, the boiler B, the funnel box F, the conning tower T, and the cold water tank t.

Figure 4 is to a smaller scale an end view of the boat.

Figure 5 is an elevation of the boat when arranged for submarine work and just 20 before the side screws begin to operate, x being the water line.

Figure 6 is an elevation of the boat when prepared for surface work; the funnel F and the conning tower T being raised project from the deck.

Sheet 2 of the Drawings shows detail of the descending apparatus.

Figure 7 is a vertical section to a large scale through the tube in which one of 25 the descending screws S works. It is driven, as will be seen, by bevilled gear from the shaft of its motor engine, which passes through the side of vessel by a stuffing box.

Figure 8 is a plan of the descending apparatus.

Figure 9 is an horizontal section of a tank t extending in front of and behind the 30 descending screw S.

Figure 10 is a vertical section of the tank t.

Sheet 3 of the Drawings shows the apparatus in connection with the bow rudders, which tends at all times when the vessel is in motion below the surface to prevent upward or downward deviation, and to cause the forward motion to be in an 35 horizontal plane.

Figure 11 is a plan of the controlling cylinder.

Figure 12 is a plan of a portion of the longitudinal stability rudders R with their cranked axis R¹. The sides of the vessel are seen in section.

Figure 13 is a vertical section of the controlling cylinder with its valve.   40

Figure 14 is a vertical section of the fore part of the vessel, and shows the cranked axis R¹ and a part of the connecting rod by which it is coupled with the piston rod of the controlling cylinder.

Figure 15 is a transverse section of the controlling cylinder and valve.

The valve V is of the rotary or plug valve class; it is fixed upon a spindle, to 45 which an arm is also attached, and the arm carries a weight W. The arm maintains approximately a vertical position, and when the vessel is horizontal the valve V occupies the position in which it is seen in Figure 13. There is a small accumulator or air vessel kept charged by a pump, and from this water under pressure is supplied to the chamber in which the valve works. Any deviation of the vessel from an 50 horizontal position causes the water under pressure to enter the cylinder and give motion to the piston and consequently to the longitudinal stability rudders R in a manner to correct the deviation.

In preparing the vessel to descend the water in the boiler B and in the hot water tanks A and A¹ has first to be heated until the pressure in them is as high 55 as they are constructed to bear. The vessel at this time may be steaming at the surface when she is navigated in the ordinary way, being propelled by the stern screw

Specification. A.D. 1881.—N° 693. 5

Nordenfelt's Improvements in Submarine or Subaqueous Boats or Vessels.

and steered by the stern rudder. When it is wished to descend the doors of the boiler furnace are closed and secured; the doors are made to shut gas tight. The funnel is then lowered and closed by a tightly fitting cover, which also fits water-tight to the side of the vessel. The conning tower also is similarly closed and
5 lowered down. Water is then admitted carefully to the tanks, and the descending apparatus S, S, is set gently to work. This apparatus will take the vessel down whilst she is still somewhat lighter than the water displaced. As soon as the gauge indicates that the vessel is descending the admission cocks to the tanks are closed, and they remain closed whilst the vessel is down, the depth at which she
10 travels beneath the surface being controlled by driving the descending apparatus a little faster or slower as may be necessary. The vessel is propelled and steered by the stern propeller and rudder as when at the surface.

The vessel contains sufficient air for the use of the navigators whilst remaining down for a considerable time, and artificial means may be resorted to to maintain
15 its purity, as is well understood. A valve is provided (to be operated by a treddle or otherwise) by which the hot water can be allowed to escape from the boiler and vessels A and A¹ into the sea. By opening this valve the vessel can in case of necessity be almost instantly brought to the surface at any time. This arrange-ment ensures safety even in the case of the vessel becoming injured by collision or
20 otherwise so as to leak seriously.

It will be seen that by burning fuel in the vessel when she is at the surface I store up power in the form of highly heated water, and that I employ this power to propel the vessel when submerged and also to regulate the depth of submergence.

25 Having thus described the nature of my said Invention and the manner of performing the same, I would have it understood that I claim as my improvements in or appertaining to submarine or subaqueous boats or vessels,—

First. Providing the said vessels with propelling engines and boiler, the latter being so arranged that after the water has been heated by the combustion of fuel
30 its furnace may be closed gas tight and the steam from the heated water used to drive the engines whilst the vessel is submerged.

Second. Providing the said vessels with descending or vertical propelling apparatus, which whilst in motion is capable of sinking the vessel beneath the surface whilst the vessel is lighter than the water which it displaces.

35 Third. Providing the said vessel with automatically acting longitudinal stability rudders controlled by hydraulic or other motor apparatus and a plumb weight.

In witness whereof, I, the said Thorsten Nordenfelt, have hereunto set my hand and seal, this Second day of August, in the year of our Lord One thousand eight hundred and eighty one.

40 THORSTEN NORDENFELT. (L.S.)

LONDON: Printed by GEORGE EDWARD EYRE and WILLIAM SPOTTISWOODE,
Printers to the Queen's most Excellent Majesty.
For Her Majesty's Stationery Office.

1881.

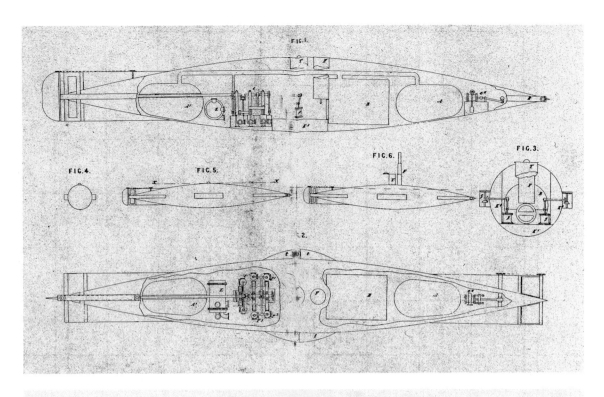

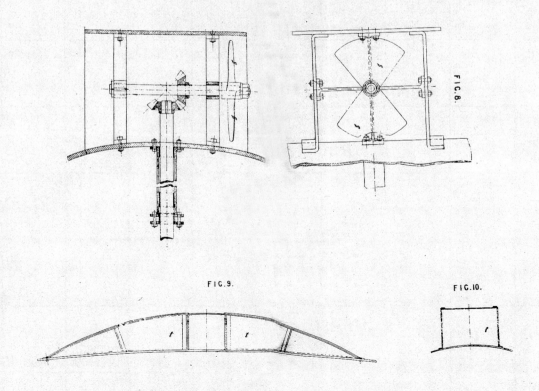

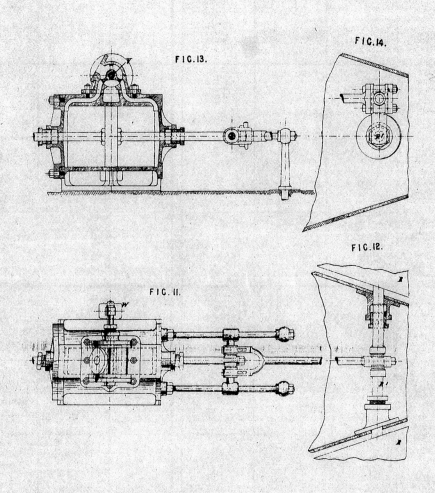

FIG.13.

FIG.14.

FIG.12.

FIG.11.

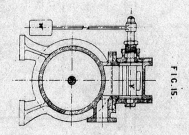

FIG.15.

APPENDIX IV

**Patent Specification for Submarine Boats for placing Torpedoes etc
taken out by George William Garrett – 8 May 1838**

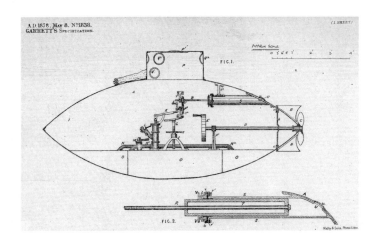

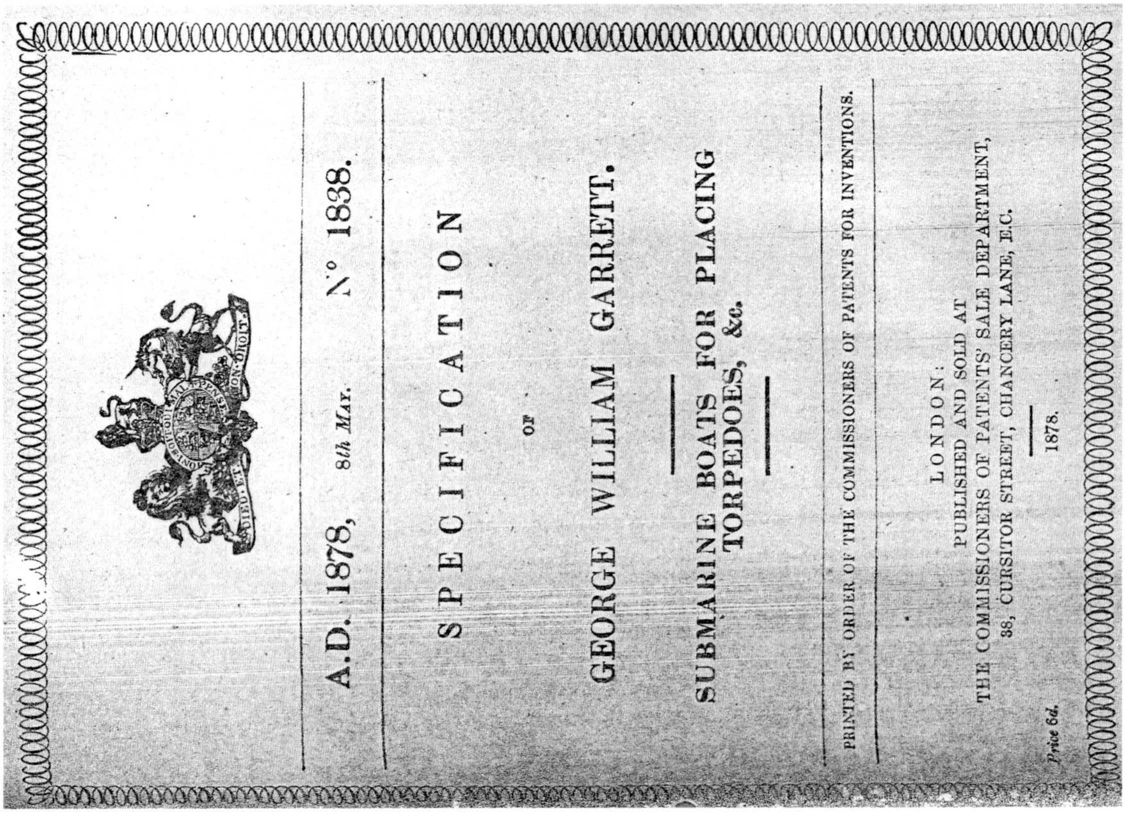

A.D. 1878, May 8. No. 1838.
GARRETT'S SPECIFICATION.

APPROX SCALE

FIG.1.

FIG.2.

(1 SHEET.)

Malby & Sons. Photo-Litho.

A.D. 1878, 8th Mar. N° 1838.

SPECIFICATION

OF

GEORGE WILLIAM GARRETT.

SUBMARINE BOATS FOR PLACING
TORPEDOES, &c.

PRINTED BY ORDER OF THE COMMISSIONERS OF PATENTS FOR INVENTIONS.

LONDON:
PUBLISHED AND SOLD AT
THE COMMISSIONERS OF PATENTS' SALE DEPARTMENT,
38, CURSITOR STREET, CHANCERY LANE, E.C.

1878.

Price 6d.

SPECIFICATION in pursuance of the conditions of the Letters Patent filed by the said George William Garrett in the Great Seal Patent Office on the 5th November 1878.

GEORGE WILLIAM GARRETT, of 82, Chorlton Road, Manchester, in the County of Lancaster, "IMPROVEMENTS IN AND APPERTAINING TO SUBMARINE OR SUBAQUEOUS BOATS OR VESSELS FOR REMOVING, DESTROYING, LAYING, OR PLACING TORPEDOES IN CHANNELS AND OTHER SITUATIONS, AND FOR OTHER PURPOSES."

This Invention relates to a novel means of constructing boats or vessels for removing or placing torpedoes in channels and like situations, but which may be also employed for diving or submarine surveying purposes.

Fig. I shews a sectional elevation of the hull, and Fig. 2 a sectional elevation of the apparatus for varying the specific gravity when submerged.

I generally construct the vessel of small dimensions, a handy size being about 14 to 20 feet long (when arranged to contain only one man), so as to be easily lifted by the davits of an ironclad or other ship, or from a pier or other structure.

In shape the hull A is nearly elliptical, or somewhat resembling the shape of an egg, with this difference that both halves are exactly alike. I prefer to construct it of thin iron, or preferably steel plates, or it might be constructed of wood. The sides can be strengthened with iron stringers, well stiffened by gusset plates, so as to resist the pressure to which they will be exposed. I prefer to make the diameter about $1/4$ of the length. Thus, a boat 14 to 20 feet long has a diameter of 5 feet at its major axis.

The boat might be propelled by means of a small gas or vapour engine of suitable construction driving a propellor or screw.

The gas can be compressed into a suitable tank. I generally prefer to use hydro-carbon gas, and add a percentage of oxygen, so that the gas can be exploded under the piston by electricity or otherwise without needing the admixture of air. I can use other explosives for operating the engine instead of hydrocarbon or similar gas.

The exhaust gas passes out into the water through a non-delivery valve, or is otherwise disposed of. Or, instead of a gas engine, an engine operated by compressed air might be used. In the Drawing, however, the boat is shewn propelled by a screw C having its shaft D passing through a stuffing box, and supported by a pedestal F bolted over the tanks hereafter described, and carrying fly wheel E, which can be rotated by hand, as shewn, or by means of a treadle. On either side of

---

A.D. 1878.—Nº 1838.

Garrett's Improvements in Submarine Boats for Placing Torpedoes, &c.

the screw I place a rudder working horizontally. These rudders are keyed or secured to a shaft b, cranked so as to allow the propellor shaft to pass it, and passing through stuffing boxes c, c, as shown. This shaft can be actuated in any suitable manner to cause the lateral deviation of the vessel.

The up-and-down or angular motion of the vessel when submerged can be given by means of side floats or fins working on horizontal pivots, and not shown in the Drawing, and I do not purpose making any claim for the steering apparatus by itself, as it is old.

To regulate the depth of flotation of the vessel I employ the following means:— Preferably at or near the centre of the vessel, and in the same horizontal plane as the centre line, or in other part of the vessel, I place a strong horizontal cylinder communicating with the water by a port or ports at its centre. Inside this cylinder I place two well packed pistons. These pistons are secured to screwed piston rods, each working through screw boxes at the ends of the cylinder. Each screw box is secured to or forms part of a toothed wheel in connection with suitable gearing, so that both wheels may be actuated by handle or otherwise, and thus cause both pistons to approach or recede from each other perfectly evenly and synchronously. When the pistons recede, the water enters, filling the cylinder, thus acting as water ballast.

The handle actuating the gearing is worked till the boat sinks deep enough. By actuating the handle the reverse way, the pistons approach each other and expel the water from the cylinder, and the boat rises. Several of these cylinders could be used and could be placed vertically if desired.

However, in a small boat, the cylinder if used alone to sink the boat would necessarily be of large size, and where economy of space is a desideratum it is well to reduce the size of the working parts as much as possible, yet still retain their efficiency. Therefore to attain this end, I prefer to cause the boat to lose her free-board by means of ballast tanks, and then regulate the depth of submersion or flotation by means of the aforesaid controlling gear. This is shewn in the Drawing, O, O, O, are the ballast tanks, preferably built into and forming an integral part of the boat. J is the pump of any suitable construction used for filling or emptying said tanks, being connected to them by the pipes N, N^1, N^2, a 4-way cock M being interposed between the pump and the tanks. L is the cock on the pipe serving to admit water to or expel it from the pump, the 4-way cock controlling the influx to or exit of water from any or all of the tanks.

S is the controlling cylinder aforesaid. I find that under great pressure the water is apt to pass the pistons if not very carefully packed, it being difficult to pack them perfectly tightly, so instead of packed pistons, I prefer to use a Bramah collar to the cylinder, and in small boats I prefer to dispense with one of the pistons and form the port, for the entrance or exit of water at one end instead of at the centre of the cylinder; also I prefer to suspend the cylinder above instead of placing it on the bottom. The arrangement is shewn in elevation in Fig. 1, and in enlarged sectional elevation in Fig. 2. S is the cylinder carried by a bracket s^3 at one end, and bolted at the other end to the hull A. U is the water port, which I prefer to cover with a grating u to prevent solid matters entering the cylinder. T is the plunger or piston working in the cylinder S, against the leathers v, v^1, which leathers are pressed together by flanged ring v^3 adjusted by screwed bolts as shewn. One end of the ring v^3 is recessed at the top, and screwed to form a stuffing box to receive the gland V.

The piston rod R is secured to the plunger as shewn, or in other desirable manner. One end is screwed and passes through a screw box in the toothed wheel s, carried by a bracket r^1 bolted to the hull. The wheel s^1 is rotated by means of handle s, driving toothed wheel s^3 operating it. The wheel s^3 is carried by bracket r^2, as shewn.

It will be seen that this arrangement occupies less room than if two pistons, rods, and screw boxes are used, and the cylinder placed horizontally on the floor of the boat as first described; though the principle is exactly the same, and both plans can

A.D. 1878.—N° 1838.

6

Garrett's Improvements in Submarine Boats for Placing Torpedoes, &c.

Having now described my Invention, and the best mode known to me of carrying it into effect, I wish it to be understood that I do not claim the use of the elastic sleeves, nor yet the arrangement of rudders shewn, or the propelling mechanism, but what I believe to be new, and desire to claim under the herein-before in part recited Letters Patent is,—

I. The mode described of varying the specific gravity of a submerged vessel, and thereby controlling the depth of submersion or floatation, by mechanically increasing or diminishing the internal containing capacity of the water ballast cylinder or chamber in free communication with the exterior water.

II. The mode described of controlling the depth of floatation of a submerged vessel, after the buoyancy or freeboard has been overcome by means of water in communication with the body in which the vessel or boat is immersed, admitted to, or expelled from a cylinder or ballast chamber, by the movement of a piston, plungers, or their mechanical equivalent, increasing or diminishing the internal capacity of said cylinder or chamber, so that the influx or efflux of a minimum quantity of water shall cause a sensible alteration in the specific gravity of the boat or vessel.

III. The combination of the cylinder S, port U, plunger or plungers T working water-tight, and gearing operating the same, for the purposes described.

IV. The general arrangement of submarine or subaqueous boat or vessel, substantially as and for the purposes described.

In witness whereof, I, the said George William Garrett, have hereunto set my hand and seal, this Second day of November, in the year of our Lord 1878.

GEORGE WILLIAM GARRETT. (L.S.)

Witness,
E. GARDNER COLTON,
Patent Agent & Engineer,
W. P. Thompson & Co.'s Patent Offices,
Liverpool & London.

LONDON: Printed by GEORGE EDWARD EYRE and WILLIAM SPOTTISWOODE,
Printers to the Queen's most Excellent Majesty.
For Her Majesty's Stationery Office.

1878.

A.D. 1878.—N° 1838.

5

Garrett's Improvements in Submarine Boats for Placing Torpedoes, &c.

be equally well worked, providing the plungers are packed as described, or so as to be tight yet easily moved. In using the boat, the tap L being turned, and the 4-way cock opened, water enters the tanks, and causes the boat to lose her buoyancy or freeboard. To cause her to sink or rise when submerged, the handle s is turned, admitting water to or expelling it from the cylinder S by the movement of the plunger T. Thus the specific gravity of the submerged boat may be adjusted with the greatest nicety, the admission or expulsion of a minimum quantity of water (when the freeboard is overcome) causing a very sensible alteration in her depth of floatation. An indicator can be fitted to this gear, so as to indicate the number of revolutions of the handle s necessary to admit a certain quantity of water to or expel it from the cylinder.

On the upper side of the boat, and preferably over the centre, I arrange a strong coming tower P fitted in the roof with a manhole P¹ for ingress and egress. I place strong glass windows or ports Q^2, Q^3, circumferentially round it, and also in the roof as shown, so that a person standing or sitting in the boat can observe objects in the water. I arrange two or more openings Q^4 in the tower fitted with elastic water-tight sleeves as shown, so that a person can get his arms through these to cut the wires of torpedoes, or place them in position, or operate an anchor or rope.

Below these holes, and in the water, I arrange a box to contain nippers and other tools for cutting wires and for other purposes. I also arrange an electric lamp, so that the occupant of the tower can swing it about in his search for torpedoes and other obstructions. I arrange the roof of the coming tower so that it is easily taken off if anything happens to the boat, so that the occupants can rise to the surface, being aided by life belts if desired.

Within the boat I arrange apparatus or chemicals for purifying the air or supplying oxygen to the occupants, or I might supply air by pumps and pipes from a distance, as with divers.

I purpose employing these boats to go before ironclads searching for torpedoes, and when found, cutting the wires connecting them to the shore, or otherwise destroying them. The boat is easily controlled at any depth by the occupant or occupants, and can be moved about as described. I might establish telegraphic or telephonic communication with the ironclads or otherwise, so that the occupants of the boat can report progress or issue orders.

A supply of insulated wire could easily be carried on a reel, and unwound as the boat proceeds. These boats could also be used for laying or placing torpedoes in various situations, or be used to cut vessels' moorings, or a number of them might be used to tow a vessel out of a roadstead, by connecting powerful cables to the keel or other part, first taking the precaution (if a steam vessel) to disable the propellor and rudder.

The propellors of these boats should be protected by guards (not shown in the Drawing), to preclude the possibility of chains and other obstructions fouling them. The boats can easily be carried on the decks of ironclads, and can be lowered into the water when required.

The occupant sits on a seat G, supported on a screwed rod working in screwed nut H working in bearings in bracket I, and by turning the hand wheel shown attached to the nut H, the height of the seat can be adjusted. The various pumps and apparatus could be otherwise placed than in the positions shown, but they should be within easy reach of the operator.

In working the boat, the occupant or occupants should take down a supply of compressed air in tins or cases, so as to allow of a pressure of air in the boat being maintained, to counteract the pressure of the water on the submerged boat. If the pressure outside increases, the pressure within can be augmented by opening one or more of the air cases, and allowing air to fill the boat till equilibrium is maintained between the pressures. Suitable gauges can be fixed to shew the pressures, and gauges to shew the depth reached, or indicators to shew the position of the screw or rudder might be used.

BIBLIOGRAPHY AND REFERENCES

Books/Papers

Vice-Admiral Sir Arther **Hezlet** KBE, DSO, DSC
The Submarine and Sea Power

H. P. **Cocker** *Royal Navy Submarines 1901 – 1982*

R. N. **Newton** *Practical Construction of Warships*

Prof Dipl. ing Ulrich **Gabler** *Unterseebootbau*

F. **Forest** and H. **Noalhat** *Bateaux Sous-Marins (Historique)*

G. L. **Pesce** *La Navigation Sous-Marin*

U. S. Navy Department *Dictionary of American Fighting Ships*

Kockums Mekaniska Verkstads *ab i Malmo Fran Hajen 1904 till Hajen 1954*

R. **Steen Steensen**, Kommandorkaptajn *Vore Undervandsbåde Gennem 50 År 1909 – 1959*

Richard **Compton-Hall** *Submarine Boats*

Antony **Preston** and John **Batchelor**
The First Submarines
The Submarine 1578 – 1919

Edward **Horton** *Illustrated History of the Submarine*

T. **Thompson** *Old Rhyl*

Simon **Lake**, M. I. N. A. *The Submarine in War and Peace*

A. H. **Burgogne** *Submarine Navigation Past and Present*

Whitaker's Almanac
Dictionary of National Biography

Cochran and Co Annan Ltd *Cochran Boilers. 50 Years at Annan 1899 – 1949*

William Scanlon **Murphy** *Father of the Submarine*

Commander F. W. **Lipscombe**, OBE, RN
The British Submarine
Historic Submarines

Arthur J. **Marder** *From Dreadnought to Scapa Flow, Vol 1*

Ebehard **Rossler** *The U Boat*

J. D. **Scott** *Vickers, a History*

Lieutenant-Commander J. M. **Maber** RN
The Royal Navy's First Submarines (Paper)
George Garrett! Who's He? or
The Curate's Submarine (Paper)
Notes on the Propulsion System of the Resurgam (Paper)
Thorsten Nordenfelt's Submarines (Paper)

United States Naval Institute *Proceedings*

Institute of Naval Architects (Now Royal Institute of Naval Architects) *Hovgaard Paper Delivered 23 March 1888* (Paper)
Account of the First Practical Submarine Boats as told by the Son of their Inventor and Commander, George William Garrett (Paper)

Turkish (Naval) Archives *Turk Denizalticilik Tarihi Vesikalar (Vesika Sura No 36)*

Robert F. **Burgess** *Beneath the Sea*

Herbert C. **Fyfe** *Submarine Warfare, London 1907*

Newspapers and Magazines

The Rhyl Record and Visitor
Rhyl Journal
Manchester Chronicle
Manchester Courier
Evening News (Manchester)
Liverpool Daily Post
Liverpool Courier
Liverpool Weekly Mercury
Liverpool Daily Post and Echo
Daily Mail
Gentleman's Magazine (Dec 1774, June 1749, Jul 1749)
Broad Arrow 3rd April 1886
The London Illustrated and Military Magazine 1886
Engineering
Rossall School Magazine
Warship International (Winter 1968)
Maritime Wales
Country Quest (August 1980)
Cheshire Life (May 1972)
Sea Breezes (March 1922)
Army and Navy Gazette
Engineer

INDEX